Inequality and Poverty in Malaysia

Measurement and Decomposition

A World Bank Research Publication

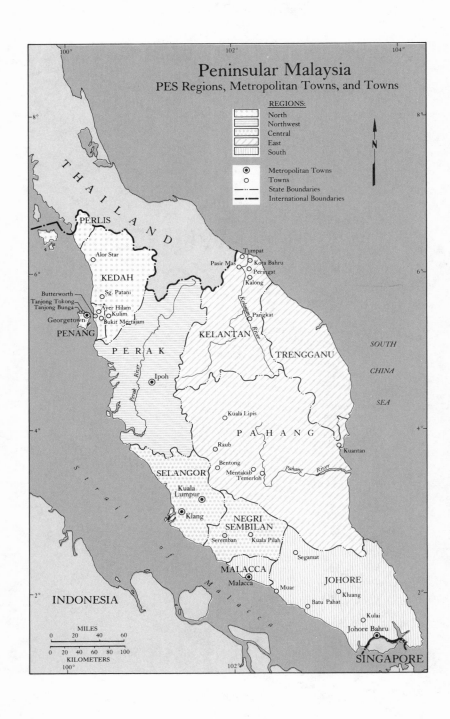

Peninsular Malaysia
PES Regions, Metropolitan Towns, and Towns

REGIONS:
North
Northwest
Central
East
South

⊙ Metropolitan Towns
○ Towns
— · — State Boundaries
— ·· — International Boundaries

N

THAILAND

PERLIS

Alor Star

KEDAH

Tumpat
Pasir Mas · Kota Bahru
Peringat
Kalong

Sg. Patani

Butterworth
Tanjong Tokong
Tanjong Bunga
Ayer Hilam
Kulim
Bukit Mertajam
Georgetown
PENANG

PERAK

KELANTAN

Pangkat

TRENGGANU

SOUTH

CHINA

SEA

Ipoh

Perak River

Kuala Lipis

PAHANG

Raub

Kuantan

Bentong
Mentakab
Temerloh

Pahang River

SELANGOR

Kuala
Lumpur

Klang

NEGRI
SEMBILAN

Seremban   Kuala Pilah

Segamat

MALACCA

Malacca

Muar

JOHORE

Kluang

Batu Pahat

Kulai

Johore Bahru

INDONESIA

Strait of Malacca

MILES
0 20 40 60
0 20 40 60 80 100
KILOMETERS

SINGAPORE

100°   102°   104°

Inequality and Poverty
in
Malaysia
Measurement and Decomposition

Sudhir Anand

Published for The World Bank
OXFORD UNIVERSITY PRESS

GIFT
7/19/83

Oxford University Press

NEW YORK OXFORD LONDON GLASGOW
TORONTO MELBOURNE WELLINGTON HONG KONG
TOKYO KUALA LUMPUR SINGAPORE JAKARTA
DELHI BOMBAY CALCUTTA MADRAS KARACHI
NAIROBI DAR ES SALAAM CAPE TOWN

Editor: Jane H. Carroll
Figures: S. A. D. Subasinghe
Map: Larry A. Bowring
Book design: Brian J. Svikhart
Binding design: Joyce C. Eisen

Typeset by Macmillan India Ltd., Bangalore

Library of Congress Cataloging in Publication Data

Anand, Sudhir, 1946–
  Inequality and poverty in Malaysia.

  (A World Bank research publication)
  Bibliography: p.
  1. Income-distribution—Malaysia. 2. Poor—
Malaysia. I. Title. II. Series.
HC445. 5. Z91513   339.2'2'09595   81–14178
ISBN 0–19–520153–1

Contents

PREFACE   *viii*

1. PERSPECTIVES ON MALAYSIA   *1*
   Economic Overview   *4*
   Political Background   *6*
   The New Economic Policy   *9*
   Inequality, Poverty, and NEP   *14*
   Reader's Guide to the Study   *17*

2. THE 1970 POST-ENUMERATION SURVEY AND COMPARISONS WITH
   OTHER SURVEYS   *21*
   The 1970 Post-Enumeration Survey   *22*
   The PES Household Income Distribution   *34*
   Intertemporal Comparisons of Inequality in Malaysia   *42*
   Appendix: PES 1970 Instructions to Field Interviewers   *53*

3. INEQUALITY IN LEVELS OF LIVING   *63*
   PES Income as a Measure of Economic Welfare   *63*
   The Population Unit and Appropriate Income Concept   *65*
   The Joint Distribution of Households by Household Income
      and Size   *67*
   The Distribution of Households by per Capita Household
      Income   *79*
   The Distribution of Individuals by per Capita Household
      Income   *81*
   The Atkinson Index   *82*
   The Methodology of Inequality Decomposition   *86*
   Interracial and Interregional Inequalities   *93*
   Rural-Urban Inequalities   *99*
   Policy Considerations   *101*

4. THE DEFINITION AND MEASUREMENT OF POVERTY   *111*
   Previous Attempts at Defining Poverty   *111*
   The Definition of a Poverty Line   *113*
   The Sen Poverty Measure   *118*
   Estimates of Poverty in Malaysia   *125*
   A Profile of Poverty in Malaysia   *126*
   Sensitivity of the Poverty Profile   *132*
   Appendix: A Profile of the Rich   *135*

5. SUBGROUPS IN POVERTY   *144*
   Rural Poverty   *145*
   Two-digit PES Subgroups   *151*
   Appendix: Urban Poverty   *167*

6. INEQUALITY IN THE PERSONAL INCOME DISTRIBUTION   *187*
   The Distribution of Income Recipients by Personal Income   *192*
   The Interpretation of Decomposition for Three Inequality
      Measures   *198*
   Decomposition by Race and Location   *202*
   Decomposition by Sex of Income Recipient   *206*
   Breakdown by Employment Status   *207*
   Interracial Earnings Differentials among Rubber Tappers   *215*
   Decomposition by Occupational Category   *216*
   Decomposition by Sector of Employment   *226*
   Multivariate Decompositions   *227*

7. EARNINGS FUNCTIONS FOR URBAN EMPLOYEES   *237*
   The Earnings Function   *238*
   The Return to Education   *241*
   Some Problems of PES Data   *243*
   Estimates by Race, Occupation, and Sex   *247*
   Estimates by Age Cohort   *255*
   Language of Instruction   *257*
   Type of Degree   *259*
   Breakdown by Region   *261*
   Appendix: Some Properties of the Earnings Function   *264*

8. CONCLUSIONS AND SOME NOTES ON POLICY   *271*
   Summary and Conclusions   *272*
   Policies to Reduce Poverty in Malaysia   *280*
   Some Implications of Employment Restructuring   *294*
   The New Economic Policy: Concluding Comments   *298*

APPENDIXES: THE MEASUREMENT OF INCOME INEQUALITY   *302*
A. A Brief Review   *303*
   Indices Based Directly on the Lorenz Diagram   *304*
   Other Indices   *306*

B. The Gini Coefficient   *311*
   Definition 1 (Geometric)   *311*
   Definition 2 (Rao, 1969)   *312*
   Definition 3 (Kendall and Stuart, 1963)   *313*
   Definition 4 (Sen, 1973a)   *314*
   Definition 5 (Fei and Ranis, 1974)   *315*
   The Effect of Changes in Certain Incomes   *316*
   The Disaggregation of Income by Factor Components   *318*
   On the Decomposition of the Gini Coefficient   *319*

C. The Decomposition of Three Inequality Measures   *327*
    The Theil Entropy Index *T*   *327*
    The Theil Second Measure *L*   *329*
    The Variance of Log-Income *V*   *330*
    Comparison of the Decompositions   *331*
D. Lorenz Dominance and Inequality   *333*
E. Lemmas on Lorenz Dominance   *341*
    The Redress of Poverty Rule   *344*
F. Mapping the Household to the per Capita Household
    Income Distribution   *346*

REFERENCES   *355*

INDEX   *365*

Preface

THERE ARE FEW STUDIES which analyze primary data on income distribution in developing countries. Work in this area has consisted largely of broad generalizations made from secondary material with little attempt to examine the underlying data sources and concepts. This study analyzes primary data on income distribution in Malaysia collected in the 1970 Post-Enumeration Survey (PES); these data have not yet been systematically analyzed or tabulated.

This book may be viewed as an anatomy of income distribution in Malaysia. It documents the state and nature of income inequality and of poverty, and develops a methodology for this purpose. Apart from detailed measurement, a decomposition by socioeconomic variables suggests the sources of inequality and poverty. In the course of the empirical work, several statistical and technical problems had to be faced—from the evaluation of the quality of data to conceptual issues of measurement and decomposition. In places I have developed general solutions or techniques of analysis that were not available in the existing literature. The final product may thus also be viewed as an application of a framework for analyzing income distribution in a developing country. It is hoped that this case study for Malaysia might serve as a benchmark for comparative studies elsewhere, as better income data begin to be collected and analyzed systematically.

The statistical and descriptive analysis of Malaysian income distribution is presented in the context of the concerns expressed by the Malaysian government in its New Economic Policy (NEP) of 1971. This policy, announced in the Second Malaysia Plan, 1971–75, consists of the twin objectives of "eradicating poverty irrespective of race" and "restructuring society to correct racial economic imbalance." In the book I have attempted to go beyond the mechanics of measurement and the exploitation of the PES data to illuminate these broader policy questions. The issues addressed, however, are confined to the objectives and strategy of the New Economic Policy and to the framework for achieving it by means of the Outline Perspective Plan, 1970–90. Because the bulk of this book was complete before publication of the Third Malaysia Plan, 1976–80, which actually incorporates some of the information contained in the first draft of this study, policy elaborated in documents published since 1977 is not discussed.

Anyone who has handled very large bodies of data on tape will know the problems of cleaning, editing, splicing, and recoding the original information to create new and usable data tapes. I have checked and rechecked the PES data (which cover 135,000 individuals by 55 distinct variables) for errors in coding and internal consistency and am confident that the edited tapes are largely free of error. In this process I was helped by Alexander Meeraus and Vinh Le-Si of the Development Research Center of the World Bank, and I would like to thank them. I would also like to acknowledge the generous assistance given in 1973 by Ramesh Chander, Dorothy Fernandez, K. G. R. Nathan, and V. T. Palan of the Department of Statistics, Malaysia, on various technical aspects of the Post-Enumeration Survey and in helping to track down and answer questions about the only surviving records of the 1957–58 Household Budget Survey.

It will be obvious that the work described in this book has entailed considerable and painstaking computational effort. For this I owe large debts of gratitude to Shail Jain and to Sam Pal; they provided outstanding research assistance in the early and later stages of this project, respectively. Thanks are also due to Meera Shah who in 1973 helped me write the initial computer program for decomposition of the three inequality measures, Theil T, Theil L, and varlog (see appendix C).

The first draft of this study took the form of four lengthy mimeographed papers (Anand, 1973, 1974*a*, 1974*b*, 1975). Parts of these papers were presented at seminars in the Department of Statistics, Kuala Lumpur; the Development Research Center of the World Bank; the Universities of London (London School of Economics), Oxford, Sussex, and Warwick; and at the Fourteenth General Conference of the International Association for Research in Income and Wealth in Aulanko, Finland. I am grateful to the participants of these seminars for their comments. The second draft, in the form of this book, was substantially complete by 1977, but its publication has been delayed for various reasons.

Many people have commented on, or discussed with me, chapters from the earlier draft. I would particularly like to thank Montek Ahluwalia, Anthony Atkinson, Clive Bell, Ramesh Chander, John Duloy, Ravi Gulhati, Heather Joshi, S. M. Kanbur, John Knight, Ian Little, Heather Milne, James Mirrlees, Graham Pyatt, Bruce Ross-Larson, Amartya Sen, T. N. Srinivasan, R. Thillainathan, A. Vaidyanathan, and Don Zagier. Helpful comments were also received in 1978 from the three referees of this book: Irma Adelman, Gian Sahota, and Donald Snodgrass.

Jean Ponchamni typed the drafts of this book with amazing speed and accuracy. She also provided valuable logistical assistance and acted as the principal contact between myself in Oxford and the World Bank in Washington, D.C. I am extremely grateful to her for undertaking these tasks with such dedication and efficiency.

There are some people without whose support or encouragement in different ways this book would have remained in mimeographed form for even longer. They are Montek Ahluwalia, John Duloy, Kaval Gulhati, Ravi Gulhati, Edward V. K. Jaycox, Jean Ponchamni, and especially Heather Milne.

SUDHIR ANAND

St. Catherine's College
Oxford, England

Inequality and Poverty in Malaysia

Measurement and Decomposition

1

Perspectives
on Malaysia

MALAYSIA IS A MULTIRACIAL SOCIETY. The main racial groups are the
Malays, who account for just more than half the population of Peninsular
Malaysia, the Chinese (36 percent), and the Indians (11 percent).[1] With
different religions, languages, cultures, and social customs, communal lines
cut across several facets of life. Except for an outbreak of racial tension in
1969, communal harmony has been maintained in the country.

The origins of ethnic pluralism in Malaysia go back to early contacts
with Indian and Chinese traders and with Portuguese and Dutch
colonialists.[2] Much of the present economic and political structure can be
traced back to the era of British colonial rule. The British settled first on the
island of Penang, later in the coastal city of Malacca and on the island of
Singapore. Penang, Malacca, and Singapore came to be known as the
Straits Settlements. Some Chinese were already involved in entrepot trade
in the Straits Settlements at that time, but the arrival of the British probably
stimulated further Chinese immigration.[3] Both communities began to
exploit local resources, especially tin, and branched out into various
commercial and economic ventures, including cash crops and spices in
nearby areas of the mainland. The British also encouraged Indians to come
to work on their new sugarcane and coffee plantations.

1. The data on which this study is based, and much of the discussion as a result, are for
Peninsular Malaysia and do not cover Malaysia's insular states: Sabah and Sarawak. The
perspective presented in this chapter does not go beyond the early 1970s.

2. See Lamb (1964) and Hirschman (1972).

3. This subcommunity, called Baba Chinese, is thought to be descended from early Chinese
immigrants to Malacca around the fifteenth century, when it was the center of an important
trading empire (Purcell, 1967). The Baba or Straits Chinese now form about 15 percent of the
Chinese population in Peninsular Malaysia.

It was not until the second half of the nineteenth century that large-scale migration to the Malay Peninsula began.[4] This coincided with the period in which the British expanded and consolidated their rule over the peninsula some hundred years after landing in Penang. An event of crucial importance in inducing large streams of migrants was the introduction of the rubber tree from Brazil in the late nineteenth century. Rubber and tin mining came to dominate the economy, with rubber soon supplanting all other commercial crops. The new economic activities required more labor, but the indigenous Malay community was largely bypassed in the satisfaction of this demand. Large numbers of foreign laborers were brought in from India to work on rubber plantations and from China to work in tin mines.

Immigration continued and even increased through the first few decades of the twentieth century, until the depression and restrictive legislation began to slow it down in the 1930s. With this tapering off, the ethnic pattern of the population started to stabilize. The proportion of Malays in the population leveled off at about 50 percent after 1931 (Arlès, 1971, p. 528). The shares of Chinese and Indians in the population stabilized, too, and the locally born proportion of these communities significantly increased. Between 1931 and 1947 the proportion of Chinese born in Malaysia rose from 30 to 64 percent, while that of Indians rose from 21 to 52 percent. At the time of independence in 1957, more than three-quarters of the Chinese population and almost two-thirds of the Indian population were locally born (Arlès, 1971). Estimates put the population of Peninsular Malaysia at approximately 250,000 in 1800, 2 million in 1900, and 6.3 million in 1957.[5] By 1970, the year to which the survey data analyzed in this study refer, the population of Peninsular Malaysia had grown to 9.2 million.[6]

The nonparticipation of Malays in the new plantation and mining sectors, and in modern activities generally, led to sectoral and geographical concentrations of the races. The Chinese and Indians became more prominent in the modern economy of tin, rubber, and commerce on the West Coast; the Malays remained in the subsistence sectors of paddy (rice) farming and fishing, mostly along the East Coast and in the North. Various reasons have been suggested for the nonparticipation of Malays in the

---

4. See Jackson (1961), Sandhu (1969), and Purcell (1967). As a point of reference, one could take 1850 as the beginning of large-scale Chinese immigration, and the 1880s as the beginning of large-scale Indian immigration (Hirschman, 1972).

5. Unadjusted total of the 1957 census.

6. Total of the 1970 census adjusted on the basis of the "1970 Census Post-Enumeration Survey" (PES) (Kuala Lumpur: Department of Statistics, n.d.; unpublished computer tapes). The population of Sabah in 1970 was about 650,000; that of Sarawak, about 975,000.

emergent modern economy: British colonial policy, covert discrimination by employers, poor conditions in the early tin mines and rubber estates, and the Malays' alleged lack of economic motivation and preference for the traditional peasant life. Obversely, the prominence of Chinese and Indians in modern sectors and occupations may in part be explained by the theory of "immigrant culture": that immigrants possess a stronger motivation to achieve and that they operate on the fringes of the established (in this case, rural) society.[7]

Whatever the reasons for the lack of Malay participation in modern activities, Malays continued to predominate in the rural sector while non-Malays came to dominate the urban sector. In 1970 Malays constituted 63 percent of the rural sector and 53 percent of the total population, but only 27 percent of the urban population. Non-Malays constituted 73 percent of the urban sector, and this in turn accounted for 29 percent of the total population of Peninsular Malaysia. The 1970 employment structure shows that nearly 80 percent of all Malays were employed in the rural sector, compared with only a little more than half of all non-Malays. Chapter 6 contains a more detailed picture of employment by sector and occupation.

Within the rural sector, Malays predominated in the smallholder segment of agriculture, although they have begun to move more into estate agriculture.[8] A majority of the Indian population has continued to be engaged as estate workers since being brought to Malaysia by the British. Almost half the Malay smallholders—about a seventh of the labor force—worked in paddy farming, which accounted for only 3 percent of the gross domestic product. Most paddy farms were, and still are, owned by Malays. In the rubber smallholder sector, Malays outnumbered Chinese by two to one, but the average size of Chinese holdings (8.3 acres) was almost twice the average size of Malay holdings. About 42 percent of Malay smallholdings were less than three acres, with another 46 percent ranging from three to ten acres.

In the urban areas, which accounted for about a third of total employment in 1970, the non-Malay share exceeded 75 percent. Chinese dominated such modern or quasi-modern sectors as mining, manufacturing, construction, and commerce. In most of the major sectors, Malays tended to be poorly represented among professionals, managers, supervisors, and clerical staff. The relative concentration of non-Malays in urban areas also gave them access to better educational facilities in the

7. Discussions of these issues may be found in Hirschman (1972), Alatas (1977), and Ross-Larson (1977).
8. Information on the ownership of the smallholding sector is scanty. See Government of Malaysia (1973), p. 11.

cities—a factor which has helped in perpetuating their edge over the Malays in the economy.

The pattern of ownership in 1970 shows an extensive participation of European capital in Malaysia's economy. While non–estate agriculture was in the hands of Malay smallholders, more than three-quarters of Malaysia's estate rubber production came from European-owned plantations. The rest originated largely in estates owned by Chinese of Malaysian or Singaporean nationality. European-owned tin mines accounted for almost three-quarters of Malaysia's tin output, and Chinese the remainder. In terms of equity capital, foreign interests accounted for more than three-fifths of the share capital of limited companies in Malaysia in 1970.

Economic Overview

The development of the Malaysian economy has depended historically on the exploitation of land and minerals, with which the country is richly endowed.[9] The main economic activities since the beginning of this century have been natural rubber production and tin mining, alongside traditional agriculture and fishing. This pattern persists. In 1970 tin and rubber accounted for 20 percent of net domestic output and 53 percent of merchandise exports; timber and palm oil accounted for another 21 percent of exports. There are abundant natural and land resources still to be exploited,[10] and the extraction of petroleum is already beginning to play an important part in Malaysian development following recent discoveries of oil and natural gas.

With such a high concentration of primary commodities in domestic production, Malaysia is heavily dependent on foreign trade: exports accounted for almost half its gross national product (GNP) in 1970. The consequent vulnerability of national income to the prices of a few exports is an important feature of the economy, although it is being reduced by progressive diversification. Palm oil production, negligible before World War II, has been developed on a large scale. In fact, Malaysia is now the world's largest exporter of palm oil, and it has consistently been the largest

9. The statistical data in this section have been obtained from recent World Bank economic reports on Malaysia. Wherever possible, economic data for 1970 are presented to allow comparison with the 1970 PES data, the analysis of which forms the subject matter of this book.

10. In addition to the 8 million acres now under cultivation, 4 million acres in Malaysia are still undeveloped and suitable for cultivation.

exporter of natural rubber and tin. Timber extraction has also expanded to take advantage of strong world demand.

Apart from diversification, the government has embarked on major programs to raise productivity of the country's traditional crops: rice and rubber. Rice production has greatly expanded as a result of double-cropping made possible by government irrigation and drainage schemes, but the country still is a net importer. In rubber there has been a far-reaching and massive program to increase productivity by replanting rubber lands with high-yielding varieties of trees. Even the decline in rubber prices by more than a third during the 1960s was absorbed with relative ease because of the dramatic improvements in productivity. Export earnings from rubber managed to grow over that decade, but the share of rubber in total exports declined from about half in 1961 to a third in 1970.[11]

Manufacturing had a relatively late start in Malaysia. Given the openness of the economy and its large import capacity, most manufactured consumer goods were freely imported. But with the need to diversify and reduce the country's dependence on the export of a few primary products, the manufacturing sector has been given increasing attention. Helped in the 1960s by uncertainty about growth in world demand for such traditional products as natural rubber and palm oil, manufacturing came to be regarded as the leading growth sector of the economy. The main stimulus for industrialization has been the protection of domestic manufacturers by selective import tariffs and quotas, as well as various investment incentives. Import substitution, chiefly of consumer goods, caused value added in the sector to expand at almost twice the rate of GNP through the 1960s. Even so, it accounted for only 13 percent of Peninsular Malaysia's GNP in 1970. More recently, manufactured goods have begun to be exported and are fast becoming a substantial export item.

The country's physical infrastructure has been adequate. Substantial investments in transport and communication facilities and in public utilities were made in the 1950s, and physical infrastructure has never represented a serious bottleneck for private development. The government's financial policies have also created and sustained favorable conditions for private initiative. There are few controls on foreign exchange, and the balance of payments position has been strong, with external reserves equal to about six months of imports in recent years. Conservative fiscal and monetary management, including a scrupulous avoidance of recourse to inflationary means for financing budget deficits,

11. In 1976 the share of rubber in total exports was down to about a quarter.

was in part responsible for the remarkable price stability in the 1960s. Between 1957 and 1970 the retail price index moved up by only 0.7 percent a year on the average.

Financial resources do not appear to have constituted a serious constraint on economic development. The external resource position has remained comfortable ever since independence, reflecting in part the inherently strong export position, an adequate and fairly elastic tax system, and careful monetary and economic management. With respect to domestic resources, the long-run marginal savings rate—that is, the increment of GNP saved—has been around 25 percent. For the 1960s as a whole, total national saving exceeded domestic investment, with private saving greater than private investment and public deficits modest. Public sector revenue grew rapidly during the 1960s, mainly as a result of vigorous taxation efforts; the ratio of government revenue to GNP was 23 percent in 1970. The First Malaysia Plan, 1966–70, was drawn up on the premise that the principal constraint on the public sector was a financial bottleneck. But a shortfall of 7 percent in the expenditure target of the plan highlighted the administrative constraint on development: an inadequate capacity for planning and implementation.

There have been shortages of technical and specialized manpower in nearly all government departments and agencies, a problem heightened by the preferential hiring of Malays over non-Malays, although the former have produced relatively few university graduates in science and engineering. Staff shortages have in turn led to problems and delays in the planning and implementation of government programs, especially in the newly established statutory bodies. Project preparation in the public sector is still weak though improving, and government staff support is sometimes inadequate.

During the 1960s Malaysia's GNP increased at about 6 percent a year in constant market prices. When adjusted for the deterioration in the terms of trade, the growth in real income in Malaysia was about 4.5 percent a year, compared with a population growth of 2.6 percent a year. The GNP per capita in 1970 was about US$380, putting Malaysia behind only Hong Kong and Singapore among countries in Southeast Asia.

Political Background

Notwithstanding the relatively high level of economic performance compared with other Asian countries, there are tensions within the Malaysian polity which can be traced to the multiracial nature of the society. In the last decade there has also been increasing concern with the problems of the poor.[12]

The interests of the three major ethnic communities have always presented a challenge to political unity in Malaysia. Well before the transfer of power by the British in 1957, differences emerged between the communities over citizenship and political representation for non-Malays. The United Malays National Organization (UMNO), formed in 1946, successfully opposed a British constitutional plan for the Malayan Union, which was to institute common citizenship for Malays and non-Malays. The Malayan Chinese Association (MCA), formed in early 1949, sought to improve the political status of the Chinese under the Federation of Malaya Agreement of February 1948. The basic problem was "the division in political and economic power, with the Malays having most of the former and the Chinese most of the latter" (Morrison, 1949, p. 253).

A modus vivendi was worked out over time, with concessions being made by both sides. The non-Malays were granted citizenship rights and the freedom to pursue their economic objectives without interference. In return, the Malays became entitled to certain privileges. Simply put, a "social contract" was agreed upon, under which the Malays would have the paramount place in the political life of the country while the Chinese would continue to enjoy their economic position and religious freedom. This basic compact was generally understood and accepted at the time of independence and is reflected in the country's constitution.

The constitution takes into account the multiracial nature of the society and the differences in economic status of the Malay and non-Malay communities. A balance is sought on the basis of a division of responsibilities and functions: the economic prominence of the non-Malays is balanced by the political supremacy of the Malays. While the basically laissez-faire environment has allowed the continuation of non-Malay predominance in commercial and industrial spheres, the constitution has protected the political supremacy of the Malays by giving them preferential access to the civil service and by granting certain rights to Malay rulers. In addition to preserving the sultanates, the constitution has made Islam the national religion. Eighty percent of the senior positions in the administrative and diplomatic services are reserved for Malays (this is intended to offset Chinese predominance in the commercial and industrial sectors). Quotas also apply in the granting of scholarships and in other public

---

12. A political expression of these problems occurred during the Baling disturbances in November 1974 and subsequent student demonstrations in Kuala Lumpur (see Peiris, 1975, pp. 29–31).

training privileges. Permits and licenses needed to operate certain businesses and trades have also been apportioned on an ethnic basis—for example, those for timber extraction and for bus, taxi, and trucking operations. Furthermore, certain land ("Malay reservation") has been earmarked for development by Malays only.[13]

The three main political parties representing the three racial groups got together under one banner shortly before independence. They formed the Alliance, composed of UMNO, MCA, and the Malayan Indian Congress (MIC).[14] The Alliance won comfortable majorities in the national elections of 1955 (under the colonial administration), 1959, and 1964. During this time, it advocated a formula for racial harmony based on the earlier social compact, and it continued to rule after Sabah, Sarawak, and Singapore joined Malaya in 1963 to form Malaysia. But political polarization was increased and this formula was weakened by events such as the separation of Singapore and its large Chinese population from Malaysia in 1965 and the adoption of Bahasa Malaysia as the national language in 1967.

In the 1969 elections the Alliance lost control of the state assembly of Penang and was stalemated in two others—Perak and Selangor—but it still obtained an overall majority. Chinese-based parties, such as the Democratic Action party and the Gerakan Rakyat Malaysia, scored significant gains. These parties, which draw support mainly from the Chinese working class, advocated racial integration and socialist reforms. The results were viewed by some as a victory for the Chinese who were seeking a greater political role for their community. The Pan Malayan Islamic party, which represents Malay nationalism with strong religious overtones, also increased its support at the expense of UMNO and the Alliance. This polarization indicated an erosion of the Alliance's strength and its formula for racial harmony. The situation led to race riots in Kuala Lumpur a few days after the elections in May 1969. The federal parliament and state assemblies were suspended and a state of emergency imposed, with the country run by a National Operations Council.

The polarization of political sentiments and the growing representation by the Chinese in politics seriously undermined the established formula for racial harmony. With the inroads made by the Chinese in the political arena, the traditional Malay dominance in politics and Chinese dominance in the economic sphere no longer applied, and the division of responsibilities and functions became lopsided. Malay nationalist sentiment mounted, and leaders of the ruling party searched for an alternative

13. These Malay privileges are provided in Articles 3, 38, 89, 152, and 153 of the constitution. See Suffian (1972) and Government of Malaysia (1972).
14. The Malayan Indian Congress was started in 1946.

formula. The government responded by proposing steps to build up the economic position of the Malays. Malay rights were reaffirmed, and the New Economic Policy was proclaimed in the Second Malaysia Plan, 1971–75. This policy sought to "correct economic imbalances between the races" by expanding Malay participation in the modern commercial and industrial sectors. Presented largely in terms of national unity, the policy had another objective: to "eradicate poverty among all races." Normal political activity was restored and Parliament was reinstituted in February 1971. The partners of the ruling party preached moderation and unity, and each tried to increase ethnic support by appealing to the middle ground.

The Malay leader of UMNO, Tun Abdul Razak, defended the New Economic Policy and Second Malaysia Plan as "the last chance for everybody's survival and the nation's survival." In the opening address of the 1971 MCA general assembly, he stated:

> The New Economic Policy must succeed. The stakes are too high to allow it to fail. It should not fail, because the Plan is not aimed at promoting any sectional interests. It is a blue-print for the progress and unity of our nation . . . Let there be no misunderstanding as to the objectives of the Second Malaysia Plan. It will not deprive any one group of its legitimate rights. It is not aimed at promoting the interests of any particular community at the expense of others (Razak, 1971, pp. 5–7).

The presidential address at the same assembly was delivered by Tun Tan Siew Sin, who explicitly recognized the other important facet of national unity: "In this day and age, it is not possible to maintain a small island of prosperity in a sea of poverty. The few who are rich cannot maintain their wealth in the midst of widespread and growing poverty. This is against the law of Nature" (Tan, 1971, p. 18).

The proclamation of the New Economic Policy helped defuse the political situation after the racial disturbances in 1969. The political structure was stable after the resumption of Parliament in 1971, and the leadership of the Alliance broadened its support by forming coalitions with opposition parties from the 1969 elections. These came together in 1972 and 1973 as the Barisan Nasional (National Front), which won an overwhelming victory in the general elections in August 1974.

The New Economic Policy

The New Economic Policy (NEP) has as its overriding goal the promotion of national unity through the two-pronged strategy of: (1) eradicating poverty by raising income levels and increasing employment opportunities for all Malaysians, irrespective of race; and (2) accelerating the process of restructuring Malaysian society to correct economic imbalance, so as to reduce and eventually eliminate the identification of race with economic function.

Announced in the Second Malaysia Plan (SMP), 1971–75, the New Economic Policy was presented largely in terms of national unity, which is seen to depend both on the reduction of racial economic imbalances and on the eradication of poverty irrespective of race. Poverty eradication and the correction of racial economic imbalances have thus been enshrined as the twin objectives of the New Economic Policy. Specifically, the objective of racial balance aims to "correct the imbalances in income distribution, employment, and ownership and control of wealth" between the Malays and non-Malays (SMP, p. 41). A fundamental premise of the New Economic Policy is that it will be undertaken in the context of rapid expansion of the economy so as to "ensure that no particular group will experience any loss or feel any sense of deprivation" (SMP, p. 1).[15]

The broad framework for achieving the objectives of the New Economic Policy was first provided in the Outline Perspective Plan (OPP), 1970–90, contained in the *Mid-Term Review of the Second Malaysia Plan* (MTR). The OPP provides a series of long-term targets designed to help restructure the racial composition of employment and the racial ownership of wealth. Such restructuring, it is believed, will help attain a better income balance between the races.

Unlike the objective of racial balance, that of poverty eradication was not elaborated in the SMP documents, nor were any specific targets set. There was no attempt at quantifying or defining poverty, and only general policies were mentioned for its alleviation: for example, "The modernization of rural areas will help Malays and the overall eradication of poverty."

The Third Malaysia Plan (TMP), 1976–80, published in late 1976, gave more explicit emphasis to poverty eradication. It goes some way toward quantifying the extent of poverty and specifying targets for its reduction during the course of the Outline Perspective Plan. It contains specific policies, programs, and projects to help the poor.

Prong 1, the eradication of poverty, needs little comment at this stage; it is discussed at length in chapters 4 and 5, where an attempt is made to define

---

15. Tun Tan Siew Sin believed that the key to the success of the New Economic Policy was "a much faster rate of economic growth, because a re-distribution of wealth to redress economic imbalances, both racial and between the haves and havenots of the same race, would be much easier if the economic cake were much larger. In this way . . . we do not have to take away from those who have in order to give to those who have not. Only the additional cake will be redistributed and this would benefit all" (Tan, 1971, pp. 20–21). The "redistribution with growth" philosophy of Chenery and others (1974) is similar in spirit to this approach.

and measure poverty in Malaysia and to suggest policies for its alleviation. Although the smp did not attempt to define or quantify the extent of poverty, the government visualized the following broad approach for its eradication:

—Expansion of employment opportunities at a rate sufficient to bring about full employment of the labor force by 1990

—Increases in productivity of traditional smallholder agriculture and traditional urban activity

—Encouragement of intersectoral movements of labor from low- to higher-productivity endeavors (Robless, 1975*b*, p. 7).[16]

Prong 2, the second objective, seeks to restructure society and narrow the differences between Malay and non-Malay incomes by reducing disparities in the ownership and control of wealth in the modern sectors and by diminishing the concentration of Malay employment in traditional agriculture while increasing it in the relatively high-income urban sector. The approach adopted by government to correct racial economic imbalances is:

—Expansion of the share of Malays in the ownership of wealth

—Restructuring of the racial pattern of employment between sectors as well as occupations, without decreasing employment opportunities for any race (Robless, 1975*b*, p. 7).

The opp specifies targets for corporate ownership and employment by racial group in 1990. Targets are laid down for the ownership of equity capital only—that is, corporate assets—and noncorporate assets are ignored. One reason presumably is that the government wishes to expand Malay participation mainly in the modern nonagricultural sectors in which Malay ownership is particularly underrepresented. Another reason probably is the lack of data on noncorporate assets.[17] The most significant feature of the structure of equity capital in 1970 was a clear dominance by foreign interests. Of the total share capital of limited companies in Peninsular Malaysia, foreign interests accounted for 60.7 percent. Chinese held 22.5

16. Dr. C. L. Robless was then deputy director-general of the Economic Planning Unit, Prime Minister's Department, Malaysia.

17. There are some data, however, on the ownership of fixed assets in modern agriculture and industry in 1970 (MTR, table 1-4). These show the noncorporate sector to account for a relatively small proportion of fixed assets: in modern agriculture, 29.6 percent of estate acreage (planted); in industry, only 11.6 percent of the value of fixed assets. Malay ownership of corporate industrial assets was only 0.9 percent, whereas it was 47.1 percent of noncorporate estate acreage. Estates are defined as landholdings of more than 100 acres.

percent of the total, Malays 1.9 percent, and Indians 1.0 percent. The remainder—about 14 percent—was held by federal and state governments, statutory bodies, and other Malaysian residents (individuals, nominees, and locally controlled companies).[18] Apart from these figures in the *Mid-Term Review of the Second Malaysia Plan*, there are no other data on the ownership of wealth in Malaysia.

The government's goal in relation to restructuring wealth is to "promote the creation of a commercial and industrial community among Malays and other indigenous people in order that, within one generation, they will own and manage at least 30 percent of the total commercial and industrial activities of the country in all categories and scales of operation."[19] The change in the Malay share of equity capital from 1.9 percent to 30 percent in twenty years obviously implies a considerable degree of restructuring. But government has emphasized that the restructuring is to be undertaken in the context of a rapidly expanding economy. There should, therefore, "be no grounds for fear or anxiety on the part of other Malaysians that government intervention in the private sector on behalf of the Malay community will lead to deprivation of the rights or prospects of non-Malays" (MTR, p. 85). The aim of increasing the share of Malay corporate ownership to 30 percent by 1990 does not entail a smaller share for the non-Malays, since the share of foreign investors is to drop from the present high level of 60.7 percent to 30 percent during the twenty-year period.

The OPP spells out the implications for increasing the Malay share of equity capital during 1970–90 when the total capital of limited companies is projected to grow at an average rate of 11.5 percent a year (MTR, table 4-8).[20] The Malay:non-Malay:foreign proportions of equity capital in 1990 are targeted to be 30:40:30, which entail annual absolute growth rates for the three totals of 27.9 percent, 11.9 percent, and 7.6 percent, respectively. Thus, despite the decline in the foreign share in relative terms, a growth rate of 7.6 percent a year is still implied in absolute terms (Robless, 1975*a*, pp. 53–55).

18. MTR, table 4-7. This table presents a breakdown by race and sector of the ownership of share capital of limited companies in Peninsular Malaysia in 1970. The share of the Malays ranged from 0.7 percent in mining to 3.3 percent in banking and insurance, with 2.5 percent and 2.2 percent in manufacturing and construction, respectively. In transport and communications, however, the Malay share was 13.3 percent. The foreign share was 75.3 percent in agriculture and 72.4 percent in mining and quarrying. In manufacturing, commerce, and banking and insurance, it varied between 50 and 60 percent.

19. MTR, p. 62. The indigenous people of Malaysia include the Kadazans of Sabah and the Ibans of Sarawak in addition to the Malays of Peninsular Malaysia.

20. In the same period, gross domestic product (GDP) is projected to grow at an average rate of 7.0 percent a year (MTR, table 4-6).

It is generally recognized that the 30 percent target for Malay ownership is ambitious. One fundamental difficulty lies in the relative shortage of Malay savings. This shortage is probably due to lower average income levels and a different spending propensity among Malays compared with non-Malays.[21] To supplement the role of individual Malay savers and entrepreneurs in restructuring the racial ownership of wealth, the government has established state-owned and -controlled enterprises and financial institutions that acquire share capital in existing and new companies to be held in trust for the Malays and other indigenous people until such time as they can acquire these shares from their own savings (MTR, pp. 14, 85). The publicly funded corporations are also expected to provide technical, financial, and management assistance to forthcoming Malay entrepreneurs, with the aim of restructuring wealth to "create a Malay entrepreneurial community equipped to play a full and wholesome role in the economic life of the nation" (Robless, 1975a, p. 53). Examples of such public corporations are the Council of Trust for the Indigenous People (MARA), the National Corporation (PERNAS), the Urban Development Authority (UDA), and state economic development corporations (SEDC).[22] These institutions are taking up equity shares in joint ventures with the private sector, shares which will "eventually be transferred to individual ownership of Malays and other indigenous people" (SMP, p. 160). The problems associated with this transfer and the mechanisms for achieving it have still to be faced.[23]

The government's long-term targets for the composition of employment have been set to "ensure that employment in the various sectors of the economy and employment by occupational levels will reflect the racial composition of the country" (MTR, p. 62). The targets for 1990 have been fixed for levels of racial employment by sector (MTR, table 4-5) and by occupational category (TMP, table 4-15).

In 1970 the racial distribution of overall employment for Malays: Chinese:Indians was 52:37:11, which is close to the ratios of the three groups in the population of Peninsular Malaysia. But large deviations from this average existed in certain sectors: Malays were overrepresented in

21. There are as yet no systematic estimates of savings rates by race.

22. UDA is in charge of commercial and property development for Malays. PERNAS was created to promote Malay participation in insurance, construction, trading, properties, engineering, and securities in addition to establishing joint ventures with the private sector.

23. For example, Puthucheary (1977, p. 10) doubts whether the Malays can save enough by 1990 to acquire the shares being held in trust for them by the public corporations. He thinks that "a great part of the 30% target for Malay ownership when achieved is likely to be owned by Malay interests which to all intents and purposes amounts to Government ownership."

agriculture, where output per worker is lowest, and underrepresented in mining, manufacturing, construction, and commerce, where output per worker is two to three times that in agriculture. In agriculture, for instance, the racial composition of employment in 1970 was 68:21:11 for Malays:Chinese:Indians; in manufacturing it was 29:65:6.[24] The OPP seeks to change the racial pattern of employment in each sector (and each occupation) so that by 1990 the three groups are more nearly represented according to their population ratios.

The targets for restructuring racial employment by sector have been chosen in such a way that "there is full employment for all races . . . in 1990" (MTR, p. 78). The *Mid-Term Review of the Second Malaysia Plan* underlines the need for rapid employment growth, particularly in the modern sectors; otherwise "the redistribution required in sectoral employment shares of the various races would lead to the displacement of workers of one racial group or another from their present employment" (MTR, p. 78). In fact, the overall rate of employment growth during 1970–90 has been targeted at an average of 3.3 percent a year, with annual rates of 7.6 percent in manufacturing, 5.0 percent in construction, 4.7 percent in commerce, but only 0.5 percent in mining and 1.2 percent in agriculture.[25] The annual rate of growth of the labor force in this period is estimated at 2.9 percent; that of population at 2.5 percent (MTR, p. 66).

Although restructuring is intended to eliminate the identification of race with economic function, the government recognizes its effects in bringing about income balance. According to MTR (p. 9), "the differences in income between the races have their origin in the concentration of the various races in different sectors of the economy and differences in their occupational position in these sectors." Hence the envisaged restructuring of racial employment, "besides bringing about employment balance, will also remove racial income differentials arising from differentials in sectoral product per worker" (MTR, p. 80).

Inequality, Poverty, and NEP

Malaysia's efforts to reduce poverty and racial imbalances will obviously have an effect on income distribution among individuals. Personal income distribution, an important subject for study in its own right, has recently concerned many governments in developing countries and is increasingly

24. MTR, table 4-4. The racial composition of employment for Malays:Chinese:Indians was 25:66:9 in mining; 22:72:6 in construction; and 24:65:11 in commerce.
25. Computed from MTR, tables 4-4 and 4-5.

the subject of academic research.[26] A study of the individual income distribution allows explicit analysis of poverty[27] and racial income imbalances, and the testing of various hypotheses concerning the effect of racial income inequality on individual income inequality.

The reduction of individual income inequality is not the chief concern of the New Economic Policy, which focuses instead on poverty and interracial inequality. The commitment to poverty eradication, however, can be viewed as a desire to improve the personal income distribution in Malaysia, at least up to the point that poverty has been eradicated. Moreover, the government itself indicates in OPP its aim "to reduce the existing inequitable distribution of income between *income classes* and races" (MTR, p. 62; italics added).[28]

What are the implications of the two prongs of NEP for individual income distribution? Figure 1-1 shows the pattern of individual income distribution for the Malays and non-Malays separately. Although intended to be illustrative, the diagram does embody most features of the actual distributions (see chapters 3 and 6). It shows a higher mean income for the non-Malays than for the Malays and a considerable overlap between the two distributions. A similar pattern of inequality is also indicated in the two distributions around their respective means. The poverty line in the diagram corresponds to the definition of poverty in chapter 4.

Prong 1, the eradication of poverty among all Malaysians irrespective of race, obviously requires the specification of a poverty line, but this has not yet been defined explicitly in the Malaysian plans (including TMP). Since the government has not specified the income levels to which the poor are to be moved in the course of poverty eradication, I define a poverty line in chapter 4 and interpret Prong 1 as simply lifting all the poor up to this level. In figure 1-1 this means moving all poor individuals, Malay and non-Malay, from the left side of the poverty line all the way up to it (but not beyond it).

Prong 2, the correction of racial economic imbalances, is a separate and logically independent goal of NEP. To restructure the racial composition of employment and the racial ownership of wealth it seeks proportional representation of racial groups according to their population ratios in each sector and each occupation. These targets are specified in and of themselves

26. See, for example, Chenery and others (1974), and the references cited therein.

27. Indeed, "relative poverty" can be defined only with reference to the overall level of, and inequality in, individual incomes.

28. Robless (1975*a*) states that an operational aim of NEP is "to raise income levels of all those in the lowest 40% of the population and reduce the present inequality in the size distribution of income."

Figure 1-1. *Individual Income Distribution for Malays and Non-Malays*

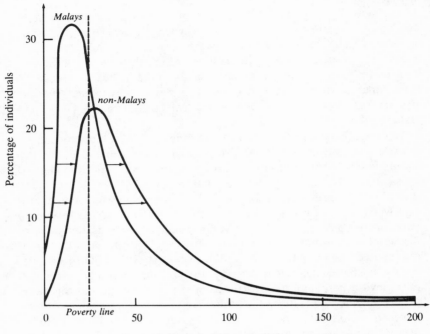

to achieve the wider objective of restructuring, but they have clear implications for racial income distribution. With proportional racial representation at every layer of the economy, a proportional racial representation is also implied at each income level—in other words, the racial groups are proportionately represented along the entire range of incomes. Thus Prong 2, racial balance, can be construed as implying a point-to-point equalization of the Malay and non-Malay income distributions. If non-Malay incomes are not to be reduced, this corresponds to a rescaling of Malay incomes so that the Malay distribution coincides with the non-Malay distribution (see figure 1-1). As Dr. Mahathir Mohamad, the prime minister, once interpreted Prong 2:

> In trying to redress the imbalance it will be necessary to concentrate your effort on the Malays, to bring out more Malay entrepreneurs and to bring out, and to make Malay millionaires, if you like, so that the number of Malays who are rich equals the number of Chinese who are

rich, the number of Malays who are poor equals the number of Chinese who are poor, and the number of unemployed Malays equals the number of unemployed Chinese, then you can say that parity has been achieved (see Low, 1971, p. 74).

Reader's Guide to the Study

In this chapter I have attempted to provide a general introduction and perspective on Malaysia as a backdrop to this study of income distribution. In particular, I have tried to trace the importance of ethnic pluralism in the country, and how this has led to special distributional concerns in the Malaysian context. The correction of racial economic imbalances has been isolated as a major objective of government policy; hence there is a clear need to control for race in the analysis. A further organizing theme of this study is the eradication of poverty irrespective of race, the other principal goal of the New Economic Policy.

Chapter 2 deals with the data source for this study: the Post-Enumeration Survey (PES) of the 1970 census. The chapter begins by describing certain technical aspects of the survey, such as sample design and the definition of income, which have not been documented elsewhere. There is then a discussion of the broad features of the PES household income distribution and a comparison of estimates of average household income based on PES and the national accounts. Next, it considers the possibility of international comparisons of income inequality among countries at approximately Malaysia's level of development. Finally, an attempt is made at intertemporal comparisons of inequality in Malaysia itself, since two earlier surveys by the Malaysian Department of Statistics have reported income data. These surveys are analyzed in some detail to determine their comparability with PES.

Chapter 3 deals with inequality in levels of living in the country. The problems associated with using PES income as a measure of economic welfare are considered, as is the choice of population unit and income concept for measuring inequality. It is argued that the distribution of individuals by per capita household income is more suitable for this purpose than the distribution of households by household income. The joint distribution of households by household income and size is presented so that the relations among the various derived distributions can be determined. Several indices of inequality are computed for these distributions, and the corresponding within-race coefficients and racial disparity ratios are noted. There is a methodological discussion on the decomposition of inequality into within-group and between-group components, and this is applied to estimate the contributions to overall inequality of interracial, interregional, and rural-urban inequalities. The final section considers the policy implications of the results of racial decomposition in terms of the two prongs of NEP and shows that the redress of poverty is also an "efficient" way to redress inequality.

Chapter 4 is concerned with the definition and measurement of poverty in Peninsular Malaysia. It seeks to explore the extent and nature of poverty in the country, so that policy measures for its alleviation can be considered. A poverty line is estimated after alternative approaches to its definition (absolute and relative) are examined. Various indices of poverty are then discussed, ranging from the simple incidence-of-poverty measure to others that take account of the poverty gap. A new index proposed by Sen (1976*a*) is derived, and alternative normalizations are suggested for it. Estimates of all these indices are presented for Peninsular Malaysia, and the simple incidence-of-poverty measure is used to construct a profile of the poor in Peninsular Malaysia. This profile identifies the poor in relation to such socioeconomic variables as race, location, employment status, occupation, and education. The chapter ends with a sensitivity analysis of the profile of poverty with respect to alternative definitions of the poverty line. An appendix contains a profile of "rich" households in Malaysia.

Chapter 5 contains a detailed picture of rural poverty, since 87.7 percent of the poor in Peninsular Malaysia reside in rural areas. The chapter begins by investigating the broad characteristics of rural poverty at the one-digit level. For an efficient design of policies that reduce leakages to the nonpoor, smaller and more homogeneous subgroups that exhibit high rates of poverty are examined. This is done by disaggregating the rural poor according to operationally and analytically relevant categories by using the employment sector and occupational variables cross-classified at the two-digit level. From this matrix are selected five major subgroups which account for about 80 percent of the rural poor: paddy smallholders, laborers on paddy and mixed-agriculture farms, rubber smallholders, workers on rubber estates and smallholdings, and fishermen. The economic problems of these subgroups, and measures to raise their productivity and incomes, are discussed with a view to identifying some major components of rural development policies and projects. The chapter has an appendix on urban poverty.

Chapter 6 analyzes the personal income distribution; that is, the distribution of income recipients by personal income. This is the distribution most directly amenable to policy intervention; it also accounts for much of the inequality in levels of living. Various inequality indices are computed for the personal income distribution, and comparisons made with distributions considered in chapter 3. Racial-disparity ratios for personal income are compared with those for household and per capita household income; the differences are explained by racial variations in average household size and participation rate. There is a decomposition of personal income inequality by race, urban or rural location, and region, and further decompositions by employment status, occupational category, and industrial sector. These help in identifying *sources* of income inequality in the country and in examining the "association of race with economic function and geographical location" (NEP Prong 2). Combinations of the variables are used to perform multivariate decompositions, which help in evaluating the appropriateness of these categories for studying inequality in developing countries.

Chapter 7 explores the empirical relations among age, education, and income of urban employees. This is done through a detailed regression analysis of earnings functions based on the human capital model. The subsample of urban employees is chosen because PES income is likely to be a good measure of earnings only for this group (data on earnings or labor income are not given separately in PES). Some properties of the earnings function are derived (in an appendix) which are useful in interpreting the regression results. The estimated equations thus provide rough orders of magnitude for private rates of return to education, for the percentage of inequality explained by the life-cycle factors of age and education, and for the peak and peakedness of the age-income profile. A disaggregation by racial group and occupation permits the testing of some interesting hypotheses about racial and occupational differences in average levels of and returns to education. Further disaggregations are by sex of employee, language of instruction, type of degree, age cohort, and region. The earnings functions illuminate various aspects of the relation between education and income and conveniently summarize much information about the urban labor market in Malaysia.

Chapter 8, the concluding chapter of the study, starts with a review of the principal findings on inequality and poverty in Malaysia. The rest of the chapter is divided roughly into policy analyses of Prongs 1 and 2 of the New Economic Policy. First there is a general discussion of policies to reduce poverty in Malaysia. Four broad types of policy are isolated which seem particularly relevant in the Malaysian context: direct income transfers, fiscal policies, intervention in commodity markets, and rural development policies. These are discussed and evaluated in the light of information about the poor from the poverty profiles and subgroups (chapters 4 and 5). There is then a short review of the implications of the employment restructuring target of Prong 2. The chapter ends with a brief discussion of the interactions and complementarities between the two prongs of NEP.

The six technical appendixes dealing with the measurement of income inequality are an integral part of the study. They are partly a unified review of recent literature relevant to this analysis of Malaysian data, and partly a presentation of results that have arisen out of measurement problems encountered in the course of this empirical work. Appendix A contains a brief review of inequality indices based on the Lorenz diagram, many of which have been estimated using data from the Post-Enumeration Survey (PES). Appendix B considers various definitions of the Gini coefficient and demonstrates their equivalence. It also derives some interesting properties of the Gini coefficient, such as its nondecomposability. Appendix C derives the decomposition of three inequality measures used in this study: Theil's entropy index T, Theil's second measure L, and the variance of log-income. Definitions are given of the between- and within-group contributions for these measures, and their decomposition formulas are deduced. Appendix D presents Atkinson's theorem and proves the equivalence of two types of ranking of income distributions (Lorenz dominance and the principle of transfers) which are important for positive measurement of inequality. Appendix E contains new results on Lorenz dominance, which enable unambiguous comparisons of inequality between related distributions defined over different population units and income concepts. This appendix also contains a statement and derivation of the redress of poverty rule. Appendix F discusses the mapping of the household to the per capita household income distribution. It derives the mathematical transformations required to effect the mapping and states conditions under which one distribution will be more or less equal than the other.

2

The 1970
Post-Enumeration Survey
and Comparisons
with Other Surveys

THE 1970 POST-ENUMERATION SURVEY (PES) is the data base for this study of Malaysian income distribution. In this chapter, I examine and evaluate the PES in detail before proceeding to a full analysis of the data in later chapters. To enable an assessment of the quality of PES data, a documentation is provided of the survey design, sampling procedure, income definition, and other technical aspects. Such documentation on the survey is not available elsewhere, and an official report on PES has not been prepared.

This chapter also presents in summary form some estimates of the PES household income distribution. It is concerned with broad facts about inequality in Malaysia, such as the degree of overall inequality and rural-urban and racial income inequality, leaving detailed analyses to later chapters. The possibility of comparing inequality in Malaysia with inequality in other countries is discussed, and an attempt is made at intertemporal comparisons in Malaysia itself using income data reported by two previous surveys: the 1967–68 Malaysian Socio-Economic Sample Survey of Households and the 1957–58 Household Budget Survey.

Recently there has been much interest and speculation about international and intertemporal inequality in developing countries,[1] but little hard evidence is available on the subject. Even where the data exist, few studies have attempted to analyze the data sources and tackle the serious problems of comparability among them. I deal with this problem head-on

1. See Kuznets (1955 and 1963), Adelman and Morris (1973), Paukert (1973), and Ahluwalia (1974a and 1976). Following Kuznets, the latter authors have attempted to establish an inverse U-shaped relation between inequality and development on the basis of cross-country experience.

in the case of Malaysian survey data, bringing to bear all relevant evidence about the earlier surveys. Since the published report on the 1957–58 Household Budget Survey is deficient in information about sample coverage, definition of income, and the like, I have reconstructed an account of this survey from unpublished records and files of the Malaysian Department of Statistics. This account is documented in detail and used to demonstrate that the 1957 survey is not comparable with the 1970 survey, and that no conclusions can be drawn from these surveys about inter-temporal changes in inequality. The exercise illustrates the danger of comparing the data on inequality from different surveys after a superficial examination which does not first establish comparability.

The chapter is divided into three major sections. The first section deals with the Post-Enumeration Survey as the data base for the entire study; it contains subsections on sample design, definition of PES income, and coding and estimation of PES income data. The second section deals with broad features of the PES household income distribution; it contains subsections on household income inequality, estimates of average household income based on PES and national accounts, and comparisons of inequality in Malaysia with that in other countries. The final section deals with intertemporal comparisons of inequality in Malaysia; it contains subsections on the Malaysian Socio-Economic Sample Survey of Households (MSSH), the Household Budget Survey (HBS), the sample design and income definition of HBS, and a detailed comparison between PES and HBS.

The 1970 Post-Enumeration Survey

The Post-Enumeration Survey (PES) is a very large sample survey covering some 135,000 individuals, or approximately 1.5 percent of the population of Peninsular Malaysia. It was conducted in September 1970, immediately after the 1970 Census of Population and Housing. Its chief purpose was to check on the undercoverage and content of the population census, but some family planning and income questions were included as well. The survey was thus primarily designed to check in detail such census items as age and education, rather than to measure income distribution accurately. Since the PES was not an income survey as such, it is possible that the usual errors associated with responses on income may have been aggravated. These are nonsampling errors which arise from incorrect or biased responses, including deliberate understatement of income at the upper end of the distribution and possible overstatement at the lower end. Such errors are generally minimized by asking a multiplicity of related questions which serve as indirect checks on the reported level of income.

It was recognized that a survey which includes only a few questions on income may suffer from poor and evasive responses. Therefore, considerable probing and prompting were attempted in the PES to obtain satisfactory income data. The following instruction was issued on this subject to field interviewers:

> Conceptually and operationally, this is the most difficult information to obtain. Very often people are afraid of telling their true income, and are often prone to understate the amount they receive. They blow up the difficulties and underplay the receipts. Many even forget certain kinds of income that have to be incorporated in the overall monthly income. Hence it is necessary to be patient, tactful, and at the same time probe to ensure no major sources of income are missed out. Ideally, we would like to ask a multitude of questions and from that derive the correct and complete income of the earning members of the household. But this is not an Income Survey, hence we will have to obtain the correct responses with the least number of questions.
>
> A large part of the accuracy of this data depends on your own ingenuity as an interviewer, and how best you can probe and probe. Let us try and explain this further. It is obvious that on visiting a particular household and talking to the respondent, you will have a feeling on two things—(a) if the household is in the very low income group, low income group, middle income group or high income group; and (b) the type of occupation in which the earning members are generally engaged.
>
> Using these two, you can judge if the reported income seems too high or too low. If you feel the reported income seems incorrect, keep probing . . . If you know a household is in a high income group, based on the Radio, Television, Air-conditioner, Cars, etc. in the place, then clearly you should keep asking simple but effective questions to trace if there are further sources of income which have not been mentioned (Department of Statistics, 1970*b*, p. 31).

To assess the reliability of data collected, an elaborate procedure of checks and rechecks was instituted at the levels of field interviewer, regional office, and headquarters (see the appendix to this chapter for some of the checks). The checks were carried out by field interviewers[2] and a small,

---

2. Field interviewers possessed at least a school certificate (that is, they had graduated from secondary school) and underwent intensive training for four weeks on the PES questionnaire. The average age of interviewers was around twenty-one years, and they were paid a monthly income of M$180 plus M$5 outstation allowance (equivalent to US$68 in 1970 U.S. dollars), which was well above the average personal income in Malaysia (see chapter 6). To avoid communication and other barriers, households were interviewed by persons of the same racial group.

well-qualified group of full-time field enumerators supervised by full-time regional supervisors. Enumerators were sent back to the field if, in the opinion of supervisors, income data had not been collected satisfactorily. Although there are bound to remain inaccuracies in the data, the PES does appear a fairly reliable source of information on personal incomes in Malaysia.

PES Sample Design

The PES sample design is not yet officially documented. Much of the description here is based on discussions with V. T. Palan, senior statistician in the Malaysian Department of Statistics, who was responsible for the survey. Briefly, the sampling procedure for PES was as follows. The interview unit (or "ultimate" sampling unit) was the household, defined as a group of people who live together with a common budget for food and other essentials of living. The following instruction was given to field enumerators on the definition:

A household may be either a one-person household or a multi-person household. (i) A *one-person household* is one where a person lives alone in a separate room or rooms and is part of a dwelling unit but does not join with any of the other occupants of the dwelling unit to form part of a multi-person household as defined below. (ii) A *multi-person household* is a group of two or more persons who combine to occupy the whole or part of a housing unit and provide themselves with food or other essentials of living. The group may pool their incomes and have a common budget to a greater or lesser extent. The group may be composed of related persons only, or only of unrelated persons, or a combination of both; as for example, a family with servants who spend their whole lives with them. The general criteria which should be used in identifying members of a multi-person household are common house-keeping arrangements, sharing the principal meals in the sense that the household's food supply is obtained for common consumption or paid for out of a common budget and having common arrangements for supplying basic living needs and are normally living together (Department of Statistics, 1970*a*, pp. 4–5).

Since the PES was a follow-up to the 1970 Population and Housing Census, its sample frame was naturally based on the latter. The country was partitioned into artificial geographical areas called enumeration blocks, which formed the "basic" (or "elementary") sampling unit. Altogether there were 15,594 enumeration blocks covering Peninsular Malaysia, with each one estimated to contain approximately sixty to eighty households.

A two-stage stratified sampling technique was employed to select the households. At the first stage the universe of 15,594 enumeration blocks was stratified into sixteen areas according to rural-urban and regional characteristics; for this purpose, Peninsular Malaysia was divided into three strata:

Metropolitan towns: those with an estimated population in excess of 75,000

Towns: those with a population between 10,000 and 75,000

Rural areas: places with a population less than 10,000

and five regions:

South: the states of Johore and Malacca
Central: Selangor and Negri Sembilan
Northwest: Perak
North: Penang, Kedah, and Perlis
East: Kelantan, Trengganu, and Pahang.

The three strata and five regions were used to delineate the following sixteen areas (see the frontispiece map):

Metropolitan towns in Peninsular Malaysia, that is, Johore Bahru, Malacca, Kuala Lumpur, Klang, Ipoh, and Georgetown (6 areas)

Towns in each region (5 areas)

Rural areas in each region (5 areas).

A sample of 1,138 enumeration blocks was selected from the stratified universe of 15,594 using probabilities proportional to the size of the block. The blocks selected contained some 670,000 persons, or approximately 8 percent of the total population.

The census books of house-listings provided the frame for the second stage of selection. The private households listed in the census book for each selected enumeration block were serially renumbered, and a random sample of households was drawn from this enumeration.[3]

This two-stage sampling procedure led to the ultimate selection for interview of about 27,000 households in the country. Owing to nonresponse,[4] however, income information was obtained for only 25,023

3. The sample represented all segments of the total population with one small exception: unattached males living in barracks in military encampments were not represented. They constituted an unknown fraction of the 45,903 military personnel that occupied military establishments.

4. Nonrespondents were those households or individuals within households who refused to provide information for PES, and those listed in the census frame who had moved out after the census. There was a gap of three to four weeks between the census and the PES.

households, or 134,186 individuals.[5] No estimates of sampling error have yet been computed. The absolute sample size is so large, however, that the sampling errors on income are likely to be quite insignificant.[6]

The check for undercoverage in the census consisted of relisting households in the enumeration blocks selected at the first stage. The first task was to relist actual houses (living quarters), which made possible an identification of those that had been missed in the census. The second task was to establish by means of interview the number of households and individuals in each house, and the results were compared with information obtained in the earlier census interviews. When there were unreconciled discrepancies, a further visit was made to the household in question. Through this process of repeated visits, individuals who had been overlooked in the census were discovered. The undercoverage check revealed an underenumeration in the census of 4.05 percent, which has a sampling error of 0.48 percentage points. Hence the PES adjusted population of Peninsular Malaysia in mid-1970 was 9,182,000, with a 95 percent probability that the true population lay within plus or minus 46,000 of this estimate.

The content check on the census consisted of re-interviewing intensively the households selected at the second stage of the PES sample. The selected households were re-interviewed on such census items as age and education, and questions were also asked on individual and household incomes. The interview was usually conducted with the household head,[7] but for income questions individual recipients were interviewed. If they were not available during the first visit, the interviewer came back at a later time to see them. The percentage of the population of Peninsular Malaysia for whom "valid" income data were thus obtained is 1.46 percent (or approximately one person in sixty-eight).

---

5. Income information was actually obtained for 25,025 households or 134,192 individuals. However, the racial group of two households (six individuals) was not available, and the effective sample size was reduced to 25,023 households or 134,186 individuals.

6. Dr. Roe Goodman, the UNDP adviser on sample surveys in the Malaysian Department of Statistics, has prepared some preliminary estimates of standard error for the sample proportions (and cumulative proportions) in twenty-three PES income intervals.

7. The household head was identified largely by the members themselves. The following instruction was given to field enumerators: "By head of household we mean a person who is accepted by the rest of the members as being the person who makes a major decision in the household. By and large, this will be the husband or in very rare cases the wife. Generally this will offer very little problem since the households themselves will tell you who is the head. Obtain the names in full. In case the household consists of unrelated persons, write the name of the person the others accept as the head. If this is not possible, write any one of their names" (Department of Statistics, 1970a).

COMPARISONS OF PES WITH OTHER SURVEYS

Definition of PES Income

The PES concept of individual and household income appears to be fairly comprehensive, including income received in kind as well as cash. A money value was imputed to receipts in kind, to own consumption from production, and to owner-occupied housing. Eleven major categories of income were distinguished to enable an accurate estimate of true income (see Department of Statistics, 1970c, sec. E on "Individual and Household Income"). They are:

1. Wages, salaries, and other receipts
2. Income from sale of produce
3. Income from jointly owned business or farm
4. Income from rent and investments (excluding capital gains)
5. Pensions, remittances, cash allowances, royalties, fees, and other receipts
6. Other periodic cash receipts, such as alimonies and scholarships
7. Money value of income in kind such as food, clothing, and housing
8. Money value of own consumption of produce
9. Money value of goods received from other sources
10. Imputed rent of owner-occupied house
11. Other concessions.

Two separate questions on income were in fact asked of respondents (see the appendix to this chapter, Questions 5 and 6 from section E of the questionnaire). The first simply asked the average monthly income (over the previous year) of each person in the household in receipt of some form of income. The response was designated as "stated income" and recorded. This is the respondent's own perception of income and probably corresponds to cash receipts (categories 1–6 above). The second question probed income recipients about each of the eleven sources of income and designated the total for each recipient as "computed income." The instruction given to field interviewers was: "This question is primarily aimed at obtaining data on income by going through each and every source of income. By so doing we hope that the respondent will be able to think about each of the categories carefully, and say if he had any income from that source" (Department of Statistics, 1970b, p. 37). In contrast to stated income, therefore, computed income includes all the imputed values on the checklist and is likely to be a better estimate of true income.[8] Although

8. Some categories of income, such as capital gains and production for own investment, seem to have been omitted from the checklist. The latter category includes own farm improvements, such as fencing and embankments for irrigation ditches, which are not easy to value, in part because there is no market for them.

information on each of the eleven components of income was collected and entered separately in the PES questionnaire form (Department of Statistics, 1970c), only the total, unfortunately, was coded onto the data tapes. The opportunity for many interesting analyses on income distribution has thereby been lost.

PES income refers to gross or pretax income for the average month, and no particular reference month is specified. Data collected in this manner suffer from the drawback that recall lapse is increased (in effect, the respondent is being asked to estimate annual income and divide it by twelve), but there is the advantage that seasonal variations in income are ironed out over the year. The need to avoid questions that are too specific has been pointed out by the senior statistician responsible for designing the PES:

> Very specific answers to even very recent instances may be un-representative and misleading. For example, information on the pre-vious month's cash income may be completely misleading if it happened to be a festival month and workers had been paid bonuses. Similarly since many activities vary seasonally, questions relating to behaviour on a particular day or week may elicit far less accurate data than questions on the usual or "average" behaviour (Palan, 1968, p. 40).

For some categories of income, the data were sought for the previous year and then converted into an average monthly figure. For example, to obtain a farmer's monthly income from sale of produce (category 2), the PES interviewer obtained data on farm output and costs on an annual basis and divided the difference by twelve. The following instruction was issued to field interviewers for the estimation of household business and farm incomes:

> If the earning members of the household are engaged in, say, a business activity, then the monthly income would be the annual profit, divided by twelve. Remember, if someone says that his wife and daughter are family workers, they will not have a separate income. The wages that should have been paid to them would have been included in the net profit. If, however, the wife and daughter are treated as employees, then their incomes would have to be accounted for separately. Again, in the case of self-employed persons, ask and compute the monetary value for the owner-occupied house (even if part of the shop), goods consumed from the shop, free electricity and water supply, etc.
>
> Similarly, in the case of a farm worker his income would be the sale of total produce for the year divided by twelve. Plus the value of the produce bartered, consumed, and stored for future use. Also include income from miscellaneous sources—like government aid, scholarships

to children, free books, subsidized items like fertilizers, etc., receipts from working sons and daughters elsewhere, etc. Farm expenses such as for seeds, fertilizers, etc. should be subtracted before obtaining the income.

Generally, a family or unpaid helper will not receive any income. But even so, confirm this with the respondent. Again, unpaid helpers sometimes work as employees for others; you should obtain the average monthly income from this (Department of Statistics, 1970*b*, p. 31).

Perhaps the most serious shortcoming of PES is that prices for the imputation of payments in kind and own consumption of produce were largely left to the discretion of respondents, with only minimal checks. This can introduce significant measurement errors in the income of subsistence and peasant farmers, as the difference between farm-gate (producer) and retail (consumer) prices is sometimes quite large. According to the senior statistician for PES, however, it is likely that market prices were used to value the own consumption of a farmer if he was a net buyer, and farm-gate prices if he was a net seller.[9] The part of a farmer's produce actually sold (income category 2) would necessarily have been valued at farm-gate prices.

The method used to impute the rental value of an owner-occupied house (income category 10) was, whenever possible, simply to take the actual rent on a similar house in the neighborhood. If no neighboring houses were rented, an attempt was made to establish the current replacement value of the property from its owner or from some other knowledgeable person in the area. The replacement value was estimated by costing the building materials, labor services, and other inputs at local prices. A monthly rental value was estimated by converting the replacement value into an annual stream at 10 percent and dividing by twelve. The procedure was sometimes difficult to follow in rural areas, owing to imperfect markets for rented housing and limited knowledge about cost structures. Where no information could be obtained, a monthly rental value between M$10 and M$15, depending on condition, was assumed for the typical kampong (village) house with attap (thatched) roof. By contrast, the monthly rent for a typical two-storied shop-house in urban areas was about M$60.

9. According to the senior statistician for PES, if the farmer consumes his entire produce and is a net buyer, he is likely to have the market price in mind rather than the farm-gate price. But if he consumes a part of his produce and is a net seller, he is more likely to have the farm-gate price in mind, as this is the price he receives for his sales. Imputation at these prices does reflect correctly the marginal value to him of consumption. When the farmer consumes his entire produce and is neither a net buyer nor a net seller, the value to him of marginal consumption lies between the retail and farm-gate prices. The satisfaction of these marginal conditions does not, of course, resolve the problem of comparing standards of living across households when their consumption has been valued at different prices.

The Coding of PES Income Data

The actual incomes received by individuals, in Malaysian dollars (M$) per month, were recorded on the completed questionnaries by interviewers. These data were then grouped and coded according to two different interval classifications with nine and ten intervals, respectively. The upper open-ended income class began at M$750 for one classification and at M$980 for the other.[10] Subsequently, the Department of Statistics prepared another, more detailed coding of incomes into twenty-three intervals with the uppermost interval beginning at M$5,000.

I have meshed the three different codings to create a new thirty-two-interval classification of PES income data. The result of combining the original two classifications is to make the intervals much finer at lower income levels. The third classification adds many more intervals at upper income levels above M$980 (see table 2-1). The new classification obviously permits more accurate estimates of Malaysian income distribution, which is especially important at the lower end of the distribution for a detailed analysis of poverty (chapters 4 and 5).[11]

Estimating the Household Income Distribution from Coded Data

To estimate the household income distribution it is necessary to know the actual income of each household. Unfortunately, this is no longer available because the income data were coded into intervals![12] The problem, therefore, is to reassign an income level to each household, given the interval in which it falls. It is assumed that all households within an interval receive the mean income for that interval; thus it remains to estimate interval means for each income class, including the open-ended one.

Interval means for the upper income classes were calculated by assuming that household incomes in this range follow a theoretical Pareto distribution.[13] Interval means for the lower income classes, which are fairly

10. See Department of Statistics (1973), pp. 4-5 and 10-11.
11. The greater number of income classes also reduces income measurement error in the estimation of earnings functions (chapter 7).
12. The problem addressed in this subsection arises solely because the income data were grouped into intervals. It is not known why actual income figures were not coded onto the data tapes.
13. There are various economic models, stochastic and deterministic, which predict a theoretical Pareto distribution for the upper income ranges. This distribution is also known to fit extremely well at high income levels in a number of countries.

narrow, were simply chosen at the interval midpoints. The truncation point for the Pareto distribution, that is, the distinction between upper and lower income classes, was determined by an ad hoc goodness-of-fit criterion.

The cumulative Pareto distribution in log-linear form can be written as

$$\log n(y) = \log A - \alpha \log y,$$

where y denotes household income, and $n(y)$, the number of households with income greater than or equal to y. This equation was estimated sequentially for an increasing number of income classes, starting from the top down. The $\overline{R}^2$'s and $\hat{\alpha}$'s were computed for each equation. Subject to the constraint that $\overline{R}^2$ exceeds 0.99, I chose the equation which maximized the fitted portion of the distribution (that is, the equation which included as many of the upper income classes as possible).[14] This somewhat arbitrary procedure led to the selection of the equation fitting the top eighteen income classes (more than M$500 per month), which account for 10.7 percent of households:

$$\log n(y) = 9.3 - 2.1455 \log y$$
t-ratio of $\hat{\alpha} = 48.59$
$\overline{R}^2 = 0.993$
Degrees of freedom $= 16$.

Mean household incomes for the top eighteen intervals were calculated using this equation with coefficient $\alpha = 2.1455$. Given a continuous Pareto distribution with coefficient α, the mean income in any interval $[a, b]$ can be shown to be

$$\frac{\alpha}{(\alpha - 1)} \frac{(b^{1-\alpha} - a^{1-\alpha})}{(b^{-\alpha} - a^{-\alpha})}.$$

Thus the mean income for the upper open-ended class ($a =$ M$5,000, $b = \infty$) was computed as M$9,365.[15] The means computed for the other seventeen intervals at the top are shown in table 2-1. Owing to the shape of the Pareto distribution, it is clear that the means computed by this method will be smaller than the interval midpoints. The differences, however, turn out to be not large.

Mean incomes for the fourteen remaining classes at the bottom of the distribution were assumed to be the interval midpoints. Since these intervals are relatively narrow, any errors from this assumption are likely to be quite small. Hence this procedure was considered as acceptable as one in which a

14. Standard practice appears to be to determine the Pareto coefficient α by fitting such an equation to the top two income classes only.

15. See the later subsection "Household Income Inequality in Malaysia" for the sensitivity of the household income distribution to alternative assumptions concerning mean income of the upper open-ended class.

Table 2-1. PES Income Intervals, Means, and Absolute Frequencies
(Malaysian dollars per month)

Code no.	Income interval	Interval midpoint	Estimated interval mean for household income distribution	Absolute frequency of households	Estimated interval mean for personal income distribution[c]	Absolute frequency of income recipients[c]
0	No income	0	0	341	0	0
1	1–39	20	20	1,336	20	6,018
2	40–49	45	45	711	45	2,103
3	50–79	65	65	2,751	65	6,889
4	80–99	90	90	1,898	90	4,273
5	100–129	115	115	2,712	115	5,693
6	130–149	140	140	1,596	140	2,373
7	150–179	165	165	2,251	165	3,217
8	180–199	190	190	1,204	190	1,395
9	200–279	240	240	3,625	233[b]	3,716
10	280–299	290	290	581	290[b]	471
11	300–399	350	350	2,175	343[b]	1,921
12	400–479	440	440	999	436[b]	846
13	480–499	490	490	168	490[b]	119
14	500–599	550	545[a]	693	545[b]	536

No.	Income range					
15	600–679	640	637[a]	412	637[b]	292
16	680–699	690	690[a]	69	690[b]	40
17	700–749	725	724[a]	160	724[b]	114
18	750–799	775	774[a]	122	774[b]	80
19	800–899	850	847[a]	246	847[b]	149
20	900–979	940	938[a]	142	938[b]	101
21	980–999	990	990[a]	29	990[b]	5
22	1,000–1,249	1,125	1,110[a]	295	1,111[b]	180
23	1,250–1,499	1,375	1,363[a]	163	1,363[b]	72
24	1,500–1,749	1,625	1,615[a]	100	1,615[b]	48
25	1,750–1,999	1,875	1,866[a]	44	1,867[b]	24
26	2,000–2,499	2,250	2,221[a]	83	2,222[b]	57
27	2,500–2,999	2,750	2,726[a]	44	2,727[b]	27
28	3,000–3,499	3,250	3,230[a]	26	3,230[b]	17
29	3,500–3,999	3,750	3,733[a]	19	3,733[b]	13
30	4,000–4,999	4,500	4,442[a]	11	4,444[b]	6
31	5,000+	—	9,365[a]	19	9,736[b]	11
All	0+	—	264	25,025	163	40,806

—Not applicable.
a. Estimated by assuming Pareto distribution with coefficient 2.1455 valid in the range.
b. Estimated by assuming Pareto distribution with coefficient 2.0559 valid in the range (see "The Distribution of Income Recipients by Personal Income," in chapter 6).
c. See chapter 6 for an analysis of the personal income distribution.

33

separate theoretical distribution, such as the lognormal, is fitted to the lower tail and the interval means computed from its estimated parameters.

Estimation of the Gini Coefficient

Various indices of inequality have been used in income distribution studies (see appendix A, "A Brief Review"). The Gini coefficient, however, remains the most popular measure in use, and it is also estimated here. My definition of the Gini coefficient is based on the Lorenz curve for an income distribution (see appendix A), which is estimated here by linear interpolation between observed points. In general, there will be thirty-two observed points corresponding to the thirty-two-interval classification of PES income data.

The Gini coefficient is defined as the ratio of the area between the Lorenz curve and the diagonal of perfect equality, to the area of the triangle below this diagonal. The actual formula used to compute the Gini coefficient G is equivalent to this definition (see appendix B, "The Gini Coefficient"):

$$G = 1 - \sum_{i=0}^{31} (F_{i+1} - F_i)(\Phi_{i+1} + \Phi_i)$$

where F_i is the cumulative population share, and Φ_i is the cumulative income share, corresponding to the ith interval. It can also be expressed as

$$G = \sum_{i=1}^{31} (F_i \Phi_{i+1} - F_{i+1} \Phi_i).$$

The approximation of the Lorenz curve by a piecewise linear interpolation of points on it underestimates the Gini coefficient. This is because the line segments in the approximation always lie above the true Lorenz curve, which is easily shown as convex (appendix A). Since there are as many as thirty-two well-spaced points on the curve, however, the piecewise linear approximation of it should be reasonably accurate. At any rate, a comparison between Gini coefficients of different distributions is unlikely to be biased when their Lorenz curves are similarly closely estimated.[16]

The PES Household Income Distribution

A detailed discussion of inequality in Malaysia is deferred until chapter 3. This section presents summary information on average income levels and

16. For this reason, I did not feel it worthwhile to estimate the Lorenz curve in a statistically more sophisticated fashion—for example, by the methods recently proposed in Kakwani and Podder (1973, 1976). Such a procedure would allow us to determine confidence limits for the parameters characterizing the Lorenz curve and Gini coefficient.

inequality, as revealed by the PES. The information is presented in terms of the household income distribution, which is the distribution reported by most surveys in Malaysia and elsewhere. It is later argued that this distribution does not provide a good indication of inequality in levels of living because it takes no account of household size and composition, and more appropriate distributions are considered in chapter 3. Primarily for comparison with other surveys, I begin by setting out some relevant features of the PES household income distribution.

Household Income Inequality in Malaysia

Table 2-2 summarizes the household income distribution from the PES and two previous Malaysian surveys (discussed in the next section). The PES shows an average household income in 1970 of M$264 (approximately US$100) per month and a Gini inequality coefficient of 0.5129.

Since estimates of the PES household income distribution are all based on interval means computed from a specific Pareto distribution, their sensitivity should really be tested with respect to alternative assumptions about the underlying theoretical distribution. The only interval mean that can be affected significantly is the one for the upper open-ended class; the other interval means are likely to remain close to the interval midpoints for distributions with "reasonable" shape. Hence I have tried to test the sensitivity of the estimates for average household income and household income inequality with respect to alternative assumptions for mean income in the class M$5,000 and over. The results show that the estimates are not unduly sensitive:

Mean assumed for income class M$5,000+ per month	Mean of household income distribution	Gini coefficient of household income distribution	Theil T index of household income distribution
5,000	261	0.5066	0.5028
9,365	264	0.5129	0.5378
10,000	265	0.5136	0.5434
15,000	268	0.5205	0.5900
20,000	272	0.5272	0.6399

As shown in appendix E, corollary 1, one expects inequality in the Lorenz sense to increase as the income of the richest person(s) in the distribution is increased. Since both the Gini coefficient and the Theil T index satisfy mean independence, population-size independence, and the Pigou-Dalton condition, they should show more inequality for a distribution which is Lorenz-dominated (see the proposition in appendix D); this is borne out by the figures above.

Table 2-2. Household Income Inequality in Malaysia

Area and race	HBS, 1957–58[a] Mean household income (M$ per month)	HBS, 1957–58[a] Gini coefficient	MSSH, 1967–68[b] Mean household income (M$ per month)	MSSH, 1967–68[b] Gini coefficient	PES, 1970 Mean household income (M$ per month)	PES, 1970 Gini coefficient
Area						
Peninsular Malaysia	199	0.3705	217	0.5624	264	0.5129
Rural Malaysia	170	0.3549	114	0.4794	200	0.4689
Urban Malaysia	261	0.3514	283	0.5224	428	0.5037
Race						
Malay	144	0.3410	130	0.5072	172	0.4664
Chinese	272	0.3322	321	0.5081	394	0.4656
Indian	217	0.3117	253	0.4974	304	0.4722
Other	n.a.	n.a.	839	0.4912	813	0.6673
Sample size (number of households)	2,760[c]		30,000[d]		25,023	

n.a. Not available.

a. There are twenty-eight size intervals in the Household Budget Survey (HBS), with no open-ended income class. The topmost income class is M$900–M$1,000. There is also no separate zero-income class, zero incomes being lumped in the range of M$0–M$25 per month (see Department of Statistics [1961?], p. 39; hereafter cited as HBS *Report*).

b. The income data for the Malaysian Socio-Economic Sample Survey of Households (MSSH) are presented in seven income classes (including a zero-income category), with the top open-ended class beginning at M$750 per month. A Pareto distribution was fitted through the last two income classes alone, giving $\hat{\alpha} = 1.7622$ and a mean of M$1,735 for the open-ended interval.

c. Of the 2,760 households sampled, 1,920 were in rural areas and 840 in urban areas. Since the HBS *Report* did not break down sample size by ethnic group and urban-rural location, I have chosen the same proportions as in the 1957 population census.

d. Approximate.

Sources: HBS *Report*; Department of Statistics (1970g); and PES, 1970.

The mean household income varies among racial groups from M$172 per month for Malays to M$813 per month for "other" communities (including Europeans, Thais, other Asians, and so on). The mean household income of Chinese is M$394 per month, and of Indians M$304 per month. Thus the oft-quoted racial disparity ratios, which are supposed to indicate average income differences between the races, are 2.29 for Chinese:Malay, and 1.77 for Indian:Malay.

Despite these large differences in average household income, the Chinese and Malay distributions appear very similar about their respective means: for Malays the Gini coefficient is 0.4664, and for Chinese it is 0.4656. The Indian distribution is just a little more unequal, with a Gini coefficient of 0.4722. The "others" distribution is very much more unequal, and its high Gini coefficient of 0.6673 reflects the large income disparities among the Europeans, Thais, and other Asians who constitute this group.[17] Further details of the PES household income distribution, with a breakdown by racial group, may be found in table 3-7.

The PES disaggregates urban areas into metropolitan towns and towns,[18] but sometimes I treat them together for uniformity of comparison with earlier surveys. The PES average household income in urban areas is M$428 per month while that in rural areas is M$200 per month, implying a disparity ratio of 2.14. Rural household incomes are distributed significantly more equally than urban household incomes (Gini coefficient of 0.4689 compared with 0.5037), and the incomes within each location are distributed more equally than in Peninsular Malaysia as a whole (Gini coefficient of 0.5129).

For the racial disparity ratios within each location, urban areas are split into metropolitan towns and towns (not shown in table 2-2). In metropolitan towns the average household income is M$495 per month, and interestingly the racial disparity ratios are quite small: 1.18 for Chinese:Malay and 1.15 for Indian:Malay. In towns the average household income is M$345 per month, but the racial disparity ratios are bigger: 1.52 for Chinese:Malay and 1.20 for Indian:Malay. In rural areas the racial

17. The relatively large European incomes account both for this inequality and for the high average income of this group (M$813 per month).

18. The PES defines metropolitan towns as Johore Bahru, Malacca, Kuala Lumpur, Klang, Ipoh, and Georgetown. Towns (with population of more than 10,000) are: Kulai, Kluang, Segamat, Muar, and Batu Pahat (in Johore); Alor Star, Sg. Patani, and Kulim (in Kedah); Kota Bahru, Pangkat Kalong, Peringat, Tumpat, and Pasir Mas (in Kelantan); Seremban and Kuala Pilah (in Negri Sembilan); Kuantan Bentong, Raub, Temerloh, Mentakab, and Kuala Lipis (in Pahang); and Butterworth, Bukit Mertajam, Ayer Hilam, Tanjong Tokong, and Tanjong Bunga (in Penang). All other areas are rural areas (see Department of Statistics, 1973, p. 1, and the frontispiece map).

disparity ratios are the largest of all locations: 2.22 for Chinese:Malay and 1.58 for Indian:Malay. The still higher overall racial disparity ratios for Peninsular Malaysia reflect the disproportionate presence of Chinese and Indians in urban areas and of Malays in rural areas. (The between-location disparity ratios are 2.48 for metropolitan towns:rural areas and 1.73 for towns:rural areas.)

Comparison of Income Estimates: PES and National Accounts

A comparison of the PES estimate of average household income in Malaysia with estimates derived from the national accounts may be suggested as a rough check on the quality of the survey data, but there are two problems associated with it. First, the correspondence is often tenuous between the income concepts of a survey and those of the national accounts. Second, the national accounts data cannot themselves be presumed sacrosanct. As is well known, they are subject to substantial error, particularly in developing countries, and this error is more pronounced for estimates of income level than for estimates of income growth, since national accounts data are at least collected on a systematic basis over time.[19]

The national accounts concept of personal income corresponds most closely to the concept of income used in surveys such as the PES. Unfortunately, however, the national accounts in Malaysia do not provide direct information on aggregate personal income. This can be estimated approximately, starting with private consumption expenditure[20] and adding to it various items such as personal saving and direct taxes on households. Aggregate personal income has been estimated in this manner by Snodgrass (1975), who calculates personal saving by a residual method (netting out from gross domestic capital formation the sum of depreciation, government saving, surpluses of public corporations, the current account deficit, and company saving). A further small correction was made to this figure for aggregate personal income to account for the part of it that accrues to persons not living in private households. Snodgrass thus obtained an estimate for average household income in 1970 of M$370 per month, which he called a "rough estimate only."

Another estimate for Malaysian average household income, also based on the 1970 national accounts, has been derived in a somewhat different

19. They are collected on a commodity flow basis, but there is a large element of discretion in allocating estimated supplies to alternative uses.

20. As a comment on the accuracy of national accounts data, a 1976 World Bank economic report on Malaysia presents three different estimates for private consumption expenditure in 1970: M$7,151 million, M$6,014 million, and M$6,349 million.

way from the Snodgrass estimate. Ahluwalia and others (1976, table IV-6)[21] have constructed a social accounting matrix for Malaysia, which is essentially a presentation of the national accounts in a disaggregated framework. Resorting to "heuristic judgment" when data were inconsistent, they arrive at a figure of M$352 per month for average household income in 1970.

The average household income computed from PES is M$264 per month (table 2-2). This is 71.4 and 75.0 percent, respectively, of the estimates of Snodgrass and Ahluwalia and others based on the national accounts. Thus, the PES income estimates seem to be about 25 percent less than those derived from the national accounts. This degree of understatement is not particularly large by the standards of household surveys in developing countries and is only fractionally larger than that recently reported in surveys from developed countries.

For six developed countries, Sawyer compares household survey estimates of income with national accounts estimates of the same categories of income. The survey estimate for pretax household income[22] as a proportion of the national accounts estimate turns out at 70.5 percent for France (1970), 81.7 percent for Germany (1969), 83.9 percent for the United Kingdom (1973) Family Expenditure Survey, and 82.8 percent for the United Kingdom (1972–73) Blue Book data (see Sawyer, 1976, app. 2). The degree of underreporting varies between categories of income and is particularly high for income from investment and self-employment. As these categories of income are "disproportionately received by the upper deciles," Sawyer concludes that "inequality will tend to be underestimated everywhere." It is not obvious that similar underreporting of income in a country such as Malaysia (if underreporting were established) would bias inequality there. The reason is that the large class of self-employed in Malaysia is spread throughout the distribution, with a substantial representation at the lower end among subsistence farmers (see chapter 4 and appendix E).

The understatement of income in PES in relation to the national accounts seems broadly in keeping with what is observed elsewhere. In Malaysia, though, there is less of a presumption that the estimates of household income based on the national accounts are more accurate than the direct estimates from PES, which are at least based on a statistically well-designed and well-implemented sample survey. The discrepancy in estimates from the two sources is not easy to resolve, but it cannot be taken as a reason for rejecting the PES.

21. A later version is Pyatt and Round (1977).
22. This is the same income concept as in PES, so that a uniform comparison can indeed be made between developed and developing countries.

International Comparisons of Inequality

Attempts at comparing income inequality in Malaysia with inequality in other countries will obviously encounter serious difficulties because income distribution data are typically noncomparable between countries. The careful study required to establish comparability and bring the data onto a common basis is a large research project in itself and plainly outside the scope of this enquiry. Here I merely mention some countries, at similar stages of development, for which it would be interesting to pursue inequality comparisons.

Table 2-3 lists some countries at similar stages of development for which income distribution data are reported in the compilation by Jain (1975). When income distribution data for a particular country are not available for 1970, the surveys carried out in the closest year are reported. Each country in the list is followed by a number in parentheses which shows the source number in Jain's compilation. According to Jain, the Gini coefficients in table 2-3 refer to the *household* income distribution and a sample coverage which is *national*. She employs a uniform method across countries to compute the Gini coefficient.[23]

Table 2-3. Household Income Inequality in Selected Economies

Economy	Year of survey	GNP per capita in 1970 (US$)	Gini coefficient
Malaysia (3)	1970	380	0.5179
Taiwan (4)	1972	390	0.2843
Philippines (4)	1971	210	0.4941
Korea, Rep. of (5)	1970	250	0.3719
Korea, Rep. of (6)	1970	250	0.3836
Thailand (1)	1962	200	0.5103
Brazil (4)	1970	420	0.5744
Brazil (7)	1970	420	0.6093
Mexico (5)	1969	670	0.5827
Mexico (4)	1968	670	0.6106
Mexico (3)	1967–68	670	0.5243
Turkey (1)	1968	310	0.5679
Zambia (1)	1959	400	0.5226

Note: Numbers in parentheses refer to source number in Jain (1975).
Sources: *1972 World Bank Atlas* (Washington, D. C.); and Jain (1975).

23. Jain (1975) computes the Gini coefficient for each distribution from an estimate for the Kakwani and Podder (1976) functional form of its Lorenz curve. My procedure in the previous section for estimating the Lorenz curve by linear interpolation between observed points could lead to a differential underestimation of the Gini coefficient across countries. This is because the number and spacing of such points can vary substantially from survey to survey.

In table 2-3 I attempted to standardize for population unit and sample coverage across surveys,[24] but major problems still remain which could lead to noncomparability. These concern differences among the surveys in sampling and nonsampling errors and, perhaps most important, in the definitions of household and income. (Is income pre- or posttax? Are own consumption of production and payments in kind included? Is owner-occupied housing imputed?) The definitions and measurement techniques, however, are not easy to verify,[25] since the published reports often do not provide adequate information on the subject (see Jain, 1975, p. xi). I have not checked the primary data sources to establish uniformity of the concepts used in the various surveys. Rather, the distribution data in table 2-3 are presented simply to give some idea of the estimates floating around as researchers try to discover "stylized facts" about inequality and development (such as the inverse U-shaped relation). It is indeed interesting to examine the extent to which levels of inequality can actually differ at similar stages of development.

Table 2-3 shows a wide range in inequality levels for countries at approximately similar levels of development. The Gini coefficient varies from 0.28 for Taiwan to 0.61 for Brazil and Mexico. Malaysia, with a per capita GNP of US$380 in 1970, shows considerably more inequality than Taiwan with a per capita GNP of US$390, but less inequality than Brazil with a per capita GNP of US$420. One estimate for Mexico shows inequality there at approximately the same level as in Malaysia, while two others show a markedly higher level of inequality. Both estimates for the Republic of Korea show less inequality than in Malaysia. The extent of inequality in Malaysia seems generally similar to that in Thailand, the Philippines, and Zambia. For what they are worth, then, these figures suggest that Malaysia displays a middle-to-high level of inequality by comparison with other countries at similar stages of development.[26] Without a good deal of further research into the underlying surveys, however, this conclusion cannot be asserted with any certainty.

24. Even such basic comparability is sometimes not established by researchers undertaking cross-country studies of inequality.

25. My experience with intertemporal comparisons in Malaysia confirms this, as shown in the next section.

26. By comparison with the three developed countries mentioned in the previous subsection, Malaysia shows significantly greater inequality. Using the distribution of household pretax income by decile shares, Sawyer (1976) computes the following Gini coefficients: France 0.416, Germany 0.396, United Kingdom Family Expenditure Survey 0.344, United Kingdom Blue Book data 0.373.

Intertemporal Comparisons of Inequality in Malaysia

Apart from PES, two previous surveys undertaken by the Malaysian Department of Statistics have reported income data: the Malaysian Socio-Economic Sample Survey of Households, 1967–68 (MSSH) and the Household Budget Survey, 1957–58 (HBS). While MSSH is easily seen to be not comparable with PES, it is more difficult to reach a judgment about the comparability between HBS and PES. The reason is that the published report on HBS (Department of Statistics, 1961?), hereafter referred to as HBS *Report*, gives totally inadequate information on the definition of income used. Several researchers have nonetheless adopted HBS as a benchmark for intertemporal inequality comparisons in Malaysia (for example, Lim, 1974; Hirschman, 1974; Lee, 1975; and Snodgrass, 1975) and reached a conclusion of worsening inequality between 1957 and 1970. Given the importance of this subject, I have attempted to construct an account of HBS income and other survey particulars along the lines of that provided earlier for PES. This account has been pieced together from unpublished records and files in the Malaysian Department of Statistics and from conversations with persons responsible for conducting the survey. It is valuable to document this information in detail, if only to apprise other researchers of the pitfalls in using HBS income data.

In table 2-2 there are large differences in measured inequality between HBS, MSSH, and PES. The Gini coefficient of the household income distribution in Peninsular Malaysia is estimated to be 0.3705 for HBS, 0.5624 for MSSH, and 0.5129 for PES. In this section it is argued that these differences are not indicative of actual changes in inequality over time, and might be wholly due to differences between the surveys in income concept and coverage. More fundamentally, I show that the three surveys are not comparable with each other, and that *no* conclusions can be drawn from them about changes in inequality.

At the outset, it is well to point out that intertemporal comparison is a hazardous business owing to differences between surveys in sample design (and size), coverage, nonresponse errors, and so on. There are other technical differences, such as the number and width of income intervals used in coding and collecting data. These differences introduce significant measurement errors in attempting comparison. But the task of comparison is made truly formidable when the definition of income itself varies substantially from one survey to another. It is shown below how the different definitions used in the three surveys render comparisons between them meaningless.

MSSH, 1967–68

The comparison of MSSH with the other two surveys is manifestly spurious. Its income concept is restricted to cash income, whereas the income definition of the other surveys is more comprehensive—even if that for HBS is partly elusive (see the later subsection, "Definition of HBS Income"). One would expect cash income to be distributed more unequally than total income, since most of the poor (such as subsistence farmers) hardly enter the cash economy, whereas the rich derive most of their income in this form. Hence the Gini ratio of MSSH may be larger than that of the other surveys[27] wholly because of differences in income concept.

This explanation seems to be corroborated by examining the (nominal) mean incomes in HBS, 1957–58; MSSH, 1967–68; and PES, 1970. Table 2-2 shows that average household income in rural Malaysia, as estimated from the surveys, declined from M$170 in 1957–58 to M$114 in 1967–68, and rose again to M$200 in 1970.[28] It is the exclusion of noncash income from MSSH, 1967–68, which probably explains the lower average household income in the middle of the 1957–70 period compared with either end. The exclusion also accounts for a similar pattern observed in the mean household income of Malays. It is clear that MSSH would have understated the income of rural and Malay households, which consist largely of self-employed groups receiving a substantial portion of their income in kind (such as own consumption of produce). The Chinese and Indians, however, probably received a large enough fraction of their income in cash for the surveys to register a growth in their incomes throughout this period.

The upshot of the preceding discussion is that MSSH should be dropped as a data source on intertemporal income distribution. It is too obviously not comparable with the other surveys, and its restricted income concept could explain the observed differences in measured inequality and mean incomes.

27. In fact, it is an underestimate in relation to the other surveys. Since there are fewer income intervals in MSSH than in the other two surveys, there are fewer points on the Lorenz curve from which its Gini coefficient is estimated.

28. The income figures in table 2-2 are in nominal, not real, terms. Price inflation during 1957–70 averaged as little as 0.7 percent a year.

HBS, 1957–58

While the comparison of MSSH with HBS or PES is easily dismissed as invalid, that between HBS and PES has been taken seriously by many researchers (for example, Lee, 1975, and Snodgrass, 1975). In my opinion, however, the published report on the survey is inadequate to allow such a comparison. There is little information in HBS *Report* on the income concept employed, sample coverage, and so on. Thus I have attempted to reconstruct an account of the HBS sample design and income definition. I then venture a comparison between PES and HBS and show that differences in income concept and coverage bias HBS inequality downward in relation to PES inequality.[29]

HBS SAMPLE DESIGN. The HBS was designed to obtain expenditure weights for the compilation of a retail price index. The collection of income data was incidental to the survey and was included only as a rough check on expenditure. The survey was based on a multistage sample which covered 2,760 households in the Federation of Malaya—1,920 in rural areas and 840 in urban areas.[30] It was conducted over a period of one year, beginning in April 1957 and ending in March 1958. A one-year period was selected in order to take account of seasonal patterns of expenditure.

The definition of household adopted in the survey may be obtained from "Course of Lectures for Training Investigators" (Department of Statistics, 1957?), hereafter cited as *Course of Lectures*:

A household may consist of one or more persons who
  (a) live within some residential building or group of adjacent buildings
  (b) consume food from same kitchen, larder, cupboard or cooking pot
  (c) incur common housekeeping expenditure or are charged on combined hotel, boarding or lodging house bill.

---

29. There is an enormous difference in sample size between PES and HBS: the HBS sample size is so small that its inequality estimate is liable to "appreciable" sampling error (HBS *Report*, p. 39). To make statistically significant comparisons of inequality, one needs to quantify confidence limits for the Gini coefficient estimates from the two surveys (for example, as in Kakwani and Podder, 1976). With the given sample sizes, the (95 percent) confidence band for the HBS estimate will obviously be much wider than for the PES estimate.

30. These figures are from the HBS *Report*. Urban areas were defined as municipalities, town councils, or town boards with a population of 10,000 or more.

A domestic servant who satisfies (a) and (b) only is regarded as a member of employer's household (*Course of Lectures*, p. 8).

A national sample frame was used to select households:[31]

The rural households were chosen as follows: First the country was divided into 16 areas of approximately equal size by population, each area consisting of a number of administrative districts. One district from each area was chosen with probability proportional to size, the mukims [subdistricts] in the selected districts were listed, and three mukims per district were chosen with probability proportional to size. The investigators then visited each selected mukim and drew a sketch map showing the villages and kampongs, and the number of houses in each. These maps were then studied carefully and each mukim was divided into four sub-areas of approximately equal number of houses. From each sub-area ten houses were chosen at random and marked on the maps or, where the houses were numbered, the house numbers were listed. Reserve houses were selected in case of a house being empty, or the head of a household refusing to co-operate; substitutes in the case of non-cooperation were only allowed after the supervisor had visited the household and had also failed to gain any co-operation.

In the urban sample, Kuala Lumpur and Georgetown were included because of their size and importance; the remaining towns of 10,000 and over were stratified into towns with population between 10,000 and 25,000, and towns with population over 25,000.

These towns were listed and since the over 25,000 group had twice the total population of the 10,000 to 25,000 group, two towns were selected from the former group and one from the latter. The towns chosen being Ipoh and Seremban, and Teluk Anson respectively. All these towns were sub-divided into smaller areas of approximately equal size, and households selected at random in a manner similar to that described for the rural areas.

The sampling scheme had to be slightly modified when it was found that Indian households in rural areas had been inadequately represented. A list of rubber estates with Indian labour was drawn up and a sample was chosen at random. An investigator was instructed to visit these estates in turn throughout the period of the survey (HBS *Report*, app. I, pp. 61–62).

---

31. There is a small qualification to this in *Course of Lectures* (p. 2): "[Owing to] the emergency . . . certain parts of Malaya are still unsafe for our investigators to work in, so we shall have to exclude all the families living in these unsafe areas from our survey. This would result in a slightly inaccurate population of households, but it cannot be helped, and luckily the number of areas which are unsafe is quite small."

This procedure apparently led to the selection of 2,760 households.[32] A breakdown of sample size between the major races was never published, nor is it now available. Where necessary, I have employed the 1957 census proportions. Other communities, such as the Europeans, were excluded from this survey.

Apart from the noncoverage of European households in HBS, there is inadequate coverage generally of the higher income groups. According to the report of the Special Advisory Committee on Cost of Living Indices, chaired by H. A. Fell (the chief statistician for HBS), there is an "omission of European budgets from the survey", and [an] unsatisfactory coverage of the higher income groups among the Malays, Chinese and Indians" (Fell and others, 1959, p. 8). In fact, there is no coverage of households with incomes above M$1,000 per month (see the later subsection "Comparison between PES and HBS"). While this may be unimportant in the construction of price indices for the lower income groups, which was the express purpose of HBS,[33] it is clearly crucial for an accurate estimation of income distribution.

No estimates of sampling error were made, nor is it now possible to make them. Since the absolute sample size was rather small, in fact, these may turn out to be fairly large. HBS *Report* (p. 2) itself draws attention to the small sample size of the survey and the possibility of error on this score: "A word of caution is . . . necessary to the user of the data . . . The sample was only one quarter percent of all the households in the Federation, and the sampling-errors must necessarily be large."

It concludes with a warning note on the reliability of the income distribution data:

32. This figure is taken from the HBS *Report*, but it is not clear whether it refers to responding households or to those actually selected for interview. Either way, it contradicts slightly the figures in the only other source I could find on this subject in Malaysia, Chew (1968). According to Chew (table 1-5, p. 43), 2,770 households were actually visited (1,920 in rural areas and 850 in urban areas); but of these, 107 did not cooperate, and information was obtained for only 2,663 households (1,818 in rural areas and 845 in urban areas).

33. The following recommendation was made by the Special Advisory Committee on Cost of Living Indices:

A separate index [should] be constructed and published for each of the three main races, i.e. the Malays, Chinese and the Indians. The weights should be based on the consumption patterns appropriate to each race as given in the household budget survey. In each case the pattern should be based on the combined consumption figures for the income groups "$1–$150 p.m." and "$151–$300 p.m." In addition, the Malay index should take account of the income group "income not clearly defined" which covers, in the main, padi planters whose average consumption was similar to the groups recommended to be covered by the indices (Fell and others, 1959, p. 3).

This sample gives sufficiently accurate results for the determination of weights to be used in the construction of retail price indices, but is subject to an appreciable *significant* margin of error as a source of information relating to income distribution. It does however give a rough broad indication of income distribution pattern and is therefore published as a matter of public interest (HBS *Report*, p. 39; emphasis in original).

DEFINITION OF HBS INCOME. In any discussion on HBS, it is important constantly to bear in mind that HBS was an expenditure survey. The collection of income data was incidental to the survey, intended solely as a rough check on expenditure. It is not surprising, therefore, that no definition of income is given in the published report on the survey. Although I have gleaned certain aspects of it in my research, I still do not have a complete or precise definition. Since a comprehensive definition was never intended, the reconstruction of one is perhaps in any case impossible.

The questionnaire for HBS consists of a booklet designed to record a household's daily expenditure and consumption, item by item, over a period of one month. There is a separate section on "special periodical expenditure" for such items as electricity, rent, and income tax. On the last page of the questionnaire there is a small section on income, with columns for salary and wages; self-employed income; rent, profit, and dividend; and other income (including pension). A final column is supposed to show the total income from all these sources.[34]

It is not known if the published income figures of HBS are net or gross of income tax. It appears the data could have been reported to interviewers in either form, with the choice left to respondents. If gross income figures were recorded in the income section of the questionnaire, however, separate figures were collected on income tax payments under special periodical expenditure. The following instruction was given to field interviewers for filling in the income tax item in the section on special periodical expenditure: "When income tax has already been deducted from the householder's income (i.e. he only gives his net income) the investigator need not put down anything for this, but where gross income is given, the amount he paid for Income Tax should be noted down here" (*Course of Lectures*, p.10). Since the income distribution data published in HBS *Report* are the figures that were recorded in the income section, they are likely to be a mixture of net and gross incomes.

It is not clear whether gifts and allowances were included as income. An instruction to field investigators in *Course of Lectures* (p. 13) says: "When

34. This information is taken from the only surviving questionnaire of HBS in the files of the Department of Statistics, Kuala Lumpur.

asking about income . . . sums obtained in the form of small monetary gifts, allowances, etc. need not be recorded in detail—just put down the amount under 'Other Income'." According to HBS *Report* (p. 3), however, "Items such as loans and gifts were not included as income in the table of income distribution."[35] There is further ambiguity in *Course of Lectures* (p. 11): "As regards allowances for a mother or other relation, the sum should be noted under expenditure for one and income for the other, and the expenditure of the latter recorded."

The rent on owner-occupied housing was *not* imputed as an item of income (or expenditure). There are published statements to this effect, and it was confirmed in private communication with the chief statistician for HBS:

> Although some households pay a full or economic rent, other households live in subsidized dwellings, or live rent-free—the latter are either owner-occupiers, or relatives of owner-occupiers who pay no rent, or employees on estates, etc. living in rent-free quarters.
>
> We can see the almost insurmountable difficulties in imputing an economic rent. An economic valuation would have to be made of a wide variety of owner-occupier dwellings in order to value the service derived from the dwelling. Original cost or present cost of building would be no guide in the case of the kampongs where labour is provided free by members of the household. Estates have indicated in another survey—national income survey—that they have little idea of the economic rent of their free-quarters (Fell and others, 1959, pp. 8–9).

There was no imputation for income in the form of free meals at one's place of work. The rationale given in this case was that "since we are here only collecting income as a check on the expenditure this need not be done" (*Course of Lectures*, p. 12).

It is worth reiterating here the principle that income questions in HBS were included only as a check on expenditure.[36] For households whose expenditure was in excess of stated income, there may have been some upward adjustment of income at the checking stage. The following instruction to HBS supervisors is suggestive of this interpretation:

35. On the assumption that loans and gifts were excluded, there might be a slight overestimation of HBS inequality if such items represent transfers mainly from rich to poor households (see Atkinson's theorem in appendix D).

36. This point has been strongly emphasized in private conversations with the chief statistician for HBS. The design of the HBS questionnaire is also consistent with the use of income data to check on the balance between income and expenditure or between receipts and payments.

When he [the supervisor] visits the investigator, he should check whether the income and expenditure roughly agrees, so far, and find out why if expenditure is greater than income. Also when the investigators hand in their record books at the end of month, the supervisor should again check to see that the stated total income and expenditure tally (*Course of Lectures*, p. 4).

The income of self-employed households probably refers to gross income, because no instructions were given to field investigators to subtract from gross revenue any input costs (such as seeds, fertilizers, rent, electricity, and loan repayments). These costs were in fact itemized under special periodical expenditure, but the purpose there was simply to compute the total expenditure of a household. Since production costs were listed under total household expenditure, the income-expenditure check would make sense only if recorded income referred to gross receipts.[37] It is quite possible, therefore, that the income of the self-employed has been overestimated and is in fact their gross income.

As regards the imputation of income in kind, the position is unclear—although actual consumption in kind does seem to have been noted under daily expenditure and consumption in the questionnaire:[38] "If some of the households interviewed grow their own vegetables, fruit, etc., or rear their own poultry for food, the amounts of these items consumed should also be entered under expenditure on food, with their own estimate of quantity and value, and the word 'free' entered in the first column in the record book" (*Course of Lectures*, p. 11). It is not known whether retail or farm-gate prices were used to value nonmarket consumption, or indeed whether such "free" consumption was included under income. There does not appear to be any provision for such imputation in the income section of the questionnaire, and no instructions for field investigators were issued to this effect.

It seems clear that problems were encountered in valuing the income of subsistence farmers. In HBS *Report* average consumption patterns are shown according to four monthly income classes (M$1–M$150, M$151–M$300, M$301–M$500, and M$501–M$1,000) and a separate category,

37. When gross income information was recorded for a respondent, his income tax was treated as an item of expenditure—again, so that the income-expenditure check would remain valid.

38. This is confirmed in a press statement on HBS issued by the Department of Statistics, probably in 1957: "We are also interested in actual consumption, so we shall try to value and take down the amount of food the family consumes from their own garden and even gifts, besides just the expenditure."

"income not definite," for which, presumably, there were difficulties in assigning an income figure. It is known from HBS *Report* (pp. 6–8) that this group consisted entirely of Malay households in rural areas. Furthermore, they are likely to have been subsistence farmers mainly, as Fell and others (1959, p. 3) state: "The income group 'income not clearly defined' . . . covers, in the main, padi planters."

Apart from the inclusions and omissions documented above, it is not known how some of the other categories of income were estimated. According to HBS *Report* (p. 3), there was some "subjective" estimation:

> The tables on income distribution of households are not as accurate and reliable as those for consumption and expenditure, and contain some subjective estimation where income was not entered on the questionnaire or was believed to be incorrect. The estimation of income had then to be *deduced from the expenditure of the household* or by reference to the type of occupation of the members of the household (italics added).

This statement reinforces my earlier point concerning upward adjustment of income of households whose expenditure exceeded reported income.

The evidence I have marshalled allows the building up of a partial picture of the income concept implicit in HBS. Although a fully comprehensive definition is likely to remain elusive, the following major limitations can be asserted with some confidence:

1. Income was sometimes recorded gross of tax and sometimes net of tax. It is not known how many households, and at what income levels, fall in each group.

2. No imputation was made for owner-occupied and free housing. This is fairly serious because the number of owner-occupied and free dwellings in Malaysia is large. According to HBS, 81 percent of the households lived in such dwellings; for Malay, Chinese, and Indian households separately the figures were 95, 56, and 75 percent, respectively (Fell and others, 1959, p. 9).

3. The income estimate for households with expenditure in excess of reported income may have been adjusted upward to the expenditure level.

4. The income of self-employed households was probably their gross income.

5. Own consumption of produce was entered under households' daily expenditure, and insofar as point 3 above was valid, a part of it may have been included under income. But the special category "income not definite" suggests this was not always practicable. It is not known how many households belong to this category.

The income distribution tables published in HBS *Report* contain twenty-eight income classes, with an upper limit on incomes of M$1,000 per month. The percentages in each income class were read from graphs of cumulative income distributions, shown in HBS *Report* (app. III): "The numbers in each income group as derived from the sample were plotted on a graph and a free-hand line drawn to remove the irregularities and so give a smooth curve. This is believed to give a better distribution of income than that from the uncorrected data" (HBS *Report*, p. 3).

Comparison between PES and HBS

The lack of a proper definition of HBS income and the ambiguities persisting on imputation and coverage are of little consequence for the basic purpose of HBS (expenditure weights for price indices), but they seriously undermine its credibility as a data source on income distribution. Furthermore, the major shortcomings of HBS income cannot be put right by adjustment or appeal to other sources. It would be necessary to go back to the completed HBS questionnaire for each household to construct a distribution which used a uniform definition of income. This is now impossible, however, because the records have long since been destroyed.

It follows that HBS should not be used as a base from which to make inequality comparisons over time. Those authors who concluded that inequality worsened between 1957 and 1970 after comparing PES with HBS have not probed sufficiently into problems leading to noncomparability. Their conclusion cannot be established because of technical differences between the surveys (for which adjustment is impossible) which bias HBS inequality downward in relation to PES inequality.[39] I have isolated six such differences:[40]

1. The noncoverage in HBS of households with incomes of more than M$1,000 per month, that is, the very rich (HBS *Report*, p. 39).[41] In fact, upper income groups were generally undersampled, and, as already

39. Some of these differences (points 1 to 3 below in the text) were already documented in Anand (1973). Lee (1975) and Snodgrass (1975) have taken account of these differences but do not recognize all the complexities. Given the importance of the subject, it is necessary to present a fuller account of the problems leading to noncomparability and to repeat my earlier admonishments.
40. For some differences between the surveys it is not possible to know the direction of bias. For example, the difference in treatment of income tax in the two surveys could bias HBS inequality in either direction. If households in HBS reported net-of-tax income, there would be a downward bias of HBS inequality in relation to PES, since PES incomes are gross of tax, and the tax system is progressive (see appendix E, corollary 2).
41. If corollary 1 in appendix E is applied to the top income class as a single group, it shows that HBS inequality is underestimated by underestimating such income.

indicated, coverage of these groups among the Malays, Chinese, and Indians was unsatisfactory.

2. The noncoverage in HBS of households belonging to "other" communities. Exclusion of this very heterogeneous and unequal group biases HBS inequality downward.[42]

3. The nonexistence in HBS of a separate zero-income category. The lowest mean income in HBS begins at M$12.50 per month, whereas in PES 1.4 percent of the households belong to the zero-income category[43] (see table 3-2). It is shown in lemma 2 in appendix E that the omission of households with zero income from a distribution always results in an underestimation of inequality.

4. The income of self-employed households in HBS may have been overestimated if it refers to their gross income. On the assumption that the self-employed are disproportionately represented among the poor (for example, subsistence farmers and urban households in the informal sector) this overestimate would tend to bias inequality downward.

5. The nonimputation of owner-occupied and free housing in HBS. It is reasonable to suppose the income elasticity of demand for housing to be greater than unity, so that omission of this component of income is likely to understate inequality (see corollary 2 in appendix E).

6. The upward adjustment of income in HBS for households whose expenditure exceeded income probably biases inequality downward. The reason is that the upward adjustment of income occurs mainly at the lower end of the distribution since expenditure is more likely to exceed income for lower income groups (see lemma 1 in appendix E).[44]

This list is not intended to be exhaustive. There might well be other differences that impart a downward bias to HBS inequality in relation to PES inequality.

42. This is certainly the case for an additively decomposable index (see chapters 3 and 6). The relative size of the "others" group was much larger in 1957 than in 1970, by which time many of the small subcommunities once classified as "others" (such as Indian Muslims, Ceylonese, and Thai Muslims) identified themselves with one of the major racial groups. Thus exclusion of the "others" is likely to have biased HBS inequality downward much more than it would have done PES inequality.

43. As noted in chapter 3, zero-income households could have supported their consumption expenditure in two ways which do not count as PES income: by running down past savings or liquidating capital assets, and by borrowing. "Distress sales" and loans are a well-known source of finance for low-income households in developing countries.

44. If income were *widely* "deduced from the expenditure of the household," the HBS income distribution would tend toward the (consumption) expenditure distribution, which is generally considered to be more equal.

It should be obvious from the evidence presented that HBS is *not* comparable with PES in income concept and coverage. The downward biases noted in HBS inequality could easily account for the entire difference in measured inequality between the two surveys. Furthermore, it is not possible to quantify the magnitude of these biases for points 4 to 6 above. Any attempt to adjust for points 1 to 3 (assuming this could be done satisfactorily) will, therefore, not be enough to prevent intertemporal comparisons of inequality from being seriously misleading. Accordingly, little significance can attach to conclusions about inequality changes between 1957 and 1970 based on these surveys.

This analysis has served to highlight the danger of making intertemporal inequality comparisons without adequate research into the comparability of the underlying data. Such comparisons have become increasingly frequent in the literature of development economics, but there have been few attempts to verify comparability or to bring the data together in a common framework. Judgments about intertemporal inequality based on a superficial examination of published data are likely to be highly suspect, as shown by this analysis of two seemingly comparable Malaysian surveys. The same cautionary note needs to be struck when making judgments about international inequality, where surveys are not conducted by the same statistical department and there is even less reason to suppose uniformity of concepts and definitions.

Appendix: PES 1970 Instructions to Field Interviewers

Individual and Household Income

[Extracted from Department of Statistics, 1970*b*, pp. 31–37.]

The questions in this section should be asked as they are written— elaborate only after you have asked the question in the stated manner. *Do not overlook even a single question.*

Questions 1 & 2:

Now, I would like to ask a few more questions about persons who have been doing some job or other for pay, profit or family gains. Please tell me their names and their relationship to the Head of Household? (ENTER THIS IN COLUMNS 1 AND 2.)

(a) Is there anyone else, like your wife, son or daughter, who has helped in the farm or field? (IF 'YES'—WRITE THEIR NAMES IN COLUMN 1.)

(b) Is there anyone else, what about (specify name)? (ENTER NAME IN COLUMN 1.)

(REPEAT THIS FOR OTHERS WHO SEEM ELIGIBLE.)

Here, first of all we want to determine the persons who are or were doing some work or other. Obviously these are the persons who will be mainly receiving some form of regular income. The names of these people should be entered in Column (1). Remember that the names mentioned here should be generally found in the household (i.e., the name must have been included with the household in Section (B), Column (9)). Very occasionally you may find someone who is normally a member of the household but did not sleep in the household on Census Night—and hence has been excluded from this household. In this case, include the person in this Section, even though he has not been included in the Household Composition. Give also a footnote to this effect.

It is also possible that there were others who worked as family workers (i.e., helping in family enterprise or farm)—if there are any, also enter their names in Column (1).

You should then flip back to Section (B) on Household Composition, and see if there are any eligible persons, whose names have not been mentioned. Then you should ask "———, what about———(name)? Did he receive any income? or has he been working somewhere?"

At the end of the question you are now reasonably sure you have not missed out any earning member in the household.

Question 3:
Let us look at those working, one by one. What type of job is (name) working. I would like to know the specific nature of his job, and where he is working. (REPEAT FOR ALL OTHERS.)

We want the type of occupation and the institution or firm in which each of the persons are working. It seems easy to get this information—but experience has shown that this is where most errors occur. This is either because the respondent does not know the precise designation of the job, or because the interviewer has not asked for sufficiently clear details. To be sure you get the required details, we will give a book of the Occupation Codes. This is an alphabetical index of the occupations and will be helpful to you.

It is important that you obtain the exact type of work done by the respondent, such as lorry driver, farm labourer, dress-maker, etc. Some of the respondents would say he is a helper or driver or mechanic, etc. In these cases you should find out what kind of a helper or driver or mechanic. For example, a driver may be a lorry driver, taxi driver, or even a chauffeur. It is necessary for purposes of classification to know the exact nature of the occupation.

Many of the occupations are found in an establishment. For example, in a school we have teachers, clerks, typists and watchmen. On the other hand, a given occupation may be found in several kinds of establishments, as in the case of, say, a typist. We want the exact nature of the job and the type of establishment.

In obtaining the responses for this question, a few points must be borne in mind:

a) Use the Occupation Classification wisely. You should make good use of the alphabetical index. For example if the respondent says he is a "driver" by occupation then refer to the occupation "driver" in the Occupational Classification Book. It shows 12 types of drivers; ask him what type does he fit into. Or again he may say that he is an engineer. If you refer to the index provided you will see that there are several types of engineers, and different levels of engineers: engineering fitter, engine fitter, engine greaser, and engine oiler. There is a good deal of difference between an engineer and an engine oiler. The basic level of the occupant can be sensed from the way he lives. Try and get at the correct description of the person's occupation using the occupation index as an aid.

b) Respondents may reply in Chinese or Malay or Tamil. It is very difficult to translate some of the words into appropriate English equivalents. Look through the occupation index provided and try to get to know some of the fairly common occupations and their equivalents in the languages in which you are conversant. In some cases you may even write on the questionnaire the actual words used by the respondents, for example, words like "Mandore," "Serang," "Amah," or "Hung Kong" can be translated in the office at a later stage.

Some examples of occupation entries are listed below as a guide. This list is not exhaustive but is intended to give an idea of the description acceptable and the degree of details required to enable the proper classification of occupations.

Attendant: Should state whether lift attendant, vehicle attendant, car park attendant, hospital attendant, woodworking machine attendant, or laboratory attendant, etc.

Clerk: Should state whether accounts clerk, correspondence clerk, store clerk, solicitors' clerk, legal clerk, tally clerk, or general office clerk, etc.

Clerical Assistant: Should also specify the type and clerical duties performed.

Conductor: Should state whether bus conductor, railway train guard, or band conductor, etc.

Driver: Should state whether lorry driver, bus driver, mail van driver, ambulance driver, taxi driver, motorcar driver, tractor driver, railway engine driver, crane driver, or bulldozer driver, etc.

Electrician: Should state whether electrical fitter or wireman. If electrical fitter, state the type of machinery or equipment handled, e.g., motors and generators, transformer, switchgear and control apparatus, electrical elevators, etc. If electrical wireman, state whether building electrician, vehicle electrician, stage studio electrician, or an electrical repairman for domestic electrical equipment, etc.

Engineer: Should state whether sanitary engineer, building construction or general construction civil engineer, general mechanical engineer, industrial machinery and tools engineer, marine and ship construction engineer, general chemical engineer, petroleum chemical engineer, mining engineer, general electrical or electronic engineer, power generation engineer, telecommunication engineer, or industrial efficiency engineer.

Factory Worker: Should state the kind of factory and the job performed, e.g., knitting machine operator, fruit press operator, lathe operator, rubber packer, rubber grader, machine labeller, etc.

Farmer: Should state whether field-crop farmer (tobacco), plantation-crop farmer (coconut), fruit tree farmer, livestock farmer, dairy farmer, poultry farmer, nursery operator, or market garden farmer, etc.

Farm Worker: Should state the type of farm as for farmer.

Fisherman: Should state whether deep sea fisherman, kelong fisherman, coastal fisherman, fishpond or prawn-pond operator/worker, shellfish gatherer, etc.

Fitter: Should state whether textile machinery fitter, internal combustion engine fitter, electrical motor and generator fitter, electronic, radio, and radar equipment fitter, gas pipe fitter, telephone fitter, or general pipe fitter, or even dress fitter, etc.

Furnaceman: Should state whether ore smelting furnaceman, steel converting and refining furnaceman, metal melting or reheating furnaceman, copola furnaceman, electric arc furnaceman, or a reverberatory furnaceman, etc.

Inspector: Should state whether public health inspector, road transport inspector, railway service inspector, bus ticket inspector, inspector of police, motor vehicle inspector, etc.

Labourer: Should state whether dock labourer, railway and road vehicle loader, aircraft loader, warehouse goods handler, building construction labourer, demolition work labourer, or manufacturing labourer, etc.

Machine Operator: If office machine operator, state whether accounting machine operator, comptometer operator, teleprinter operator. If metalworking machine operator, state whether lathe operator, metal-weaving machine operator, honing-machine operator. If woodworking machine operator, state whether precision sawyer, wood lathe setter-operator, wood-shaping and planing machine operator. If other industrial machine operator, state whether bottle-washing machine operator, knitting-machine operator, etc.

Manager: Should state whether production manager, sales manager, administration manager, finance manager, personnel manager, advertising manager, farm manager, wholesale trade manager, retail trade manager, or manager of hotel, restaurant, etc.

Mechanic: Should state whether motor-car mechanic, bus mechanic, radio and television mechanic, aircraft engine mechanic, office machines mechanic, plant maintenance mechanic, textile machinery mechanic, or metal-working machine tool mechanic, etc.

Printer: Should state whether hand compositor, linotype operator, typecasting machine operator, cylinder pressman, pattern pressman, rotary pressman, stereotyper or electrotyper, etc.

Repairman: Should state whether bicycle repairman, motor repairman, clock and watch repairman, electrical domestic appliance repairman, camera repairman, or shoe repairman, etc.

Salesman: Should state whether wholesale trade salesman, retail trade salesman, technical salesman, manufacturer's agent, manufacturer's sales representative, insurance salesman, or advertising salesman, real estate agent, market stall-holder.

Sewer/Seamstress: Should state whether hand sewer or machine operator and the type of article the sewer specialises in, e.g., hand sewer, garments; hand sewer, house furnishings; etc.

Supervisor: Should state whether general clerical supervisor, accounts section supervisor, typing pool supervisor, sales supervisor (wholesale or retail trade), road transport supervisor, supervisor of metal processing industry, supervisor of construction work, or supervisor of food processing industry, field supervisor, etc.

Technician: Should state whether surveyor's technician, radio and television technician, air-conditioning engineering technician, chemical engineering technician, or mining technician, etc. ("Technician" should not be used to describe a Mechanic or a Repairman.)

Welder: Should state whether gas welder or electric arc welder.

Working Proprietor: Should state whether working proprietor of wholesale trade or retail trade, working proprietor of coffeeshop, bar, canteen, nightclub, boardinghouse, etc.

Question 4:

What is (<u>name</u>) working as? Is he an Employer, Employee, Own Account Worker, or Family Worker? Please be careful; a Family Worker should be one who has contributed to family gain and not one doing housework. (ENTER IN COLUMN 4.)

Here we want to know the earning member's Employment Status—and he may be an Employer, Employee, Own Account Worker, or Unpaid Family Worker. This is a way of describing the person's position in the business, factory, farm, etc. and his relationship to other persons in that organization.

An Employer is a person who employs one or more persons and pays them to work (in cash and/or kind). Such workers (employees) may assist in operating his business, farm or enterprise.

An Employee is a person who works for somebody else and is paid a fixed wage or salary or paid in kind. Included as Employees would be Government Servants, Managing Directors and Directors of Companies, and others in a similar position. Even though they can hire and fire people, they are still employees of the Government or the Company.

Own Account Worker is a person who works for himself and does not employ anybody else. However, he may have a partner and still be counted as self-employed. The important point is that no labour is hired. Family workers are not to be regarded as hired labour.

An Unpaid Family Worker is a person who works without pay in a business run by another member of the family.

Question 5:

We now come to an important part of the interview. I would like to know the average monthly income of each of the persons you have mentioned. (Name), what do you think is his average monthly income? Please think carefully. (REPEAT FOR OTHERS. ENTER IN COLUMN 5.)

This is an exceedingly difficult question, and needs great tact in asking. We want to know what the respondent thinks is the monthly income of each of the persons living in the household and earning. While we want to know what he thinks is the income, you should prompt certain questions that he should bring into his calculation. Emphasise that you want the average monthly income.

Generally, this question needs to be carefully thought out by the respondent; hence be patient and don't rush him to give you a response.

Question 6:

Let us see, (name) is a (empl. status). What do you think would be his monthly income from:

(a) Wages and salaries and other receipts.
(b) From sale of produce. (Note: this should be an average for the month.)
(c) From jointly owned businesses or farm.
(d) From rent, investments, etc.
(e) Pension, remittances and cash allowances, royalties, fees and other receipts.
(f) Other periodic cash receipts—e.g., alimonies, scholarships, etc.
(g) Monetary value for food, clothing, housing, etc.
(h) Monetary value ($) of goods used for own consumption.
(i) Monetary value ($) of goods for consumption received from other sources.
(j) Value of owner-occupied house.
(k) Other concessions.

This question is primarily aimed at obtaining data on income by going through each and every source of income. By so doing we hope that the respondent will be able to think about each of the categories carefully, and say if he had any income from that source. . . .

You should note that not all categories mentioned from (a) to (k) are applicable to all members. In fact only a few of them would be. You should apply your common sense to know what categories to ask and what not to ask. For example, if the respondent is a clerk—his monthly income would be mainly in wages, and he may have other sources of revenue from rent, investment, etc. Clearly, sale of produce generally will not be applicable to him though it is possible. A farmer on the other hand will receive the bulk of his income from sale of own produce. You should know whom to ask what question.

Report the details in the Second Block at the bottom of the page in Section (E).

Interviewer's Assessment of Household

[Extracted from Department of Statistics, 1970*b*, pp. 38–39.]

When all the five Sections (A to E) have been completed, you should now be in a position to assess the quality of the overall interview with the respondent. You should always attempt to answer the questions in this section as accurately as possible because we want to know the inconsistencies in the respondents' answers, and also the reliability of the answers.

Your assessment of the interview should refer to the overall interview, and not to a particular respondent. In case a particular respondent's answers were particularly bad, indicate this under comments.

Question 1—Reliability of Respondents' Answers:

The problem here is how to assess the respondents' answers as reliable or otherwise. If the respondent answers your questions without much hesitation and in a relaxed manner, there is reason to believe the accuracy of the data given by him. When the respondent gives his answers, you should be able to tell whether his answers are reliable or not. Sometimes, you can sense the respondent's reluctance, especially when he tries to evade giving you a direct answer. If he understood fully the purpose of the survey and right from the start he was willing to co-operate, the chances are his answers would be reliable.

It is also possible that right from the start, the respondent refuses to co-operate and he answers your questions with a "yes" or "no" and with indifference. It is here that you have to be careful for if he continues to respond in this manner, it is possible that his answers may be unreliable. This does not mean that a smiling and co-operative respondent will not give unreliable data. This is also possible. You have to look at the type of responses to decide the degree of reliability of the data you obtain for the household.

Question 2—Respondent's Understanding of Questions:

If the respondent is able to answer your questions directly and exactly, he must have comprehended the questions well.

But if he needs simple explanations to the questions and ultimately he gives a correct answer, then he clearly has understood your questions only fairly well.

Finally, if even after you have explained and re-worded your questions in greater detail, the respondent still gives some answers not pertaining to the questions, then it is obvious that his understanding is extremely bad.

Another factor which can broadly indicate whether the respondent understands the question is "Time Factor." How long does he take to answer a question? The longer he takes to answer, the greater the likelihood he finds difficulty in following the question. This may not be so in all cases. He may take a long time if he wants to think carefully before answering.

Generally speaking, understanding will be a function of the fluency in a language. Lack of understanding of a question may be because you are not conducting the interview in the language the respondent understands best. If you get even the slightest doubt of language problem, excuse yourself politely and report this to your regional supervisor as soon as possible.

Question 3—Respondent's Confidence in You:
Confidence is the most important factor in helping you to obtain correct and accurate information, and also ensures a smooth interview. Therefore, it is your duty to establish rapport with the respondents. Once the respondent trusts the purpose of the Survey and he feels very free to answer your questions, then you can rest assured that he will be very co-operative in replying to your questions. Build this confidence through the way you perform your interview. A few useful hints would be:

(a) Be sure that you are dressed properly and appear clean and smart
(b) Be polite and pay respects to the elders if any, at the place of interview
(c) If you use a motor-scooter or other vehicles, be sure that it is not jazzy and offensive to simple people
(d) Do not engage in controversies and never discuss religion or politics even as a side line
(e) Offer all common courtesies—e.g., if the respondent is a smoker, offer him a cigarette if you have one. Don't ignore the respondent.
(f) Be attentive to what he says, and be patient, and put on a smile as often as possible.

Remember that if the respondent lacks the assurance and the confidence in the contents of the questions and the manner you ask the questions, he is bound to give you some problems in obtaining reliable information.

Question 4—Language:
If right from the start you face language problems, then do not interview the household at all. You are to inform your regional supervisor as soon as possible. Try to find out the dialect of the respondent, for this will enable the regional supervisor to send an appropriate interviewer to do the job.
Should the problem crop up during the interview, then you are to mark down the individual questions which give you trouble. This will enable the regional supervisor to check these questions and see whether a second visit to the household is necessary or not. If, however, you really get stuck in the middle of an interview and you are unable to proceed any further, excuse yourself politely and report to your regional supervisor. He will make some alternative arrangements.

Question 5—Comments:

This column is meant for you to write all the problems faced by you in the interview and other field problems.

Try to express your difficulties and if possible suggest a few solutions. Little comments can help a lot in planning the future Surveys, therefore, do not hesitate to contribute your ideas and solutions pertaining to field problems.

Indicate also any customs or traditions or fears expressed by the persons. This will help future planning of Surveys.

3

Inequality in
Levels of Living

IN THE PREVIOUS CHAPTER, which presented a broad picture of inequality in
Malaysia as revealed by the PES, the household income distribution was
used to enable comparison with other surveys. In this chapter, to analyze
inequality in levels of living or economic welfare among the population, the
per capita household income distribution is considered more appropriate.
Various inequality indices are estimated for this distribution, and there is a
discussion on the decomposition of inequality, which is applied to estimate
the contribution of interracial, interregional, and rural-urban inequalities
to overall inequality. The final section discusses the implications of the
racial decompositions for the two prongs of the New Economic Policy and
shows how the redress of poverty rule (from appendix E) is also "efficient"
for redressing inequality.

PES Income as a Measure of Economic Welfare

There appear to be three shortcomings in using PES income as a proxy for
levels of living or economic welfare. First, welfare levels at a point in time
are likely to be better indicated by current consumption than by current
income as defined in most surveys including PES. (Unfortunately, data on
the consumption distribution are not available in sufficient detail in PES.)
The problem is highlighted in PES by the existence of a small number (1.4
percent) of households with zero current income. Obviously, the consumption of such households cannot be taken as zero, and presumably their
consumption expenditure was financed from sources that do not count as
PES income. The two most important of these are likely to have been
borrowing and dissaving,[1] which are omitted from the eleven income

---

1. The consumption expenditure could also have been financed by other unrecorded
transfers or by asset decumulation. Surveys which use the net change in assets or balance-sheet
approach to define income are likely to catch this aspect.

categories listed in PES (see chapter 2, "Definition of PES Income"). Borrowing and dissaving are fairly common phenomenons among low-income households in developing countries, but surveys do not usually include these sources in their definition of income. PES current income is also an imperfect proxy if one is interested in a lifetime measure of welfare levels. This requires data on the profile of income over time, which irons out life-cycle variations associated with age and experience[2] as well as purely random fluctuations around the age profile. Again, current consumption might be a better proxy than current income, if a version of the "permanent income" hypothesis is accepted.

The second problem associated with using PES income as a surrogate for economic welfare concerns its nonadjustment for tax incidence and public expenditure benefits (including transfer payments).[3] If it is to be a measure of welfare, PES income should ideally be adjusted for direct and indirect tax incidence and public goods and services, which have a differential impact according to income class. Unfortunately, it has not been possible to make such corrections here, and unadjusted PES income is used as a proxy for welfare levels.

A potential third problem is that owing to geographical variation in prices, especially between rural and urban areas, the PES (money) income distribution could turn out to be somewhat different from the real income distribution in the country. Unfortunately, there are no regional price surveys in Malaysia to enable estimates of real income, but it seems that regional price differences are in fact fairly small for the average consumption bundle.[4] Hence the error introduced by neglecting such price differences may not be particularly significant.

2. Income differences arising from age and experience are an important part of observed inequality among urban employees in Malaysia (see chapter 7).

3. There appears to be some adjustment on the subsidy side: the PES field interviewers were instructed to "include income from miscellaneous sources—like government aid, scholarships to children, free books, subsidized items like fertilizers, etc." (Department of Statistics, 1970*b*, p. 31; also quoted in chapter 2).

4. This was the opinion of senior officials in the Malaysian Ministry of Agriculture (including Mr. Selvadurai, the senior economist, and Mr. Haridas). For example, the difference in rice prices between states in 1970 was at most 5 percent because the price of paddy was nationally controlled. The prices of other food items apparently varied by about 10–15 percent, but there are likely to have been compensating variations across regions. On the one hand, clothing and imported goods (such as sugar and kerosene) are likely to have been more expensive in the rural hinterland because of transport costs (and also because goods are often bought on credit in rural areas). On the other hand, fruits and vegetables (which are locally produced) were probably cheaper in rural than in urban areas. For the average consumption bundle, therefore, the difference in rural-urban prices may not have been very large. This question is briefly discussed again in chapter 4, in connection with the definition of a poverty line.

The Population Unit and Appropriate Income Concept

Income distributions have typically been defined over different types of population unit.[5] The choice of unit obviously depends on the purpose at hand, which in this chapter is to analyze inequality in levels of living. The distribution of households by household income is most widely used for this purpose, but for two reasons this distribution does not provide a good indication of differences in levels of living in the population. First, the distribution is defined with respect to the *household*, whereas the primary interest here is in differences among *individuals*. Second, even when the household is the unit of concern, its living standard is not properly measured by household income. Household income needs to be adjusted to take account of variations in household size and composition, and economies of scale in consumption. For example, a large household with a certain household income is not as well-off as a small household with the same total income.[6] Even if household size is the same, a unit of income can produce different amounts of household utility or well-being, depending on the age-sex composition of its members.[7]

Even though the primary interest is in inequality among individuals, it is still necessary to consider the household income of households to which the individuals belong.[8] This is because the household performs a redistributive function among its members, with the income accruing to individual recipients getting pooled. Indeed, in some cases income accrues directly to the household as a unit and not to individual members within it. In family

5. Several different types of unit have been distinguished for the purpose of measuring inequality: households, individuals, income recipients, economically active population, and so on. To avoid confusion, throughout this book I have tried to describe distributions explicitly in terms of both the population unit and the income concept. For example, I refer to the distribution of households by per capita household income. This terminology arises naturally from the underlying frequency distribution, in which households are "distributed" across class intervals of per capita household income. The alternative terminology based on "distributing" per capita household income among households is less elegant: first, it is not per capita household income that is distributed among households, but a total (which, in this case, is not the total household income in the economy); second, mentioning this total does not obviate the need to mention the income concept according to which the total is distributed.

6. An exception to this occurs if household income is a "public good."

7. The welfare level of a household depends both on the total income of the household and on its size and composition. Among those who have tried to derive equivalence scales for households by formalizing this dependence is Muellbauer (1976).

8. The income actually received by individuals does not provide much information about differences in levels of living. About 70 percent of them get zero income, including many well-off individuals belonging to rich households.

farms and enterprises, for example, the income is jointly received by the household, and family workers are typically unpaid. The income from other jointly owned physical or financial assets can also be attributed only to the household collectively. For these reasons, then, the household must be regarded as the basic income-sharing unit.

The welfare level of an individual depends on the size of his or her share of household income, but information about sharing among members is not easily obtainable. I make the assumption that it is shared equally, although its distribution undoubtedly depends on characteristics of individual members such as earner status, power, age, sex, weight, and so on.[9] Hence the procedure is adopted of ranking individuals according to their per capita household income.[10]

The welfare level of a household is also measured by its per capita household income.[11] No allowance is thus made for the age and sex composition of its members, nor for economies of scale in household consumption. Some correction should have been made for household composition, but with present data this has proved impossible. An estimation of equivalence scales requires detailed household expenditure data, which are not yet available.[12] Neglect of composition effects

9. Little is known about the intrafamily income distribution. Some sociological literature from village India suggests considerable inequality in the sharing of household food. This is explained by the differing needs of working and nonworking members of the household, with the working members consuming more to sustain higher levels of physical activity.

10. This income concept defined over the population of individuals certainly gives a better idea of inequality in levels of living than does the distribution of income recipients by personal income. For certain purposes, such as an analysis of education and earnings (chapter 7), the personal income distribution would also be of interest. It is shown in appendix E, lemma 3, that the distribution of individuals according to per capita household income is more equal (in the Lorenz sense) than their distribution according to personal income.

11. If household income is strictly a "public good," however, then for welfare measurement individuals and households should be ranked according to household income, not per capita household income.

12. Such scales would allow estimates of the household income per equivalent adult. For inequality measurement, however, there is still the problem of assigning this income concept to the appropriate population unit: households, individuals, or equivalent adults (including fractional ones). In other words, which of the three distributions should be chosen to measure inequality: the distribution of households by household income per equivalent adult, the distribution of individuals by household income per equivalent adult, or the distribution of equivalent adults by household income per equivalent adult? The present methodology for estimating equivalence scales is based on income-scaling factors that keep *household* utility constant for variations in household size and composition. For consistency with the derivation of equivalence scales, therefore, the distribution of *households* by household income per equivalent adult may be regarded more appropriate for the measurement of inequality.

probably leads to a relative underestimation of welfare levels of households with a high proportion of children and female members.[13] In Malaysia, these are not necessarily the large households, owing to the prevalence of the joint family system and other institutions.[14]

Three separate distributions are considered:

1. The distribution of households according to household income
2. The distribution of households according to per capita household income
3. The distribution of individuals according to per capita household income.

The first distribution has already been discussed in the previous chapter. It is briefly included again to facilitate comparison with the other distributions: table 3-1 shows the distribution of households by household income class and racial group. (For a disaggregation of this distribution by urban-rural location, see tables 3-12 and 3-13 at the end of the chapter.) The second and third distributions will generally differ from the first and from each other, except when household size is constant in the economy. Their derivation requires full information on the *joint* distribution of households by household income and size (see appendix F).

The Joint Distribution of Households by Household Income and Size

The joint distribution of households by household income and size is presented in table 3-2. Each cell refers to a particular household income and size class and shows the absolute frequency of households in it. The rows of the table show the household size distribution within each income class. The columns of the table show the income distribution within each household size class, together with the average household income, Gini coefficient, average number of income recipients, and so on.

13. This assumes that children and women count for less than a "standard adult" or, in other words, their "equivalent adult" factors are smaller than unity. But it is not clear how different from unity these might be for children in certain age groups. While children eat less food on average than adults (those, at any rate, who are not yet teenagers), they incur larger expenditures on other items such as education (including books), health, toys, and so on.

14. The welfare level of members from large households is, however, underestimated if economies of scale in consumption are neglected. But I have not seen a convincing treatment that allows for scale economies. In fact, in the context of existing models that have been used to estimate equivalence scales, it seems impossible to distinguish scale effects from composition effects.

Table 3-1. Distribution of Households
by Household Income Class and Racial Group
(number of households)

Household income class (M$ per month)	Malay	Chinese	Indian	All races including "other"
No income	190	110	32	341
1–39	1,145	104	56	1,336
40–49	617	46	34	711
50–79	2,316	270	141	2,751
80–99	1,525	245	122	1,898
100–129	1,834	537	333	2,712
130–149	996	373	218	1,596
150–179	1,204	661	379	2,251
180–199	576	409	217	1,204
200–279	1,478	1,564	573	3,625
280–299	238	267	74	581
300–399	744	1,163	264	2,175
400–479	317	555	120	999
480–499	54	97	17	168
500–599	201	398	88	693
600–679	123	228	55	412
680–699	17	43	9	69
700–749	46	92	20	160
750–799	27	76	19	122
800–899	47	169	22	246
900–979	32	91	16	142
980–999	7	18	3	29
1,000–1,249	59	180	43	295
1,250–1,499	29	97	27	163
1,500–1,749	12	67	17	100
1,750–1,999	11	29	3	44
2,000–2,499	8	49	13	83
2,500–2,999	3	25	7	44
3,000–3,499	2	15	3	26
3,500–3,999	2	8	4	19
4,000–4,999	1	3	5	11
5,000+	2	14	2	19
All income classes	13,863	8,003	2,936	25,025[a]

Note: See tables 3-12 and 3-13 for a disaggregation by urban-rural location.
a. Includes two households for which the racial group was not available.

The row showing average household income for different household sizes indicates a steady rise in average income with household size, except for a slight fall for the nine-member group. The row showing the Gini coefficient for each household size indicates inequality to be highest among

Table 3-2. Joint Distribution of Households by Household Income and Size
(number of households)

Household income class (M$ per month)	Household size										All household sizes
	1	2	3	4	5	6	7	8	9	10+	
No income	29	54	53	46	57	39	24	13	8	18	341
1–39	495	352	163	127	82	53	32	18	8	6	1,336
40–49	124	148	156	102	87	43	26	11	11	3	711
50–79	354	407	489	462	374	279	181	102	52	51	2,751
80–99	175	217	288	301	261	244	195	96	64	57	1,898
100–129	269	260	360	393	397	368	257	189	113	106	2,712
130–149	128	121	193	237	228	232	180	119	78	80	1,596
150–179	187	168	254	313	296	290	249	217	144	133	2,251
180–199	71	82	119	151	182	151	137	137	77	97	1,204
200–279	173	233	340	440	463	491	406	385	287	407	3,625
280–299	22	35	45	56	59	81	79	68	59	77	581
300–399	92	112	176	230	240	250	270	255	185	356	2,175
400–479	38	47	65	119	116	128	116	106	85	179	999
480–499	6	12	10	18	13	19	23	14	10	43	168
500–599	24	33	57	64	75	75	82	69	59	155	693
600–679	13	25	34	46	46	38	39	35	30	106	412
680–699	3	4	9	9	7	7	5	3	3	19	69
700–749	2	7	12	15	18	18	14	20	14	40	160
750–799	2	6	6	10	16	18	17	9	10	28	122
800–899	3	12	19	26	21	36	25	22	20	62	246
900–979	4	6	9	15	20	22	12	7	10	37	142
980–999	0	1	2	4	1	3	2	2	5	9	29

(Table continues on the following page.)

Table 3-2 (continued).

Household income class (M$ per month)	Household size										All household sizes
	1	2	3	4	5	6	7	8	9	10+	
1,000–1,249	7	20	25	32	28	47	28	30	17	61	295
1,250–1,499	5	5	12	17	22	18	16	20	12	36	163
1,500–1,749	1	6	4	12	12	15	12	7	7	24	100
1,750–1,999	1	1	1	5	2	12	3	4	1	14	44
2,000–2,499	3	9	10	8	8	11	8	4	4	18	83
2,500–2,999	0	2	2	3	9	4	5	5	2	12	44
3,000–3,499	0	3	5	3	0	4	1	5	0	5	26
3,500–3,999	0	2	0	4	2	0	3	2	1	5	19
4,000–4,999	0	1	0	0	2	1	1	2	0	4	11
5,000 +	0	0	2	0	0	3	2	3	0	9	19
All income classes	2,231	2,391	2,920	3,268	3,144	3,009	2,450	1,979	1,376	2,257	25,025
Average household income	137	181	207	231	243	282	289	326	315	496	264
Gini coefficient	0.5111	0.5621	0.5178	0.4927	0.4837	0.4920	0.4634	0.4592	0.4031	0.4728	0.5129
Average number of income recipients[a]	0.99	1.24	1.37	1.46	1.54	1.64	1.73	1.90	2.02	2.76	1.63

Standard deviation of number of income recipients[a]	0.11	0.50	0.64	0.75	0.82	0.91	0.99	1.07	1.18	2.09	1.10
Average participation rate[a,b]	0.99	0.62	0.46	0.37	0.31	0.27	0.25	0.24	0.22	0.23	0.40
Standard deviation of participation rate[a]	0.11	0.25	0.21	0.19	0.16	0.15	0.14	0.13	0.13	0.20	0.28
Average dependency ratio[a,c,d]	1.00	1.72	2.47	3.18	3.83	4.44	5.03	5.38	5.82	5.97	3.76
Standard deviation of dependency ratio[a,d]	0	0.45	0.76	1.08	1.40	1.73	2.07	2.41	2.76	3.57	2.37

a. Per household.
b. The participation rate for a household is the ratio of number of income recipients to household size.
c. The dependency ratio for a household is the ratio of household size to number of income recipients.
d. The average dependency ratio per household and the standard deviation of dependency ratio per household were calculated by excluding the zero-income households; otherwise they are not calculable.

two-member households (Gini coefficient of 0.5621).[15] Inequality seems to fall as one moves to larger-sized households, dropping sharply between the eight-member and the nine-member groups, and rising again for the largest size (ten or more members). For one-member households inequality is fairly high with a Gini coefficient of 0.5111, which is only slightly lower than the overall Gini coefficient of 0.5129 for all households.

Tables 3-3 to 3-5 show the average number of income recipients, the average participation rate, and the average dependency ratio[16] by household income class and racial group; table 3-2 shows these averages by household size class. The average number of income recipients rises uniformly with household size, from 0.99 for one-member households to 2.76 for households of ten or more. This rate of increase, however, does not prevent the average participation rate falling from 0.99 for one-member households to 0.23 for households with ten or more members. The obverse of this finding is the increase in average dependency ratio from 1.01 to 5.97 over the same range.

Across income classes, the average number of income recipients per household rises from 1.10 in the lowest positive class (M$1 – M$39) to 8.37 in the uppermost (M$5,000 and over), although it fluctuates somewhat above the M$600 level. Over the same range, the average participation rate displays a nonmonotonic relationship, which might be described as approximately U-shaped.[17] The participation rate first falls from 0.62 in the lowest class, then fluctuates between 0.36 and 0.44 at middle income levels, and finally rises back up to 0.52. The average dependency ratio follows a more or less inverse pattern to this. For all households, the average number of income recipients is 1.62, the average participation rate is 0.40, and the average dependency ratio is 3.76.[18]

---

15. Ignoring composition effects, the Gini coefficient for any household size does give a valid indication of inequality in living standards within it, since there is no variation in the number of members.

16. The participation rate for a household is defined here as the ratio of number of income recipients to household size. The dependency ratio for a household is the reciprocal of the participation rate. This definition of participation rate is somewhat different from that used in labor economics generally. The latter refers to the ratio of actual to potential labor force participants in a household (or a population). My definition is of an "income" participation rate, where everyone is viewed as a potential income recipient (for example, through remittances or gifts).

17. These data make it possible to conduct analyses explaining the participation rate in terms of economic and demographic variables. This would be important for making projections about labor supply and unemployment.

18. The average dependency ratio is not equal to the reciprocal of the average participation rate: in general, the average of a reciprocal is not equal to the reciprocal of the average.

Table 3-3. Average Number of Income Recipients per Household
by Household Income Class and Racial Group

Household income class (M$ per month)	Malay	Chinese	Indian	All races including "other"	Standard deviation[a]
No income	0	0	0	0	0
1–39	1.11	1.02	1.02	1.10	0.33
40–49	1.17	1.04	1.09	1.16	0.39
50–79	1.24	1.07	1.15	1.22	0.50
80–99	1.33	1.18	1.17	1.30	0.59
100–129	1.41	1.21	1.17	1.34	0.60
130–149	1.49	1.31	1.34	1.43	0.65
150–179	1.52	1.35	1.47	1.46	0.68
180–199	1.63	1.54	1.69	1.62	0.80
200–279	1.70	1.70	1.82	1.72	0.85
280–299	1.72	2.01	2.16	1.91	0.95
300–399	1.81	2.07	2.24	2.00	1.04
400–479	2.00	2.33	2.21	2.20	1.26
480–499	2.32	2.23	2.29	2.26	1.20
500–599	2.02	2.61	2.02	2.36	1.36
600–679	2.42	2.61	2.07	2.47	1.51
680–699	2.00	2.35	2.22	2.25	1.18
700–749	2.07	2.79	2.65	2.58	1.38
750–799	2.41	2.82	1.95	2.59	1.47
800–899	2.51	2.92	2.77	2.79	1.77
900–979	2.41	3.01	2.06	2.75	1.74
980–999	2.00	3.11	2.67	2.72	1.31
1,000–1,249	2.49	2.95	2.63	2.76	1.68
1,250–1,499	3.10	3.13	3.11	3.03	1.71
1,500–1,749	4.00	3.31	4.29	3.52	2.16
1,750–1,999	3.64	3.59	3.33	3.52	1.69
2,000–2,499	3.13	2.94	3.85	2.86	2.28
2,500–2,999	3.67	3.44	4.71	3.30	2.73
3,000–3,499	3.00	2.93	3.33	2.65	1.41
3,500–3,999	2.00	4.75	2.50	3.53	2.59
4,000–4,999	1.00	2.67	6.60	4.18	4.00
5,000+	2.00	10.50	2.50	8.37	13.43
All income classes	1.46	1.90	1.72	1.63	1.10

Note: See tables 3-12 and 3-13 for a disaggregation by urban-rural location.
a. Standard deviation of number of income recipients per household for all races including "other."

Table 3-4. Average Participation Rate per Household
by Household Income Class and Racial Group

Household income class (M$ per month)	Malay	Chinese	Indian	All races including "other"	Standard deviation[a]
No income	0	0	0	0	0
1–39	0.61	0.79	0.76	0.62	0.33
40–49	0.44	0.80	0.71	0.48	0.30
50–79	0.38	0.71	0.57	0.42	0.28
80–99	0.34	0.59	0.45	0.38	0.27
100–129	0.33	0.50	0.44	0.38	0.27
130–149	0.33	0.44	0.42	0.37	0.26
150–179	0.34	0.39	0.41	0.37	0.26
180–199	0.35	0.40	0.36	0.37	0.26
200–279	0.35	0.38	0.38	0.36	0.25
280–299	0.34	0.40	0.37	0.37	0.25
300–399	0.35	0.39	0.41	0.38	0.25
400–479	0.36	0.41	0.43	0.40	0.26
480–499	0.44	0.36	0.49	0.40	0.26
500–599	0.40	0.40	0.45	0.41	0.27
600–679	0.42	0.41	0.45	0.42	0.25
680–699	0.54	0.43	0.32	0.44	0.30
700–749	0.35	0.40	0.57	0.41	0.24
750–799	0.41	0.42	0.37	0.41	0.25
800–899	0.44	0.41	0.54	0.43	0.25
900–979	0.43	0.43	0.38	0.43	0.25
980–999	0.32	0.36	0.58	0.37	0.22
1,000–1,249	0.44	0.47	0.56	0.47	0.27
1,250–1,499	0.42	0.48	0.59	0.48	0.25
1,500–1,749	0.67	0.47	0.63	0.52	0.25
1,750–1,999	0.51	0.51	0.53	0.50	0.20
2,000–2,499	0.45	0.45	0.59	0.49	0.26
2,500–2,999	0.52	0.42	0.50	0.44	0.23
3,000–3,499	0.44	0.44	1.00	0.48	0.26
3,500–3,999	0.43	0.52	0.38	0.50	0.27
4,000–4,999	0.09	0.41	0.49	0.47	0.29
5,000+	0.28	0.56	0.58	0.52	0.27
All income classes	0.37	0.43	0.43	0.40	0.28

Note: The participation rate for a household is the ratio of number of income recipients to household size.

a. Standard deviation of participation rate per household for all races including "other."

Table 3-5. Average Dependency Ratio per Household
by Household Income Class and Racial Group

Household income class (M$ per month)	Malay	Chinese	Indian	All races including "other"	Standard deviation[a]
No income	—	—	—	—	—
1–39	2.43	1.99	1.88	2.40	1.76
40–49	3.22	1.64	2.21	3.07	1.90
50–79	3.74	2.20	2.97	3.55	2.13
80–99	4.11	2.78	3.64	3.91	2.30
100–129	4.24	3.23	3.75	3.98	2.35
130–149	4.21	3.70	3.82	4.04	2.40
150–179	4.22	4.00	3.79	4.09	2.42
180–199	4.08	4.01	4.07	4.05	2.45
200–279	4.17	4.03	3.80	4.06	2.47
280–299	4.27	3.83	3.66	3.98	2.48
300–399	4.14	3.79	3.68	3.90	2.44
400–479	4.11	3.62	3.70	3.78	2.46
480–499	3.16	4.17	2.76	3.70	2.46
500–599	3.74	3.73	3.55	3.70	2.48
600–679	3.65	3.51	3.42	3.53	2.55
680–699	2.78	3.73	4.50	3.60	2.43
700–749	4.02	3.38	2.51	3.45	2.27
750–799	3.31	3.23	3.76	3.33	1.79
800–899	3.30	3.40	2.92	3.31	2.33
900–979	3.31	3.20	4.11	3.31	2.10
980–999	3.57	3.53	2.75	3.44	1.62
1,000–1,249	3.17	3.13	2.56	3.07	2.13
1,250–1,499	3.75	3.05	2.39	3.02	2.52
1,500–1,749	2.01	2.76	2.14	2.53	1.57
1,750–1,999	2.24	2.43	2.64	2.41	1.31
2,000–2,499	2.72	2.91	2.45	2.68	1.51
2,500–2,999	3.78	3.44	2.18	3.14	2.05
3,000–3,499	3.13	2.85	1.00	2.69	1.53
3,500–3,999	2.83	2.43	2.90	2.59	1.24
4,000–4,999	11.00	2.50	2.73	3.24	2.79
5,000+	9.00	2.78	1.75	3.37	3.94
All income classes	3.88	3.61	3.60	3.76	2.37

— Not applicable.

Note: The dependency ratio for a household is the ratio of household size to number of income recipients.

a. Standard deviation of dependency ratio per household for all races including "other."

The average household size by household income class and racial group is shown in table 3-6. Excluding the zero-income class, average household size increases with income up to the M$980–M$999 class, after which it fluctuates a little. Households in the M$1 – M$39 class have an average of

Table 3-6. Average Household Size
by Household Income Class and Racial Group

Household income class (M$ per month)	Malay	Chinese	Indian	All races including "other"	Standard deviation[a]
No income	4.24	5.16	4.47	4.51	2.52
1–39	2.62	2.01	1.93	2.57	1.87
40–49	3.54	1.70	2.35	3.36	1.94
50–79	4.28	2.36	3.33	4.04	2.22
80–99	4.90	3.12	4.04	4.61	2.37
100–129	5.29	3.67	4.23	4.84	2.51
130–149	5.51	4.42	4.69	5.15	2.54
150–179	5.62	4.85	5.10	5.31	2.63
180–199	5.79	5.33	5.95	5.67	2.70
200–279	6.02	5.85	6.32	6.00	2.87
280–299	6.24	6.40	6.92	6.39	2.84
300–399	6.33	6.54	6.94	6.51	3.08
400–479	6.66	6.84	6.36	6.71	3.34
480–499	6.43	7.54	6.59	7.08	3.63
500–599	6.31	7.69	5.93	7.05	3.63
600–679	7.14	7.60	6.22	7.25	4.12
680–699	5.06	7.51	8.33	7.01	4.57
700–749	6.67	8.07	5.65	7.34	3.50
750–799	7.30	7.66	6.47	7.39	3.85
800–899	6.45	8.17	5.77	7.49	3.91
900–979	7.25	8.02	6.56	7.61	4.80
980–999	6.71	10.28	6.67	8.79	4.79
1,000–1,249	7.05	7.46	5.63	7.02	3.94
1,250–1,499	8.17	7.91	6.22	7.42	4.28
1,500–1,749	6.75	7.88	7.47	7.53	4.57
1,750–1,999	8.27	7.52	7.33	7.59	3.43
2,000–2,499	8.13	7.20	6.85	6.53	4.02
2,500–2,999	7.33	9.12	8.14	7.82	4.33
3,000–3,499	11.00	7.40	3.33	6.54	4.14
3,500–3,999	4.50	10.13	6.50	7.47	4.18
4,000–4,999	11.00	6.33	13.20	9.36	5.36
5,000+	11.00	14.79	4.50	13.11	12.55
All income classes	5.084	5.839	5.453	5.363	3.09

Note: See tables 3-12 and 3-13 for a disaggregation by urban-rural location.
a. Standard deviation of household size for all races including "other."

2.57 members, while those in the M$980–M$999 class have an average of 8.79 members. For incomes above M$1,000, the average household size drops slightly and varies before climbing again to reach its maximum of 13.11 for those with incomes of M$5,000 and over; the average household size for the entire sample is 5.36 members.[19] Across income classes, a correlation coefficient of 0.81 has been computed between average household size and income level.

Table 3-6 indicates a large variation in household size at each income level, measured by the standard deviation of household size within each income class. The variability in size at a given income level causes large-sized households to be ranked below small-sized ones in the ordering by per capita household income. Apart from the variability within income classes, size variability *across* income classes can also cause a reordering of households. Thus a large-sized high-income household can turn out to have a lower per capita income than a small-sized low-income household. Both factors can lead to substantial reordering of households when ranked by per capita household income rather than by household income.

Starting from the joint distribution function $f(y, m)$ of households with household income y and size m, I derive in appendix F the theoretical distribution of households and of individuals according to per capita household income. I show there the exact mathematical transformations required to effect these mappings. Sufficient conditions are specified for the per capita household income distribution to be identical to the household income distribution. Furthermore, I disprove (by counterexample) the widely held but erroneous belief that if average household size increases with household income, the per capita household income distribution is more equal than the household income distribution.

The last proposition needs some elaboration. As noted above, it is not merely the variation of average household size *across* income classes that causes the household and per capita household income distributions to diverge. They can diverge even if average household size is constant across income classes, so long as there is a nonzero variance around this average *within* income classes.[20] Except in certain special cases, however, it is difficult to predict the direction of divergence (in terms of inequality) when one moves from the household to the per capita household income distribution.

19. Since the sample size thins out in upper income classes, statistics for these groups are subject to increasingly large sampling error. For example, there were only 19 households in the top income class (M$5,000+), of which one had 56 members, 53 of whom were income recipients.

20. The larger this variance, other things being equal, the larger is the inequality in the per capita household income distribution (see appendix F).

Table 3-7. Distribution of Households by Household Income and per Capita Household Income

Households	Average household or per capita household income (M$ per month)	Average household size	Gini coefficient	Percentage share of income by percentile group				Sample size (number of households)
				Lowest quintile	Lowest 40 percent	Highest quintile	Highest 5 percent	
Household income								
All	264	5.363	0.5129	3.5	11.5	55.7	28.3	25,023
Malay	172	5.084	0.4664	4.3	13.2	51.6	24.0	13,863
Chinese	394	5.839	0.4656	4.8	13.8	52.6	25.5	8,003
Indian	304	5.453	0.4722	5.0	14.8	54.0	28.2	2,936
Other	813	4.416	0.6673	0.5	2.2	68.2	26.0	221
Per capita household income								
All	62		0.5374	4.9	10.9	59.2	30.5	25,023
Malay	41		0.4926	4.5	13.0	56.0	26.0	13,863
Chinese	86		0.4834	4.7	13.0	54.0	26.5	8,003
Indian	79		0.5382	4.0	11.3	59.2	31.0	2,936
Other	249		0.6998	0.5	1.9	72.0	29.2	221

Note: Further information on these distributions is provided in tables 3-14 to 3-16.
a. The standard deviations of household income are: all, 417; Malay, 226; Chinese, 548; Indian, 451; and other, 1,190.

The Distribution of Households
by per Capita Household Income

For Malaysia, there is an increase in inequality among households in going from the household income distribution to the per capita household income distribution. The Gini coefficient is 0.5129 for the household income distribution, and 0.5374 for the per capita household income distribution (table 3-7; see also tables 3-15 and 3-16). The Lorenz curves for the two distributions are drawn in figure 3-1. Since they intersect, their

Figure 3-1. *Lorenz Curves for the Household and per Capita Household Income Distributions*

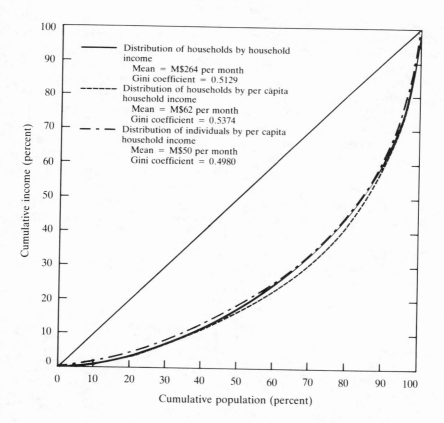

inequality ranking is not unambiguous in the sense that different measures of inequality could rank the distributions differently. The use of Lorenz comparability in this study is basically positive, however, not normative. It relies on the proposition that if the Lorenz curves of two distributions are nonintersecting (that is, one Lorenz curve dominates, or lies above, the other), then all measures of inequality which satisfy mean independence, population-size independence, and the Pigou-Dalton condition will show less inequality for the Lorenz-dominant distribution (see appendix D for a proof). Without drawing any welfare implications about the underlying distributions, I use Lorenz dominance simply to establish an unambiguous ranking of inequality by all indices belonging to this wide class. Indeed, in most cases it is impossible to undertake meaningful welfare comparisons between the underlying distributions because they refer to different population units or income concepts. It is still useful, however, to show Lorenz dominance where possible, as this allows automatic comparison by most well-known inequality measures.

The increase in inequality among households in going from the household income distribution to the per capita household income distribution occurs despite the fact that average household size increases with household income, and at a rate which is less than proportionate with income (see table 3-6). In these circumstances an unambiguous decrease in inequality would be expected if household size were constant at each income level (see appendix F, proposition 1). Hence I conclude that it is the variation of household size within income classes which produces the observed increase in inequality by substantially reordering households.

Table 3-7 presents summary information on the distribution of households by per capita household income (see also table 3-16). The average per capita household income in Malaysia is M$62 per month, but the importance of this number seems limited: it is simply the unweighted mean of per capita household incomes. The true per capita income (PCI) in

Table 3-8. Distribution of Individuals
by per Capita Household Income

Individuals	Per capita income (M$ per month)	Gini coefficient	Lowest quintile	Lowest 40 percent	Highest quintile	Highest 5 percent	Sample size (number of individuals)
All	50	0.4980	4.3	12.3	54.8	28.5	134,186
Malay	34	0.4553	5.2	14.8	52.2	24.6	70,474
Chinese	68	0.4542	5.3	14.3	52.8	26.8	46,726
Indian	57	0.5003	5.0	13.7	56.7	29.5	16,010
Other	185	0.7071	0.5	2.3	75.5	31.0	976

Malaysia is the mean of distribution 3, which has been computed as M$50 per month. This is the weighted mean of per capita household incomes, where the weights are the household sizes. It is easy to see that PCI is equal to average household income divided by average household size, but there is obviously no reason for average per capita household income to equal this. The relations among the different mean incomes of the three distributions in tables 3-7 and 3-8 can be expressed as follows: Let y_h be the income of household h and m_h its size, for $h = 1, 2, \ldots, H$. Then

Average household income, $\bar{y} = \dfrac{1}{H} \displaystyle\sum_{h=1}^{H} y_h = \text{M\$264.}$

Average per capita household income, $(\overline{y/m}) = \dfrac{1}{H} \displaystyle\sum_{h=1}^{H} (y_h/m_h) = \text{M\$62.}$

Per capita income, $\text{PCI} = \left(1 \Big/ \displaystyle\sum_{h=1}^{H} m_h \right) \displaystyle\sum_{h=1}^{H} m_h(y_h/m_h) = \text{M\$50}$

$$= \bar{y}/\bar{m}, \text{ where } \bar{m} = \dfrac{1}{H} \displaystyle\sum_{h=1}^{H} m_h = 5.363.$$

The Distribution of Individuals by per Capita Household Income

Since inequality in levels of living among individuals is of ultimate interest, it is necessary to examine the distribution of individuals by per capita household income. In further discussion of discrepancies in living standards in Malaysia, I restrict attention to this distribution, the summary characteristics of which are set out in table 3-8.

The Gini coefficient of the distribution is 0.4980, which implies a fairly high degree of inequality in the country. Individuals in the 40 percent of the population with the lowest incomes receive only 12.3 percent of total income, whereas those in the top 5 percent receive 28.5 percent of total income. The lowest quintile get a mere 4.3 percent, and the ratio of the shares of the highest to the lowest quintile (a frequent measure of inequality[21]) is almost 13.

The extent of inequality in distribution 3 seems lower than that indicated in distributions 1 and 2. Since the Lorenz curve for distribution 3 intersects

---

21. An obvious defect of this measure is that it satisfies only the "weak" principle of transfers, which states that transfers from rich to poor should either reduce the measure or leave it unchanged. For example, transfers among the 60 percent of the population in the middle income range (or within the top or bottom quintiles) leave the index unchanged.

the Lorenz curves for the other two distributions, however, an unambiguous comparison is not possible; compare the shares of the highest 5 percent in 1 and 3, and the shares of the lowest quintile in 2 and 3 (see tables 3-7 and 3-8). In fact, it might have been expected that distribution 3 would Lorenz-dominate distribution 1 (see appendix F, proposition 2); but, as noted earlier, the reordering of households when they are ranked by per capita household income prevents this outcome (because the hypothesis of proposition 2 is not met).

A breakdown by racial group of the distribution of individuals by per capita household income has been effected in table 3-8. It shows the per capita income of the Chinese community (M\$68 per month) to be twice that of the Malay community (M\$34 per month). The per capita income of the Indians (M\$57 per month) is around 1.7 times that of the Malays. These disparity ratios are lower than those calculated on the basis of average household income.[22] The reason for this is evident from table 3-7, since the per capita income of a group is simply its average household income divided by its average household size. As the Malays have a lower average household size (5.084 members) than the Chinese (5.839 members) and the Indians (5.453 members), the disparity ratios in per capita income will be smaller than the disparity ratios in household income. Hence disparity ratios in Malaysia are lower than is indicated by researchers who neglect racial differences in household size.

The distribution of individuals by per capita household income *within* racial groups shows that Malay and Chinese incomes are distributed very similarly around their respective means. The corresponding fractile shares are close to one another, and the Gini coefficient for the Malay distribution (0.4553) is very similar to that for the Chinese distribution (0.4542). Indian incomes are distributed somewhat more unequally (Gini coefficient of 0.5003), and "other" incomes are distributed extremely unequally (Gini coefficient of 0.7071).

The Atkinson Index

So far I have attempted to measure inequality largely by positive or descriptive indices such as various fractile shares. Another type of index (Atkinson, 1970) is based explicitly on a social welfare evaluation of income

---

22. On the basis of average household income, the Chinese-Malay disparity ratio is 2.29, and the Indian-Malay ratio is 1.77 (see chapter 2 or table 3-7).

distribution.[23] Let $\mathbf{y} = (y_1, y_2, \ldots, y_n)$ denote an income distribution among n individuals, where $y_i \geq 0$ is the income of individual i $(i = 1, \ldots, n)$. Denote the mean income level by μ, so that

$$n\mu = \sum_{i=1}^{n} y_i.$$

Given a social welfare function, the Atkinson index is constructed by computing the equally distributed equivalent income, y_{EDE}, of the distribution. This is defined as the level of income per head which, if equally distributed, would give the same level of social welfare as the existing distribution. Atkinson's index is then defined as the difference between y_{EDE} and the mean income μ of the distribution, in proportionate terms. This definition is independent of the actual welfare function chosen, but in practice Atkinson restricts himself to the class of additively separable and symmetric functions of individual income. Formally, y_{EDE} is defined through

$$nU(y_{EDE}) = \sum_{i=1}^{n} U(y_i),$$

which is the level of social welfare associated with the existing distribution $\mathbf{y}$, and the Atkinson index I is defined as $1 - (y_{EDE}/\mu)$.

If I is required to be a mean-independent inequality index, the function $U(y)$ must be limited to the constant elasticity marginal utility form, that is,

$$U(y) = \begin{cases} \dfrac{1}{1-\varepsilon} y^{1-\varepsilon}, & \varepsilon \neq 1 \\ \log y, & \varepsilon = 1 \end{cases}$$

up to a positive linear transformation. Only values of $\varepsilon \geq 0$ are considered so that $U(y)$ is concave (that is, it displays nonincreasing marginal utility). This condition implies $y_{EDE} \leq \mu$. The choice of a particular value for ε is obviously a value judgment; ε measures the degree of inequality aversion. As ε rises, more weight is attached to transfers at the lower end of the distribution and less weight to transfers at the top. As $\varepsilon \to \infty$ we get the so-called Rawlsian function $\min_i \{y_i\}$, and as $\varepsilon \to 0$ we get the linear utility function which ranks distributions solely according to total income.

23. This is the pioneering contribution on normative measurement of inequality. Roughly speaking, Atkinson shows that normative inequality comparisons between two distributions can be made without reference to a prespecified social welfare function (as long as it is strictly concave) if, and only if, the corresponding Lorenz curves are nonintersecting except at the end points (that is, one Lorenz curve dominates the other). A formal statement and proof of this theorem are provided in appendix D.

The choice of ε within the range 0 to ∞ remains arbitrary. In the empirical sections of his paper, Atkinson (1970) restricts himself to values for ε between 1.0 and 2.5. Others advocate a value of about 2.0. Stern (1977) reviews the literature on the elasticity of marginal utility of income and presents a number of arguments in support of values between 1.5 and 2.5. It seems, therefore, that a value for ε of 2.0 might be reasonable and broadly acceptable.

Unfortunately, the Atkinson index cannot be computed on the Malaysian data for values of ε > 1 because of the presence of zero-income individuals in distribution 3.[24] Welfare falls to minus infinity, and the equally distributed equivalent income y_{EDE} is not defined in this case.[25] This is not simply a technical problem which can be got around by assigning a small positive income to zero-income individuals, as is sometimes suggested. The value of the inequality index will depend crucially on the particular income assigned, and it can be made arbitrarily close to unity (perfect inequality) by choosing a small enough level.

When there are zero-income individuals, the Atkinson index can perhaps be extended to a lexicographic ordering of inequality. Thus distributions might be ranked by first comparing the number of zero-income individuals in each. If the number of zero-income individuals is the same in both distributions, the usual Atkinson index computed for the positive-income individuals can be used to rank them. The natural index for this extended ordering is one which shows the number of zero-income individuals before the decimal point, and the Atkinson index for positive-income recipients after the decimal point. However, the value judgment implicit in this extension is open to serious question. For example, it might be difficult to accept that a distribution with a greater number of zero-income individuals is necessarily worse, independently of the number of *near*-zero-income individuals in the other distribution. The difference between a zero-income level and an infinitesimally small income level is unlikely to be a decisive one in economic terms.[26]

With zero-income individuals, therefore, it seems that we can properly use the Atkinson index only if ε is chosen to be less than (or equal to)

24. There are 1,366 zero-income individuals (corresponding to 341 zero-income households) in this sample of 134,186 individuals.

25. For the case of ε = 1, y_{EDE} is simply the geometric mean income of the distribution, and the Atkinson index is 1 minus the ratio of the geometric to the arithmetic mean income. With a single zero-income individual, the geometric mean is zero and the Atkinson index takes the value unity.

26. A discontinuity at the subsistence level of income might be perfectly defensible, however, if the difference is interpreted as one between life and death.

Table 3-9. Equally Distributed Equivalent Income
and Atkinson Inequality Index for the Distribution
of Individuals by per Capita Household Income
(M$ per month)

Individuals	0.00	0.25	0.50	0.75	0.90	0.99	Sample size (number of individuals)
All	49.9	44.1	39.3	34.8	30.9	11.9[a]	134,186
		(0.1162)	(0.2124)	(0.3026)	(0.3807)	(0.7615)	
Malay	34.3	31.0	28.2	25.3	22.6	8.1	70,474
		(0.0962)	(0.1778)	(0.2623)	(0.3411)	(0.7638)	
Chinese	68.4	61.8	56.2	50.9	45.9	18.7	46,726
		(0.0964)	(0.1783)	(0.2558)	(0.3289)	(0.7266)	
Indian	56.5	49.7	44.3	39.6	35.9	17.7	16,010
		(0.1203)	(0.2159)	(0.2991)	(0.3646)	(0.6867)	
Other	185.4	143.1	104.4	71.5	52.0	10.3	976
		(0.2281)	(0.4368)	(0.6143)	(0.7195)	(0.9444)	

Note: Figures in parentheses are the Atkinson inequality index.
a. When the 1,366 zero-income individuals are omitted, the equally distributed equivalent income y_{EDE} for $\varepsilon = 0.99$ is as high as M$33.1.

unity.[27] Table 3-9 presents the equally distributed equivalent income y_{EDE} for six different values of ε less than unity (from 0.0 to 0.99) and the corresponding Atkinson inequality index I (in parentheses). For $\varepsilon = 0$, y_{EDE} is simply the mean income (μ) of the distribution, which has earlier been called PCI. For $\varepsilon = 0.5$, $y_{EDE} = $ M$39.3, which means that if incomes were equally distributed, it would require only M$39.3 per person to achieve the same level of social welfare as the existing distribution with a mean income of M$49.9. Thus a proportionate income "loss" of $(\mu - y_{EDE})/\mu = 21.24$

27. The restriction might lead some to reject values for ε which are greater than unity—or $U(y)$ functions which are unbounded below. The problem raised by zero-income individuals is not simply that current income is an imperfect proxy for levels of living. It could arise even with current consumption as the proxy, if the reference period of the survey were very short. This leads naturally to an interest in levels of living over the longer run, but for a normative measurement of their inequality, essentially the same underlying problem of welfare economics would have to be faced. How does one evaluate in welfare terms a level of living which falls below the long-run subsistence minimum and implies starvation and premature death? Such levels of living are certainly consistent with a positive level of long-run or "permanent" consumption. This suggests the original problem is not in essence the empirical one of zero incomes, but it raises deep questions of welfare economics which are difficult to handle in a dynamic context.

percent arises from the inequality in the distribution, which gives a value of 0.2124 for I.

The table also shows y_{EDE} and I for each racial group separately. For $\varepsilon = 0.5$, the Atkinson inequality index for Malays, Chinese, Indians, and others, respectively, is 0.1778, 0.1783, 0.2159, and 0.4368. Again, the Malay inequality coefficient is close to that of the Chinese. This reinforces the earlier observation about the similarity of the Malay and Chinese distributions about their respective means.

As the inequality aversion parameter ε increases, y_{EDE} decreases and I increases; with zero-income individuals, neither is defined for $\varepsilon > 1$. In this case, y_{EDE} can be made arbitrarily close to zero, and I to unity, by choosing ε sufficiently close to unity. Witness the sharp drop in y_{EDE} as ε approaches unity in table 3-9.[28] When $\varepsilon = 1$, in fact, y_{EDE} is the geometric mean of the distribution, which is zero with zero-income individuals, and in this case I is equal to unity.

The Methodology of Inequality Decomposition

Traditionally the study of between-group inequality in Malaysia has been conducted in terms of differences in mean income between the groups. Thus, for example, the previously noted racial disparity ratios between non-Malays and Malays simply reflect mean income differences between the groups. Such ratios completely ignore income differences within racial groups, which could turn out to be quite large. It is interesting, therefore, to ask how much of total inequality in Malaysia consists of between-group inequality and how much of within-group inequality.

The obvious way to answer this question is to decompose total inequality into between-group and within-group inequality. The between-group contribution might then be defined as the ratio of between-group to total inequality (and similarly the within-group contribution). The inequality indices considered so far, however, are not neatly decomposable into between- and within-group terms. For example, the Gini coefficient cannot in general be written as the sum of a between-group component and a within-group component, where the two components have a natural meaning (see "On the Decomposition of the Gini Coefficient" in appendix B). I attempt to give a consistent definition for these terms.

28. When zero-income individuals are omitted from the distribution, the value of y_{EDE} for $\varepsilon = 0.99$ is M\$33.1 (note to table 3-9). With zero-income individuals omitted, y_{EDE} is defined for all $\varepsilon \geqslant 0$. Its values for $\varepsilon = 0.5, 1.0, 2.0,$ and 3.0 are M\$40.1, M\$33.0, M\$23.2, and M\$16.0, respectively. Since there are 1,366 fewer individuals in this case and the same total income, the arithmetic mean μ is slightly higher at M\$50.4 (compared with M\$49.9).

The between-group component can be defined as the value of the inequality index when all within-group income differences are artificially suppressed. In other words, it is the value of the inequality index for the hypothetical income distribution which assigns to each person within a group the mean income of the group. In this way, within-group inequality is eliminated, and the resultant distribution shows only the inequality arising from between-group income differences.

Likewise, the within-group component can be defined as the value of the inequality index when all between-group income differences are suppressed. Thus a hypothetical income distribution is constructed in which the group mean incomes are equalized to the overall mean through an equiproportionate change in the income of every person within a group. In this way, between-group inequality is eliminated, but the inequality within each group remains constant (assuming the inequality index is mean-independent).[29] The within-group component is then the value of the index for this hypothetical distribution.

An inequality index may be said to be additively decomposable if for any grouping total inequality can be written as the sum of between-group and within-group inequality. This property allows the unambiguous measurement of the contribution of a particular grouping (or variable) to overall inequality.[30]

The Gini coefficient does not satisfy the property of additive decomposability as shown by a racial grouping of distribution 3. The between-race component according to the above definition is 0.1648, which is the value of the Gini coefficient when each member of a group receives the mean income of that group; that is, all 70,474 Malays get M$34 per month, all 46,726 Chinese get M$68 per month, all 16,010 Indians get M$57 per month, and all 976 others get M$185 per month. The within-race component according to the above definition has not been computed, but it is at least as large as 0.4621, which is the population-weighted average of Gini coefficients of the four racial groups.[31] Hence the sum of the between-group and within-group components is at least as large as 0.6269, whereas the overall Gini

29. With a mean-independent inequality index, in fact, it does not matter to what income level all the group mean incomes are equalized in constructing the hypothetical distribution, provided the level is non-zero.

30. Notice the analogy with regression analysis, where the total variance is decomposed into the sum of the "explained" variance and the "unexplained" variance, and R^2 is the fraction of the total variance explained by the independent variable(s). The analogy is discussed further in chapter 6.

31. The section "On the Decomposition of the Gini Coefficient" in appendix B proves that the Gini coefficient of a composite group is always greater than or equal to the population-weighted average of subgroup Gini coefficients.

coefficient is only 0.4980 (table 3-8). The Gini coefficient is not decomposable into the sum of between- and within-group inequality and therefore cannot provide an adequate basis for assessing the relative importance of these two sources of inequality.[32]

It would be an interesting exercise to characterize the complete class of inequality measures decomposable according to the strict definition given above. I suspect the class is quite restrictive, although Theil's second measure L (discussed below) belongs to it as does the variance of the logarithm of income (variance of log-income).[33] The latter satisfies the above decomposition property if the means in the definitions of between-group component and within-group component are interpreted to be *geometric* means.[34]

The decomposition formulas for Theil's second measure L and the variance of log-income are shown in appendix C, "The Decomposition of Three Inequality Measures." The within-group component for these measures is a weighted average of the inequality indices for each group, where the weights are simply the population shares of the groups.[35]

Unfortunately, neither Theil's second measure L nor the variance of log-income can be used as inequality measures in this chapter, although I will use them in chapters 6 and 7. The reason is a technical one, namely, the existence of individuals with zero per capita household income. This causes log-income and the logarithm of geometric mean income to blow up to minus infinity, so that the measures become uncomputable. It is exactly the

---

32. By the above definition, the between-group contribution of racial inequality is 33.1 percent (0.1648 divided by 0.4980). Yet if interracial inequality were to be eliminated, with intraracial inequalities kept constant, overall inequality as measured by the Gini coefficient would reduce by *less than 7.2 percent* (0.4980 minus 0.4621, all divided by 0.4980). In this sense, the between-group contribution to overall inequality would be less than 7.2 percent! This inconsistency in interpretation arises because the Gini coefficient is not decomposable. The two interpretations are consistent for any inequality index which satisfies the above decomposition property. See the section "The Interpretation of Decomposition for Three Inequality Measures" in chapter 6.

33. The variance of log-income satisfies mean independence and population-size independence, but it does not satisfy the Pigou-Dalton condition over the entire range of incomes (see appendix A).

34. In other words, the between-group component is the variance of log-income for the hypothetical distribution in which each person within a group gets the geometric (not arithmetic) mean income of the group. Likewise, the within-group component is the variance of log-income for the hypothetical distribution in which the group geometric mean incomes are equalized (to the overall geometric mean) through an equiproportionate change in the income of every person within a group.

35. The definition given earlier for within-group component does not restrict it to be of this form a priori.

same reason which prevented the use of the Atkinson index for values of ε greater than unity.

I relax slightly the definition of within-group component so that other measures of inequality, which are computable when there are zero incomes, can be classified as decomposable. Keeping the definitions of between-group component and additive decomposability the same as before, a weaker definition is provided for within-group component, which extends the class of decomposable measures. It requires only that the within-group component be constructed from the individual inequality indices, population sizes, and total incomes of each group, as an additively separable function over groups so that the contribution of each to overall inequality can be identified. The only functional form possible, if the measure is also to satisfy the basic properties of mean independence and population-size independence,[36] seems to be a weighted sum of inequality indices for each group, where the weights depend only on the population *share* and income *share* of the groups. This form of decomposability is clearly desirable in that overall inequality is built up as a sum of its constituent parts, which isolates the contribution of each; thus knowledge of changes in constituent parts allows us directly to predict changes in overall inequality.

There are several measures which satisfy this definition of decomposability as well as other desirable properties for an inequality index, namely, mean independence, population-size independence, and the Pigou-Dalton condition. Among such inequality measures are:

—Theil's entropy index T (see Theil, 1967, pp. 91–95)
—Theil's second measure L, which is the logarithm of the ratio of arithmetic mean income to geometric mean income (see Theil, 1967, pp. 125–27)
—The squared coefficient of variation C^2
—Any index A of the form

$$A = 1 - \left[\frac{y_{EDE}}{\mu} \right]^{1-\varepsilon} \quad \text{for} \quad 0 < \varepsilon < 1,$$

where μ is the arithmetic mean income, and y_{EDE} is the Atkinson equally distributed equivalent income corresponding to the additively sep-

---

36. The property of population-size independence implies that the index depends only on the *proportions* of the population at each income level. Thus doubling, or replicating   times, the number of people at each income level does not affect the value of the inequality index. Mean independence and population-size independence together imply that the index depends only on the Lorenz curve of the distribution (see the proof of the proposition in appendix D).

arable welfare function with constant elasticity marginal utility ε. As in the previous section, y_{EDE} is defined through

$$y_{EDE}^{1-\varepsilon} = \frac{1}{n} \sum_{i=1}^{n} y_i^{1-\varepsilon}.$$

Thus if I is the Atkinson index,

$$A = 1 - (1-I)^{1-\varepsilon}.$$

I show the decomposition formulas for these measures when the population is divided into two groups. (The extension is obvious for a partition of the population into more than two groups.) Let the overall population size be n and the overall arithmetic mean income μ. Let n_1 and n_2 denote the sizes of the two groups and μ_1 and μ_2 their mean incomes. Finally, let the labels 1, 2 on an inequality measure denote the value of the measure for groups 1, 2, respectively. Then

$$n = n_1 + n_2$$
and
$$n\mu = n_1\mu_1 + n_2\mu_2.$$

Theil's entropy index T can be written as:[37]

$$\begin{aligned}
T &= \sum_{i=1}^{n} \frac{1}{n} \frac{y_i}{\mu} \log \frac{y_i}{\mu} \\
&= \frac{n_1\mu_1}{n\mu} T_1 + \frac{n_2\mu_2}{n\mu} T_2 + \frac{n_1\mu_1}{n\mu} \log \frac{\mu_1}{\mu} + \frac{n_2\mu_2}{n\mu} \log \frac{\mu_2}{\mu} \\
&= T_W + T_B.
\end{aligned}$$

The between-group component T_B is the Theil index of the distribution with n_1 persons at income level μ_1 and n_2 persons at income level μ_2. The within-group component T_W is a weighted average of the Theil indices for each group, where the weights are the income shares of each group in total income.

Theil's second measure L is the logarithm of the ratio of the arithmetic mean μ to the geometric mean $\tilde{\mu}$. As shown in appendixes A and C, L simply reverses the roles of income share and population share in the entropy index T. L can be written and decomposed as follows:[38]

---

37. See appendixes A and C.

38. L is also a simple monotonic increasing transform of Atkinson's (1970) index I when the inequality aversion parameter ε is equal to unity. In this case, the Atkinson equally distributed equivalent income is just the geometric mean income $\tilde{\mu}$ of the distribution, and $I = 1 - (\tilde{\mu}/\mu)$. Hence, $L = -\log(1-I)$.

$$L = \sum_{i=1}^{n} \frac{1}{n} \log \frac{\mu}{y_i}$$

$$= \log \mu - \frac{1}{n} \sum_{i=1}^{n} \log y_i$$

$$= \log \frac{\mu}{\tilde{\mu}}.$$

Since $\log \tilde{\mu} = \frac{n_1}{n} \log \tilde{\mu}_1 + \frac{n_2}{n} \log \tilde{\mu}_2$, it follows that

$$L = \frac{n_1}{n} \log \frac{\mu_1}{\tilde{\mu}_1} + \frac{n_2}{n} \log \frac{\mu_2}{\tilde{\mu}_2} + \log \mu - \frac{n_1}{n} \log \mu_1 - \frac{n_2}{n} \log \mu_2$$

$$= \frac{n_1}{n} L_1 + \frac{n_2}{n} L_2 + \frac{n_1}{n} \log \frac{\mu}{\mu_1} + \frac{n_2}{n} \log \frac{\mu}{\mu_2}$$

$$= L_W + L_B.$$

The between-group component L_B is the L measure of the distribution with n_1 persons at income level μ_1, and n_2 persons at income level μ_2. The within-group component is a weighted average of the L measures for each group, where the weights are the population shares of each group.

The squared coefficient of variation C^2 is the variance σ^2 of the distribution divided by the square of the arithmetic mean, μ^2. It can be built up from the variance σ^2 as follows:

$$\sigma^2 = \frac{1}{n} \sum_{i=1}^{n} (y_i - \mu)^2$$

$$= \frac{n_1}{n} \sigma_1^2 + \frac{n_2}{n} \sigma_2^2 + \frac{n_1}{n} (\mu_1 - \mu)^2 + \frac{n_2}{n} (\mu_2 - \mu)^2$$

$$= \sigma_W^2 + \sigma_B^2, \text{ as in standard analysis of variance.}$$

Therefore,

$$C^2 = \frac{\sigma^2}{\mu^2}$$

$$= \frac{n_1}{n} \frac{\mu_1^2}{\mu^2} C_1^2 + \frac{n_2}{n} \frac{\mu_2^2}{\mu^2} C_2^2 + \frac{1}{\mu^2} \left[\frac{n_1}{n} (\mu_1 - \mu)^2 + \frac{n_2}{n} (\mu_2 - \mu)^2 \right]$$

$$= C_W^2 + C_B^2.$$

The between-group component C_B^2 is the squared coefficient of variation for the distribution with n_1 persons at income level μ_1 and n_2 persons at income level μ_2. The within-group component is a weighted sum of the squared coefficients of variation for each group, where the weights depend only on the population share and income share of the groups. The within-group component is not strictly a weighted average, as the weights do not add up to unity. In fact, the sum of the weights is

$$\frac{1}{\mu^2}\left[\frac{n_1}{n}\mu_1^2+\frac{n_2}{n}\mu_2^2\right]=1+\frac{\dfrac{n_1}{n}(\mu_1-\mu)^2+\dfrac{n_2}{n}(\mu_2-\mu)^2}{\mu^2}$$

$$=1+C_B^2.$$

Thus the weights on the squared within-group coefficients of variation sum to a number greater than unity, by an amount which is equal to the between-group component C_B^2.[39]

The index A based on the Atkinson equally distributed equivalent income y_{EDE} can be decomposed using the following relation between y_{EDE} and y_{1EDE}, y_{2EDE}, the equally distributed equivalent incomes for the two groups:

$$y_{EDE}^{1-\varepsilon}=\left[\frac{n_1}{n}\right]y_{1EDE}^{1-\varepsilon}+\left[\frac{n_2}{n}\right]y_{2EDE}^{1-\varepsilon}.$$

Hence, for $0<\varepsilon<1$,

$$A=1-\left[\frac{y_{EDE}}{\mu}\right]^{1-\varepsilon}$$

$$=\frac{n_1}{n}\left[\frac{\mu_1}{\mu}\right]^{1-\varepsilon}A_1+\frac{n_2}{n}\left[\frac{\mu_2}{\mu}\right]^{1-\varepsilon}A_2+1-\frac{n_1}{n}\left[\frac{\mu_1}{\mu}\right]^{1-\varepsilon}-\frac{n_2}{n}\left[\frac{\mu_2}{\mu}\right]^{1-\varepsilon}$$

$$=A_W+A_B.$$

Thus for every ε between 0 and 1, we have an index $A(\varepsilon)$[40] decomposable into the sum of a within-group and a between-group component. The between-group component A_B is the A index evaluated for the distribution with n_1 persons at income μ_1 and n_2 persons at income μ_2. The within-group component is simply a weighted sum of the A indices for each group, where the weights depend only on the population share and income share of the groups. Although A is decomposable in the weak sense, the Atkinson index itself (I in the previous section) is not decomposable.

39. This, according to Theil (1967, p. 125), is "a disadvantage, because one should prefer a measure for which the within-set components, including their weights, are independent of the between-set component."

40. The limiting measures $A(\varepsilon)$ when $\varepsilon\to0$ and $\varepsilon\to1$ correspond to the indices T and L, respectively.

Interracial and Interregional Inequalities

Of the inequality measures presented in the last section, Theil's second measure L and the variance of log-income are not computable in this chapter owing to the presence of zero-income individuals. Of the remaining measures, perhaps the most suitable one is the Theil entropy index T. Unlike the squared coefficient of variation and the family of $A(\varepsilon)$ measures, the within-group component for the Theil T index is a weighted average, and not just a weighted sum, of the inequality indices for each group. The property of the weights summing to unity is attractive, if not essential, for a decomposable measure. It does make the use and interpretation of the within-group component a little easier. Accordingly, I adopt the Theil T index for all empirical decompositions here.[41]

The decompositions by any of the above four indices are purely descriptive. While they permit an ex post accounting of inequality, there is no statistical model behind them which allows tests of significance. For the Theil T index, this seems in any case problematic because it does not follow a known statistical distribution. By contrast, the variance of log-income *can* be decomposed in accordance with standard analysis of variance, since the ratio of between-group to within-group variance is known to follow an F-distribution. Given the very large number of degrees of freedom here, however, the estimated between-group contributions should be highly significant. Of course, the different measures of inequality will still give rise to different numerical contributions for between-group inequality. For reassurance about the magnitude of the contribution, alternative indices should be employed for decomposition where possible. This will be feasible in chapter 6 where, in addition to the Theil T index, we can use the Theil L measure and the variance of log-income, the within-group weights of which also sum to unity.

Table 3-10 presents the Gini coefficient,[42] Theil T index, mean income, and sample size for a racial and regional breakdown of the distribution of individuals by per capita household income. The Theil T index for all communities in Malaysia is 0.5161, and the Gini coefficient, as noted earlier,

41. For the important variable of race, I also use the measure $A(\varepsilon)$ for decomposition in this chapter, even though its within-group weights do not sum to unity; see note 44 below.

42. The Gini coefficient is presented although it is not decomposable. This is in deference to its widespread usage; it provides a familiar reference point for comparisons of inequality.

Table 3-10. Decomposition by Region and Race of Inequality in the Distribution of Individuals by per Capita Household Income

State	Item	Malay	Chinese	Indian	Other	All racial groups	Between-race component of Theil T	Between-race contribution to inequality according to Theil T (percent)
Johore	Gini	0.4280	0.3840	0.4120	0.6026	0.4366		
	Theil T	0.3430	0.2888	0.3508	0.6527	0.3725	0.0481	12.9
	Arithmetic mean	33	55	51	210	44		
	Sample size	10,021	7,703	1,904	94	19,722		
Kedah	Gini	0.4040	0.4349	0.4295	0.4982	0.4449		
	Theil T	0.3226	0.4071	0.3633	0.5686	0.4090	0.0482	11.8
	Arithmetic mean	28	54	38	36	35		
	Sample size	9,782	3,574	1,164	160	14,680		
Kelantan	Gini	0.4349	0.4707	0.5028	0.6344	0.4689		
	Theil T	0.3693	0.3745	0.7597	0.8784	0.4454	0.0616	13.8
	Arithmetic mean	25	86	88	24	28		
	Sample size	10,259	387	64	168	10,878		
Malacca	Gini	0.4421	0.4406	0.4831	0.3826	0.4691		
	Theil T	0.4377	0.3852	0.5758	0.2655	0.4594	0.0404	8.8
	Arithmetic mean	35	64	51	77	49		
	Sample size	3,235	2,746	527	34	6,542		
Negri Sembilan	Gini	0.4267	0.4342	0.4553	0.1937	0.4917		
	Theil T	0.3356	0.3932	0.4041	0.0618	0.4974	0.1294	26.0
	Arithmetic mean	33	80	59	854	53		
	Sample size	3,221	1,909	1,136	11	6,277		
Pahang	Gini	0.4449	0.3809	0.4461	0.4154	0.4569		
	Theil T	0.3716	0.2626	0.3563	0.3905	0.3797	0.0533	14.0

Arithmetic mean	40	77	74	50	53	
Sample size	4,604	1,933	567	13	7,117	
Penang						
Gini	0.3964	0.4665	0.4781	0.5229	0.4799	
Theil T	0.2955	0.4476	0.4318	0.4710	0.4854	0.0708 14.6
Arithmetic mean	37	59	59	341	54	
Sample size	3,683	6,596	1,545	96	11,920	
Perak						
Gini	0.4403	0.4326	0.4219	0.5217	0.4654	
Theil T	0.3688	0.3814	0.4038	0.4652	0.4414	0.0589 13.4
Arithmetic mean	32	62	41	299	47	
Sample size	10,276	9,841	4,178	60	24,355	
Perlis						
Gini	0.3833	0.2603	0.0658	0.4493	0.3922	
Theil T	0.2657	0.1489	0.0105	0.3513	0.2781	0.0218 7.8
Arithmetic mean	26	40	16	10	26	
Sample size	1,544	92	19	102	1,757	
Selangor						
Gini	0.4929	0.4794	0.5630	0.5281	0.5206	
Theil T	0.4816	0.4706	0.6837	0.4834	0.5627	0.0506 9.0
Arithmetic mean	57	89	73	369	78	
Sample size	8,557	11,733	4,836	228	25,364	
Trengganu						
Gini	0.4237	0.5082	0.5559	0.6571	0.4623	
Theil T	0.3429	0.4872	0.7792	0.9907	0.4524	0.0737 16.3
Arithmetic mean	29	95	59	294	32	
Sample size	5,292	203	70	10	5,580	
Peninsular Malaysia						
Gini	0.4553	0.4542	0.5003	0.7071	0.4980	
Theil T	0.4114	0.4228	0.5448	0.9371	0.5161	0.0671 13.0
Arithmetic mean	34	68	57	185	50	
Sample size	70,474	46,726	16,010	976	134,186	
Between-state component of Theil T	0.0338	0.0196	0.0298	0.4457	0.0467	
Between-state contribution to inequality according to Theil T (percent)	8.2	4.6	5.5	47.6	9.1	

95

is 0.4980.[43] The Theil T index for the Malay and Chinese communities is 0.4114 and 0.4228, respectively, which again demonstrates the similarity of these distributions about their means. The Indians show a higher level of inequality, with a Theil T index of 0.5448, while the "others" show a considerably higher level of inequality, with a Theil T index of 0.9371.

Heuristically, the interracial component of overall inequality is obtained by suppressing all within-race income differences and measuring the inequality in the resultant distribution. Inequality in this distribution arises solely from between-race income differences, and its Theil T index works out at 0.0671 (table 3-10). The intraracial component is an income-weighted average of Theil T indices for each racial group, and this works out at 0.4490. The between- and within-race components sum to the overall Theil T index of 0.5161 since the index is decomposable in the weak sense. The ratio of the between-race component (0.0671) to overall inequality (0.5161) is the between-race contribution, which is, therefore, 13.0 percent according to the Theil T index.[44] (In chapter 6, overall inequality in the personal income distribution is decomposed according to the Theil T index, the Theil L measure, and the variance of log-income, and the between-race contributions are 9.2, 9.6, and 7.9 percent, respectively; see table 6-4.) The result is important because it shows that almost 90 percent of the inequality in the country arises from disparities in income *within* each racial group. Thus it is not very helpful to invoke the relatively large income disparity ratios *between* the races in attempting to explain individual income inequality in the country.

43. The two measures of inequality presented in table 3-10, the Gini coefficient and Theil T index, show virtually the same ranking for every comparison of distributions. A comparison of the ranking of distributions by the Gini coefficient (G) and the Theil index (T) may be obtained by computing the Spearman rank correlation coefficient (r_{GT}) between the two measures of inequality. Taking the eleven state distributions as observations, the following rank correlation coefficients are obtained:

All racial groups:	$r_{GT} = 0.9636$, significant at 0.01 level
Malay:	$r_{GT} = 0.9727$, significant at 0.01 level
Chinese:	$r_{GT} = 0.8364$, significant at 0.02 level
Indian:	$r_{GT} = 0.9364$, significant at 0.01 level
Other:	$r_{GT} = 0.9364$, significant at 0.01 level.

Thus the ranking of distributions by the Gini coefficient and the Theil T index turns out to be very similar.

44. The between-race contribution to overall inequality according to the index $A(\varepsilon)$, for $0 < \varepsilon < 1$, can be computed from table 3-9. For different values of ε, the between-race contribution is: 13.8 percent for $\varepsilon = 0.25$; 14.2 percent for $\varepsilon = 0.50$; 13.8 percent for $\varepsilon = 0.75$; 12.2 percent for $\varepsilon = 0.90$; and 4.4 percent for $\varepsilon = 0.99$.

Before examining the between- and within-region decomposition of inequality, I consider regional variations in mean income and Gini coefficient. It is evident from table 3-10 that significant disparities exist in per capita income across states. The northern states of Kedah, Kelantan, Perlis, and Trengganu are poorest, with per capita incomes of M$35, M$28, M$26, and M$32 per month, respectively. The richest state by far is Selangor, with a per capita income of M$78 per month. The Malaysian per capita income, as noted before, is M$50 per month.

There are also significant variations in the Gini coefficient among states. Interestingly, the highest Gini coefficient (0.5206) is associated with Selangor, the state with the highest per capita income, and the lowest Gini coefficient (0.3922) is associated with Perlis, the state with the lowest per capita income. There is a correlation of 0.766 between these two variables, and a cross-state regression equation indicates a significantly positive association between inequality and the level of per capita income. The following equation was estimated using the eleven states as observations:

$$G = 0.3870 + 0.0017 \text{ (PCI).} \qquad R^2 = 0.5868$$
$$(17.47) \quad (3.58) \qquad\qquad \text{SEE} = 0.0220$$
$$\bar{G} = 0.4626$$

G here denotes the Gini coefficient, PCI is per capita income, and the numbers in parentheses are t-ratios.

A quadratic form in PCI was also tried in order to test the hypothesis of an inverse U-shaped relation between inequality and development. This hypothesis (Kuznets, 1955) states that income inequality first increases and then decreases with development (see also the recent tests on cross-country data by Ahluwalia, 1974a and 1976, and a critique of these tests by Anand and Kanbur, 1978). The estimated equation shows little support for this hypothesis on Malaysian interstate data, and for positive levels of PCI, inequality seems to be always increasing with development:

$$G = 0.3990 + 0.0011 \text{ (PCI)} + 0.00003 \text{ (PCI)}^2. \quad R^2 = 0.5889$$
$$(6.21) \quad (0.42) \qquad\qquad (0.20) \qquad\qquad \text{SEE} = 0.0233$$
$$\bar{G} = 0.4626$$

The contribution of between-state inequality to overall inequality and to inequality within each racial group is shown in the last row of table 3-10. The between-state contribution to inequality in Peninsular Malaysia is 9.1 percent, which seems relatively low. The explanation, as in the case of race, is that there are substantial inequalities *within* the states (see table 3-10). The between-state contribution to inequality within each racial group is even

Table 3-11. Decomposition by Race and Location of Inequality in the Distribution of Individuals by per Capita Household Income

Racial group	Item	Metropolitan towns	Towns	Rural areas	Peninsular Malaysia	Between-location contribution to inequality according to Theil T (percent)
Malay	Gini	0.4505	0.4358	0.4272	0.4553	11.6
	Theil T	0.3913	0.3446	0.3622	0.4114	
	Arithmetic mean	77	50	30	34	
	Sample size	4,120	5,882	60,472	70,474	
Chinese	Gini	0.4862	0.4449	0.4045	0.4542	6.0
	Theil T	0.4727	0.4065	0.3236	0.4228	
	Arithmetic mean	92	70	55	68	
	Sample size	13,027	9,871	23,828	46,726	
Indian	Gini	0.5648	0.4924	0.4115	0.5003	10.6
	Theil T	0.6480	0.4506	0.3704	0.5448	
	Arithmetic mean	92	56	44	57	
	Sample size	3,799	1,895	10,316	16,010	
Other	Gini	0.5270	0.6759	0.7896	0.7071	12.5
	Theil T	0.4782	0.9040	1.3057	0.9371	
	Arithmetic mean	328	122	124	185	
	Sample size	297	151	528	976	
All racial groups	Gini	0.5082	0.4582	0.4505	0.4980	13.7
	Theil T	0.5214	0.4173	0.4135	0.5161	
	Arithmetic mean	92	62	38	50	
	Sample size	21,243	17,799	95,144	134,186	
Between-race contribution to inequality according to Theil T (percent)		5.8	3.5	11.4	13.0	

smaller than 9.1 percent, except for the "other" group.[45] For the Chinese community it is only 4.6 percent, and for the Indians and Malays it is 5.5 percent and 8.2 percent, respectively. Thus it appears that with the exception of the "others," interstate variation in racial incomes is small in relation to intrastate variation.

Decomposition the other way, namely, the between-race contribution to inequality within each state, is also shown in table 3-10. Race accounts for a variable proportion of inequality within the states, ranging from 7.8 percent in Perlis to 26.0 percent in Negri Sembilan.[46] But, in general, the racial contribution is clustered around the 13 percent between-race contribution for Peninsular Malaysia as a whole. In summary, it appears that neither between-race nor between-region disparities account for much of the inequality in levels of living in the country. Most of the inequality seems to arise within the racial groups and within the regions.

From the information in table 3-10, it is also possible to derive a two-way decomposition of inequality by both race and region (four racial groups in each of the eleven state groups). In other words, the between-group component here is the value of the inequality index for the hypothetical distribution which assigns to each individual within a state-cum-racial group the mean income of that group. It is an easy exercise to check that between-group inequality in this case accounts for 20.2 percent of overall inequality.

Rural-Urban Inequalities

To consider the extent to which rural-urban disparities contribute to income inequality in Malaysia, a similar decomposition is attempted for race and rural-urban location (table 3-11) as in the previous section for race and region. It shows a between-location contribution to income inequality of 13.7 percent. This finding tends to refute the views of those who claim that large rural-urban income differences in developing countries, and dualism in general, are responsible for the high levels of inequality there.[47]

45. From the "other" column in table 3-10 it is apparent that the between-state variation in mean incomes is very large for this group, ranging from M$10 per month in the poor northern state of Perlis to M$854 per month in Negri Sembilan. This reflects the heterogeneity of this group, with, for example, poor Thais resident in the northern states bordering Thailand, and rich Europeans in the plantations and urban centers of the southern states.

46. This result for Negri Sembilan is obviously due to the unusually large income there for the "other" group.

47. See, for example, Lipton (1977). It could be argued, however, that the inequalities *within* urban areas and *within* rural areas are not independent of the large income differences *between* urban and rural areas.

The point is that there are large inequalities *within* rural and *within* urban areas. For rural areas, one might expect the maldistribution of land to account for a substantial part of these inequalities. For urban areas, there could be several important factors, including the maldistribution of human capital (see chapter 7) and of other income-yielding assets. The segmentation of the urban labor market into the organized and the informal sectors might also account for some of the observed inequality in urban areas.

The between-location contribution to inequality within each racial group is slightly lower than 13.7 percent, and among the Chinese it is significantly lower at 6.0 percent. The Chinese display a smaller variation in average income across location (and states) than the other racial groups.

Table 3-11 shows that the mean income in metropolitan towns is M$92 per month; in towns it is M$62 per month, and in rural areas, M$38 per month.[48] If the "other" group is excluded, racial disparity ratios in metropolitan towns are quite small. In fact, the Chinese and Indians have the same per capita income of M$92 per month, while the Malay per capita income is only 16 percent lower at M$77 per month. The Chinese-Malay disparity ratio is larger in towns, and larger still in rural areas.[49] For all locations taken together (Peninsular Malaysia), the disparity ratios are even larger; this is explained by the disproportionate presence of the racial groups in the three locations. The between-race contribution to inequality in each location broadly reflects the racial disparity ratios in it.

If metropolitan towns and towns are taken to constitute urban areas, table 3-11 shows that inequality is on the whole greater in urban than in rural areas (measured by the Gini coefficient or the Theil T index). This is true not only for all racial groups together, but also for each considered separately (with the exception of "other"). Indeed, there is a gradual reduction in inequality for each racial group (except "other"), and for all taken together, as one passes from metropolitan towns to towns, and from towns to rural areas.[50] Perhaps one can conclude from this evidence that urbanization in Malaysia has tended to increase inequalities. At any

48. Metropolitan towns are Johore Bahru, Malacca, Kuala Lumpur, Klang, Ipoh, and Georgetown. Towns are all others of more than 10,000 population (see chapter 2, note 18, for a listing). All other areas are considered rural.

49. There is less racial disparity but more overall inequality as one moves to increasingly urban areas.

50. Exactly the opposite is true for the "other" group. This is probably explained by the simultaneous presence in rural areas of rich European estate owners and managers and poor peasants of Thai or other Asian origin. The higher per capita income of the "others" in rural areas (M$124 per month) than in towns (M$122 per month) indicates the presence of at least some relatively rich persons there.

rate, higher stages of urbanization seem to be associated with higher levels of inequality.[51]

Policy Considerations

A general discussion on distribution policy in Malaysia is postponed until the final chapter, where all the major findings of the study are reviewed. Here I discuss some particular aspects of policy suggested by the results of the racial decomposition of inequality. These are important to isolate because some of the later analysis is motivated by these results.

With the aid of the inequality measures estimated in this chapter, I have shown the Malay and Chinese income distributions to be very similar about their respective means. In particular, the Malay distribution displays just as much inequality as the Chinese, although it is often suggested that Malay incomes are less dispersed. I have also estimated various racial-disparity ratios and shown the mean income of the Chinese to be twice that of the Malays. Despite such disparities in average income, there turns out to be a considerable overlap between the Malay and non-Malay distributions, which reflects the large inequalities within the racial groups. This pattern of income distribution was illustrated in figure 1-1.

The racial balance objective (Prong 2) of the New Economic Policy was depicted in figure 1-1 as a rescaling of the Malay distribution so that it coincides with the non-Malay distribution. The restructuring targets of Prong 2 imply proportional racial representation at every income level.[52] Since the Malay and Chinese distributions are almost identical about their respective means, proportional racial representation at every income level can be achieved by a simple rescaling of the Malay distribution until it coincides with the non-Malay distribution.[53] This shift implies leaving unchanged the inequality within each race but eliminating altogether the inequality in (arithmetic) mean incomes between the races.

51. The variations noted earlier in per capita income among states are likely to be correlated with their degree of urbanization. This could be tested if a rural-urban breakdown of table 3-10 were done. It might also help explain the positive association across states between Gini coefficient and per capita income (noted earlier), since urban incomes are more unequally distributed than rural incomes.

52. See the section "Inequality, Poverty, and NEP" in chapter 1. See also Dr. Mahathir Mohamad's view of racial balance quoted there.

53. Given the fundamental premise of NEP that no group in Malaysian society should "experience any loss or feel any sense of deprivation," it is the Malay distribution that must be shifted toward the non-Malay distribution, and not vice versa.

The methodology of *strictly* decomposable indices can be invoked precisely to measure the effects of such a shift on overall inequality. But for *weakly* decomposable indices such as Theil's T index, the within-group component depends on the income share of each group, which changes with the approximate doubling of Malay incomes required to eliminate between-race inequality.[54] Thus the between-group component for a weakly decomposable index does *not* indicate the reduction in overall income inequality when group means are equalized but within-group inequalities are kept constant. The between-group component for a strictly decomposable index *does* measure the reduction because the weights on group inequality indices are population shares which remain constant when the group mean incomes are changed. I compute two strictly decomposable indices for the personal income distribution in chapter 6.

For the distribution of individuals by per capita household income, I have computed the new Gini coefficient and Theil T index after all Malay incomes are raised by a factor of 1.96, which is the racial disparity ratio between the non-Malays and Malays. The new Gini coefficient is 0.4697, which implies a reduction of inequality by 5.7 percent from its pre-Prong 2 value of 0.4980. The new value for the Theil T index is 0.4528, which implies a reduction of inequality by 12.3 percent from its pre-Prong 2 value of 0.5161. Thus policies designed to achieve racial balance will have a limited effect in reducing individual income inequality.

The implementation of the racial balance prong is unlikely to be carried out by proportional increases in *all* Malay incomes at each stage of the restructuring process. Different parts of the Malay distribution are likely to move at different speeds toward the non-Malay distribution. Government documents do not discuss the time-phasing of racial income equalization, but present policies suggest that the top end may move faster toward equalization than the bottom end.[55] In the transition toward implementation of Prong 2, it is thus possible that intra-Malay inequality will widen, although there will be some narrowing of between-race inequality. The effect on overall inequality will depend on the relative strength of the two components, so that in the short run there might even be an increase in individual income inequality as a result of implementing Prong 2.

54. Apart from the two-to-one Chinese-Malay disparity there are other racial income disparities between the Indians and Malays and between the "others" and Malays. The racial income disparity between all the non-Malays and Malays is 1.96.

55. Indeed, it has been asserted that restructuring is likely to lead (and to some extent has already led) to the creation of Malay millionaires without bringing comparable benefits to the Malay working class and peasantry. (See, for example, Chandra Muzaffar, 1977; see also *Far Eastern Economic Review*, September 2, 1977, pp. 57–61.)

In general, because the racial contribution to individual income inequality in Malaysia is relatively small and approximately 90 percent of such inequality arises from income differences *within* racial groups, NEP Prong 2 can at best play a minor role in rectifying individual income inequality. If the redress of inequality were taken as the sole objective of policy, it would be possible to identify in abstract terms the most "efficient" rule for redressing individual income inequality (where "efficiency" corresponds to the reduction in inequality achieved). Obviously some constraint must be imposed on the type of redistribution considered feasible: a program of razing all incomes to zero achieves perfect equality! On this point I take a cue from the NEP, the premise of which is that no group in Malaysian society should experience any loss or feel any sense of deprivation. Thus I take it as a constraint that existing incomes cannot be reduced and only increments to national income can be considered for distribution.

The solution to this distribution problem is fairly obvious and is derived in appendix E ("The Redress of Poverty Rule"). The most efficient rule for redressing individual income inequality is to distribute the incremental income from the bottom upward. In other words, the rule is: Give the incremental income to the poorest person until his or her income reaches that of the second poorest person; distribute the remainder equally between them until their incomes reach that of the third poorest person; and so on, until all the available income is exhausted. This rule can be shown to yield a distribution which Lorenz-dominates the distribution of any other rule.[56] Hence it secures the maximum reduction in inequality by any index which satisfies mean independence, population-size independence, and the Pigou-Dalton condition (see appendix D).[57] Most standard indices of inequality satisfy these properties, including the ones used in this study.

Thus the best strategy for redressing individual income inequality turns out to be a strategy to redress poverty, in which the poverty gap is filled from the bottom upward. This strategy is strikingly close to NEP Prong 1, which seeks to "eradicate poverty irrespective of race."

---

56. Essentially, any other rule implies giving some of the incremental income to a person who is not among the "equal poorest." But then a sequence of transfers from rich to poor yields the distribution corresponding to the redress of poverty rule, which is therefore Lorenz-dominant (by Atkinson's theorem).

57. It follows, therefore, that equal expenditure on racial balance will bring about a smaller reduction in individual income inequality. The inefficiency of attempting to redress individual income inequality by improving racial balance has also been illustrated by the racial decomposition results in this chapter.

Table 3-12. Number of Urban Households, Average Household Size,
and Average Number of Income Recipients per Household by Household Income Class and Racial Group

Household income class (M$ per month)	Number of urban households				Average household size				Average number of income recipients per household			
	Malay	Chinese	Indian	Total[a]	Malay	Chinese	Indian	Total[a]	Malay	Chinese	Indian	Total[a]
No income	23	61	17	104	4.17	4.64	4.35	4.44	0	0	0	0
1–39	42	33	18	93	2.33	1.91	2.44	2.20	1.14	1.03	1.00	1.08
40–49	28	18	8	55	2.75	1.72	2.63	2.36	1.21	1.11	1.13	1.16
50–79	105	138	34	279	3.55	2.23	3.65	2.90	1.33	1.05	1.27	1.19
80–99	95	111	32	239	4.46	2.74	4.22	3.62	1.42	1.14	1.09	1.25
100–129	145	264	103	513	4.83	3.36	3.92	3.89	1.30	1.19	1.08	1.20
130–149	106	155	80	347	4.80	3.89	4.71	4.40	1.37	1.32	1.19	1.30
150–179	183	329	116	631	4.63	4.41	4.72	4.53	1.26	1.33	1.21	1.29
180–199	93	201	57	352	5.11	4.81	5.47	5.01	1.34	1.50	1.28	1.43
200–279	311	733	164	1,213	5.58	5.53	5.71	5.57	1.54	1.61	1.48	1.57
280–299	59	129	21	211	5.90	5.95	5.81	5.90	1.49	2.05	1.52	1.83
300–399	234	556	98	891	5.86	6.11	6.63	6.11	1.70	2.05	1.87	1.94
400–479	103	300	59	467	6.88	6.41	6.05	6.46	1.97	2.13	1.86	2.06
480–499	22	51	12	85	6.27	7.73	5.50	7.04	2.36	2.37	1.92	2.31
500–599	70	218	48	340	6.66	7.11	5.85	6.82	2.10	2.56	1.81	2.36

Income class												
600–679	58	130	34	226	7.57	6.85	6.35	6.96	2.26	2.47	2.18	2.36
680–699	5	25	5	35	6.00	6.72	6.80	6.63	2.40	2.40	1.80	2.31
700–749	25	60	13	98	6.96	7.53	5.00	7.05	2.08	2.58	2.31	2.42
750–799	12	49	13	74	6.67	7.27	6.31	7.00	2.42	2.94	1.69	2.64
800–899	21	111	16	156	5.86	7.59	6.44	7.06	2.33	2.92	3.31	2.82
900–979	18	53	6	78	7.72	7.25	8.00	7.39	2.56	2.74	2.17	2.64
980–999	3	11	3	18	8.00	9.09	6.67	8.17	2.00	3.18	2.67	2.78
1,000–1,249	36	131	37	214	7.44	7.45	5.73	7.08	2.44	2.89	2.68	2.73
1,250–1,499	16	74	19	115	8.81	7.38	6.74	7.30	3.69	3.24	3.32	3.23
1,500–1,749	9	53	14	80	7.44	7.60	8.36	7.55	4.22	3.34	4.57	3.60
1,750–1,999	5	21	2	29	8.60	7.57	6.00	7.48	3.40	3.57	4.00	3.48
2,000–2,499	6	37	8	60	7.00	6.68	8.50	6.30	3.17	2.73	5.00	2.87
2,500–2,999	2	21	6	32	7.50	9.24	8.33	8.50	4.00	3.67	5.17	3.81
3,000–3,499	1	13	3	20	19.00	7.00	3.33	6.90	4.00	2.92	3.33	2.85
3,500–3,999	2	6	3	15	4.50	11.00	5.33	7.53	2.00	5.50	2.33	3.87
4,000–4,999	1	3	5	10	11.00	6.33	13.20	9.80	1.00	2.67	6.60	4.40
5,000+	1	10	2	14	16.00	8.30	4.50	8.50	1.00	3.70	2.50	3.29
All income classes	1,840	4,105	1,056	7,094								

a. All races including "other."

105

Table 3-13. Number of Rural Households, Average Household Size, and Average Number of Income Recipients per Household by Household Income Class and Racial Group

Household income class (M$ per month)	Number of rural households				Average household size				Average number of income recipients per household			
	Malay	Chinese	Indian	Total[a]	Malay	Chinese	Indian	Total[a]	Malay	Chinese	Indian	Total[a]
No income	167	49	15	237	4.25	5.80	4.60	4.54	0	0	0	0
1–39	1,103	71	38	1,243	2.63	2.06	1.68	2.59	1.11	1.01	1.03	1.10
40–49	589	28	26	656	3.58	1.68	2.27	3.45	1.17	1.00	1.08	1.16
50–79	2,211	132	107	2,472	4.31	2.49	3.23	4.17	1.24	1.10	1.11	1.23
80–99	1,430	134	90	1,659	4.93	3.43	3.98	4.76	1.33	1.20	1.20	1.31
100–129	1,689	273	230	2,199	5.33	3.97	4.37	5.06	1.41	1.22	1.21	1.37
130–149	890	218	138	1,249	5.59	4.80	4.67	5.36	1.51	1.30	1.43	1.46
150–179	1,021	332	263	1,620	5.80	5.29	5.26	5.61	1.56	1.37	1.58	1.53
180–199	483	208	160	852	5.92	5.84	6.13	5.94	1.69	1.59	1.83	1.70
200–279	1,167	831	409	2,412	6.14	6.13	6.57	6.21	1.74	1.78	1.96	1.79
280–299	179	138	53	370	6.35	6.82	7.36	6.67	1.79	1.97	2.42	1.95
300–399	510	607	166	1,284	6.54	6.93	7.11	6.79	1.86	2.08	2.46	2.04
400–479	214	255	61	532	6.56	7.35	6.66	6.93	2.00	2.56	2.54	2.33
480–499	32	46	5	83	6.53	7.33	9.20	7.13	2.28	2.07	3.20	2.22
500–599	131	180	40	353	6.13	8.38	6.03	7.27	1.98	2.66	2.28	2.36
600–679	65	98	21	186	6.75	8.60	6.00	7.60	2.57	2.81	1.91	2.60
680–699	12	18	4	34	4.67	8.61	10.25	7.41	1.83	2.28	2.75	2.18
700–749	21	32	7	62	6.33	9.06	6.86	7.81	2.05	3.19	3.29	2.82
750–799	15	27	6	48	7.80	8.37	6.83	8.00	2.40	2.59	2.50	2.52
800–899	26	58	6	90	6.92	9.28	4.00	8.24	2.65	2.93	1.33	2.74
900–979	14	38	10	64	6.64	9.11	5.70	7.88	2.21	3.40	2.00	2.88
980–999	4	7	0	11	5.75	12.41	—	9.82	2.00	3.00	—	2.64

1,000–1,249	23	49	6	81	6.44	7.49	5.00	6.85	2.57	3.10	2.33	2.85
1,250–1,499	13	23	8	48	7.39	9.61	5.00	7.69	2.39	2.78	2.63	2.56
1,500–1,749	3	14	3	20	4.67	8.93	3.33	7.45	3.33	3.21	3.00	3.20
1,750–1,999	6	8	1	15	8.00	7.38	10.00	7.80	3.83	3.63	2.00	3.60
2,000–2,499	2	12	5	23	11.50	8.83	4.20	7.13	3.00	3.58	2.00	2.83
2,500–2,999	1	4	1	12	7.00	8.50	7.00	6.00	3.00	2.25	2.00	1.92
3,000–3,499	1	2	0	6	3.00	10.00	—	5.33	2.00	3.00	—	2.00
3,500–3,999	0	2	1	4	—	7.50	10.00	7.25	—	2.50	3.00	2.25
4,000–4,999	0	0	0	1	—	—	—	5.00	—	—	—	2.00
5,000+	1	4	0	5	6.00	—	—	—	3.00	27.50	—	22.60
All income classes	12,023	3,898	1,889	17,931		31.00		26.00				

— Not applicable.
a. All races including "other."

Table 3-14. Average Household Income by Racial Group and Location
(M$ per month)

Households	Metropolitan towns	Towns	Rural areas	Peninsular Malaysia
All	495	345	200	264
Malay	419	263	149	172
Chinese	496	399	331	394
Indian	483	316	235	304
Other	1,503	678	505	813

Table 3-15. Decomposition by Region and Race of Inequality
in the Distribution of Households by per Capita Household Income

State	Item	Malay	Chinese	Indian	Other	All racial groups	Between-race contribution to inequality according to Theil T (percent)
Johore	Gini	0.4779	0.4356	0.4790	0.4418	0.4915	
	Theil T	0.4329	0.3761	0.4472	0.3540	0.4720	14.0
	Arithmetic mean	42	72	72	331	58	
	Sample size	1,721	1,244	361	20	3,346	
Kedah	Gini	0.4451	0.5208	0.4880	0.5588	0.5109	
	Theil T	0.4024	0.5862	0.4524	0.6363	0.5641	15.0
	Arithmetic mean	32	79	55	48	44	
	Sample size	2,000	598	209	27	2,834	
Kelantan	Gini	0.4549	0.4371	0.6605	0.6062	0.4912	
	Theil T	0.4092	0.3181	1.0018	0.7908	0.5105	15.9
	Arithmetic mean	28	92	199	29	32	
	Sample size	2,250	78	14	45	2,387	
Malacca	Gini	0.5208	0.4608	0.5805	0.3600	0.5233	
	Theil T	0.6534	0.3958	0.8558	0.2296	0.5881	7.1
	Arithmetic mean	46	82	88	98	65	
	Sample size	588	456	105	5	1,154	
Negri Sembilan	Gini	0.4659	0.4711	0.5040	0.1926	0.5373	
	Theil T	0.4020	0.4393	0.5123	0.0609	0.5929	28.8
	Arithmetic mean	40	99	83	876	68	
	Sample size	629	343	204	5	1,181	
Pahang	Gini	0.4895	0.4235	0.4502	0.3589	0.4982	
	Theil T	0.4516	0.3206	0.3547	0.2862	0.4503	14.1
	Arithmetic mean	48	101	93	82	66	
	Sample size	944	387	121	2	1,454	

Penang	Gini	0.4448	0.4982	0.4836	0.5061	0.5218	18.2
	Theil T	0.4016	0.5012	0.4336	0.4455	0.5676	
	Arithmetic mean	44	74	79	417	68	
	Sample size	749	1,062	277	26	2,114	
Perak	Gini	0.4801	0.4657	0.5012	0.5182	0.5062	12.4
	Theil T	0.4369	0.4236	0.5348	0.4649	0.5104	
	Arithmetic mean	40	76	59	396	58	
	Sample size	1,989	1,712	726	13	4,440	
Perlis	Gini	0.3951	0.3819	0.0806	0.4912	0.4148	9.5
	Theil T	0.2777	0.2889	0.0131	0.4252	0.3114	
	Arithmetic mean	29	56	16	12	29	
	Sample size	338	16	2	24	380	
Selangor	Gini	0.5033	0.4906	0.5751	0.5776	0.5345	9.8
	Theil T	0.4808	0.4807	0.6804	0.5819	0.5821	
	Arithmetic mean	71	108	95	456	97	
	Sample size	1,550	2,048	898	51	4,548[a]	
Trengganu	Gini	0.4629	0.5307	0.6157	0.4812	0.5253	25.4
	Theil T	0.4088	0.4828	0.7042	0.5997	0.5872	
	Arithmetic mean	33	138	159	478	40	
	Sample size	1,102	45	15	2	1,165[a]	
Peninsular Malaysia	Gini	0.4926	0.4834	0.5382	0.6998	0.5374	14.5
	Theil T	0.4814	0.4638	0.6016	0.9081	0.5924	
	Arithmetic mean	41	86	79	249	62	
	Sample size	13,860	7,989	2,932	220	25,003	
Between-state contribution to inequality according to Theil T (percent)		8.3	3.3	4.4	47.5	8.7	

a. The racial affiliation of one household in this state was not available.

109

Table 3-16. Decomposition by Race and Location of Inequality in the Distribution of Households by per Capita Household Income

Racial group	Item	Metropolitan towns	Towns	Rural Areas	Peninsular Malaysia	Between-location contribution to inequality according to Theil T (percent)
Malay	Gini	0.4636	0.4808	0.4674	0.4926	
	Theil T	0.4156	0.4256	0.4341	0.4814	10.5
	Arithmetic mean	95	62	36	41	
	Sample size	742	1,097	12,021	13,860	
Chinese	Gini	0.4909	0.4995	0.4429	0.4834	
	Theil T	0.4743	0.4964	0.3780	0.4638	4.7
	Arithmetic mean	110	94	69	86	
	Sample size	2,392	1,705	3,892	7,989	
Indian	Gini	0.5568	0.5415	0.4837	0.5382	
	Theil T	0.6266	0.5337	0.5004	0.6016	8.2
	Arithmetic mean	122	85	61	79	
	Sample size	716	337	1,879	2,932	
Other	Gini	0.5346	0.6182	0.7803	0.6998	
	Theil T	0.4938	0.6794	1.2385	0.9081	12.3
	Arithmetic mean	439	218	161	249	
	Sample size	64	27	129	220	
All racial groups	Gini	0.5168	0.5116	0.4978	0.5374	
	Theil T	0.5374	0.5109	0.5052	0.5924	13.0
	Arithmetic mean	115	83	46	62	
	Sample size	3,915[a]	3,166	17,922[a]	25,003	
Between-race contribution to inequality according to Theil T (percent)		7.7	4.8	11.9	14.5	

a. The racial affiliation of one household was not available.

4

The Definition and Measurement of Poverty

IN THE LAST CHAPTER, the redress of poverty was seen to be the most efficient method of redressing inequality (see also "The Redress of Poverty Rule" in appendix E). The eradication of poverty irrespective of race is, in fact, one of the two objectives of the government's New Economic Policy (MTR, p. 1). In the present chapter I explore the extent and nature of poverty in Malaysia, so that policy measures for its alleviation might be considered.[1]

This chapter is specifically concerned with the definition and measurement of poverty in Malaysia. A poverty line is estimated after considering both the absolute and relative approaches to the definition. Various indices of poverty are then discussed, ranging from the simple incidence-of-poverty measure (that is, the percentage of the population in poverty) to others that take account of the poverty gap. A new index proposed by Sen (1976a) is derived, and alternative normalizations are suggested for it. Estimates of all these measures are presented for Malaysia. Finally, the simple incidence-of-poverty measure, which is decomposable, is used to construct a profile of the poor in Malaysia.

The profile adumbrates the poor in terms of variables that can provide a basis for policy action, describing the poor by such characteristics as race, location, employment status, occupation, and education. Such information should help not only to trace the correlates of poverty, but also to identify areas of government intervention for the redress of poverty.

Previous Attempts at Defining Poverty

One of the earliest recorded discussions of poverty in Malaysia was written fifty years ago by the literary figure Za'ba. In an article entitled

---

1. This chapter was presented as a paper (Anand, 1975) to the Fourteenth General Conference of the International Association for Research in Income and Wealth, Aulanko, Finland, August 1975.

"The Poverty of the Malays" in the *Malay Mail* of December 1, 1923, Za'ba drew attention to the fact of Malay poverty, but made no attempt to define or measure poverty.[2]

More recent explorations of the nature and causes of poverty in Malaysia have been made by Ungku A. Aziz. In a couple of stimulating contributions to the *Kajian Ekonomi Malaysia*, he has discussed various aspects of the problem (Aziz, 1964 and 1965). Although his approach is somewhat different from mine, Aziz recognizes the need to define and measure poverty.[3] Indeed, he has proposed the so-called sarong index of poverty, which is based on the long cloths that are traditionally worn by Malaysian men and women.

> There is one index that I have found to be convenient for purposes of measuring the extent of poverty among Malays in any kampong. This is the per capita sarong index. If we take the number of sarongs in a household and divide it by the number of persons above the age of one living in the household, then we can obtain a ratio of sarongs per capita. Any figure below one sarong per capita would indicate a condition of extreme poverty. Wealthy kampong dwellers like landlords, boatlords or the better-off Government employees generally have rates of 7–15 sarongs per capita. The index can be refined by taking a valuation of the sarongs and by differentiating between the types of sarongs. To measure the effect of a rural development programme on a particular kampong we could compare the per capita sarong indices before and after implementation of the programme. This index is a fairly good measure of any reduction in poverty (Aziz, 1964, pp. 79–80).

The sarong index of poverty, albeit ingenious, is too susceptible to the vagaries of fashion to be of much practical use!

In any case, poverty has to do with *incomes* that are low in some sense, rather than the amounts consumed or held of a single commodity. It can, of course, happen that some commodity has a perfect, or near-perfect, correlation with income. A definition of poverty could then be based on the consumption of this commodity. But since there do not seem to be any obvious advantages in this approach—not even easier data collection—

2. Za'ba wrote: "The Malays, as a whole, are a particularly poor people. Poverty is their most outstanding characteristic and their greatest handicap" (as cited in Aziz, 1975a, p. 9). His 1923 article is described by Ungku A. Aziz in *Jejak-Jejak di Pantai Zaman* (Kuala Lumpur: University of Malaya Press, 1975).

3. Aziz asserts that there are three basic causes of poverty: "neglect, low productivity and exploitation" (via his "MM," now modified to "OO," system). He also develops an intriguing "MV scale" to explain the phenomenon (Aziz, 1964).

attention might as well be focused on income itself, rather than on some commodity which is supposed to be a proxy for it. Even Aziz himself appears to have abandoned the sarong index and now favors the position that "if we adopt the income gap approach, we can minimize the quantum of nebulous quiddities and think more effectively" (Aziz, 1975*b*, p. 6).

The Definition of a Poverty Line

My analysis of poverty is based on an examination of the lower end of the Malaysian income distribution. The precise truncation point depends on the definition of poverty, to which there are essentially two approaches, an *absolute* and a *relative* one. In the absolute approach a certain minimal living standard is specified in terms of nutritional level, clothing, and the like, and the income required to support it is calculated. The relative approach interprets poverty in relation to the prevailing living standards of the society, recognizing explicitly the interdependence between the poverty line and the entire income distribution. My estimate of a poverty line is a compromise between these two considerations. It should elicit agreement about a definition of the poor in Malaysia.

The crudest definition of a relative poverty line is that income level which cuts off the lowest p percent of the population in the national income distribution. There are two objections to this method of defining the poor. First, the method prejudges the *extent* of poverty (it is p percent by definition!). Second, it implies that "the poor are always with us." In a trivial statistical sense there is always a bottom p percent in the income distribution, and thus one could never actually eradicate poverty. Even so, it could still be perfectly reasonable for a government to be continually concerned with the lowest p percent of the population. Indeed, with a Rawlsian criterion of justice, one is concerned precisely with improving the welfare levels of the worst-off group—defined in this case as the lowest p percent.[4]

The choice of percentile p in the distribution is, of course, somewhat arbitrary. In the context of developing countries, the figure of 40 percent has sometimes been suggested.[5] For Malaysia, the per capita household income level which cuts off the bottom 40 percent of the population from

4. See Rawls (1971) for the now famous "maximin" criterion of social welfare. Strictly speaking, the Rawlsian welfare function as interpreted by economists is concerned with increasing the income level of the worst-off *individual*.

5. The popularity of this particular figure seems to stem from Robert McNamara's plea that special policies be initiated to increase the income growth of the lowest 40 percent in developing countries (McNamara, 1972).

the rest is very slightly under M$25 per month. I have rounded this off to an income level of M$25 per month. The percentage of individuals who fall below this level of per capita household income is thus a little higher, at 40.2 percent. The percentage of *households* falling below such a poverty line is 36.5 percent, however, because the poor have larger households on average than the nonpoor (see the later section entitled "A Profile of Poverty in Malaysia").

Another method, which does not make it a matter of definition that the poor are always with us, is to define poverty in relation to contemporary living standards by drawing the poverty line at, say, half the average income level of the society.[6] In this case, although the poverty line rises with the general level of incomes, it is no longer true that poverty cannot be eliminated. In fact, it is "quite possible to imagine a society in which no one has less than half the average income—in which there is no poverty according to this definition" (Atkinson, 1975, p. 189). The per capita income in Malaysia has been estimated at M$50 per month, so the relative poverty line according to this definition is also M$25 per month.

An absolute poverty line has been estimated by the Ministry of Welfare Services (Department of Social Welfare) in Malaysia. The ministry is considering a public assistance program, a major objective of which is to institute "a scheme of social assistance based on principles of social justice whereby all those in poverty through circumstances beyond their control should be eligible for assistance in the quantum related to their needs" (Department of Social Welfare, 1975, p. 105).[7] For this purpose, the ministry identified a poverty line in terms of the income required to maintain a family in "good nutritional health" as well as to satisfy "minimum conventional needs in respect of clothing, household management, transport and communication." The minimum basket of food to maintain good nutritional health was devised with assistance from the Institute of Medical Research in Malaysia. The items of food chosen were costed at prices prevailing in August 1974, and a minimum food budget was thus obtained.

The minimum food budget was estimated separately for adults (male and female) by ethnic group,[8] and for children (divided into two age groups),

---

6. See Atkinson (1975). This suggestion has the merit that perceptions of poverty are tied up with perceptions of inequality.

7. Other objectives of the scheme are to "suggest various formulae and structures for the sharing of financial and technical responsibility by State and Federal Governments," and eventually to "integrate this social assistance with social insurance to form a nationwide social security scheme in the full sense of the term."

8. The breakdown by ethnic group allows for the different dietary habits and conventions of the three major communities in Malaysia.

Table 4-1. Cost of Nutritionally Adequate Diet at 1970 Prices
(M$ per month)

Location	Malay Male	Malay Female	Chinese Male	Chinese Female	Indian Male	Indian Female	Children 0–6 years	Children 7–11 years
Rural	25.39	24.13	24.56	23.29	25.67	24.41	14.95	21.04
Urban	25.85	24.59	25.00	23.74	26.41	25.15	15.29	21.46
Average	25.62	24.36	24.78	23.51	26.04	24.78	15.09	21.25

Source: Department of Social Welfare (1975), app. V.

both according to rural and urban location. It was found, however, that there was very little difference in cost between the food baskets of the three ethnic groups. There was also "very little variation between urban and rural prices for the items considered" (Department of Social Welfare, 1975, para. 16, p. 119).[9] Accordingly, the average cost was taken of the food baskets for the three ethnic groups in rural and urban areas.[10]

A food price index provided by the Department of Statistics was used to deflate the food budgets back to 1970, the year to which the survey data refer. Table 4-1 shows the estimates obtained of the monthly cost of food at 1970 prices for Malays, Chinese, and Indians in rural and urban areas.

The average monthly cost in 1970 of a nutritionally adequate diet for a male was M$25.37, for a female M$24.21, for a child M$18.17, and the average for an individual in the population at large was M$22.58. The food

9. Details of urban and rural market prices for individual food items are set out in Department of Social Welfare (1975 or 1976, app. II). Rural market prices, however, do not necessarily apply to the food baskets of peasant farmers, whose income from own consumption of produce is valued at farm-gate prices (see "Definition of PES Income" in chapter 2).

10. Details of the monthly food basket for each racial group are shown in Department of Social Welfare (1975), app. II (males) and app. III (females). There are separate food baskets in app. IV for children of 0–6 years and 7–11 years, which are not broken down by racial group. In choosing items for the food basket,

the cheapest items were chosen, particularly for vegetables. In the case of fish, the two varieties of fish chosen, i.e. ikan cincaru and ikan kembong, may not be the cheapest available in the market but they are the two most common types, which are consumed by the people in the low income group. In the case of milk, sweetened condensed milk was chosen for adults, as it is used as sweetener in coffee or tea; and for children, powdered milk, as recommended by the nutritionist. For meat, a combination of pork and chicken for Chinese, beef and chicken for Malays, and mutton and chicken for Indians was adopted (Department of Social Welfare, 1975, pp. 118–19).

budget for a household thus depends on its composition as well as its size. The ministry, however, assumes a fixed relation between size and composition,[11] so that, for instance, the average-size five-member household is assumed to consist of two adults and three children. The minimum food budget for such a household in 1970 was thus M$104.09 per month.

An estimate of nonfood expenditure is also required to calculate the total poverty budget. Three different methods have been used for this purpose, all based on expenditure data obtained from the 1973 Household Expenditure Survey (HES). In the first method, the proportion of total expenditure on food was estimated for families in the 1973 HES with monthly incomes less than M$200. The poverty line for each household size class was then calculated by multiplying the reciprocal of this proportion by the minimum food budget for that household size class.[12]

In the second method, the nonfood budget was restricted to four essential items: clothing and footwear; rent, fuel, and power; household equipment and operation; and transport and communications. The ratio of expenditure on each of these items to food expenditure was then estimated from the 1973 HES for families with less than M$200 monthly income. These ratios were applied to the minimum food budget for each household size class to calculate the nonfood portion of its poverty budget. This method is thus similar to the first except that all nonfood items other than the above four are excluded from the poverty budget.[13] Naturally, it leads to a lower poverty line.

The third method estimates the nonfood part of the poverty line budget by taking the absolute expenditure incurred on the four items by households in the 1973 HES with monthly incomes less than M$200. These were adjusted upward for price increases between July 1973 and August 1974 to obtain the nonfood component corresponding to the (August 1974) minimum food budget. The adjusted value was divided by the average household size in the less than M$200 monthly income class to yield the nonfood cost per person. Finally, the poverty line for each household size class was calculated by adding the minimum food budget for that size class to the product of nonfood cost per person and household size. Thus the nonfood budget of a household was assumed to be shared equally among its members.

11. See Department of Social Welfare (1975), app. VI.
12. This method of blowing up minimum food expenditure to get the total poverty budget is due to Orshansky (1965).
13. Excluded, for example, are the following categories of expenditure: beverages and tobacco; medical care and health needs; education and cultural services; recreation and entertainment.

The nonfood budget has been estimated at 1970 prices for each of the three methods. Different price indices provided by the Department of Statistics have been applied to deflate the different nonfood items. A breakdown of the nonfood cost per person in 1970 arrived at by the third method is:

	Cost per person (M$ per month)
Clothing and footwear	0.98
Rent, fuel, and power	4.74
Household equipment and operation	0.58
Transport and communications	1.44
Total nonfood cost per person for essential items	7.74

For a five-member household in 1970, therefore, the poverty line according to the third method is M$104.09 + (5 × M$7.74) = M$142.79 per month. The 1970 poverty line for a household of five persons according to the first method has been estimated at M$207.70 per month, and according to the second method at M$163.24 per month.

It is difficult to defend the first method on the basis of an absolute subsistence definition of poverty. The nonfood budget includes many items which might be considered inessential for subsistence. The second and third methods come closer to the subsistence notion of poverty inasmuch as they specify only certain nonfood items deemed to be essential. Even for these methods, however, the food basket chosen is obviously not a nutritional minimum.[14] The food budget estimated by the ministry appears to be based more on general consumption patterns in the society than on an absolute minimum required for subsistence. It is likely, therefore, to be higher than is strictly implied by the latter definition.

In fact, the concept of "minimum" is itself difficult to fix, since minimum requirements, in terms of the intake of calories and proteins, vary with the amount of physical activity of an individual. There are also large interindividual variations in requirements stemming from physiological factors, such as age, sex, body weight and size, and metabolism. Taking an average of minimum requirements for all individuals in society as the per capita subsistence level (or poverty line) leads to familiar problems of misclassification. Individuals above their own minimum requirement may be

---

14. The diet for the minimum food budget was obtained "basically from the diet provided in Government Hospitals for a 'normal average adult' " (Department of Social Welfare, 1975, p. 118). For children it was the "diet required for normal growth and maintenance of good nutritional health."

below the per capita subsistence level and therefore misclassified as poor; conversely, individuals below their own minimum requirement may be above the per capita subsistence level and therefore misclassified as nonpoor.[15] These classification errors are reduced by taking the household as the survey unit—because of the averaging of individual requirements when persons are considered as part of a household.

The eventual choice of a poverty line must to some extent remain arbitrary. Per person, the absolute poverty line under the second method is M\$32.6 per month, and under the third method it is M\$28.6 per month (dividing by five the household poverty line for the average five-member household). The estimates suggested by this absolute approach turn out to be fairly close to the M\$25 poverty line of the relative approach considered earlier. In view of this, and for computational convenience, I choose a poverty line of M\$25 per month household income per capita.[16] Later in the chapter, I conduct some sensitivity analysis around this poverty line.

The Sen Poverty Measure

Two types of indices have hitherto been used to measure the extent of poverty after the poverty line has been defined. The commonest index is the percentage of the population in poverty, also referred to as the incidence of poverty. The other index is the poverty gap, which is the total income needed to bring all the poor up to the poverty line. (In the United States, the poverty gap is sometimes expressed as a fraction of GNP.) The former index ignores the amounts by which the incomes of the poor fall short of the poverty line, while the latter index ignores the number actually in poverty. Both, moreover, are insensitive to a transfer of income from the poor to the very poor. In other words, neither measure is sensitive to the income distribution among the poor. A new measure of poverty has recently been proposed by Sen (1976a) which incorporates all three of these concerns into a single index.

The index is axiomatically derived after the general form for the poverty measure is taken to be a "normalized weighted sum of the income gaps of the poor." Two axioms then suffice to derive the index. The first specifies the income-weighting scheme, and the second stipulates the normalization procedure. Sen chooses the rank-order-weighting scheme, in which the weight on the income gap of a poor person is simply his or her rank in the income ordering below the poverty line. It should come as no surprise that

15. Note the analogy with Type I and Type II errors in statistical inference.
16. In 1970 U.S. dollars, this is equivalent to a poverty line of about US\$110 a year.

this weighting scheme will yield the Gini coefficient of the income distribution among the poor. Sen's normalization axiom requires that when all the poor have the same income, the index takes a value equal to the proportion of persons in poverty multiplied by the proportionate average shortfall of their income from the poverty line.

The following notation is introduced to set up the Sen index and relate it to other poverty measures:

n = total population size
μ = mean income of the population
π = poverty line
q = number of people in poverty (that is, with income less than or equal to π)
v = mean income of the poor
G_p = Gini coefficient of the income distribution among the poor.

Relabel the population (if necessary) in nondescending order of income so that

$$y_1 \leqslant y_2 \leqslant \ldots \leqslant y_n.$$

Then $y_q \leqslant \pi$, but $y_{q+1} > \pi$. The proportion of the population in poverty is (q/n), and the poverty gap is

$$\sum_{i=1}^{q} g_i$$

where $g_i = (\pi - y_i)$ is the income gap of person i. Thus the poverty gap is equal to

$$\sum_{i=1}^{q} (\pi - y_i) = q (\pi - v).$$

Therefore, the average poverty gap is $(\pi - v)$; the proportionate average income shortfall from the poverty line is $(\pi - v)/\pi$; and the normalized value of the Sen index is $(q/n) (\pi - v)/\pi$.

The rank-order-weighting scheme implies a weight of $(q + 1 - i)$ on the income gap g_i of person i, since there are $(q + 1 - i)$ persons among the poor with incomes at least as large as that of person i. The Sen index P is then

$$A \sum_{i=1}^{q} (q + 1 - i) (\pi - y_i)$$

where A is a parameter depending on the normalization selected. The normalized value of the index, when each $y_i = v$, is

$$\frac{q}{n} \cdot \frac{\pi - v}{\pi} = A(\pi - v)\frac{q(q+1)}{2}, \qquad \text{since} \sum_{i=1}^{q} (q+1-i) = \frac{q(q+1)}{2}.$$

Thus $A = 2/[(q+1)n\pi]$. Now the Gini coefficient G_p of the income distribution among the poor can be written as:

$$G_p = \frac{q+1}{q} - \frac{2}{q^2 v} \sum_{i=1}^{q} (q+1-i) y_i$$

(see definition G_4 of the Gini coefficient in appendix B).[17] Therefore,

$$P = \frac{q}{n} \cdot \frac{1}{\pi} \left[\pi - v + \frac{q}{q+1} v G_p \right].$$

For large q, $q/(q+1) \simeq 1$, and the index P reduces to

$$P = \frac{q}{n} \cdot \frac{1}{\pi} [\pi - v(1 - G_p)].$$

The effect of the weighting scheme is to *augment* the average poverty gap by the Gini coefficient times mean income of the poor. Thus an additional income "loss" arises when inequality in the income distribution among the poor is taken into account. The correction for this loss involves deflating the mean income v of the poor by $(1 - G_p)$, which yields the familiar equally distributed equivalent income (see Atkinson, 1970) corresponding to the rank-order welfare function. Hence the weighted income gap is calculated by taking the difference, not between the poverty line and the mean income of the poor, but between the poverty line and the equally distributed equivalent income of the poor.

The index P lies between 0 and 1. It assumes the value 0 when everyone's income is above the poverty line π (that is, when $q = 0$), and the value 1 when everyone has zero income (implying $v = 0$ and $q = n$).

The rank-order welfare function is rather special in that the relative weight on a person's income depends only on the rank of the person in the income ordering and not on the amount of the person's income as such.

---

17. If G is the Gini coefficient for the whole population, and G_{np} the Gini coefficient of the income distribution among the nonpoor, the following relation holds:

$$G = \left(\frac{q}{n}\right)\left(\frac{qv}{n\mu}\right)G_p + \left(\frac{n-q}{n}\right)\left(\frac{n\mu - qv}{n\mu}\right)G_{np} + \left(\frac{q}{n}\right)\left(\frac{\mu - v}{\mu}\right)$$

(see note 5 in the section "On the Decomposition of the Gini Coefficient" in appendix B). Thus the Gini coefficient for the nonpoor G_{np} can be inferred from a knowledge of G (table 3-8) and G_p (table 4-2).

Other welfare functions with relative weights that do depend directly on the size of a person's income may be found more acceptable. The weighting schemes implied by them produce different expressions for equally distributed equivalent income and, by the same token, different indices of inequality. It is evident that the weighted income gap under any welfare function is simply the difference between the poverty line and the corresponding equally distributed equivalent income. Hence for each different welfare function there corresponds by this approach a different *index of poverty*.

An obvious consequence of using such income-weighting schemes should be mentioned. In the Sen index P, for example, there is clearly a tradeoff between the mean income (v) of the poor and equality $(1 - G_p)$ in their income distribution, the tradeoff being given by $v(1 - G_p)$. Thus it is perfectly possible for the Sen index to register a decline in poverty when the poor have become poorer in absolute terms (that is, v has decreased) so long as equality in their income distribution $(1 - G_p)$ has increased more than proportionately. Put another way, the index implies a reduction in poverty even if there are transfers of income from the poor to the nonpoor (or the amount taken from the poor is simply thrown away) so long as the remaining incomes of the poor are sufficiently better distributed. A maximum reduction of $(1 - G_p)$ percent can be made in the total income of the poor, yet an improvement in distribution can still neutralize the effect of this income loss on the Sen index. These implications, while acceptable when weighting the incomes of the entire population as in the Atkinson inequality index, may be more difficult to swallow when applied only to those below the poverty line, especially if this is interpreted as an absolute minimum. In this case, one may not wish to weight the incomes of poor people differently, preferring instead the value judgment of equal or unit weights on all their income gaps. Treating the incomes of the poor similarly yields a poverty measure which is simply the normalized value of the Sen index.

It was noted earlier that a commonly used index of poverty is the percentage of GNP needed to close the poverty gap. A slightly different normalization from the one used by Sen produces a poverty measure which generalizes this index to correct for income inequality among the poor. The normalization can be modified so that when incomes below the poverty line are equal the measure reduces to the poverty gap expressed as a fraction of the total income of society; that is, $(q/n)(\pi - v)/\mu$. With this normalization, A takes the value: $A = 2/[(q + 1)n\mu]$.[18] The rank-order weighting pro-

---

18. Sen himself (1973*b*) alludes to this kind of normalization, but his equations (8) and (9) imply a different value for A, namely, $A = 2/n^2\mu$.

cedure now yields the modified Sen measure given by

$$M = \frac{q}{n} \cdot \frac{1}{\mu} [\pi - v(1 - G_p)].$$

The relation between P and M is $M = (\pi/\mu) P$, and the measure M lies between the limits 0 and π/μ.[19]

The measure M reduces to the proportion of total income needed to close the poverty gap in either of two circumstances: (1) incomes below the poverty line are equally distributed (implying $G_p = 0$), or (2) the same weight of unity attaches to the income gap of every person below the poverty line.

Instead of expressing the income required to close the poverty gap as a fraction of total income, define an index F (after Fishlow, 1972, 1973) which expresses the gap as a fraction of the income of the nonpoor:

$$F = \frac{q}{n\mu - qv} [\pi - v(1 - G_p)]$$

$$= \frac{\pi}{\mu - \frac{q}{n}v} P.$$

The idea behind this index is the elimination of poverty through a direct transfer of income from the nonpoor to the poor.[20] The ratio reflects the burden on the nonpoor since it represents the proportionate reduction in their income if the poverty gap is to be closed through redistribution alone.

Three comments are appropriate about these indices M and F. First, they are not so much measures of poverty as indicators of the economy's capacity for its alleviation. Failure to distinguish the measurement of poverty from the prospects for its alleviation can lead to the following

19. If one adopts Atkinson's suggestion for defining a relative poverty line (discussed earlier in this chapter), π and μ stand in constant relation to each other, namely, $\pi/\mu = 1/2$. In this case, M and P are related as $M = P/2$, and M lies between the limits of 0 and $1/2$.

20. If poverty is to be eliminated by transfers alone, the income of the nonpoor must be large enough not to drag the nonpoor themselves into poverty in the course of income transfers. This motivates yet another normalization for the Sen index, in which the poverty gap is expressed as a fraction of the income of the nonpoor *in excess of* the poverty level. This measure is easily seen to reduce to

$$\frac{\pi}{\mu - \frac{q}{n}v - \pi\left(1 - \frac{q}{n}\right)} P$$

where P is the Sen index.

anomalous consequence. With no change in the number or the incomes of the poor, an increase in the incomes of people above the poverty line will lead to a fall in both the indices M and F. Yet no reduction in poverty has actually occurred since the position of the poor remains unchanged.[21] What has happened is that a smaller fraction of society's income is now required to eliminate poverty, and to that extent the task may be regarded as potentially easier. The measurement of poverty thus needs to be conceptually separated from the possibilities for its alleviation.

Second, the values of F and M could exceed unity if the poverty line happens to be drawn at a level higher than the mean income of society. Then, the augmented poverty gap could exceed the income of the nonpoor (or even the total income of society), implying a value of F (or of M) larger than unity. A sufficient condition for the poverty problem to be tractable through transfers is that the mean income of society exceed the poverty-line income. There is then enough income to bring everyone in the population above the poverty line. With this condition satisfied, both the indices M and F are bounded above by unity.

Third, the assumption implicit in the indices M and F is that the redistribution of income to close the poverty gap does not affect the size of total income in the economy. Yet any transfer scheme based on the taxation system is likely to influence both the (pretransfer) poverty gap and the (pretransfer) income of the nonpoor through its disincentive effects. A full income support program implies a 100 percent marginal rate of taxation at and below the poverty line, as well as changes in taxation at higher income levels (to raise the required revenue). The work disincentive effects of such changes in the tax schedule could substantially increase the pretransfer poverty gap and reduce the size of pretransfer income of the nonpoor. This, of course, would alter the values of the indices M and F. Indeed, for each different tax schedule/transfer scheme that is contemplated to eliminate poverty, there will correspond different values for M and F. To calculate these and the optimum tax schedule requires information on individual labor supply functions, the distribution of skills, and so on.[22]

21. There might even be an increase in poverty if one takes a relative view of poverty. The Sen poverty measure P is unchanged in this case since the income gap of the poor is normalized on the poverty line π and not on the mean income μ of the entire community. Only an actual reduction in the number of poor, or an increase in their incomes, or an improvement in their income distribution, or an increase in the number of nonpoor can lead to a fall in the Sen poverty index.

22. See Mirrlees (1971) for the pioneering contribution in the theory of optimum income taxation. The optimum tax schedule mentioned here is different from that of Mirrlees because of the additional constraint that no one's posttax income should fall below an exogenously chosen poverty line.

Table 4-2. Estimates of Poverty by Racial Group

Racial group	Proportion of persons in poverty (q/n)	Average poverty gap per person, (M$ per month) ($\pi-\mu$)	Weights of unity on income gaps of the poor			Gini coefficient of income distribution among the poor	Rank-order weights on income gaps of the poor		
			Index P	Index M	Index F		Index P	Index M	Index F
Peninsular Malaysia	0.402	9.05	0.145	0.073	0.083	0.2126	0.200	0.100	0.115
Malay	0.562	9.74	0.219	0.161	0.215	0.2200	0.294	0.216	0.290
Chinese	0.183	6.80	0.050	0.018	0.019	0.1677	0.072	0.026	0.028
Indian	0.334	7.28	0.097	0.043	0.048	0.1658	0.137	0.060	0.067
Other	0.433	12.44	0.215	0.029	0.030	0.3328	0.288	0.039	0.040

Estimates of Poverty in Malaysia

The indices discussed above have been estimated for the Malaysian population in poverty. It is assumed first that the weights attaching to each person's income gap are unity. The indices then reduce to the poverty gap expressed as a fraction of various income aggregates. Estimates of these measures, as well as the proportion in poverty and the average poverty gap, are presented in table 4-2 for Peninsular Malaysia and each ethnic group separately.

The percentage of the population in poverty was calculated as 40.2 percent, and the average poverty gap as M$9.05 per month. The poverty gap as a fraction of the total income needed to support everyone in the population at the poverty level is 14.5 percent. The index M for the country was estimated as 0.073, which implies that the poverty gap in Malaysia stands at 7.3 percent of total personal income. If poverty were to be eliminated by transfers from the nonpoor to the poor, the nonpoor would need to sacrifice 8.3 percent of their income (or 12.7 percent of their income in excess of the poverty level).[23]

These indices have also been computed separately for each ethnic group. The average income gap is largest for the small and heterogeneous community of "others" (Europeans, Thais, other Asians, and so forth), while the incidence of poverty is highest among Malays. The product of these two measures divided by poverty-line income gives the Sen index in the case of unit weights, which shows that poverty is more acute among Malays than among "others."

The values of M and F for the communities show the poverty gap of each racial group as a fraction of various income aggregates for that group. For policy purposes, however, it is probably more useful to express the poverty gap of each racial group as a fraction of the *overall* poverty gap. Of the overall income shortfall, the Malays account for 79.0 percent, the Chinese for 11.9 percent, the Indians for 8.0 percent, and other races for 1.1 percent.[24] Of the overall number in poverty, however, the Malays account for 73.5 percent, the Chinese for 15.8 percent, the Indians for 9.9 percent, and other races for 0.8 percent. The difference between these two sets of figures obviously reflects the difference between races in their average poverty gaps.

23. See note 20 above.
24. In a poverty relief program, allocation to communities in these percentages will reduce their income gaps equiproportionately.

Assume now that rank-order weights attach to the income gaps of poor persons. The average poverty gap then needs to be augmented by the mean income times the Gini coefficient of the income distribution among the poor. This adjustment yields values for P, M, and F shown in the last three columns of table 4-2. The Sen poverty measure takes the value 0.200 for Peninsular Malaysia. It is difficult to judge whether the degree of poverty which this represents is large or small in the absence of estimates for other countries.[25] In fact, one of the main reasons for evaluating the Sen measure in the unit weights (or distribution-free) case is that it has a straightforward interpretation there. Its value under rank-order weighting indicates the magnitude of the correction to the unit weights case, which arises from the inequality in incomes among the poor.

According to the Sen index, poverty is greatest among Malays, followed by "others," Indians, and Chinese, respectively. Although the Sen index points to the severity of the problem within each racial group, it cannot be used to indicate the contribution of a group to overall poverty. Yet, in the design of policies to redress poverty, it would seem important to be informed of the extent to which a particular group accounts for overall poverty. An index which does permit poverty to be "decomposed" as a weighted average of poverty in each group is the simple incidence-of-poverty measure (unlike the case for an inequality index, there is obviously no between-group component for a poverty index).[26] In the next section, this index is adopted to characterize the nature of poverty in Malaysia.

A Profile of Poverty in Malaysia

A characterization of poverty requires answers to questions such as: Who are the poor? Where are they located? In which sectors do they work? What

25. Like most indices of inequality, the Sen poverty measure is useful mainly for comparisons across countries or over time. Unlike indices of inequality, which are relative, however, indices of poverty (including the one by Sen) are sensitive to the choice of poverty line. This needs to be borne in mind when making intercountry comparisons of poverty. So far I have seen an estimate of the Sen index for only one other country: from National Sample Survey data on consumption in 1970–71, Ahluwalia (1977) estimates the Sen index for rural India as 0.176 and the incidence of rural poverty as 47.5 percent.

26. The overall incidence of poverty can be written as a weighted average of the poverty incidence in each group, where the weights are the population shares of the groups. The income gap measures (aggregate and proportionate) are similarly decomposable (with income share weights), but the Sen index, which uses the Gini coefficient to correct for inequality among the poor, is not. Because the Gini coefficient is not decomposable (see chapter 3 and "On the Decomposition of the Gini Coefficient" in appendix B), the Sen index cannot indicate the proportion of poverty accounted for by a particular group.

are the characteristics of the poor that are different from those of the nonpoor? The profile of poverty in this section identifies the poor in terms of socioeconomic variables such as race, location, employment status, occupation, sector of employment, and education. It also indicates the extent of poverty accounted for by separate values of each variable (or characteristic)—made possible by the decomposability of the incidence-of-poverty measure.

Since the household is the basic income-sharing unit, it appears more appropriate for policy purposes to describe the population in poverty in terms of *households*, rather than *individuals*. Accordingly, the population unit in the poverty profile is chosen to be the household, and poor households are those with per capita household incomes below M$25 per month. While the percentage of persons in poverty is 40.2 percent (table 4-2), the percentage of households in poverty is 36.5 percent (table 4-3). This is because the poor have a larger average household size than the nonpoor [see point 8(3) below].[27]

Table 4-3 shows two distinct aspects of poverty. In column 2 the percentage distribution of poverty among the values of each variable is shown, which indicates concentrations of poverty. Column 4 shows which groups suffer from a particularly high incidence of poverty; these are so-called high-risk groups which may, in fact, account for only a small proportion of overall poverty. Clearly, both types of information are important in the design of policies to redress poverty.

The following picture of the poor emerges from an examination of the characteristics of households and their heads in table 4-3.

1. The problem is overwhelmingly a Malay one, with 78.1 percent of poor households being Malay. There are six Malay households in poverty for every one Chinese. Malays, who constitute 55.4 percent of all households, are overrepresented among poor households by a factor of 1.41 (see column 5 on the relative incidence of poverty). More than half (51.4 percent) of Malay households suffer from poverty, while the incidence among Chinese is 14.7 percent, and among Indians, 24.8 percent.

2. Poverty is also overwhelmingly a rural phenomenon, with 87.7 percent of poor households living in rural areas.[28]

---

27. Whereas there is a negative correlation between average household size and per capita household income, there is a positive correlation between average household size and household income (see chapter 3).

28. Separate profiles of the urban and rural poor reveal that the ethnic distribution of urban poverty is quite different from that of rural poverty (see chapter 5). The Chinese form the most numerous group among the urban poor, but the incidence of urban poverty among Malays is almost twice that among Chinese (table 5-4).

Table 4-3. Profile of Poverty at a Poverty Line of M$25

Selected characteristic of household	Percentage distribution among all households (1)	Percentage distribution among poverty households (2)	Percentage distribution among nonpoverty households (3)	Incidence of poverty (percent) (4)	Relative incidence of poverty (2)/(1) (5)
Race					
Malay	55.4	78.1	42.4	51.4	1.41
Chinese	32.0	12.9	42.9	14.7	0.40
Indian	11.7	8.0	13.9	24.8	0.68
Other	0.9	1.0	0.8	40.3	1.11
Total	100.0	100.0	100.0		
Location					
Urban	28.4	12.3	37.6	15.8	0.43
Rural	71.6	87.7	62.4	44.6	1.22
Total	100.0	100.0	100.0		
State					
Johore	13.4	12.1	14.1	32.9	0.90
Kedah	11.3	15.1	9.2	48.6	1.34
Kelantan	9.5	17.0	5.2	65.2	1.79
Malacca	4.6	4.1	4.9	32.0	0.89
Negri Sembilan	4.7	4.2	5.1	32.1	0.89
Pahang	5.8	4.9	6.3	30.7	0.84
Penang	8.5	6.9	9.4	29.7	0.81
Perak	17.8	16.8	18.3	34.5	0.94
Perlis	1.5	2.4	1.0	58.9	1.60
Selangor	18.2	9.5	23.2	19.1	0.52
Trengganu	4.7	7.0	3.3	54.6	1.49
Total	100.0	100.0	100.0		
Employment status of head					
Employer	2.7	0.4	4.0	5.1	0.51
Employee	51.8	38.2	59.3	26.3	0.74
Own-account worker	39.3	55.3	30.4	50.1	1.41
Housewife or houseworker	2.6	2.2	2.8	30.5	0.85
Unemployed	3.6	3.9	3.5	38.0	1.08
Total	100.0	100.0	100.0		
Occupation of head[a]					
Professional and technical	5.7	1.1	8.2	6.7	0.19
Administrative and managerial	3.3	0.4	4.9	4.4	0.12
Clerical and related	4.0	0.3	6.1	2.7	0.08

Selected characteristic of household	Percentage distribution among all households (1)	Percentage distribution among poverty households (2)	Percentage distribution among nonpoverty households (3)	Incidence of poverty (percent) (4)	Relative incidence of poverty (2)/(1) (5)
Sales	11.5	6.4	14.3	20.0	0.56
Service	8.3	3.4	10.9	14.9	0.41
Farmers	27.6	47.9	16.4	61.9	1.74
Farm laborers	21.6	29.5	17.3	48.6	1.37
Production	18.0	11.0	21.9	21.9	0.61
Total	100.0	100.0	100.0		
Sector of employment of head[b]					
Agriculture	24.1	41.7	14.4	61.5	1.73
Agricultural products	25.7	33.4	21.4	46.2	1.30
Mining and quarrying	1.8	0.9	2.3	18.1	0.50
Manufacturing	8.6	5.2	10.4	21.8	0.60
Construction	3.2	2.0	4.0	21.5	0.63
Public utilities	1.6	1.0	2.0	21.0	0.63
Commerce	12.6	7.2	15.6	20.2	0.57
Transport and communications	5.5	3.3	6.7	21.2	0.60
Services	16.9	5.3	23.2	11.1	0.31
Total	100.0	100.0	100.0		
Education of head					
None	32.1	43.2	25.7	49.0	1.35
Some primary	33.1	35.6	31.7	39.1	1.08
Completed primary	20.4	18.4	21.6	32.8	0.90
Lower secondary (forms I–III)	6.7	2.1	9.3	11.7	0.31
Some upper secondary (forms IV–V)	3.0	0.4	4.4	5.2	0.13
School certificate or higher	4.7	0.3	7.3	2.1	0.06
Total	100.0	100.0	100.0		
Sex of head					
Male	81.7	77.5	84.2	34.6	0.95
Female	18.3	22.5	15.8	44.9	1.23
Total	100.0	100.0	100.0		

(Table continues on the following page.)

Table 4-3 (*continued*).

Selected characteristic of household	Percentage distribution among all households (1)	Percentage distribution among poverty households (2)	Percentage distribution among nonpoverty households (3)	Incidence of poverty (percent) (4)	Relative incidence of poverty (2)/(1) (5)
Age of head					
Under 20	1.5	1.3	1.6	31.5	0.87
20–29	15.3	11.5	17.5	27.4	0.75
30–39	25.2	26.7	24.4	38.5	1.06
40–49	22.9	25.4	21.5	40.4	1.11
50–59	19.1	18.0	19.7	34.3	0.94
60+	16.0	17.1	15.3	39.0	1.07
Total	100.0	100.0	100.0		
Household size					
1	8.9	5.7	10.7	23.5	0.64
2	9.5	6.1	11.6	23.2	0.64
3	11.7	9.4	12.9	29.5	0.80
4	13.1	11.4	14.0	31.8	0.87
5	12.6	13.8	11.9	40.0	1.10
6	12.0	13.8	11.0	41.8	1.15
7	9.8	12.5	8.2	46.7	1.28
8	7.9	9.9	6.8	45.6	1.25
9	5.5	6.1	5.2	40.3	1.11
10+	9.0	11.3	7.7	45.7	1.26
Total	100.0	100.0	100.0		
Number of children under age 15					
0	24.7	14.0	30.9	20.7	0.57
1	17.0	14.3	18.5	30.7	0.84
2	15.5	14.9	15.8	35.2	0.96
3	13.6	15.5	12.5	41.5	1.14
4	11.5	15.3	9.3	48.4	1.33
5+	17.7	26.0	13.0	53.5	1.47
Total	100.0	100.0	100.0		
Number of income recipients					
0	1.3	3.4	0.0	99.0	2.62
1	57.8	66.5	52.9	41.9	1.15
2	26.4	22.5	28.6	31.1	0.85
3	9.1	5.6	11.1	22.4	0.62
4+	5.4	2.0	7.4	13.3	0.37
Total	100.0	100.0	100.0		

Note: The poverty line is defined at a per capita household income of M$25 per month; 36.5 percent of all households fall below this line.

a. See note to table 6-11 for a definition of this one-digit occupation classification.

b. See note to table 6-9 for a definition of this one-digit employment sector classification.

3. The four northern states of Kedah, Kelantan, Perlis, and Trengganu stand out as having above average incidences of poverty. Together they account for 41.5 percent of poverty households, but for only 27.0 percent of all households.

4. Of poor households, 93.5 percent are headed by employees or own-account (self-employed) workers.[29] The incidence of poverty among households whose heads are own-account workers is 50.1 percent, which is higher than that among households whose heads are employees (26.3 percent). The unemployment rate among heads of poverty households is a mere 3.9 percent, and the rate of poverty among households with unemployed heads is 38.0 percent.[30]

5. Farmers head 47.9 percent of poor households, and farm laborers, 29.5 percent. The incidence of poverty among households headed by farmers and farm laborers is 61.9 percent and 48.6 percent, respectively. The higher incidence of poverty among households headed by farmers reflects something of a dual economy in the rural sector. The category of farm laborers includes both relatively well-paid estate workers, who form a significant proportion of the rural labor force, as well as casual and other laborers. The category of farmers includes all peasants and smallholders.

6. The incidence of poverty is well above average among households with heads in the agricultural sector (61.5 percent) and in the agricultural products sector (46.2 percent). These two sectors account for three-quarters (75.1 percent) of poverty households but less than half (49.8 percent) of all households.[31]

7. Persons whose schooling does not extend beyond primary school head 97.2 percent of all poverty households. Of these, 43.2 percent have had no education at all. There is a strong negative correlation between education and poverty incidence, and the decline in incidence is particularly marked for households whose heads have acquired even *some* secondary education. Of households whose heads have received some upper secondary

---

29. For definitions of the various employment status categories, see the appendix to chapter 2.

30. Thus the problem of poverty needs to be distinguished from the problem of unemployment. A policy of absorbing unemployed heads of households into the labor market will not make a significant dent in poverty. Of course, a general expansion of formal sector employment, which also absorbs subsistence sector own-account and family workers, could contribute appreciably to a reduction in poverty.

31. This is in accordance with the finding of 77.4 percent of poverty households headed by farmers or farm laborers. The breakdown by employment status of head of household includes categories (own-account workers and employees) that overlap with the occupations of farmer and farm laborer. The overlap or *joint* distribution of categories must obviously be borne in mind when policy interpretations are attempted.

education, only 5.2 percent are poor, and of those whose heads have received the school certificate, only 2.1 percent are poor.

8. The distribution and incidence of poverty as a function of household composition show the following features: (1) Households headed by females are somewhat more poverty-prone (44.9 percent) than those headed by males (34.6 percent). (2) The incidence of poverty does not show wide variation according to age of household head, but it is lowest for the 20–29 age group. (3) The incidence of poverty increases with household size up to seven-member households, after which the relation is unclear (owing to the effect of additional income recipients); but the incidence is above average for all size classes above five and below average for all lower size classes. A comparison of the percentage distribution of household size among poverty and nonpoverty households shows a larger average household size for the poor. (4) The incidence of household poverty increases steadily with the number of children under age fifteen (who are unlikely to be income recipients).[32] (5) Almost all (99 percent) of the households with no income recipients are in poverty, and the incidence rate falls with the number of recipients. Among poor households, 66.5 percent have just one income recipient, and 22.5 percent have two.

When several of the characteristics associated with high degrees of poverty are taken together, the chances of being poor can become extremely high. Thus, for example, a Malay farmer in rural Kelantan has a worse than three-fourths probability of being poor. In order to design policies and projects to help the poor selectively and with minimal leakage, it is necessary to identify smaller, more homogeneous groups such as these, with particularly high incidences of poverty (see chapter 5).

Sensitivity of the Poverty Profile

Before zeroing in on subgroups in poverty, it should be established that the picture of poverty in table 4-3 does not hinge crucially on the chosen poverty line of M$25 per capita household income per month. Accordingly, I consider two further poverty lines, at M$15 and M$33 per month, and conduct sensitivity analysis on the profile of poverty.[33] This is partially

32. This relation might weaken if the per equivalent adult household income had been used instead of per capita household income to measure living standards. But the relation between poverty incidence and household size need not be affected by this very much. Because of the prevalence of the joint family system in Malaysia, larger households do not necessarily have a larger proportion of children.

33. This is an obvious but somewhat neglected exercise in the growing empirical literature on poverty. As attempts to estimate poverty in developing countries get under way and cross-

possible through table 4-4, which shows the percentage of households falling below these poverty lines with a breakdown by location and racial group.

The M$15 poverty line cuts off roughly the bottom 20 percent of the population, and may be said to identify the "very poor" in Malaysia. Since the redress of poverty rule requires filling the poverty gap from the bottom upward, this poorest group may be of special interest. Some 15.5 percent of households, containing 17.3 percent of individuals, receive a per capita household income of less than M$15 per month. The average per capita income of these individuals is slightly less than M$10 per month, while that of the other 82.7 percent is M$58 per month. A transfer of just 1.8 percent of the income of this upper group can bring all the very poor up to the income level of M$15 per month.

The M$33 poverty line corresponds to that of the second method used earlier in this chapter to define an absolute poverty line. The proportion of households falling below M$33 per month is 49.3 percent.[34] Thus when the poverty line is raised from M$25 to M$33, the incidence of poverty rises from 36.5 to 49.3 percent, and when it is lowered from M$25 to M$15, the incidence of poverty falls from 36.5 to 15.5 percent. Hence, the incidence of poverty is fairly sensitive to changes in the poverty line, showing an elasticity of 1.1 for upward movement from M$25 and an elasticity of 1.4 for downward movement from M$25.

The profile of poverty is much less sensitive to variations in the poverty line than is the incidence of poverty.[35] As the poverty line is lowered from M$33 to M$25 and then to M$15, Malays account for 75.3, 78.1, and 85.3 percent, respectively, of poverty households, while the reverse trend is in evidence for the Chinese, who account for a decreasing percentage of poverty households.[36] As the poverty line is lowered, the rural concentration of poverty also increases a little: 85.2 percent of M$33 poverty

---

country comparisons begin to be made, it becomes important to establish the robustness of estimates through sensitivity analysis. In some countries it is possible that the estimates are highly sensitive to small variations in the poverty threshold.

34. This is the figure for poverty incidence mentioned in the Third Malaysia Plan (TMP) (see Government of Malaysia, 1976, p. 160). In addition to this, the TMP (tables 9-1, 9-2, 9-3, and 9-6) quotes detailed poverty incidence figures from my M$33 poverty profile (see Anand, 1974a, or table 4-6 below). The plan document, however, does not mention that these figures correspond to a poverty line of M$33 income per month.

35. It is the presence of bunching, or excessive inequality, in the lower portions of the income distribution that could cause profile characteristics and the incidence of poverty to move discontinuously as a function of the poverty line. Since the Sen index specifically incorporates inequality among the poor, it may be relatively immune to such jumps.

36. These findings are consistent with the racial pattern of income distribution depicted in figure 1-1.

Table 4-4. Household Percentages in Four per Capita Household Income Classes by Racial Group and Location

Per capita household income class (M$ per month)	Percentage of households in income class	Percentage distribution among racial groups					Percentage of urban households in income class	Percentage of rural households in income class
		Malay	Chinese	Indian	Other	Total		
0–15	15.5	85.3	7.8	5.4	1.5	100.0	5.0	19.6
Urban	1.4	42.6	34.7	21.6	1.1	100.0		
Rural	14.1	89.6	5.1	3.8	1.5	100.0		
0–25	36.5	78.1	12.9	8.0	1.0	100.0	15.8	44.6
Urban	4.5	37.4	41.9	19.6	1.1	100.0		
Rural	32.0	83.9	8.8	6.3	1.0	100.0		
0–33	49.3	73.0	16.9	9.3	0.8	100.0	25.5	58.6
Urban	7.3	34.5	47.0	17.7	0.8	100.0		
Rural	42.0	79.6	11.7	7.9	0.8	100.0		
185+	5.0	21.5	55.8	16.9	5.8	100.0	11.4	2.6
Urban	3.2	14.9	61.9	17.3	5.9	100.0		
Rural	1.8	33.2	44.9	16.3	5.6	100.0		
All income classes (0+)	100.0	55.4	32.0	11.7	0.9	100.0	100.0	100.0
Urban	28.4	25.9	57.9	14.9	1.3	100.0		
Rural	71.6	67.1	21.7	10.5	0.7	100.0		

households reside in rural areas, compared with 87.7 and 91.0 percent, respectively, of M$25 and M$15 poverty households. It seems that racial and rural-urban features of poverty are not very sensitive to the choice of poverty line within a reasonably wide range, although they are accentuated as the poverty line is dropped.

The distribution of poverty according to other characteristics also remains relatively stable as the poverty line rises from M$15 to M$33 (see tables 4-5 and 4-6).[37] Kedah, Kelantan, Perlis, and Trengganu remain the states worst affected by poverty. As the poverty line rises, the relative incidence of poverty in these states drops slightly but remains well above unity. Households whose heads are own-account workers continue to be overrepresented among the poor as the poverty line is raised, with the relative incidence dropping a little from 1.61 to 1.32. The relative incidence of poverty among households whose heads are employees increases (from 0.61 to 0.81) but remains well below unity. With respect to sectors of employment, the relative incidence among households with heads in agriculture declines from 2.12 to 1.56, while for those in agricultural products it remains virtually stationary around 1.30. By occupational category, the relative incidence of poverty for households headed by farmers declines from 2.07 to 1.58 as the poverty line is raised, while for those headed by farm laborers it oscillates from 1.34 to 1.37 to 1.32. Finally, the educational and demographic characteristics of poverty households display similarly small variations as the poverty line is altered.

Thus the picture of poverty in table 4-3 does not seem very sensitive to the variations considered in the poverty line. One can remain fairly confident about the profile it depicts, and in subsequent discussion on poverty I adhere to the original line of M$25 per month. Such changes in emphasis as there are in the poverty profile suggest that households headed by farmers and those in agriculture form the hard core of the poor. This highlights the need to study rural poverty in greater detail—which is the subject of the next chapter.

Appendix: A Profile of the Rich

For comparative purposes, it is interesting to look briefly at the top end of the per capita household income distribution. Defining rich households as those belonging in the top 5 percent of this distribution, that is, those

---

37. Separate rural and urban poverty profiles for the M$15 and M$33 poverty lines were presented in Anand (1974*a*); they are included as tables 5-7, 5-8, 5-9, and 5-10 in the next chapter.

Table 4-5. Profile of Poverty at a Poverty Line of M$15

Selected characteristic of household	Percentage distribution among all households (1)	Percentage distribution among poverty households (2)	Percentage distribution among nonpoverty households (3)	Incidence of poverty (percent) (4)	Relative incidence of poverty (2)/(1) (5)
Race					
Malay	55.4	85.3	49.9	23.9	1.54
Chinese	32.0	7.8	36.4	3.8	0.24
Indian	11.7	5.4	12.9	7.2	0.46
Other	0.9	1.5	0.8	25.3	1.67
Total	100.0	100.0	100.0		
Location					
Urban	28.4	9.0	32.0	5.0	0.32
Rural	71.6	91.0	68.0	19.6	1.27
Total	100.0	100.0	100.0		
State					
Johore	13.4	11.7	13.7	13.5	0.87
Kedah	11.3	15.8	10.5	21.7	1.40
Kelantan	9.5	21.4	7.4	34.8	2.25
Malacca	4.6	3.4	4.8	11.4	0.74
Negri Sembilan	4.7	3.9	4.9	12.7	0.83
Pahang	5.8	4.6	6.0	12.4	0.79
Penang	8.5	5.1	9.1	9.3	0.60
Perak	17.8	15.5	18.2	13.6	0.87
Perlis	1.5	3.0	1.2	31.1	2.00
Selangor	18.2	7.1	20.2	6.0	0.39
Trengganu	4.7	8.5	4.0	28.2	1.31
Total	100.0	100.0	100.0	100.0	
Employment status of head					
Employer	2.7	0.3	3.1	1.8	0.11
Employee	51.8	31.6	55.2	8.7	0.61
Own-account worker	39.3	63.1	35.3	23.1	1.61
Housewife or houseworker	2.6	1.7	2.8	9.1	0.65
Unemployed	3.6	3.3	3.6	13.2	0.92
Total	100.0	100.0	100.0		
Occupation of head					
Professsional and technical	5.7	0.6	6.5	1.6	0.11
Administrative and managerial	3.3	0.1	3.9	0.5	0.03
Clerical and related	4.0	0.1	4.7	0.2	0.03

Selected characteristic of household	Percentage distribution among all households (1)	Percentage distribution among poverty households (2)	Percentage distribution among nonpoverty households (3)	Incidence of poverty (percent) (4)	Relative incidence of poverty (2)/(1) (5)
Sales	11.5	4.6	12.7	6.0	0.40
Service	8.3	2.3	9.3	4.0	0.28
Farmers	27.6	57.0	22.5	30.6	2.07
Farm laborers	21.6	28.9	20.4	19.8	1.34
Production	18.0	6.4	20.0	5.3	0.36
Total	100.0	100.0	100.0		
Sector of employment of head					
Agriculture	24.1	51.1	19.5	30.9	2.12
Agricultural products	25.7	33.5	24.4	18.9	1.30
Mining and quarrying	1.8	0.3	2.1	2.4	0.17
Manufacturing	8.6	3.5	9.4	6.0	0.41
Construction	3.2	1.0	3.6	4.3	0.31
Public utilities	1.6	0.2	1.9	1.5	0.13
Commerce	12.6	5.1	13.9	5.9	0.41
Transport and communications	5.5	2.2	6.0	5.7	0.40
Services	16.9	3.1	19.2	2.7	0.18
Total	100.0	100.0	100.0		
Education of head					
None	32.1	48.2	29.1	23.2	1.50
Some primary	33.1	34.0	33.0	15.8	1.03
Completed primary	20.4	15.1	21.4	11.4	0.74
Lower secondary (forms I–III)	6.7	1.9	7.5	4.5	0.28
Some upper secondary (forms IV–V)	3.0	0.4	3.5	2.0	0.13
School certificate or higher	4.7	0.4	5.5	1.2	0.09
Total	100.0	100.0	100.0		
Sex of head					
Male	81.7	73.5	83.2	13.9	0.90
Female	18.3	26.5	16.8	22.5	1.45
Total	100.0	100.0	100.0		

(*Table continues on the following page.*)

Table 4-5 (*continued*).

Selected characteristic of household	Percentage distribution among all households (1)	Percentage distribution among poverty households (2)	Percentage distribution among nonpoverty households (3)	Incidence of poverty (percent) (4)	Relative incidence of poverty (2)/(1) (5)
Age of head					
Under 20	1.5	1.4	1.5	14.9	0.93
20–29	15.3	11.6	16.0	11.6	0.76
30–39	25.2	28.4	24.7	17.4	1.13
40–49	22.9	25.2	22.5	17.0	1.10
50–59	19.1	17.7	19.3	14.3	0.93
60 +	16.0	15.7	16.0	15.2	0.98
Total	100.0	100.0	100.0		
Household size					
1	8.9	0.7	10.4	1.3	0.08
2	9.5	10.5	9.4	17.0	1.11
3	11.7	9.6	12.1	12.7	0.82
4	13.1	7.1	14.2	8.4	0.54
5	12.6	15.5	12.0	19.1	1.23
6	12.0	17.0	11.1	21.9	1.42
7	9.8	11.8	9.4	18.7	1.20
8	7.9	11.0	7.3	21.7	1.39
9	5.5	6.6	5.3	19.6	1.20
10 +	9.0	10.2	8.8	17.6	1.13
Total	100.0	100.0	100.0		
Number of children under age 15					
0	24.7	10.5	27.3	6.6	0.43
1	17.0	14.3	17.5	13.1	0.84
2	15.5	13.2	15.9	13.2	0.85
3	13.6	18.4	12.7	21.0	1.35
4	11.5	17.0	10.5	22.8	1.40
5 +	17.7	26.6	16.1	23.3	1.50
Total	100.0	100.0	100.0		
Number of income recipients					
0	1.3	8.0	0.0	98.7	6.15
1	57.8	67.7	56.1	18.1	1.17
2	26.4	18.9	27.8	11.1	0.72
3	9.1	4.0	10.0	6.7	0.44
4 +	5.4	1.4	6.1	4.1	0.26
Total	100.0	100.0	100.0		

Note: The poverty line is defined at a per capita household income of M$15 per month; 15.5 percent of all households fall below this line.

Table 4-6. Profile of Poverty at a Poverty Line of M$33

Selected characteristic of household	Percentage distribution among all households (1)	Percentage distribution among poverty households (2)	Percentage distribution among nonpoverty households (3)	Incidence of poverty (percent) (4)	Relative incidence of poverty (2)/(1) (5)
Race					
Malay	55.4	73.0	38.4	64.8	1.32
Chinese	32.0	16.9	46.6	26.0	0.53
Indian	11.7	9.3	14.0	39.2	0.79
Other	0.9	0.8	1.0	44.8	0.89
Total	100.0	100.0	100.0		
Location					
Urban	28.4	14.8	41.6	25.5	0.52
Rural	71.6	85.2	58.4	58.6	1.19
Total	100.0	100.0	100.0		
State					
Johore	13.4	12.4	14.3	45.7	0.93
Kedah	11.3	14.6	8.2	63.2	1.29
Kelantan	9.5	14.8	4.5	76.1	1.56
Malacca	4.6	4.2	5.0	44.9	0.91
Negri Sembilan	4.7	4.3	5.1	44.8	0.91
Pahang	5.8	5.1	6.5	43.2	0.88
Penang	8.5	7.5	9.4	43.7	0.88
Perak	17.8	17.5	18.0	48.6	0.98
Perlis	1.5	2.3	0.8	73.9	1.53
Selangor	18.2	10.8	25.4	29.2	0.59
Trengganu	4.7	6.5	2.8	68.9	1.38
Total	100.0	100.0	100.0		
Employment status of head					
Employer	2.7	0.5	4.8	8.8	0.19
Employee	51.8	41.8	61.2	39.1	0.81
Own-account worker	39.3	51.9	27.4	64.0	1.32
Housewife or houseworker	2.6	2.3	2.9	42.8	0.88
Unemployed	3.6	3.5	3.7	47.2	0.97
Total	100.0	100.0	100.0		
Occupation of head					
Professional and technical	5.7	1.2	9.8	10.6	0.21
Administrative and managerial	3.3	0.7	5.8	9.5	0.21
Clerical and related	4.0	0.9	6.9	10.7	0.23

(Table continues on the following page.)

Table 4-6 (*continued*).

Selected characteristic of household	Percentage distribution among all households (1)	Percentage distribution among poverty households (2)	Percentage distribution among nonpoverty households (3)	Incidence of poverty (percent) (4)	Relative incidence of poverty (2)/(1) (5)
Sales	11.5	7.2	15.5	30.5	0.63
Service	8.3	4.6	11.7	27.0	0.55
Farmers	27.6	43.5	12.7	76.4	1.58
Farm laborers	21.6	28.5	15.2	63.8	1.32
Production	18.0	13.4	22.4	36.0	0.74
Total	100.0	100.0	100.0		
Sector of employment of head					
Agriculture	24.1	37.5	11.5	75.4	1.56
Agricultural products	25.7	32.7	19.1	61.7	1.27
Mining and quarrying	1.8	1.3	2.3	34.0	0.72
Manufacturing	8.6	5.7	11.2	32.3	0.66
Construction	3.2	2.4	4.0	36.6	0.75
Public utilities	1.6	1.3	2.0	37.0	0.81
Commerce	12.6	7.9	17.1	30.3	0.63
Transport and communications	5.5	4.2	6.8	36.6	0.76
Services	16.9	7.0	26.0	20.3	0.41
Total	100.0	100.0	100.0		
Education of head					
None	32.1	40.6	23.8	62.3	1.26
Some primary	33.1	36.2	30.2	53.7	1.09
Completed primary	20.4	19.8	21.0	47.7	0.97
Lower secondary (forms I–III)	6.7	2.6	10.6	19.0	0.39
Some upper secondary (forms IV–V)	3.0	0.5	5.4	7.6	0.17
School certificate or higher	4.7	0.3	9.0	3.3	0.06
Total	100.0	100.0	100.0		
Sex of head					
Male	81.7	79.2	84.2	47.7	0.97
Female	18.3	20.8	15.8	56.1	1.14
Total	100.0	100.0	100.0		

Selected characteristic of household	Percentage distribution among all households (1)	Percentage distribution among poverty households (2)	Percentage distribution among nonpoverty households (3)	Incidence of poverty (percent) (4)	Relative incidence of poverty (2)/(1) (5)
Age of head					
Under 20	1.5	1.2	1.8	38.3	0.80
20–29	15.3	11.8	18.7	37.9	0.77
30–39	25.2	26.6	23.9	51.9	1.06
40–49	22.9	25.4	20.5	54.5	1.11
50–59	19.1	18.1	19.9	46.9	0.95
60+	16.0	16.9	15.2	51.9	1.06
Total	100.0	100.0	100.0		
Household size					
1	8.9	4.3	13.4	23.5	0.48
2	9.5	7.8	11.3	40.2	0.82
3	11.7	9.3	13.9	39.3	0.79
4	13.1	11.6	14.5	43.8	0.89
5	12.6	14.5	10.7	56.7	1.15
6	12.0	13.8	10.3	56.5	1.15
7	9.8	10.4	9.2	52.3	1.06
8	7.9	10.4	5.5	65.0	1.32
9	5.5	7.3	3.7	65.5	1.33
10+	9.0	10.6	7.5	57.8	1.18
Total	100.0	100.0	100.0		
Number of children under age 15					
0	24.7	14.4	34.8	28.6	0.58
1	17.0	14.8	19.1	43.0	0.87
2	15.5	15.2	15.3	40.2	0.99
3	13.6	15.8	11.4	57.3	1.16
4	11.5	14.5	8.6	62.2	1.26
5+	17.7	25.3	10.3	70.4	1.43
Total	100.0	100.0	100.0		
Number of income recipients					
0	1.3	2.5	0.0	99.0	1.92
1	57.8	64.0	51.9	54.4	1.11
2	26.4	24.2	28.6	45.1	0.92
3	9.1	6.7	11.4	36.0	0.74
4+	5.4	2.6	8.1	23.9	0.48
Total	100.0	100.0	100.0		

Note: The poverty line is defined at a per capita household income of M$33 per month; 49.3 percent of all households fall below this line.

with per capita household income above M$185 per month, certain characteristics of "richness" are apparent from table 4-4. Of the 5.0 percent rich households, 3.2 percent reside in urban areas and 1.8 percent in rural areas. As many as 11.4 percent of urban households, but only 2.6 percent of rural households, are rich. Only 2.0 percent of Malay households are rich, compared with 8.8 percent of Chinese, 7.3 percent of Indian, and 33.5 percent of other races.[38] Of rich households 55.8 percent are Chinese, compared with 21.5 percent Malay, 16.9 percent Indian, and 5.8 percent others. Further characteristics (not shown in table 4-4) of the top 5 percent of households are:[39]

1. Almost three-quarters (73.8 percent) of the rich are concentrated in the four states of Johore, Penang, Perak, and Selangor, with Selangor itself accounting for 37.7 percent.

2. Households whose heads are employers are overrepresented among the rich by a factor of 4.26 (that is, they show a relative incidence of richness of 4.26), and those whose heads are own-account workers are underrepresented (with a relative incidence of 0.33). Among rich households 2.3 percent have heads who are unemployed, and 3.4 percent of households with unemployed heads are rich.

3. With respect to sector of employment, heads of rich households are highly concentrated in services (46.7 percent), commerce (20.3 percent), and manufacturing (12.0 percent). Few of them are to be found in agriculture (3.1 percent) or agricultural products (5.4 percent), which also accords with the occupational finding that few are farmers (2.3 percent) or farm laborers (1.2 percent). Indeed, an extremely small percentage of households whose heads are farmers (0.5 percent) or farm laborers (0.3 percent) are rich.[40] In contrast, the professional and technical and the administrative and managerial categories each have an incidence of richness above 30 percent.

4. Education of the household head seems positively correlated with the household's being rich. Only 1.2 percent of households whose heads have no education belong to the M$185 + group, compared with 45.5 percent of

---

38. This last fact, together with 40.3 percent of "others" being poor (table 4-3), confirms the wide income inequality within this racial group noted in chapter 3.

39. A detailed profile of the rich is contained in Anand (1974a), pp. 29-37, which also has a disaggregation according to separate urban and rural profiles.

40. The incidence of richness among urban households whose heads are farmers is 2.8 percent, whereas that among rural households whose heads are farmers is 0.4 percent. This is to some extent explained by different cropping patterns in urban and rural areas, with urban farmers probably growing high-value perishables such as fruits and vegetables for nearby markets.

those whose heads have a school certificate (form V) or more.[41] The chances of being rich improve significantly for households whose heads have completed even some secondary education.

5. Other, demographic features of richness stand in mirror image to those associated with poverty.

41. The strong relation persists even when rural areas are considered separately from urban areas: 36.9 percent of rural households whose heads have a school certificate or higher education are rich (51.1 percent of urban households). While I have partially tested for the effect of education on income in urban areas (see chapter 7), no such test has been conducted for rural areas. The evidence here, however, suggests that even in rural areas living standards are positively correlated with education.

5

Subgroups in Poverty

WITH 87.7 PERCENT OF POOR HOUSEHOLDS located in rural areas, it seems probable that rural development will form a major instrument for the redress of poverty in Malaysia. The possibilities for absorption of the rural poor into the modern industrial sector are obviously limited by its small absolute base and growth, whereas several million acres of land are still available for cultivation and development in the country. Chapter 8 contains a general analysis of alternative policy instruments to alleviate poverty in Malaysia, including tax, price, and transfer policies. But in the present chapter I anticipate the conclusions of that discussion to a large extent, and assume that rural development through land (re-)settlement and the further development of existing agriculture will form a major means for raising the income levels of the poor. Hence it is clear that a detailed statistical picture of rural poverty is needed.

This chapter begins by investigating the broad characteristics of rural poverty at the one-digit level of detail for the variables of industry and occupation.[1] From the general features of this poverty map, I then zero in on specific subgroups that display especially high rates of poverty. The purpose is not merely better diagnosis of the problem, but more efficient design of rural development policies—which reduce leakages to the nonpoor. Improvement in the targeting of such policies requires the identification of smaller and more homogeneous groups than those shown in the one-digit profile. This is done here by two methods: (1) increasing the selected level of detail to characterize relevant variables (when this is possible), and (2) cross-classifying these variables to obtain a multidimensional profile of the poor. The rural poor in Malaysia are thus disaggregated into operationally and analytically meaningful subgroups with selected values of the industrial sector and occupational variables cross-classified at the two-digit level.[2] From the two-digit matrix which is

1. See notes to tables 6-9 and 6-11.
2. A caveat must be entered here. The PES classification is determined by the occupation or industry which accounts for the bulk of the individual's income, although the individual may

generated, I select the five largest subgroups in poverty, which together account for as many as 79 percent of poor rural households with known occupations. These subgroups are further disaggregated regionally to determine their concentration by state.

The five subgroups are paddy farmers, laborers on paddy and mixed-agriculture farms, rubber smallholders, workers on rubber estates and smallholdings, and fishermen. The economic problems of these subgroups, and measures to raise their productivity and income, are discussed case by case. This allows the identification of some major components of rural development policies and projects in Malaysia. The chapter ends with a brief discussion of other rural subgroups in poverty.

Urban poverty is examined separately in the appendix to this chapter. Although urban poverty accounts for a relatively small proportion of overall poverty (12.3 percent of all poor households are urban), its dimensions are quite different from those of rural poverty and consequently antipoverty policies are likely to be different in the two locations. Furthermore, given the attention recently placed on the growing problem of urban poverty in developing countries (see, for example, McNamara, 1975), a separate discussion of this question seems warranted in the Malaysian context.

The emphasis placed in this chapter on particular subgroups takes for granted the importance of the microapproach to the alleviation of poverty. Such an approach helps us not only to understand better the causes and circumstances of poverty, but also to suggest policy packages in specific cases (such as land settlement and certain types of agricultural development). In a recent survey paper on distributional issues in development planning, Michael Bruno (1977) concludes:

> With all my natural bias in favour of a general equilibrium approach I believe some of the most vexing problems in this area had best be studied by concentrating on specific social or regional groups in which poverty is most concentrated. This of necessity entails a partial equilibrium or micro approach to the problem . . . With our present knowledge and resource limitations this may be the avenue of highest marginal social product.

Rural Poverty

The broad characteristics of rural poverty are examined in this section at the one-digit level of detail for the industrial sector and occupational

---

have income from other occupations or industries. This can affect policy conclusions premised on a classification by a single occupation or industry.

variables. Since rural poverty accounts for the bulk of overall poverty, considering the rural poor in isolation does not give a picture very different from that of overall poverty. Table 5-1 presents a full profile of rural poverty at the one-digit level.[3]

The incidence of poverty in rural Malaysia (44.6 percent) is higher than in the country as a whole (36.5 percent), and it is higher for each racial group considered separately. Malays constitute an even larger fraction of rural poor households (83.9 percent) than they do of all poor households (78.1 percent). In this sense, rural poverty seems largely synonymous with Malay poverty, and government policies to redress rural poverty will also help to narrow racial income imbalances slightly (see chapter 8).

Households whose heads are farmers or farm laborers account for 82.8 percent of the rural poor, with the former accounting for 51.6 percent and the latter for 31.2 percent. Households headed by farmers show a higher poverty incidence (62.5 percent) than those headed by farm laborers (49.3 percent). This phenomenon is probably attributable to the dual economy noted earlier within the rural sector.[4] Farm laborers are both those who work on paddy and rubber smallholdings and vegetable farms, and those employed in the plantation sector, which is largely unionized and relatively well paid. Farmers include not merely owner-operators but also tenant farmers (sharecroppers), who pay half (*bagi dua*) to two-thirds (*bagi tiga*) of their gross income as rent—a fact often invoked to explain their poverty. Furthermore, landlessness is not widespread, and those employed at relatively low wages on smallholdings constitute a small fraction of all farm laborers.[5] Hence, the farm laborer category is less prone to poverty than the farmer category.[6]

3. Table 5-10 in the appendix to this chapter presents the rural poverty profile corresponding to the M$33 per month poverty line implicit in the Third Malaysia Plan (TMP).

4. Another possible explanation would be that farmers suffered temporary poverty owing to adverse price movements in 1970, whereas the majority of farm laborers (estate workers) were shielded against price fluctuations through their unions' sliding-scale agreements with the estates. This suggestion must be rejected, however, because 1970 was not an abnormal year for rubber prices, and paddy prices continued to be supported at a stable level.

5. In the Muda project area, for instance, less than 10 percent of the work force consisted of landless laborers. A possible explanation for the limited extent of landlessness in Malaysia may be found in Muslim inheritance law. Under this law, land tends to be equally divided among the heirs, in contrast to the practice of primogeniture, and often results in uneconomic holdings and endemic poverty.

6. In India, however, landlessness is prevalent, and agricultural laborers show the highest incidence of poverty in rural areas (Dandekar and Rath, 1971).

Interestingly, this finding does not hold for each racial group separately. For the Chinese, the incidence of poverty is higher among households headed by farm laborers (22.5 percent) than among those headed by

(*Text continues on page 150.*)

Table 5-1. Profile of Rural Poverty at a Poverty Line of M$25

Selected characteristic of household	Percentage distribution among all rural households (1)	Percentage distribution among rural poverty households (2)	Percentage distribution among rural nonpoverty households (3)	Incidence of rural poverty (percent) (4)	Relative incidence of rural poverty (2)/(1) (5)
Race					
Malay	67.1	83.9	53.5	55.8	1.25
Chinese	21.7	8.8	32.2	18.1	0.41
Indian	10.5	6.3	13.8	27.0	0.60
Other	0.7	1.0	0.5	59.7	1.43
Total	100.0	100.0	100.0		
State					
Johore	13.8	11.9	15.2	38.6	0.86
Kedah	13.6	16.3	11.5	53.3	1.20
Kelantan	11.5	17.7	6.5	68.6	1.54
Malacca	5.2	4.3	5.9	37.0	0.83
Negri Sembilan	5.6	4.4	6.6	35.0	0.79
Pahang	6.4	5.3	7.2	37.2	0.83
Penang	6.1	5.5	6.6	40.4	0.90
Perak	17.5	16.7	18.1	42.6	0.95
Perlis	2.1	2.8	1.6	58.7	1.33
Selangor	13.1	8.1	17.2	27.5	0.62
Trengganu	5.1	7.0	3.6	61.2	1.37
Total	100.0	100.0	100.0		
Employment status of head					
Employer	1.6	0.4	2.6	10.3	0.25
Employee	47.8	36.3	56.8	33.3	0.76
Own-account worker	45.6	58.1	35.8	55.9	1.27
Housewife or houseworker	2.1	1.8	2.2	38.9	0.86
Unemployed	2.9	3.4	2.6	50.6	1.17
Total	100.0	100.0	100.0		

(*Table continues on the following page.*)

Table 5-1 *(continued)*.

Selected characteristic of household	Percentage distribution among all rural households (1)	Percentage distribution among rural poverty households (2)	Percentage distribution among rural nonpoverty households (3)	Incidence of rural poverty (percent) (4)	Relative incidence of rural poverty (2)/(1) (5)
Occupation of head					
Professional and technical	4.1	0.9	6.6	9.5	0.22
Administrative and managerial	2.5	0.4	4.1	7.4	0.16
Clerical and related	2.1	0.2	3.6	3.9	0.10
Sales	7.9	5.1	10.2	28.4	0.65
Service	5.5	2.1	8.2	16.8	0.38
Farmers	36.4	51.6	24.4	62.5	1.42
Farm laborers	27.8	31.2	25.2	49.3	1.12
Production	13.7	8.5	17.7	27.4	0.62
Total	100.0	100.0	100.0		
Sector of employment of head					
Agriculture	31.1	44.6	20.6	62.7	1.43
Agricultural products	34.1	36.7	32.1	46.9	1.08
Mining and quarrying	1.9	0.8	2.7	19.3	0.42
Manufacturing	5.8	4.2	7.1	31.7	0.72
Construction	2.2	1.4	2.8	28.3	0.64
Public utilities	1.1	0.6	1.5	23.1	0.55
Commerce	8.7	5.8	11.0	29.2	0.67
Transport and communications	3.9	2.4	5.0	27.3	0.62
Services	11.2	3.5	17.2	13.6	0.31
Total	100.0	100.0	100.0		
Education of head					
None	35.0	43.7	28.0	55.6	1.25
Some primary	34.6	35.5	33.9	45.7	1.03
Completed primary	21.5	18.7	23.8	38.8	0.87
Lower secondary (forms I–III)	4.7	1.7	7.0	16.5	0.36
Some upper secondary (forms IV–V)	1.6	0.2	2.7	7.0	0.13
School certificate or higher	2.6	0.2	4.6	2.8	0.08
Total	100.0	100.0	100.0		

Selected characteristic of household	Percentage distribution among all rural households (1)	Percentage distribution among rural poverty households (2)	Percentage distribution among rural nonpoverty households (3)	Incidence of rural poverty (percent) (4)	Relative incidence of rural poverty (2)/(1) (5)
Sex of head					
Male	82.5	78.8	85.4	42.6	0.96
Female	17.5	21.2	14.6	53.8	1.21
Total	100.0	100.0	100.0		
Age of head					
Under 20	1.4	1.2	1.5	39.1	0.86
20–29	15.2	12.0	17.7	35.4	0.79
30–39	25.1	26.5	23.9	47.1	1:06
40–49	22.6	24.8	21.0	48.8	1.10
50–59	19.0	18.2	19.7	42.6	0.96
60 +	16.7	17.3	16.2	46.1	1.04
Total	100.0	100.0	100.0		
Household size					
1	8.0	5.8	9.8	32.3	0.73
2	9.9	6.3	12.7	28.6	0.64
3	12.1	9.9	13.8	36.7	0.82
4	13.3	12.0	14.4	40.1	0.90
5	13.0	14.1	12.1	48.4	1.08
6	12.6	13.9	11.5	49.2	1.10
7	9.9	12.5	7.9	56.2	1.26
8	7.9	9.6	6.5	54.3	1.22
9	5.3	6.0	4.7	50.6	1.13
10 +	8.0	9.9	6.6	54.8	1.24
Total	100.0	100.0	100.0		
Number of children under age 15					
0	22.8	14.4	29.6	28.1	0.63
1	17.5	15.0	19.5	38.3	0.86
2	15.8	15.6	15.8	44.3	0.99
3	13.8	15.6	12.4	50.3	1.13
4	12.0	14.9	9.7	55.4	1.24
5 +	18.1	24.5	13.0	60.3	1.35
Total	100.0	100.0	100.0		
Number of income recipients					
0	1.3	2.8	0.0	98.7	2.15
1	59.7	67.2	53.7	50.2	1.13
2	26.9	23.0	30.2	38.0	0.86
3	8.1	5.3	10.3	29.4	0.65
4 +	4.0	1.7	5.8	19.5	0.43
Total	100.0	100.0	100.0		

Note: The poverty line is defined at a per capita household income of M$25 per month; 44.6 percent of all rural households fall below this line.

farmers (18.5 percent), although the reverse holds for the other communities. These figures probably reflect the economic situation in the predominantly Chinese "New Villages," in which a majority of the residents are thought to be underemployed laborers engaged on smallholdings or nonunionized estates where wages are low.[7] The obverse of this situation for farm laborers is the fact that Chinese farmers have larger landholdings than Malay farmers. In the rubber sector, for which some data are available, the average Chinese smallholding is almost twice as large as the average Malay smallholding.

In accordance with the results for the occupational variable, households whose heads are in the one-digit industrial sectors of agriculture and agricultural products account for 81.3 percent of the rural poor. Households headed by those in agriculture account for 44.6 percent of the rural poor and show a poverty rate of 62.7 percent, while households headed by those in agricultural products account for 36.7 percent of the rural poor and show a poverty rate of 46.9 percent. The importance of these sectors in accounting for relatively high rates of poverty survives the breakdown by racial group (and, in fact, the breakdown by location; see the appendix to this chapter, "Urban Poverty"). Given that the industrial sector and occupational variables are both economically and operationally relevant in identifying target groups, the one-digit categories agriculture and agricultural products, and farmers and farm laborers, should be disaggregated further, especially since they each account for more than 80 percent of rural poverty. This is done in the next section, which considers the occupational and industrial sector variables at the two-digit level and, further, cross-classifies them to obtain a still more precise definition of target groups.

The breakdown of rural poverty by the employment status of the household head is consistent with the above findings. Households headed by own-account workers and employees make up 58.1 and 36.3 percent, respectively, of the rural poor and show poverty incidences of 55.9 and 33.3 percent, respectively. Households with unemployed heads account for a very small percentage (3.4 percent) of the rural poor and show a poverty incidence (50.6 percent) which is lower than for households headed by own-account workers. In fact, the phenomenon of open unemployment is insignificant (2.9 percent) among household heads in rural areas. Underemployment, both among households (in terms of low participation rates and number of income recipients) and among individuals within households, is much more important as a factor determining the degree of

7. These New Villages, now some 465 in number with a total population of about 1 million, were established in 1950–52 to contain the communist insurgency. Resettled with Chinese, the villages suffer from a severe land shortage, and many of the farm families earn a livelihood through market gardening, the cultivation of tapioca, and the like.

poverty. Thus, the incidence of poverty drops markedly with additional income recipients, from 98.7 percent for households with no recipients to 19.5 percent for households with four or more recipients. The incidence of poverty tends to rise, however, with household size.[8] Together with the previous finding, this suggests that poverty incidence is likely to be negatively correlated with the participation rate of a household. A manifestation of the increase in poverty with the household dependency ratio is the fact that the poverty percentage rises with the number of children under age fifteen, from 28.1 percent for no children to 60.3 percent for five or more children.

Other features of rural poverty remain largely unaltered in comparison with overall poverty.[9] The four poorest states of Kedah, Kelantan, Perlis, and Trengganu account for 43.8 percent of rural poverty, compared with 41.5 percent of overall poverty. The educational characteristics of the rural poor show that 97.9 percent of rural poverty, compared with 97.2 percent of overall poverty, is concentrated in households where the head has primary education or less. The demographic characteristics of poverty, that is, those pertaining to age or sex of household head, are virtually the same in rural areas as in Peninsular Malaysia as a whole.

The one-digit profile presented of the rural poor gives a broad indication of groups which account for a significant proportion of poverty and also suffer a high incidence. But these groups are too widely defined for the purpose of designing effective poverty action programs. Further targeting is needed within these categories by relevant variables. For example, farmer households, which account for more than half of rural poverty, need to be narrowed down at least by region and sector (or commodity) at the two-digit level. Such cross-classifications will allow subgroups such as paddy farmers in Trengganu and rubber smallholders in Kelantan to be singled out. The cross-tabulations will also permit estimates of poverty among subgroups traditionally thought to be poor, such as fishermen along the East Coast of Peninsular Malaysia and rubber farmers in Perak.

Two-digit PES Subgroups

In the following subsections the PES is used to isolate specific subgroups in poverty with a view to discussing policy measures to raise their incomes.

8. Among poverty households in rural areas the average number of income recipients is 1.36 and the average household size, 5.77. The comparable figures for all households in Malaysia are 1.63 and 5.36, respectively (tables 3-3 and 3-6).

9. The incidence of rural poverty, however, is greater than that of overall (or urban) poverty in each category, owing to rural incomes being lower than overall (or urban) incomes and the degree of inequality being fairly similar in the two locations.

To minimize leakages, groups selected should be homogeneous and show high rates of poverty. To keep the number of separate groups and policies down to a manageable level, the subgroups selected should account for a significant fraction of total poverty. First, the one-digit classification of rural poor is refined according to the industrial sector and occupational variables. Selected values of these variables are disaggregated to the two-digit level (the finest level of detail available in PES) and then cross-classified to generate a matrix of rural poverty (table 5-2). Although this procedure does not allow estimates of poverty among all the subgroups in the population believed to be poor, it does isolate the major target groups in the rural sector by commodity and occupation.[10]

Table 5-2 shows the incidence of poverty, the number of households in poverty, and the total number of households for each occupational-industrial subgroup. The two-digit industrial groups are a disaggregation of the one-digit categories, agriculture and agricultural products; and the two-digit occupational groups are a disaggregation of the one-digit categories, farmers and farm laborers.[11] Some of the subgroups defined by the cells of the matrix correspond to groups identified by the Economic Planning Unit (EPU) of the government of Malaysia in its "Survey of Rural Poverty."[12] In that survey, EPU estimated poverty among six rural subgroups in 1970 using the one-digit figures contained in Anand (1974a), supplemented where possible by information from existing socioeconomic surveys of the Ministry of Agriculture. Now that I have computed a two-digit matrix of poverty, it can be compared with EPU's estimates for some of these groups.

According to table 5-2 the five largest subgroups in poverty are:

Paddy smallholders and livestock and mixed-agriculture farmers (01×61)

Laborers on paddy and livestock and mixed-agriculture farms (01×62)

Rubber smallholders (11×61)

Laborers on rubber estates and smallholdings (11×62)

Fishermen (04×64).

10. Aziz (1975*b*), for example, intuitively singled out the following subgroups as poor: Chinese rubber and vegetable farmers and residents of the New Villages, Teochow farmers in mainland Penang, several fishing communities along the West Coast of Peninsular Malaysia, vegetable farmers in the Cameron Highlands, pineapple farmers in South Johore, and Trengganu fishermen.

11. The one-digit categories, agriculture and agricultural products, make up codes 01–09 and 11–19, respectively, of the PES two-digit industrial classification (see table 6-9). The one-digit categories, farmers and farm laborers, make up codes 61 and 62–69, respectively, of the PES two-digit occupational classification (see table 6-11).

12. This survey (EPU, 1975) was prepared as a background paper to the Third Malaysia Plan.

These five subgroups together account for as much as 79 percent of impoverished rural households whose heads have known occupations: 5,123 out of 6,481 households.[13] A few small subgroups in sectors such as coconut, oil palm, forestry, tea, and coffee can also be singled out by means of table 5-2. The economic problems of the five largest subgroups in poverty, located by state, and measures to raise their incomes, are discussed in the following subsections.

Paddy Farmers

The paddy farmer subgroup has probably attracted greatest attention in the context of Malaysian poverty. The relatively low incomes in paddy are revealed by the fact that whereas 20 percent of the working population is engaged in this subsector, only 5 percent of GDP originates there (Selvadurai, 1972*a*). Socioeconomic surveys of paddy farms in different parts of the country distinguish between specialized paddy growers and others.[14] According to Selvadurai (1972*a*), specialized paddy farms (those with more than three-quarters of the farm acreage in paddy) constitute about 50 percent of all farms cultivating paddy. The nonspecialized paddy farms are generally engaged in mixed agriculture (including fruits and vegetables), livestock, and miscellaneous crops.

The two-digit commodity classification in PES does not distinguish between purely paddy farmers and those who grow paddy along with other crops (table 5-2). For the combined category of paddy smallholders and livestock and mixed-agriculture farmers, the poverty incidence is an alarming 65.8 percent—in other words, two out of three such farmers are poor.[15] The group is predominantly Malay (88.5 percent), with an ethnic composition and poverty incidence as follows:

	Malay	*Chinese*	*Indian*	*Other*	*All races*
Incidence of poverty (percent)	69.8	24.8	37.9	87.3	65.8
Number of poor households	2,204	79	11	55	2,349
Total number of households	3,159	319	29	63	3,570

13. For some 1,500 rural households in poverty, either the head is not in the labor force or the occupation is not available.

14. Purcal (1971) contains a valuable description of several socioeconomic surveys of paddy households. Some of the important surveys are Selvadurai (1972*b*, 1972*c*, and 1975); Narkswasdi and Selvadurai (1968); Selvadurai and Ani (1969); Selvadurai, Ani, and Nik Hassan (1969).

15. EPU (1975) estimated poverty among paddy cultivators separately from that among mixed-agriculture farmers. Its estimates for these groups are 75 and 78 percent, respectively.

Table 5-2. Incidence of Poverty by Two-digit Industrial Sector and Occupational Group

Code number	Two-digit industrial sector [a]	Two-digit occupational group [a]				Subtotal of occupations 61–64	Total of all occupations
		61 Farmers	62 Farm laborers	63 Forestry workers	64 Fishermen, hunters, and related workers		
01	Paddy, livestock, and mixed agriculture						
	Incidence of poverty (percent)	65.8	63.9	—[b]	—	65.5	63.9
	Number of poor households	2,349	327	0	—	2,676	2,710
	Total number of households	3,570	512	1	0	4,083	4,238
02	Forestry						
	Incidence of poverty (percent)	—[b]	—[b]	33.3	—[b]	31.4	30.5
	Number of poor households	0	0	20	2	22	36
	Total number of households	1	4	60	5	70	118
04	Fishing						
	Incidence of poverty (percent)	—[b]	—	—	50.9	50.8	50.7
	Number of poor households	0	—	—	315	315	317
	Total number of households	1	0	0	619	620	625
11	Rubber						
	Incidence of poverty (percent)	55.6	47.5	—	—	50.9	47.3
	Number of poor households	981	1,151	—	—	2,132	2,196
	Total number of households	1,764	2,423	0	0	4,187	4,641
12	Oil palm						
	Incidence of poverty (percent)	—[b]	23.5	—	—	23.1	20.9
	Number of poor households	1	44	—	—	45	49
	Total number of households	8	187	0	0	195	235

13	Coconut, copra, and coconut oil						
	Incidence of poverty (percent)	49.3	61.9	—	—	56.0	55.8
	Number of poor households	68	99	—	—	167	174
	Total number of households	138	160	0	0	298	312
14	Tea						
	Incidence of poverty (percent)	—	15.4	—	—	15.4	10.0
	Number of poor households	—	2	—	—	2	2
	Total number of households	0	13	0	0	13	20
15	Coffee						
	Incidence of poverty (percent)	44.4	60.0	—	—	50.0	46.7
	Number of poor households	8	6	—	—	14	14
	Total number of households	18	10	0	0	28	30
	Subtotal of industries 01–15						
	Incidence of poverty (percent)	61.9	49.2	32.8	50.8	56.6	53.8
	Number of poor households	3,407	1,629	20	317	5,373	5,498
	Total number of households	5,500	3,309	61	624	9,494	10,219
	Total of all industries						
	Incidence of poverty (percent)	61.9	48.5	32.4	50.8	56.1	
	Number of poor households	3,423	1,767	23	318	5,531	
	Total number of households	5,529	3,641	71	626	9,867	

— Not applicable.

a. The two-digit occupational classification is from Department of Statistics (1971a), and the two-digit industrial classification is from Department of Statistics (1971b).

b. Denotes sample size too small for statistically valid inference.

Many of the Chinese farmers are so-called market gardeners growing fruits and vegetables for market sales.

The distribution by state of paddy smallholders and mixed-agriculture farmers is shown in table 5-3. Although paddy is grown in all eleven states of Peninsular Malaysia, the northern states are the most important producers of this crop. Whereas for Peninsular Malaysia as a whole, 14 percent of cultivated land is under paddy, the corresponding percentages for the northern states of Perlis, Kedah, Kelantan, and Trengganu are 75, 36, 35, and 26 percent, respectively.[16] These four states account for 65 percent of the paddy land in Peninsular Malaysia and are sometimes called the rice bowl of the country. From table 5-3 it is clear that these states account for the bulk of poverty in paddy and mixed agriculture (70.1 percent). The poverty incidence in the rice-bowl states varies from 64.8 percent for Perlis to 79.0 percent for Trengganu.

The average size of paddy farms in Malaysia has been estimated at 3.1 acres (Selvadurai, 1972a, p. 41). About 55 percent of the farms are less than three acres, and 80 percent are less than five acres. The size of landholding is a major factor affecting the income level of paddy farmers.[17] Small and fragmentary holdings are to a large extent the result of the system of inheritance in the country. Consolidation of existing land and resettlement on larger holdings of land newly developed by the Federal Land Development Authority (FELDA) are possible solutions to this problem.

Another major factor contributing to poverty among paddy farmers is the low productivity of paddy in relation to other crops.[18] To some extent the problem of low incomes can be tackled by increasing yields on paddy land. An important government program to assist this subgroup is

16. See Selvadurai (1972a), table 2-2. Except for Penang, which has 24 percent, other states have a considerably smaller percentage of land under paddy.

17. The problems of paddy smallholders, and measures to raise their incomes, are discussed extensively in FAO/World Bank (1975), annex E.

18. The tenurial status of farmers is sometimes said to affect the incomes they earn. About 40 percent of paddy land in Peninsular Malaysia is leased to tenant farmers under fixed rent (in cash or paddy) or crop-sharing leases. Two alleged features of sharecropping in developing countries are: (1) reduced incentives for the use of inputs and for on-farm investment (such as to improve land for double-cropping); and (2) very high rentals which cause poverty among tenant farmers. Recent empirical work by Huang, however, casts doubt on the validity of these arguments for Malaysia. Huang (1975, table 5) finds that productivity is not adversely affected by tenancy, and that tenants and owner-tenants (those who both own and rent land) have significantly higher yields than owner-cultivators. Tenants also appear to use more fertilizer than owner-cultivators and to adopt double-cropping just as readily. Finally, Huang finds that the poverty of paddy tenants is due not to exorbitant rentals but to the relatively low profitability of paddy farming compared with other crops or wage employment.

therefore irrigation and drainage to provide for double-cropping. The extension of irrigation facilities was initiated during the Second Malaysia Plan,[19] when it was intended to increase the double-cropped area from one-third of all paddy land in the country to two-thirds. The scope for double-cropping is, however, limited by the availability of surface water and the topography.[20] In any case, double-cropping needs to be supplemented by direct measures to improve yield.[21] The FAO/World Bank (1975) report suggests that average yields fall short of best-practice yields on the order of 40 percent; it emphasizes the use of higher-yielding varieties and more fertilizer and pesticides. The adoption of these inputs clearly depends on the quality and intensity of extension services and the availability of credit. Policies aimed at alleviating poverty by raising productivity also help fulfill the government's target of self-sufficiency in rice.

There is a residual category of paddy farmers who cannot be lifted out of poverty by productivity-raising measures: those whose holdings are too small to generate sufficient income even with double-cropping and best-practice yields. The long-term solution to this problem lies in encouraging such smallholders to switch to more remunerative crops or occupations.

Laborers in Paddy and Mixed Agriculture

The two-digit occupation-industry matrix shows a poverty incidence of 63.9 percent for farm laborer households in paddy, livestock, and mixed agriculture (table 5-2).[22] This small subgroup consists mainly of employees on the larger smallholdings who, unlike estate workers, are neither unionized nor covered by formal wage agreements. Some farm laborers may possess fractional parcels of land, but these make only a modest contribution to their total income. On the whole, the subgroup is landless and relies on wage employment for support. The conditions of employment are diverse, and many work as agricultural laborers on vegetable, poultry, and mixed-agriculture farms. Many are also employed as seasonal laborers in paddy, especially in the double-cropping areas.[23]

19. Large irrigation works have begun in Muda (the states of Kedah and Perlis), Kemubu (Kelantan), and Besut (Trengganu).

20. The limit has been estimated by EPU (1975) at about 75 percent of total paddy area. Remunerative off-season crops need to be identified for the 25 percent which cannot be double-cropped. Tobacco has been successfully tried among Kelantan farmers; other crops such as fruits and vegetables could also be tried.

21. See Selvadurai (1972a), table 2-6, p. 21, for estimates of yield variation across states.

22. The EPU (1975, p. 33) estimate of poverty incidence for this subgroup is 80 percent, but this is stated to be based on "shaky" information.

23. For tasks such as transplanting and harvesting of paddy, family labor is often insufficient, and it is necessary to hire outside labor.

Table 5-3. Incidence of Poverty among Five PES Subgroups by State

State	Paddy smallholders and livestock and mixed-agriculture farmers (01 × 61)	Laborers on paddy, livestock, and mixed-agriculture farms (01 × 62)	Rubber smallholders (11 × 61)	Laborers on rubber estates or smallholdings (11 × 62)	Fishermen (04 × 64)
Johore					
Incidence of poverty (percent)	39.2	44.6	49.5	42.1	53.1
Number of poor households	38	29	164	246	43
Total number of households	97	65	331	584	81
Kedah					
Incidence of poverty (percent)	66.8	77.7	49.6	51.9	59.1
Number of poor households	588	87	70	182	39
Total number of households	880	112	141	351	66
Kelantan					
Incidence of poverty (percent)	78.7	84.3	63.4	64.6	79.7
Number of poor households	702	75	123	93	51
Total number of households	892	89	194	144	64
Malacca					
Incidence of poverty (percent)	57.6	—[a]	38.7	41.9	35.3
Number of poor households	34	8	29	54	6
Total number of households	59	11	75	129	17
Negri Sembilan					
Incidence of poverty (percent)	55.1	—[a]	58.7	37.7	—[a]
Number of poor households	49	4	105	81	2
Total number of households	89	8	179	215	3

Pahang					
Incidence of poverty (percent)	62.0	—[a]	54.2	48.8	59.3
Number of poor households	134	5	110	60	16
Total number of households	216	15	203	123	27
Penang					
Incidence of poverty (percent)	57.3	57.9	—[a]	58.7	36.9
Number of poor households	110	22	2	37	38
Total number of households	192	38	9	63	103
Perak					
Incidence of poverty (percent)	56.4	44.1	66.2	50.5	43.8
Number of poor households	216	26	278	249	64
Total number of households	383	59	420	493	146
Perlis					
Incidence of poverty (percent)	64.8	80.6	—[a]	—[a]	44.1
Number of poor households	142	25	0	5	15
Total number of households	219	31	2	6	34
Selangor					
Incidence of poverty (percent)	44.9	40.7	39.8	42.0	46.2
Number of poor households	122	22	51	86	6
Total number of households	272	54	128	205	13
Trengganu					
Incidence of poverty (percent)	79.0	80.0	59.8	52.7	53.8
Number of poor households	214	24	49	58	35
Total number of households	271	30	82	110	65
Peninsular Malaysia					
Incidence of poverty (percent)	65.8	63.9	55.6	47.5	50.9
Number of poor households	2,349	327	981	1,151	315
Total number of households	3,570	512	1,764	2,423	619

a. Denotes sample size too small for statistically valid inference.

This subgroup accounts for only 5.8 percent of households in all five subgroups (512 households out of 8,888). Its ethnic composition and poverty breakdown are:

	Malay	Chinese	Indian	Other	All races
Incidence of poverty (percent)	69.6	34.4	31.6	—	63.9
Number of poor households	297	22	6	2	327
Total number of households	427	64	19	2	512

Table 5-3 shows that over half the subgroup is found in the rice-bowl states, which suggests that a large proportion of it probably consists of paddy laborers. Landlessness in these areas is also higher than in other states, and the incidence of poverty there is about 80 percent. There are few direct policy measures which would specifically benefit this subgroup. One measure would be to select them for new land development schemes in paddy, oil palm, rubber, and the like. Even before they are settled, they could be employed as unskilled labor for preparatory work on development sites. A drawback to this measure, however, is that it might remove a valuable supply of agricultural labor at peak periods. Moreover, land-rich states are frequently reluctant to accept residents of other states as settlers. It might be preferable to create nonagricultural employment in the off-peak season through rural public works and the stimulation of local small-scale industry.

Rubber Smallholders

The two-digit occupation-industry matrix (table 5-2) allows us to isolate the important rural subgroup of rubber farmers. Since only a negligible proportion of the rubber farmers (less than 0.5 percent) are estate owners[24] (Barlow and Chan, 1968), the subgroup can be taken as consisting of smallholders. The incidence of poverty among rubber smallholders is thus 55.6 percent, with Malays constituting an overwhelming majority (96.1 percent) of rubber smallholders in poverty. The ethnic composition and breakdown of poverty for this subgroup are:

	Malay	Chinese	Indian	Other	All races
Incidence of poverty (percent)	63.8	11.8	22.7	—	55.6
Number of poor households	943	31	5	2	981
Total number of households	1,477	262	22	3	1,764

Information on the distribution of smallholdings by size is scanty. EPU (1975) estimates 45 percent of smallholdings to be less than five acres, and 90 percent to be less than ten acres.[25] The average size of rubber

---

24. In Malaysia, an estate is defined as a farm larger than 100 acres.

25. FAO/World Bank (1975, p. 70), however, estimates 28 percent of smallholdings to be less than five acres.

smallholdings has been put at 6.6 acres by Barlow and Chan (1968). Of the 2.7 million acres in the country under smallholder rubber, about 60 percent are planted with high-yielding stocks which yield an average of 800 pounds per acre compared with 500 pounds per acre elsewhere. EPU (1975) has calculated poverty percentages separately for the two categories of smallholding: it estimates a 30 percent incidence for owners with high-yielding stock and a 70 percent incidence for those with low-yielding stock.[26] Overall it has estimated a poverty percentage for rubber small-holders of 50 percent, which is reasonably close to my own estimate of 55.6 percent from PES.

Table 5-3 shows that the largest concentration of poor rubber smallhold-ers is in Perak, followed by Johore, Kelantan, Pahang, and Negri Sembilan. These five states account for 79.5 percent of rubber smallholder households in poverty. The poverty incidence is highest in Perak (66.2 percent), followed by Kelantan (63.4 percent), Trengganu (59.8 percent), Negri Sembilan (58.7 percent), and Pahang (54.2 percent). The states with the heaviest concentrations of poor rubber smallholders are different from those with the heaviest concentrations of poor paddy smallholders.

The extent to which smallholder acreages are replanted with high-yielding stock affects the level of poverty. Those with very small-size holdings have been reluctant to take part in government replanting programs, apparently because—although those with larger smallholdings can afford to replant in stages—small growers find it difficult to forgo rubber income during the six to seven years needed for replanting. Government grants are not geared to the maintenance of smallholder income during the long immaturity period but only to the estimated cash outlays required for replanting (cutting and burning old trees, buying new trees, fertilizer, pesticides, and so forth). If smallholders are not to be deterred from replanting, grants need to be set at levels which maintain current income.[27]

The Rubber Industry Smallholders Development Authority (RISDA) has initiated schemes for block replanting that can also increase the financial incentives to replant. Apart from reducing the unit cost of replanting, such schemes might allow smallholders to spread replanting in the block so that some rubber income is maintained during the gestation period. Since the group replanting schemes cannot be implemented, however, without the

26. Estimates of nonrubber income were based on the only available socioeconomic survey of rubber smallholdings: Selvadurai (1972*d*).

27. Some smallholders are ineligible for replanting grants because they are squatters. Although they have no title to their lands they are unlikely ever to be removed from them; if the status of such people were legitimized, they could be included in replanting programs.

consent of the multiple owners of plots, some measures to make participation obligatory for unwilling co-owners might have to be considered.

There appears to be scope for raising smallholder incomes further by
improving production practices. Smallholder yields (800 pounds per acre
for high-yielding stock) are still well below estate yields (about 1,200
pounds per acre) or yields on organized settlement projects with intensive
technical guidance. RISDA could help to raise these yields by increased
extension services, particularly beyond the replanting period.[28]

Some holdings are too small to provide poverty-line incomes, even if they
are replanted with high-yielding stock. EPU (1975) calculations suggest that
holdings of four to five acres in high-yielding materials are sufficient to
generate the 1970 poverty-line income for an average-size household
(earning a "typical" amount of nonrubber income). The Barlow and Chan
(1968) study comes up.with a goal of six to eight acres under high-yielding
materials, which it considers "optimum."[29] To the extent that farm size is
the constraint, fringe alienation schemes might be supported near present
holdings. A government agency such as RISDA could acquire and con-
solidate existing land to create viable-size plots. In the longer term, those
with subeconomic holdings could be encouraged to switch to alternative
crops which generate higher and more stable incomes. Although this policy
might conflict with the government's desire to protect rubber production, it
may nonetheless be the best way of alleviating poverty among this group of
smallholders.

A change in the indirect taxation of rubber is another policy that might
be considered to alleviate poverty among smallholders (discussed in
chapter 8 under general policies[30]). The farm-gate price of smallholder
rubber could be raised significantly by reducing or eliminating the rubber
export tax, which falls almost wholly on producers. This measure would
also stimulate the production of rubber. A general reduction of rubber
taxes would benefit all producers, however, and not just those in poverty.
To minimize leakages, one needs to consider ways of revising the export
duty on rubber so that its incidence is reduced on small producers, say,

28. Various institutional and administrative reforms, such as improved marketing of
smallholder rubber and better coordination of responsible agencies, are discussed in the
FAO/World Bank (1975) report.

29. Such acreage figures suggest that the present allotment of twelve acres on government
(FELDA) land settlement schemes is considerably above that needed to lift a family out of
poverty. It would seem desirable to reduce the land allocation on these schemes to, say, six
acres, and increase the number of families settled.

30. See the subsection entitled "Fiscal Policies" in chapter 8. The possibility of *stabilizing*
the price received by rubber producers is discussed in the subsection entitled "Intervention in
Commodity Markets."

those with acreages below ten to fifteen acres. One method might be to adopt a system of rebates below the acreage limit fixed, possibly in the form of subsidized inputs or higher replanting grants. Another method is to change the base of the tax from a product to a special revenue or production tax on estates, which might be redefined to begin at fifteen to twenty acres instead of a hundred acres as at present.

Laborers on Rubber Estates and Smallholdings

The intersection of the two-digit farm laborer group with the rubber subsector in table 5-2 generates the subgroup of laborers on rubber estates and smallholdings. The definition of a rubber smallholding used by the Malaysian Department of Statistics is "an area contiguous, aggregating less than 100 acres, planted with rubber, or on which the planting of rubber is permitted under a single ownership." Rubber estates account for 1.6 million acres out of the 4.3 million acres in Malaysia planted with rubber in 1970.[31] Smallholdings account for 2.7 million acres, or 63 percent of acreage, but produce only 49 percent of total rubber output. Smallholdings of fewer than ten acres probably account for half the rubber produced by all smallholdings. Most smallholdings between ten and a hundred acres can be expected to hire significant numbers of nonfamily laborers.

The PES, unfortunately, does not distinguish between estates and smallholdings. For the combined subgroup of laborers on estates *and* smallholdings, it shows a poverty incidence of 47.5 percent. The ethnic composition and poverty breakdown for this subgroup are :

	Malay	Chinese	Indian	Other	All races
Incidence of poverty (percent)	64.0	18.6	30.1	—	47.5
Number of poor households	889	79	183	0	1,151
Total number of households	1,390	425	607	1	2,423

The relatively large percentage of Indians in this subgroup reflects their dominant position as estate workers (Ministry of Labour and Manpower, 1972). Malays are not far behind Indians in estate employment, with a share in 1972 of 33 percent compared with the Indians' 40 percent. When laborers on smallholdings are included, Malays form the largest ethnic community (57.4 percent of all households), which reflects their over-whelming majority as laborers on the smallholdings.

Fairly complete information is available on the cash incomes of rubber estate workers. Monthly cash incomes, as recorded in the Ministry of Labour's annual survey, are shown at about M$115 for 1970. Subsidized

---

31. Rubber land in turn accounts for two-thirds of total planted area in the country.

housing and fringe benefits (such as electricity, water, and medical care) are additional and have been estimated by EPU (1975) at approximately M$30 per month for 1970. With further assumptions about household size and number of income recipients, the EPU estimates a poverty incidence of 20 percent among estate worker households. Households below the poverty line are those with few recipients or a large household size, or both, and include some living off the estates who receive negligible nonmonetary benefits. Contract workers and workers on nonunionized estates also constitute some of the poor in this subgroup.

About half of all estate workers are covered by a wage agreement between the National Union of Plantation Workers (NUPW) and the Malayan Agricultural Producers Association (MAPA). This agreement includes a basic wage, an output incentive, and a sliding-scale adjustment for rubber prices. It has succeeded in raising the incomes of unionized workers considerably above those of workers on smallholdings. Even among estate workers not covered by the agreement, wages have clearly been influenced by union scales (EPU, 1975, p. 19). The EPU's poverty estimate of 20 percent for estate workers together with a PES poverty incidence of 47.5 percent for *all* rubber laborers implies a rather high incidence for workers on smallholdings.[32] One policy measure that might help is to extend union-management agreements and Ministry of Labour regulations to smallholdings,[33] but the employment costs of this measure would need to be considered.

Another problem that faces rubber workers is one of redundancy. Estate work has become increasingly mechanized with a general improvement in rubber technology. There has also been a structural shift in recent years from rubber to the less labor-intensive oil palm. The problem of redundancy is likely to continue in the future, yet there are indications of relative immobility, especially among estate workers.[34] One approach is to provide vocational and other training for younger estate workers to prepare them for job mobility. Another approach is to settle poor estate workers on government (FELDA) land schemes.[35] Their previous experience on estates is likely to facilitate the transition.

32. EPU (1975) estimates a poverty incidence of something like 80 percent for all nonestate agricultural laborers.

33. Ministry of Labour regulations might be extended by reducing the minimum acreage defining an estate from the present hundred acres to fifteen to twenty acres.

34. According to FAO/World Bank (1975, p. 39), immobility is "supplemented in many cases by the reluctance of rubber tappers to take on the much harder work of oil palm harvesting."

35. FAO/World Bank (1975, p. 42) notes that special efforts should be made to settle more Indians on public land schemes. It points to the fact that whereas non-Malays have

Fishermen

In table 5-2 the subgroup of fishermen is generated by the intersection of the two-digit occupational code for fishermen, hunters, and related workers with the two-digit industrial code for fishing. It shows that the subgroup of fishing households in Peninsular Malaysia is relatively small (accounting for 7.0 percent of households in all five subgroups), and that its poverty incidence is 50.9 percent. The EPU has also estimated poverty among fishermen by using two socioeconomic surveys of this group.[36] From these surveys EPU (1975) estimates an overall poverty incidence of 65 percent in 1970, with separate incidences of 90 and 40 percent, respectively, for the East and West coasts of the peninsula. This implies that more than two-thirds of poor fishing households reside on the East Coast.

My estimate of overall poverty diverges from that of EPU, and its distribution across states also turns out to be somewhat different. Whereas according to EPU the largest number of poor fishermen reside in Trengganu, followed by Kelantan and East Johore, table 5-3 indicates a different ordering: Perak, Kelantan, and Johore—with heavy concentrations in Kedah and Penang. The PES results also question the view that East Coast fishermen are much poorer (poverty incidence 90 percent) than West Coast fishermen (poverty incidence 40 percent). According to table 5-3, the East Coast states display poverty incidences around 55 percent (Trengganu 53.8 percent and Pahang 59.3 percent); but almost equally high incidences seem to obtain in the West Coast states (Kedah 59.1 percent, Perlis 44.1 percent, and Perak 43.8 percent), with Johore, which is on both coasts, at 53.1 percent.

The subgroup of fishermen shows an ethnic composition and poverty breakdown as follows:

	Malay	*Chinese*	*Indian*	*Other*	*All races*
Incidence of poverty (percent)	60.3	25.9	—	—	50.9
Number of poor households	269	43	2	1	315
Total number of households	446	166	6	1	619

The ethnic breakdown for the subgroup has also been computed for each state separately, although this is not shown here. Between the two coasts there are significant differences in the racial composition of the fishing

---

constituted about 4 percent of settlers in FELDA schemes, their share of applications has run at around 25 percent.

36. See Fisheries Division (1971), and Universiti Sains Malaysia (1972). In fact, these are the only socioeconomic surveys of this group át present available.

population. In the eastern states almost all fishing households are Malay, while in the western states, particularly Penang and Perak, about half the fishermen in poverty are Chinese. On the whole, however, poverty among fishermen in Malaysia is predominantly a Malay problem.

The poorest fishermen are usually small-time operators engaged in inshore fishing, who use traditional gear and net low catches. One policy measure to help this subgroup might consist in modernization: better boats and engines, a greater variety of nets and gear for different types of fish and weather conditions, and practical training in the use of this equipment. Extension of bank credit, grants and subsidies, and training courses would need to be provided by the government. There are dangers, however, in excessive modernization. An expansion in trawling, for instance, will not necessarily benefit traditional fishermen. Trawlers are relatively capital intensive and their crews need not be experienced fishermen; thus traditional poor fishermen may not be provided with employment. Moreover large-scale trawling poses a threat to inshore fishing resources, on which small fishermen rely for their livelihood.

The danger of depleting fishing resources suggests that poverty alleviation programs should not concentrate on increasing output from existing fishing activities (see Khoo, 1976). Rather, the possibilities of alternative employment and sources of income for poor fishermen should be considered. Fishermen can be encouraged to emigrate to other occupations by providing vocational training for those willing to move (for example, through MARA, the new Rural and Industrial Development Authority). Fishermen could also be accommodated on the state and federal land settlement schemes.[37] Another measure would be to help fishing households obtain more part-time employment, for example, in agricultural crops such as cashew nuts and tobacco. Any such program would naturally have to be tailored to the situation in particular fishing villages.[38] In addition, the possibilities of aquaculture could be explored. Aquaculture would have the advantage of allowing fishermen continuity with the old way of life; it would also help boost fish supplies.

---

37. Unlike rubber estate workers, fishermen appear ready to move, but few so far have been absorbed in such schemes.

38. It is customary for many fishing households in the traditional sector to augment their incomes by working as part-time laborers. In some seaside places, notably Penang, the growth of tourism has brought new opportunities for earning cash through various services to tourists. In most rural fishing areas, however, agriculture is the only extra source of income available to the community, but fishermen often do not possess enough land. In Kelantan, a number of fishermen have managed to raise their family incomes substantially by cultivating tobacco on previously unused plots of bris soil.

Other Subgroups

A few other rural subgroups in poverty can be isolated by commodity in table 5-2. The two-digit industrial code for coconut, copra, and coconut oil isolates the coconut subsector as a whole. It shows a poverty incidence of 56.0 percent and accounts for about 2 percent of total rural poverty. When the subsector is disaggregated by two-digit occupational group, a poverty incidence of 49.3 percent is found among coconut farmers (mainly smallholders), and a poverty incidence of 61.9 percent among coconut farm laborers. EPU (1975) has identified coconut smallholders as a rural poverty group, and from a single survey on coconut smallholdings (Selvadurai, 1968), it has estimated a poverty incidence of 45 percent for this group in 1970. The problems of coconut smallholders, and measures to raise their incomes, are discussed in the FAO/World Bank (1975) report. Chief among these measures are the replanting and rehabilitation of old coconut trees to raise yields, and intercropping with suitable plants such as cocoa, pineapples, and coffee.

The other subgroups isolated through table 5-2 are even smaller, with the oil palm subsector next in size. More than 95 percent of households in the oil palm subsector are headed by laborers on estates or smallholdings and show a poverty incidence of 23.5 percent. The oil palm subsector has not been singled out by EPU as a target group; this seems justified in view of its comparatively low rate of poverty.

Individual estimates of poverty in the subsectors of forestry, coffee, and tea have also been computed in table 5-2. The EPU (1975) study has estimated poverty for two of these three subsectors: forestry and coffee. In table 5-2 the estimate of poverty incidence among forestry workers is 33.3 percent, compared with EPU's 29 percent. In table 5-2 the estimate of poverty incidence in the coffee subsector is 50.0 percent and among coffee smallholders 44.4 percent; EPU's estimate for coffee smallholder poverty is 45 percent. Finally, the estimate of poverty incidence in the tea subsector is 15.4 percent. The PES sample size for the last subgroup is rather small (thirteen households), however, and begins to stretch the limits of reasonable statistical inference. Little confidence can attach to estimates based on an absolute sample size this small.

Appendix: Urban Poverty

Although quantitatively small (12.3 percent of all poor households are urban), urban poverty could become an increasingly serious problem in

Malaysia. With the present emphasis on job creation in the modern sector, it is likely that large numbers of rural poor will migrate to the cities.[39] These migrants will probably join the urban informal or unorganized sector while searching and waiting for modern sector job openings. Thus the urban informal sector is a potential receptacle for the poor.

Table 5-4 presents a one-digit profile of the urban poor in Malaysia.[40] It shows urban poverty to be characterized by features quite different from those associated with rural poverty. The incidence of urban poverty is considerably lower than that of rural poverty (15.8 percent compared with 44.6 percent). In addition, several salient features stand out.

The ethnic distribution of urban poverty is quite different from that of rural poverty, with the Chinese (41.9 percent) rather than the Malays (37.4 percent) as the most numerous racial group among the urban poor. This reflects the larger proportion of Chinese in urban areas, where they constitute as much as 57.9 percent of the household population, while the Malays make up only 25.9 percent. The incidence of poverty among Malays (22.9 percent), however, is twice that among Chinese (11.5 percent). The Indians, too, show a high incidence of poverty (20.9 percent) in urban areas.

The distribution of urban poverty by region shows Selangor with the heaviest concentration although a low relative incidence. Selangor contains almost a third of all urban households in Malaysia, owing to the large urban conurbation around Kuala Lumpur. Penang and Perak also account for sizable percentages of the urban poor; this simply reflects their share in the urban population since the two states show near-average rates of poverty.

Employees make up 53.9 percent of the heads of urban poor households, whereas own-account workers make up only 32.7 percent. This is the reverse of the situation for the country as a whole, in which a greater

39. A theoretical explanation for such migration is provided by Todaro (1969) and Harris and Todaro (1970). An econometric test of the Harris-Todaro model for Indian data is contained in Anand (1971).

40. This is the profile corresponding to the poverty line of M$25 per capita household income. Tables 5-7 and 5-8 present urban poverty profiles corresponding to the poverty lines of M$15 and M$33, respectively. The poverty line implicit in TMP is M$33 for both urban and rural areas, and no urban-rural differential in the cost of living has been assumed (despite the claim to the contrary in TMP, para. 507, p. 166). Note that an urban poverty line of M$33 together with a rural poverty line of M$25 implies an urban-rural cost of living differential of 32 percent, which is the approximate figure assumed for some developing countries.

proportion of heads of poverty households are own-account workers. The relative incidence of poverty among these groups is broadly similar in urban and rural areas, respectively: 0.87 and 0.76 for employees and 1.43

(*Text continues on page 172.*)

Table 5-4. Profile of Urban Poverty at a Poverty Line of M$25

Selected characteristic of household	Percentage distribution among all urban households (1)	Percentage distribution among urban poverty households (2)	Percentage distribution among urban nonpoverty households (3)	Incidence of urban poverty (percent) (4)	Relative incidence of urban poverty (2)/(1) (5)
Race					
Malay	25.9	37.4	23.8	22.9	1.44
Chinese	57.9	41.9	60.9	11.5	0.72
Indian	14.9	19.6	14.0	20.9	1.32
Other	1.3	1.1	1.3	13.0	0.85
Total	100.0	100.0	100.0		
State					
Johore	12.5	13.4	12.3	17.1	1.07
Kedah	5.5	6.5	5.3	18.7	1.18
Kelantan	4.6	12.7	3.1	43.6	2.76
Malacca	3.1	2.0	3.3	10.6	0.65
Negri Sembilan	2.5	2.4	2.5	15.3	0.96
Pahang	4.4	2.0	4.9	7.0	0.45
Penang	14.4	16.5	14.0	18.2	1.15
Perak	18.5	17.8	18.6	15.3	0.96
Perlis	0.0	0.0	0.0	0.0	0.00
Selangor	31.0	19.9	33.1	10.2	0.64
Trengganu	3.5	6.8	2.9	30.6	1.94
Total	100.0	100.0	100.0		
Employment status of head					
Employer	5.6	0.5	6.4	1.1	0.09
Employee	62.2	53.9	63.5	12.3	0.87
Own-account worker	22.9	32.7	21.3	20.3	1.43
Housewife or houseworker	4.0	5.5	3.8	19.3	1.38
Unemployed	5.3	7.4	5.0	19.8	1.40
Total	100.0	100.0	100.0		

(*Table continues on the following page.*)

Table 5-4 (*continued*).

Selected characteristic of household	Percentage distribution among all urban households (1)	Percentage distribution among urban poverty households (2)	Percentage distribution among urban nonpoverty households (3)	Incidence of urban poverty (percent) (4)	Relative incidence of urban poverty (2)/(1) (5)
Occupation of head					
Professional and technical	10.0	2.8	11.1	3.6	0.28
Adminstrative and managerial	5.6	0.3	6.3	0.7	0.05
Clerical and related	9.3	1.5	10.4	2.0	0.16
Sales	21.3	19.0	21.7	11.3	0.89
Service	15.9	16.5	15.8	13.1	1.04
Farmers	3.3	11.4	2.2	43.3	3.45
Farm laborers	4.6	13.0	3.3	36.4	2.83
Production	30.0	35.5	29.2	15.0	1.18
Total	100.0	100.0	100.0		
Sector of employment of head					
Agriculture	4.9	15.3	3.3	40.8	3.12
Agricultural products	2.8	5.1	2.5	23.6	1.82
Mining and quarrying	1.6	1.6	1.5	14.0	1.00
Manufacturing	16.1	14.8	16.3	12.0	0.92
Construction	6.0	6.8	5.9	14.7	1.13
Public utilities	3.1	4.4	2.9	18.9	1.42
Commerce	23.3	19.4	23.9	10.9	0.83
Transport and communications	9.9	11.2	9.8	14.7	1.13
Services	32.3	21.4	33.9	8.7	0.66
Total	100.0	100.0	100.0		
Education of head					
None	24.7	39.6	22.0	25.4	1.60
Some primary	29.5	36.8	28.1	19.7	1.25
Completed primary	17.6	16.0	17.8	14.5	0.91
Lower secondary (forms I–III)	11.7	5.1	13.0	6.9	0.44
Some upper secondary (forms IV–V)	6.4	1.4	7.3	3.5	0.22
School certificate or higher	10.1	1.1	11.8	1.7	0.11
Total	100.0	100.0	100.0		

Selected characteristic of household	Percentage distribution among all urban households (1)	Percentage distribution among urban poverty households (2)	Percentage distribution among urban nonpoverty households (3)	Incidence of urban poverty (percent) (4)	Relative incidence of urban poverty (2)/(1) (5)
Sex of head					
Male	79.9	68.1	82.1	13.5	0.85
Female	20.1	31.9	17.9	25.2	1.59
Total	100.0	100.0	100.0		
Age of head					
Under 20	1.7	1.7	1.7	15.8	1.00
20–29	15.8	7.9	17.2	8.0	0.50
30–39	25.6	28.1	25.2	17.4	1.10
40–49	23.5	29.7	22.3	20.1	1.26
50–59	19.2	16.5	19.7	13.6	0.86
60+	14.2	16.1	13.9	17.9	1.13
Total	100.0	100.0	100.0		
Household size					
1	11.2	5.3	12.3	7.5	0.47
2	8.8	4.3	9.7	7.8	0.49
3	10.7	5.9	11.6	8.7	0.55
4	12.4	7.1	13.4	9.1	0.57
5	11.4	11.4	11.4	15.8	1.00
6	10.6	13.3	10.1	19.9	1.25
7	9.4	12.6	8.8	21.3	1.34
8	8.0	11.8	7.2	23.6	1.48
9	6.0	6.7	5.9	17.6	1.12
10+	11.5	21.6	9.6	29.7	1.88
Total	100.0	100.0	100.0		
Number of children under age 15					
0	29.5	11.4	32.9	6.1	0.39
1	15.7	9.3	16.9	9.4	0.59
2	14.8	10.0	15.7	10.8	0.68
3	13.0	14.7	12.7	18.0	1.13
4	10.2	17.7	8.8	27.5	1.74
5+	16.8	36.9	13.0	34.9	2.20
Total	100.0	100.0	100.0		
Number of income recipients					
0	1.3	8.0	0.0	100.0	6.15
1	53.1	61.2	51.6	18.3	1.15
2	25.1	19.9	26.1	12.6	0.79
3	11.5	7.3	12.3	10.0	0.63
4+	9.0	3.6	10.0	6.5	0.40
Total	100.0	100.0	100.0		

Note: The poverty line is defined at a per capita household income of M$25 per month; 15.8 percent of all urban households fall below this line.

Table 5-5. Distribution of Urban Poverty
by Two-digit Occupational Classification

Selected occupation of head of household	Percentage distribution among urban poverty households
Working proprietors in whosesale and retail trade	3.6
Salesmen, shop assistants, canvassers, news vendors, and street vendors (such as hawkers and cold-drink sellers)	15.0
Cooks, waiters, maids, and housekeeping service workers (including amahs and ayahs)	5.8
Protective service workers (such as doormen, porters, ushers, and attendants) and other service workers (including undertakers and embalmers)	7.9
Farmers, farm laborers, and fishermen	24.4
Bricklayers, carpenters, and other construction workers	6.2
Material handlers, dockers and freight handlers, transport equipment operators	13.8
Total	76.7

and 1.27 for own-account workers. As might be expected, open unemployment of household heads is greater in urban areas (5.3 percent) than in rural areas (2.9 percent); and unemployment among household heads is a larger contributor to urban poverty (7.4 percent) than to rural poverty (3.4 percent).[41] The incidence of urban poverty is slightly lower among households with unemployed heads (19.8 percent) than among households whose heads are own-account workers (20.3 percent). This indicates the importance of secondary earners in determining the size of household income.

The occupational breakdown of heads of urban poverty households shows, somewhat surprisingly, that as many as 24.4 percent of them are farmers or farm laborers.[42] In fact, farming households in urban areas have substantially higher rates of poverty than any other occupational group, clustering around the national avarage of 36.5 percent rather than the urban average of 15.8 percent. Groups with which urban poverty is generally thought to be associated are informal or unorganized sector workers, such as hawkers, stallkeepers, shoe repairers, trishaw pedalers, and houseboys. Workers in traditional manufacturing are also considered poverty prone, but those in organized manufacturing are regarded as on the whole immune. The two-digit occupational classification in table 5-5 supports the view that the urban poor are engaged largely in the informal

41. The fact that this contribution is nonetheless small tends to support the observation that the poor in developing countries cannot "afford" to be unemployed.
42. Urban areas are defined as towns with a population in excess of 10,000.

Table 5-6. Distribution of Urban Poverty
by Two-digit Industrial Classification

Selected industrial sector of head of household	Percentage distribution among urban poverty households
Agriculture and agricultural products	20.4
Retail trade (in food, drink, tobacco, footwear, and so on, including hawkers and temporary stall-holders)	18.6
Government and community services (including local administration, education, medical and health services, religious and welfare organizations)	10.8
Personal services (including domestic and miscellaneous laundry services; eating and drinking stalls)	8.1
Water and sanitary services (including garbage collection and disposal and sewage disposal)	3.2
Transport (including taxi and trishaw services)	10.8
Construction (contractors and services)	6.8
Manufacture of wood, rattan, and attap products (except furniture and footwear)	3.6
Total	82.3

sector, and are underemployed or self-employed on a casual basis.[43]

Consistent with the occupational breakdown, the sector of employment of heads of urban poverty households shows that 20.4 percent of them are in agriculture and agricultural products (table 5-4). The two-digit industrial classification in table 5-6 shows another 40.7 percent in commerce and services, 10.8 percent in transport, and 10.4 percent in construction and light manufacturing. The distribution of urban poverty by two-digit occupational and industrial categories (tables 5-5 and 5-6) confirms that, apart from agriculture and related activities, the poor are engaged in a variety of services, many of which are supplied in the informal sector. Agriculture and agricultural products account for about a quarter, and the informal service sector for about a half, of urban poor households. The rest of the urban poor are found in miscellaneous nonservice activities, including construction and manufacturing.

The strong inverse relation between education of household head and poverty incidence persists in urban areas, and, as for overall poverty, there is a marked decline in incidence for households whose heads have acquired even some secondary education. The percentage of heads of poor

(*Text continues on page 186.*)

43. Their underemployment may in fact represent a quasi-voluntary queuing for the attractive but infrequent modern sector jobs. Material on urban unemployment in Malaysia (Mazumdar, 1975), which shows the unemployed as long-time urban dwellers with some education, lends support to the queuing hypothesis.

Table 5-7. Profile of Urban Poverty at a Poverty Line of M$15

Selected characteristic of household	Percentage distribution among all urban households (1)	Percentage distribution among urban poverty households (2)	Percentage distribution among urban nonpoverty households (3)	Incidence of urban poverty (percent) (4)	Relative incidence of urban poverty (2)/(1) (5)
Race					
Malay	25.9	42.6	25.1	8.3	1.64
Chinese	57.9	34.7	59.1	3.0	0.60
Indian	14.9	21.6	14.5	7.3	1.45
Other	1.3	1.1	1.3	4.3	0.85
Total	100.0	100.0	100.0		
State					
Johore	12.5	13.2	12.4	5.3	1.06
Kedah	5.5	7.0	5.4	6.4	1.27
Kelantan	4.6	17.1	4.0	18.6	3.72
Malacca	3.1	1.4	3.1	2.3	0.45
Negri Sembilan	2.5	1.7	2.5	3.4	0.68
Pahang	4.4	1.9	4.6	2.2	0.43
Penang	14.4	13.7	14.4	4.8	0.95
Perak	18.5	18.5	18.5	5.0	1.00
Perlis	0.0	0.0	0.0	0.0	0.00
Selangor	31.0	17.1	31.8	2.8	0.55
Trengganu	3.5	8.4	3.3	11.9	2.40
Total	100.0	100.0	100.0		
Employment status of head					
Employer	5.6	1.0	5.7	0.6	0.18
Employee	62.2	44.9	62.8	2.4	0.72
Own-account worker	22.9	38.5	22.3	5.5	1.68
Housewife or houseworker	4.0	6.8	4.0	5.5	1.70
Unemployed	5.3	8.8	5.2	5.4	1.66
Total	100.0	100.0	100.0		

Selected characteristic of household	Percentage distribution among all urban households (1)	Percentage distribution among urban poverty households (2)	Percentage distribution among urban nonpoverty households (3)	Incidence of urban poverty (percent) (4)	Relative incidence of urban poverty (2)/(1) (5)
Occupation of head					
Professional and technical	10.0	3.2	10.3	0.9	0.32
Administrative and managerial	5.6	0.6	5.7	0.3	0.11
Clerical and related	9.3	1.3	9.5	0.4	0.14
Sales	21.3	16.8	21.5	2.3	0.79
Service	15.9	18.7	15.8	3.4	1.18
Farmers	3.3	14.2	3.0	12.4	4.30
Farm laborers	4.6	20.0	4.1	12.8	4.35
Production	30.0	25.2	30.1	2.4	0.84
Total	100.0	100.0	100.0		
Sector of employment of head					
Agriculture	4.9	26.1	4.3	15.4	5.33
Agricultural products	2.8	6.2	2.7	6.4	2.21
Mining and quarrying	1.6	1.9	1.5	3.5	1.19
Manufacturing	16.1	8.7	16.3	1.6	0.54
Construction	6.0	3.1	6.1	1.5	0.52
Public utilities	3.1	1.2	3.1	1.2	0.39
Commerce	23.3	16.2	23.6	2.0	0.70
Transport and communications	9.9	11.8	9.9	3.5	1.19
Services	32.3	24.8	32.5	2.2	0.77
Total	100.0	100.0	100.0		
Education of Head					
None	24.7	45.9	23.6	9.4	1.85
Some primary	29.5	30.1	29.5	5.1	1.02
Completed primary	17.6	13.5	17.8	3.9	0.77
Lower secondary (forms I–III)	11.7	7.1	12.0	3.0	0.61
Some upper secondary (forms IV–V)	6.4	1.7	6.6	1.3	0.27
School certificate or higher	10.1	1.7	10.5	0.8	0.17
Total	100.0	100.0	100.0		

(Table continues on the following page.)

Table 5-7 (*continued*).

Selected characteristic of household	Percentage distribution among all urban households (1)	Percentage distribution among urban poverty households (2)	Percentage distribution among urban nonpoverty households (3)	Incidence of urban poverty (percent) (4)	Relative incidence of urban poverty (2)/(1) (5)
Sex of head					
Male	79.9	50.1	81.5	3.2	0.63
Female	20.1	49.9	18.5	12.5	2.48
Total	100.0	100.0	100.0		
Age of head					
Under 20	1.7	3.1	1.6	9.2	1.82
20–29	15.8	10.9	16.0	3.5	0.69
30–39	25.6	26.6	25.6	5.2	1.04
40–49	23.5	24.1	23.4	5.2	1.03
50–59	19.2	17.9	19.3	4.7	0.93
60+	14.2	17.4	14.1	6.1	1.23
Total	100.0	100.0	100.0		
Household size					
1	11.2	2.8	11.7	1.3	0.25
2	8.8	9.5	8.8	5.4	1.08
3	10.7	8.7	10.7	4.1	0.81
4	12.4	8.1	12.6	3.3	0.65
5	11.4	12.0	11.4	5.3	1.05
6	10.6	14.3	10.4	6.8	1.35
7	9.4	8.4	9.5	4.5	0.89
8	8.0	10.9	7.8	6.9	1.36
9	6.0	6.5	6.0	5.4	1.08
10+	11.5	18.8	11.1	8.2	1.63
Total	100.0	100.0	100.0		
Number of children under age 15					
0	29.5	11.5	30.5	2.0	0.39
1	15.7	13.4	15.8	4.3	0.85
2	14.8	10.6	15.0	3.6	0.72
3	13.0	17.7	12.8	6.8	1.36
4	10.2	15.4	9.9	7.6	1.51
5+	16.8	31.4	16.0	9.4	1.87
Total	100.0	100.0	100.0		
Number of income recipients					
0	1.3	25.2	0.0	100.0	19.38
1	53.1	48.4	53.4	4.6	0.91
2	25.1	18.2	25.5	3.6	0.73
3	11.5	4.8	11.9	2.1	0.42
4+	9.0	3.4	9.2	1.9	0.38
Total	100.0	100.0	100.0		

Note: The poverty line is defined at a per capita household income of M$15 per month; 5.0 percent of all urban households fall below this line.

Table 5-8. Profile of Urban Poverty at a Poverty Line of M$33

Selected characteristic of household	Percentage distribution among all urban households (1)	Percentage distribution among urban poverty households (2)	Percentage distribution among urban nonpoverty households (3)	Incidence of urban poverty (percent) (4)	Relative incidence of urban poverty (2)/(1) (5)
Race					
Malay	25.9	34.5	23.0	33.9	1.33
Chinese	57.9	47.0	61.6	20.8	0.81
Indian	14.9	17.7	13.9	30.4	1.19
Other	1.3	0.8	1.5	16.3	0.62
Total	100.0	100.0	100.0		
State					
Johore	12.5	13.4	12.1	27.5	1.07
Kedah	5.5	6.7	5.1	31.3	1.22
Kelantan	4.6	9.4	3.0	52.1	2.04
Malacca	3.1	2.1	3.4	17.5	0.68
Negri Sembilan	2.5	2.0	2.6	20.9	0.80
Pahang	4.4	2.7	5.0	15.6	0.61
Penang	14.4	17.0	13.5	30.2	1.18
Perak	18.5	19.3	18.2	26.7	1.04
Perlis	0.0	0.0	0.0	0.0	0.00
Selangor	31.0	21.2	34.4	17.5	0.68
Trengganu	3.5	6.1	2.7	43.7	1.74
Total	100.0	100.0	100.0		
Employment status of head					
Employer	5.6	0.6	7.1	2.9	0.11
Employee	62.2	58.5	63.3	22.4	0.94
Own-account worker	22.9	29.6	20.8	30.8	1.29
Housewife or houseworker	4.0	5.0	3.8	29.5	1.25
Unemployed	5.3	6.3	5.0	28.1	1.19
Total	100.0	100.0	100.0		

(*Table continues on the following page.*)

Table 5-8 (*continued*).

Selected characteristic of household	Percentage distribution among all urban households (1)	Percentage distribution among urban poverty households (2)	Percentage distribution among urban nonpoverty households (3)	Incidence of urban poverty (percent) (4)	Relative incidence of urban poverty (2)/(1) (5)
Occupation of head					
Professional and technical	10.0	2.7	12.1	6.0	0.27
Administrative and managerial	5.6	0.6	7.0	2.4	0.11
Clerical and related	9.3	3.6	10.8	8.5	0.39
Sales	21.3	19.1	22.0	19.6	0.90
Service	15.9	17.2	15.6	23.6	1.08
Farmers	3.3	8.8	1.8	57.3	2.67
Farm Laborers	4.6	10.0	3.0	47.9	2.17
Production	30.0	38.0	27.7	27.8	1.27
Total	100.0	100.0	100.0		
Sector of employment of head					
Agriculture	4.9	11.9	2.9	54.8	2.43
Agricultural products	2.8	4.2	2.4	33.1	1.50
Mining and quarrying	1.6	2.2	1.3	32.6	1.38
Manufacturing	16.1	15.1	16.4	21.3	0.94
Construction	6.0	7.6	5.6	28.4	1.27
Public utilities	3.1	4.5	2.6	33.1	1.45
Commerce	23.3	19.5	24.5	18.9	0.84
Transport and communications	9.9	12.2	9.3	27.8	1.23
Services	32.3	22.8	35.0	16.0	0.71
Total	100.0	100.0	100.0		
Education of head					
None	24.7	35.8	20.9	37.0	1.45
Some primary	29.5	37.6	26.7	32.5	1.27
Completed primary	17.6	18.2	17.4	26.3	1.03
Lower secondary (forms I–III)	11.7	5.7	13.8	12.4	0.49
Some upper secondary (forms IV–V)	6.4	1.6	8.0	6.4	0.25
School certificate or higher	10.1	1.1	13.2	2.8	0.11
Total	100.0	100.0	100.0		

Selected characteristic of household	Percentage distribution among all urban households (1)	Percentage distribution among urban poverty households (2)	Percentage distribution among urban nonpoverty households (3)	Incidence of urban poverty (percent) (4)	Relative incidence of urban poverty (2)/(1) (5)
Sex of head					
Male	79.9	72.9	82.3	23.3	0.91
Female	20.1	27.1	17.7	34.4	1.35
Total	100.0	100.0	100.0		
Age of head					
Under 20	1.7	1.4	1.8	21.7	0.82
20–29	15.8	8.7	18.2	14.2	0.55
30–39	25.6	28.8	24.6	28.7	1.13
40–49	23.5	29.7	21.3	32.3	1.26
50–59	19.2	16.5	20.1	21.9	0.86
60 +	14.2	14.9	14.0	26.7	1.05
Total	100.0	100.0	100.0		
Household size					
1	11.2	3.3	13.9	7.5	0.29
2	8.8	5.6	9.9	16.3	0.64
3	10.7	5.6	12.4	13.4	0.52
4	12.4	7.4	14.1	15.3	0.60
5	11.4	13.2	10.8	29.7	1.16
6	10.6	13.4	9.7	32.1	1.26
7	9.4	9.8	9.3	26.6	1.04
8	8.0	13.2	6.1	42.6	1.65
9	6.0	10.2	4.6	43.1	1.70
10 +	11.5	18.3	9.2	40.5	1.59
Total	100.0	100.0	100.0		
Number of children under age 15					
0	29.5	10.6	36.0	9.2	0.36
1	15.7	9.6	17.8	15.6	0.61
2	14.8	11.7	15.8	20.3	0.79
3	13.0	16.2	12.0	31.7	1.24
4	10.2	16.6	8.0	41.4	1.63
5 +	16.8	35.3	10.4	53.8	2.10
Total	100.0	100.0	100.0		
Number of income recipients					
0	1.3	5.0	0.0	100.0	3.85
1	53.1	60.5	50.6	29.1	1.14
2	25.1	21.7	26.3	22.0	0.86
3	11.5	8.6	12.5	19.1	0.75
4 +	9.0	4.2	10.6	12.0	0.47
Total	100.0	100.0	100.0		

Note: The poverty line is defined at a per capita household income of M$33 per month; 25.5 percent of all urban households fall below this line.

Table 5-9. Profile of Rural Poverty at a Poverty Line of M$15

Selected characteristic of household	Percentage distribution among all rural households (1)	Percentage distribution among rural poverty households (2)	Percentage distribution among rural nonpoverty households (3)	Incidence of rural poverty (percent) (4)	Relative incidence of rural poverty (2)/(1) (5)
Race					
Malay	67.1	89.6	61.6	26.3	1.33
Chinese	21.7	5.1	25.8	4.6	0.24
Indian	10.5	3.8	12.1	7.1	0.36
Other	0.7	1.5	0.5	40.3	2.14
Total	100.0	100.0	100.0		
State					
Johore	13.8	11.5	14.3	16.5	0.83
Kedah	13.6	16.7	12.9	24.1	1.23
Kelantan	11.5	21.8	9.0	37.3	1.90
Malacca	5.2	3.6	5.6	13.5	0.69
Negri Sembilan	5.6	4.1	6.0	14.3	0.73
Pahang	6.4	4.9	6.7	15.2	0.77
Penang	6.1	4.2	6.6	13.6	0.69
Perak	17.5	15.3	18.0	17.1	0.87
Perlis	2.1	3.3	1.8	31.1	1.57
Selangor	13.1	6.1	14.8	9.1	0.47
Trengganu	5.1	8.5	4.3	32.6	1.67
Total	100.0	100.0	100.0		
Employment status of head					
Employer	1.6	0.3	1.9	3.4	0.19
Employee	47.8	30.7	51.7	12.0	0.64
Own-account worker	45.6	64.7	41.2	26.5	1.42
Housewife or houseworker	2.1	1.3	2.2	11.8	0.62
Unemployed	2.9	3.0	3.0	18.7	1.03
Total	100.0	100.0	100.0		

Selected characteristic of household	Percentage distribution among all rural households (1)	Percentage distribution among rural poverty households (2)	Percentage distribution among rural nonpoverty households (3)	Incidence of rural poverty (percent) (4)	Relative incidence of rural poverty (2)/(1) (5)
Occupation of head					
Professional and technical	4.1	0.5	4.9	2.2	0.12
Administrative and managerial	2.5	0.1	3.0	0.5	0.04
Clerical and related	2.1	0.0	2.6	0.0	0.00
Sales	7.9	3.9	8.9	9.5	0.49
Service	5.5	1.4	6.5	4.7	0.25
Farmers	36.4	59.3	31.0	31.2	1.63
Farm laborers	27.8	29.4	27.5	20.2	1.06
Production	13.7	5.4	15.6	7.6	0.39
Total	100.0	100.0	100.0		
Sector of employment of head					
Agriculture	31.1	52.6	26.1	31.7	1.69
Agricultural products	34.1	35.0	33.8	19.3	1.03
Mining and quarrying	1.9	0.2	2.3	2.1	0.11
Manufacturing	5.8	3.3	6.4	10.6	0.57
Construction	2.2	0.8	2.5	7.1	0.36
Public utilities	1.1	0.1	1.4	1.8	0.09
Commerce	8.7	4.5	9.7	9.7	0.52
Transport and communications	3.9	1.6	4.4	7.8	0.41
Services	11.2	1.9	13.4	3.2	0.17
Total	100.0	100.0	100.0		
Education of head					
None	35.0	48.5	31.7	27.1	1.39
Some primary	34.6	34.4	34.6	19.4	0.99
Completed primary	21.5	15.2	23.1	13.8	0.71
Lower secondary (forms I–III)	4.7	1.5	5.4	6.0	0.32
Some upper secondary (forms IV–V)	1.6	0.2	2.0	2.4	0.13
School certificate or higher	2.6	0.2	3.2	1.7	0.08
Total	100.0	100.0	100.0		

(Table continues on the following page.)

Table 5-9 (*continued*).

Selected characteristic of household	Percentage distribution among all rural households (1)	Percentage distribution among rural poverty households (2)	Percentage distribution among rural nonpoverty households (3)	Incidence of rural poverty (percent) (4)	Relative incidence of rural poverty (2)/(1) (5)
Sex of head					
Male	82.5	75.9	84.1	18.1	0.92
Female	17.5	24.1	15.9	27.0	1.38
Total	100.0	100.0	100.0		
Age of head					
Under 20	1.4	1.3	1.4	17.7	0.93
20–29	15.2	11.6	16.0	15.0	0.76
30–39	25.1	28.5	24.3	22.3	1.14
40–49	22.6	25.4	22.0	21.9	1.12
50–59	19.0	17.7	19.3	18.2	0.93
60+	16.7	15.5	17.0	18.2	0.93
Total	100.0	100.0	100.0		
Household size					
1	8.0	0.5	9.8	1.3	0.06
2	9.9	10.6	9.7	21.1	1.07
3	12.1	9.7	12.7	15.8	0.80
4	13.3	7.0	14.9	10.3	0.53
5	13.0	15.8	12.3	23.9	1.22
6	12.6	17.2	11.4	26.9	1.37
7	9.9	12.1	9.4	24.0	1.22
8	7.9	11.1	7.1	27.6	1.41
9	5.3	6.6	5.0	24.6	1.25
10+	8.0	9.4	7.7	23.0	1.18
Total	100.0	100.0	100.0		
Number of children under age 15					
0	22.8	10.5	25.8	9.0	0.46
1	17.5	14.4	18.3	16.2	0.82
2	15.8	13.4	16.3	16.8	0.85
3	13.8	18.5	12.7	26.3	1.34
4	12.0	17.1	10.8	28.0	1.43
5+	18.1	26.1	16.1	28.4	1.44
Total	100.0	100.0	100.0		
Number of income recipients					
0	1.3	6.3	0.0	98.2	4.85
1	59.7	69.6	57.3	22.9	1.17
2	26.9	19.0	28.9	13.9	0.71
3	8.1	3.9	9.1	9.4	0.48
4+	4.0	1.2	4.7	6.0	0.30
Total	100.0	100.0	100.0		

Note: The poverty line is defined at a per capita household income of M$15 per month; 19.6 percent of all rural households fall below this line.

Table 5-10. Profile of Rural Poverty at a Poverty Line of M$33·

Selected characteristic of household	Percentage distribution among all rural households (1)	Percentage distribution among rural poverty households (2)	Percentage distribution among rural nonpoverty households (3)	Incidence of rural poverty (percent) (4)	Relative incidence of rural poverty (2)/(1) (5)
Race					
Malay	67.1	79.6	49.3	69.6	1.19
Chinese	21.7	11.7	36.0	31.5	0.54
Indian	10.5	7.9	14.1	44.1	0.75
Other	0.7	0.8	0.6	65.1	1.14
Total	100.0	100.0	100.0		
State					
Johore	13.8	12.2	15.8	52.3	0.88
Kedah	13.6	15.9	10.4	68.3	1.17
Kelantan	11.5	15.7	5.6	79.9	1.37
Malacca	5.2	4.6	6.2	51.3	0.88
Negri Sembilan	5.6	4.7	6.9	49.1	0.84
Pahang	6.4	5.5	7.6	50.8	0.86
Penang	6.1	5.9	6.5	56.2	0.97
Perak	17.5	17.2	17.8	57.8	0.98
Perlis	2.1	2.7	1.3	73.9	1.29
Selangor	13.1	9.0	18.9	40.2	0.69
Trengganu	5.1	6.6	3.0	75.9	1.29
Total	100.0	100.0	100.0		
Employment status of head					
Employer	1.6	0.5	3.2	16.8	0.31
Employee	47.8	39.1	59.7	47.5	0.82
Own-account worker	45.6	55.4	32.0	70.4	1.21
Housewife or houseworker	2.1	1.9	2.3	52.8	0.90
Unemployed	2.9	3.1	2.8	60.4	1.07
Total	100.0	100.0	100.0		

(Table continues on the following page.)

Table 5-10 (*continued*).

Selected characteristic of household	Percentage distribution among all rural households (1)	Percentage distribution among rural poverty households (2)	Percentage distribution among rural nonpoverty households (3)	Incidence of rural poverty (percent) (4)	Relative incidence of rural poverty (2)/(1) (5)
Occupation of head					
Professional and technical	4.1	1.0	8.3	14.6	0.24
Administrative and managerial	2.5	0.7	5.0	15.4	0.28
Clerical and related	2.1	0.5	4.3	14.2	0.24
Sales	7.9	5.6	11.1	41.1	0.71
Service	5.5	2.9	9.1	30.5	0.53
Farmers	36.4	48.3	20.0	77.0	1.33
Farm laborers	27.8	31.0	23.5	64.7	1.12
Production	13.7	10.0	18.7	42.5	0.73
Total	100.0	100.0	100.0		
Sector of employment of head					
Agriculture	31.1	41.1	17.3	76.6	1.32
Agricultural products	34.1	36.8	30.2	62.6	1.08
Mining and quarrying	1.9	1.1	3.0	34.5	0.58
Manufacturing	5.8	4.4	7.8	43.5	0.76
Construction	2.2	1.7	2.9	44.6	0.77
Public utilities	1.1	0.8	1.6	40.8	0.73
Commerce	8.7	6.3	12.1	41.5	0.72
Transport and communications	3.9	3.0	5.1	44.8	0.77
Services	11.2	4.8	20.0	24.8	0.43
Total	100.0	100.0	100.0		
Education of head					
None	35.0	41.5	25.8	69.4	1.19
Some primary	34.6	36.0	32.6	60.9	1.04
Completed primary	21.5	20.1	23.6	54.6	0.93
Lower secondary (forms I–III)	4.7	2.0	8.4	25.5	0.43
Some upper secondary (forms IV–V)	1.6	0.2	3.6	8.7	0.13
School certificate or higher	2.6	0.2	6.0	4.1	0.08
Total	100.0	100.0	100.0		

Selected characteristic of household	Percentage distribution among all rural households (1)	Percentage distribution among rural poverty households (2)	Percentage distribution among rural nonpoverty households (3)	Incidence of rural poverty (percent) (4)	Relative incidence of rural poverty (2)/(1) (5)
Sex of head					
Male	82.5	80.3	85.5	57.0	0.97
Female	17.5	19.7	14.5	65.9	1.13
Total	100.0	100.0	100.0		
Age of head					
Under 20	1.4	1.1	1.8	46.4	0.79
20–29	15.2	12.3	19.2	47.7	0.81
30–39	25.1	26.3	23.4	61.3	1.05
40–49	22.6	24.7	19.9	63.7	1.09
50–59	19.0	18.4	19.8	56.8	0.97
60+	16.7	17.2	15.9	60.4	1.03
Total	100.0	100.0	100.0		
Household size					
1	8.0	4.4	13.1	32.3	0.55
2	9.9	8.2	12.2	48.6	0.83
3	12.1	10.0	15.0	48.4	0.83
4	13.3	12.3	14.7	54.2	0.92
5	13.0	14.7	10.7	66.0	1.13
6	12.6	13.9	10.7	64.6	1.10
7	9.9	10.5	9.2	61.9	1.06
8	7.9	10.0	5.0	74.0	1.27
9	5.3	6.8	3.1	75.6	1.28
10+	8.0	9.2	6.3	67.6	1.15
Total	100.0	100.0	100.0		
Number of children under age 15					
0	22.8	15.0	33.9	38.5	0.66
1	17.5	15.7	20.0	52.7	0.90
2	15.8	15.7	15.7	58.6	0.99
3	13.8	15.8	11.1	66.8	1.14
4	12.0	14.2	9.0	69.1	1.18
5+	18.1	23.6	10.3	76.5	1.30
Total	100.0	100.0	100.0		
Number of income recipients					
0	1.3	2.1	0.0	98.7	1.62
1	59.7	64.6	52.8	63.4	1.08
2	26.9	24.7	30.2	53.7	0.92
3	8.1	6.3	10.7	45.5	0.78
4+	4.0	2.3	6.3	34.5	0.58
Total	100.0	100.0	100.0		

Note: The poverty line is defined at a per capita household income of M$33 per month; 58.6 percent of all rural households fall below this line.

households with no education is smaller in urban (39.9 percent) than in rural areas (43.7 percent), and a larger percentage have some upper secondary education or better (2.5 percent compared with 0.4 percent).

The demographic features of urban poverty are a little different from those of rural poverty. Women head a significantly larger percentage of poor households in urban areas (31.9 percent) than in rural areas (21.2 percent). The age profile of poverty is similar in the two locations, but the "alternating periods of want and comparative plenty" are more pronounced in urban areas.[44] The highest relative incidence of urban poverty occurs for the 40–49 year age group. The household size distribution shows a larger average size for urban poor households (6.77 members) than for rural poor households (5.77 members).[45] As many as 21.6 percent of urban poor households have ten or more members. The relative incidence of poverty among large households is higher in urban than in rural areas, which might reflect the fact that unpaid family helpers can make more of a contribution to household income in rural areas (by working on their own land) than they can in an urban environment. Another manifestation of the heavier concentration of poverty in large households in urban than in rural areas is the higher *relative* incidence of urban poverty in households with three or more children under age 15. Finally, the incidence of urban poverty declines in a predictable manner with the number of income recipients in the household. As many as 8.0 percent of urban poverty households have no recipients compared with 2.8 percent of rural poverty households. These findings suggest higher average dependency ratios and lower average participation rates for urban than for rural poor households.

44. Five alternating periods of want and comparative plenty in the life of a laborer were indicated by Rowntree (1922) in his study of poverty in nineteenth-century Britain. The cross-section data in table 5-4 tend to corroborate the cycle of poverty noted by Rowntree:

An initial period of want when [the laborer] is too young to work [under 20 years] is followed by a period of comparative prosperity when he is earning money which continues [20–29 years] until he has two or three children. The next period of poverty [30–49 years] will last until his first child begins to earn. While the children are earning, the man enjoys another period [50–59 years] of prosperity . . . only to sink back again into poverty when his children have married, and he is too old to work.

45. There is, however, a larger percentage of one-member households in urban (11.2 percent) than in rural areas (8.0 percent).

6

Inequality
in the
Personal Income Distribution

IN THE PRECEDING CHAPTERS inequality in levels of living and poverty have been measured by the distribution of individuals or households according to per capita household income. I now consider the distribution of income recipients according to personal income, also referred to as the personal income distribution. An income recipient is defined here as a person who receives income from any of the eleven sources listed in the PES questionnaire (see "Definition of PES Income" in chapter 2); personal income is defined as the *sum* of the income received from these eleven sources.[1] The category of income recipient thus includes both working and nonworking persons, and personal income includes both earned and unearned income.[2] Household income in PES is the sum of personal income received by all the income recipients in a household.

The distribution of income recipients according to personal income provides little information on inequality in levels of living in a country,[3] which is usually the eventual concern of analysis. Nevertheless, it is of some importance to analyze the personal income distribution. It comes closest to the distribution generated by the production and payments system of the

1. Personal income thus includes wages and salaries plus income from rent, property, gifts, and so on. The terminology is borrowed from the national accounts notion of personal income to which this PES concept of income approximately corresponds.

2. There is a problem with imputing income from jointly owned assets such as land or a family house. In practice, such income is likely to have been attributed wholly to the household head, and unpaid family workers, for example, would not count as income recipients unless they were in receipt of income from other sources. This should be borne in mind in the interpretation of some of the findings in this chapter (see, for example, note 9).

3. Nor does this distribution even provide accurate information on inequality in levels of living among recipients themselves. The reason is that income is redistributed from high-income recipients to low- (including zero-) income recipients in each household, and the percentage transfer varies from recipient to recipient according to household circumstances.

economy and hence is relevant for understanding the distributional nature of that system. It is also the distribution most directly amenable to policy intervention, because most instruments of economic policy operate via the production and payments system and affect household or per capita household income only through personal incomes.

Ultimately, of course, the personal income distribution needs to be translated into the household or per capita household income distribution so that welfare implications can be considered.[4] But this mapping is not an easy task since it requires matching income recipients (from different parts of the distribution) who belong to the same household, as well as information on the size of the household. Without a satisfactory theory that would allow a prediction of the per capita household income distribution from the personal income distribution, it is possible to make only the following *suggestive* type of calculation. Its purpose is to describe the inequality across households in per capita income in terms of the inequality in income per recipient and the proportion of recipients (or participation rate). Since only the distribution of positive income recipients is considered, households with no recipients, that is, zero-income households, are excluded.

Using standard notation, for household h let y_h denote the household income, m_h the household size, and n_h the number of income recipients. As households with no recipients are excluded, the per capita income of household h can be expressed as

$$y_h/m_h = y_h/n_h \cdot n_h/m_h$$

where y_h/n_h is the income per recipient of household h, and n_h/m_h the proportion of recipients in it. Taking logarithms of both sides,

$$\log y_h/m_h = \log y_h/n_h + \log n_h/m_h.$$

Now forming the variance across households,

$$\begin{aligned} \operatorname{var}(\log y_h/m_h) = {}& \operatorname{var}(\log y_h/n_h) + \operatorname{var}(\log n_h/m_h) \\ & + 2\operatorname{cov}(\log y_h/n_h, \log n_h/m_h). \end{aligned} \tag{1}$$

The variance of the logarithm of income (or any positive variable) is a well-known measure of inequality (appendix A); I call this measure "varlog." Therefore this equation expresses the inequality across households in per capita income as a sum of three terms: the inequality in income per recipient; the inequality in proportion of income recipients, or participation rate; and

---

4. Mapping the personal to the household income distribution is important for determining not only welfare levels among the population, but also consumer demands in the economy—the household being the appropriate decisionmaking unit in both cases.

twice the covariance between the logarithms of income per recipient and proportion of recipients.

Table 6-1 presents the means and varlogs of these variables for Malaysian households, with a disaggregation by racial group. The inequality level, or varlog, of 0.8453 in per capita income across *all* households is the sum of inequality levels of 0.7154 in income per recipient and 0.4251 in participation rate, minus a number (0.2952) that reflects the negative correlation between the logarithms of these variables. A large part of inequality in per capita household income is thus accounted for by inequality in income per recipient. Moreover, changes in economic policy that reduce inequality in income per recipient are also likely to reduce inequality in per capita household income.[5] The negative correlation between the logarithm of income per recipient and the logarithm of participation rate is not strong enough to compensate for the reduction of inequality in income per recipient.

The correlation coefficient ρ between $\log y_h/n_h$ and $\log n_h/m_h$ is defined as:

$$\rho[\text{var}(\log y_h/n_h)]^{1/2}[\text{var}(\log n_h/m_h)]^{1/2} = \text{cov}(\log y_h/n_h, \log n_h/m_h).$$

Substituting in the variance equation (1) above, and differentiating partially with respect to $\text{var}(\log y_h/n_h)$ under the assumption of a constant ρ,[6] we get:

$$\frac{\partial \text{var}(\log y_h/m_h)}{\partial \text{var}(\log y_h/n_h)} = 1 + \rho\frac{[\text{var}(\log n_h/m_h)]^{1/2}}{[\text{var}(\log y_h/n_h)]^{1/2}}$$

$$> 0 \text{ if } \text{var}(\log y_h/n_h) > -\text{cov}(\log y_h/n_h, \log n_h/m_h).$$

The latter condition is easily satisfied in Malaysia (0.7154 > 0.1476), as can be verified from table 6-1. Provided the negative correlation coefficient persists, therefore, a change of inequality in income per recipient should lead (other things being equal) to a change of inequality in per capita household income in the *same direction*.

In Malaysia the average number of income recipients per household is 1.651, and the average participation rate, or proportion of income recipients, per household is 40.3 percent (table 6-1).[7] Malay households

5. However, since poor households have significantly fewer income recipients than nonpoor households (table 4-3), there might be considerable scope for alleviating poverty by raising the per capita incomes of poor households through policies which affect their participation rate in paid employment.

6. This might be a reasonable prediction to make on the basis of a household-utility-maximizing theory of participation rates, in which the participation rate turns out to be negatively related to income per recipient.

7. The reciprocal of the participation rate is the dependency ratio, which shows the number of household members m_h supported by income recipients n_h. But, since the average value of a reciprocal is not equal to the reciprocal of the average value, the average dependency ratios in Malaysia cannot be inferred from the average participation rates shown in table 6-1.

Table 6-1. Means and Varlogs of per Capita Household Income, Household Income per Recipient, and Household Participation Rate

Racial group	$\bar{y}_h$	$\bar{m}_h$	$\bar{n}_h$	$\overline{(y_h/m_h)}$	$\overline{(y_h/n_h)}$	$\overline{(n_h/m_h)}$	Var (log y_h/m_h)	Var (log y_h/n_h)	Var (log n_h/m_h)	2cov (log y_h/n_h, log n_h/m_h)	ρ	Sample size[a]
All households	267.9	5.381	1.651	61.9	169.1	0.403	0.8453	0.7154	0.4251	−0.2952	−0.2676	24,682
Malay	174.5	5.097	1.481	41.0	124.2	0.378	0.6921	0.6624	0.3931	−0.3634	−0.3545	13,673
Chinese	399.6	5.863	1.919	86.7	228.8	0.431	0.6651	0.5371	0.4572	−0.3292	−0.3322	7,893
Indian	307.8	5.472	1.731	78.6	188.2	0.434	0.8050	0.5373	0.4631	−0.1954	−0.1959	2,904
Other	847.3	4.528	1.542	256.8	584.1	0.442	3.1277	2.5857	0.4020	+0.1400	+0.0687	212

a. The 341 zero-income households have been excluded from the calculations in this table. See the related estimates in tables 3-3 to 3-5 based on all 25,023 households.

have a significantly lower participation rate (37.8 percent) than either Chinese households (43.1 percent) or Indian households (43.4 percent).[8] There is also less inequality in the participation rate among Malay households [var$(\log n_h/m_h) = 0.3931$] than among Chinese households (0.4572) or Indian households (0.4631). But Malay households display a stronger negative association between participation rate and income per recipient (correlation coefficient of -0.3545) than the other races.[9] If correlation coefficients remain stable, participation rates for Malay households are likely to fall more than those for other households in response to an increase in income per recipient.

For each racial group separately, a large part of the inequality in per capita household income arises from inequality in income per recipient—notwithstanding the negative covariances (table 6-1). The inequality in income per recipient is therefore likely to play an important role in the explanation of differences in levels of living among households. But the distribution of households by income per recipient is not a tractable distribution for purposes of analysis. Since personal income is received directly by individual recipients, the individual is clearly a more satisfactory population unit than the household.

Two types of individual unit may be distinguished in an analysis of personal income inequality: the actual recipients and all individuals in the population. The difference between the distribution of actual recipients by personal income and the distribution of all individuals by personal income is the addition of dependents who receive no personal income.[10] The addition of zero-income individuals to the distribution of recipients leads to an increase in the percentage of people falling below each income level, but it leads to no change in aggregate income. Thus to each previous cumulative income share there now corresponds a larger cumulative population share, and the new Lorenz curve lies horizontally to the right of the old one (see appendix E, lemma 2 for a formal proof). This implies that the distribution

---

8. The significance of these racial differences in average participation rate has been determined at the 95 percent level of confidence, using a t-test based on the standard deviation of the estimates.

9. This finding may be related to the possibility that the PES attributed the income from a family farm or business entirely to the household head, and that unpaid family workers were not in receipt of income from other sources and thus do not count as income recipients. The participation rate in such households would tend to be underestimated and the income per recipient correspondingly overestimated. The larger negative correlation between the logarithms of these variables for Malay households may thus be partly due to the disproportionate number of family farm or family business households among the Malays.

10. Although such individuals receive no personal income (that is, income from one or more of the eleven sources listed in chapter 2, the section "Definition of PES Income"), they obviously get that part of household income which is transferred to them as household members.

of income recipients by personal income Lorenz-dominates the distribution of all individuals by personal income. Thus the former distribution shows less inequality than the latter distribution according to any index that satisfies mean independence, population size independence, and the Pigou-Dalton condition.[11] Since the relation between the two distributions is straightforward, we can drop the zero-income individuals and confine our attention to the distribution of actual recipients.

Before doing so, however, note the relation between the distribution of all individuals by personal income and the distribution of all individuals by per capita household income (chapter 3). It can be shown that the distribution of all individuals by per capita household income always Lorenz-dominates their distribution by personal income (see appendix E, lemma 3). This follows from a direct application of Atkinson's theorem (appendix D), because the first distribution is obtained from the second distribution by a sequence of progressive transfers from rich to poor. The transfers in this case are within each household from the high-income recipients to the low- or zero-income recipients.

Figure 6-1 shows the Lorenz curves for (a) the distribution of income recipients by personal income and (b) the distribution of all individuals by per capita household income. Although both distributions Lorenz-dominate the distribution of all individuals by personal income, in general there is no relation between the two distributions themselves.[12]

The Distribution of Income Recipients by Personal Income

PES data for the personal income distribution have been coded as absolute frequencies in thirty-two income intervals (see table 2-1 and "The Coding of PES Income Data" in chapter 2). As in the case of the household income distribution, I estimated interval means for the upper-income classes of the personal income distribution by fitting a theoretical Pareto distribution. The same procedure was adopted as in chapter 2 of maximizing the portion

---

11. In this sense, Lorenz dominance implies "unambiguous" ranking of inequality (see the proposition in appendix D).

12. Although in figure 6-1 distribution (b) appears to Lorenz-dominate distribution (a), this is not the case. In fact, for a short stretch at the bottom, the Lorenz curve for distribution (a) lies above that for distribution (b). The reason is that about 1 percent of individuals in distribution (b) have no income (see chapter 3) whereas everyone in distribution (a) receives positive income.

Figure 6-1. *Lorenz Curves for the Personal and per Capita Household Income Distributions*

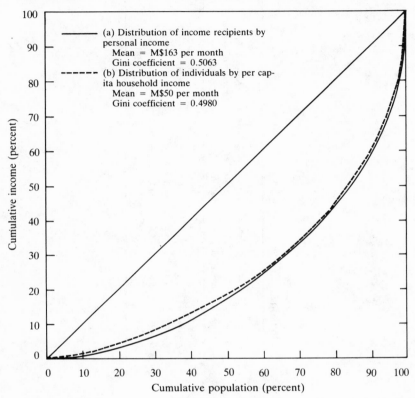

of the distribution fitted from above, subject to an $\bar{R}^2$ greater than 0.99. This led to the following equation:

$$\log n(y) = 8.8 - 2.0559 \log y$$
$$(56.48)$$

where $n(y)$ denotes the number of recipients with personal income greater than or equal to y; the t-ratio is shown in parentheses, $\bar{R}^2 = 0.994$, and the degrees of freedom = 21. This equation refers to the top twenty-three income intervals (more than M$200 per month) and accounts for 21.7 percent of all recipients. Mean incomes for the top twenty-three intervals were calculated by assuming that a Pareto distribution with the coefficient of 2.0559 was valid in this range; hence the mean calculated for the open-

Table 6-2. Distribution of Income Recipients by Personal Income

| Racial group | Arithmetic mean income (M$ per month) | Gini coefficient | Percentage share of | | | | Sample size (number of income recipients) |
			Lowest quintile	Lowest 40 percent	Highest quintile	Highest 5 percent	
All income recipients	163.0	0.5063	3.5	11.3	55.0	28.5	40,806
Malay	118.2	0.4751	3.3	12.8	51.9	23.5	20,321
Chinese	209.1	0.4908	4.0	12.6	54.6	27.5	15,190
Indian	180.4	0.4693	5.0	14.8	54.2	29.0	4,994
Other	573.5	0.7048	0.5	3.9	75.5	31.0	301

ended class M$5,000 and over per month was M$9,736. Mean incomes for the remaining eight intervals at the bottom of the distribution were taken to be at interval midpoints. The means for each income interval are shown in table 2-1. I have also conducted a sensitivity analysis of the personal income distribution with respect to alternative assumptions for interval mean in the upper open-ended class M$5,000 and over per month (compare table 2-1 and the section "Household Income Inequality in Malaysia" in chapter 2). The results are:

Interval mean assumed for income class M$5,000 and over per month	Mean of personal income distribution	Gini coefficient of personal income distribution	Theil T index of personal income distribution
5,000	162	0.5024	0.5103
9,736	163	0.5063	0.5360
10,000	163	0.5065	0.5375
15,000	164	0.5105	0.5686
20,000	166	0.5145	0.6019

As the assumed mean for the top income interval (that is, the income of the richest persons) increases, so does inequality in the Lorenz sense (see appendix E, corollary 1), and hence inequality as measured by the Gini coefficient and the Theil T index, which belong to the Lorenz class of indices (see the proposition in appendix D).

Table 6-2 summarizes the distribution of income recipients by personal income in terms of traditional inequality indices such as the Gini coefficient and the shares of various fractile groups. For the same distribution, table 6-3 presents the equally distributed equivalent income and Atkinson inequality index for values of ε between 0 and 3. In each table there is a breakdown by ethnic group.

The arithmetic mean of the personal income distribution in Malaysia is M$163 per month, and the Gini coefficient is 0.5063. The income share of the lowest quintile is 3.5 percent while that of the top quintile is 55.0 percent; this implies a ratio of almost 16 between the top and the bottom quintiles. For different values of the inequality aversion parameter ε, the Atkinson index is as follows: 0.2196 for $\varepsilon = 0.5$, 0.3785 for $\varepsilon = 1$, 0.5975 for $\varepsilon = 2$, and 0.7159 for $\varepsilon = 3$.[13] These indices all point to a high degree of personal

13. In chapter 3 the Atkinson index could not be computed for any value of ε greater than unity because of the presence of zero-income people in the distribution of individuals by per capita household income. There are, however, no zero-income people in the personal income distribution, which is defined over actual recipients, and the Atkinson index can be computed for all values of $\varepsilon \geqslant 0$. In table 6-3 notice the comparatively small change in going from $\varepsilon = 0.9$ to $\varepsilon = 0.99$ or $\varepsilon = 1.00$. In table 3-9, however, there is a sharp drop in y_{EDE} and a sharp rise in I as ε goes from 0.9 to 0.99; further, when $\varepsilon = 1.00$, $y_{EDE} = 0.0$ and $I = 1.0$.

Table 6-3. Equally Distributed Equivalent Income and Atkinson Inequality Index
for the Distribution of Income Recipients by Personal Income
(M$ per month)

Income recipients	ε									Sample size (number of income recipients)
	0.00	0.50	0.90	0.99	1.00	1.50	2.00	2.50	3.00	
All	163.0	127.2	105.9	101.7	101.3	81.1	65.6	54.3	46.3	40,806
		(0.2196)	(0.3503)	(0.3760)	(0.3785)	(0.5024)	(0.5975)	(0.6668)	(0.7159)	
Malay	118.2	95.7	81.0	78.1	77.7	63.4	52.5	44.6	39.1	20,321
		(0.1903)	(0.3147)	(0.3392)	(0.3426)	(0.4636)	(0.5558)	(0.6226)	(0.6692)	
Chinese	209.1	166.1	140.1	134.9	134.3	108.6	87.5	71.1	59.0	15,190
		(0.2056)	(0.3299)	(0.3548)	(0.3577)	(0.4806)	(0.5815)	(0.6599)	(0.7178)	
Indian	180.4	145.2	126.0	122.3	121.9	103.8	88.3	74.8	63.5	4,994
		(0.1951)	(0.3015)	(0.3220)	(0.3242)	(0.4246)	(0.5105)	(0.5853)	(0.6480)	
Other	573.5	330.2	196.2	174.7	172.5	98.4	66.6	51.4	43.1	301
		(0.4242)	(0.6578)	(0.6953)	(0.6992)	(0.8284)	(0.8838)	(0.9103)	(0.9248)	

Note: The Atkinson inequality index is shown in parentheses.

income inequality in Malaysia; this inequality is higher than the inequality in per capita household incomes (chapter 3). It should be stressed that all the indices used here, including the Atkinson index, refer to a statistical and not a normative measurement of inequality. The underlying distribution is in any case not the relevant one for a measurement of inequality based on social welfare. Thus even the Atkinson index is used here in a purely positive sense to summarize inequality in the personal income distribution.[14]

The ethnic breakdown of the personal income distribution shows a Chinese mean income (M$209) which is 1.77 times the Malay mean income (M$118). At the same time, the Indian-Malay ratio of mean incomes is 1.53. These racial disparity ratios for personal income are *smaller* than for per capita household income, where they are 2.00 and 1.65, respectively. The reason is that the participation rates of the Chinese and Indian communities are higher than that of the Malay community (table 6-1).[15] Table 6-4 presents the racial disparity ratios according to the three different income concepts. The disparity ratios were reduced in going from household income to per capita household income because of a larger average household size $(\bar{m}_h)$ for the Chinese and Indians than for the Malays (chapter 3). They are further reduced in going from per capita household income to personal income because of a higher ratio of average number of

Table 6-4. Racial Disparity Ratios

	Household income $(\bar{y}_h)$	Per capita household income $(\bar{y}_h/\bar{m}_h)$	Personal income[a] $(\bar{y}_h/\bar{n}_h)$
Chinese-Malay	2.29	2.00	1.77
Indian-Malay	1.77	1.65	1.53

a. There are negligible discrepancies between these disparity ratios and the same ones calculated from table 6-1. The discrepancies arise from independent estimation of the Pareto coefficients and interval means for the household income distribution and the personal income distribution (see table 2-1). For example, the mean personal income in Malaysia as calculated from the household income distribution is $\bar{y}_h/\bar{n}_h$ = M$162.3 (table 6-1), but M$163.0 when calculated directly (table 6-2).
Source: Tables 3-7, 3-9, and 6-2.

14. The Atkinson index for constant elasticity of marginal utility $\varepsilon > 0$ satisfies all the desirable properties for a "positive" inequality measure specified in appendix A: mean independence, population-size independence, and the Pigou-Dalton condition.

15. This should be interpreted with some caution. The participation rate of Malays may be underestimated and their mean personal income overestimated, relative to that of Chinese and Indians, because of the nonimputation of income to unpaid family workers (see note 9 above). Hence racial disparity ratios for personal income may be underestimated.

income recipients to average household size $(\bar{n}_h/\bar{m}_h)$ for the Chinese and Indians than for the Malays. Hence, in terms of incomes that can be influenced by economic policy, the disparity ratios are a good deal smaller than is popularly believed.

These considerations also suggest that the between-race contribution to personal income inequality should be smaller than the between-race contribution to per capita household income inequality, unless, of course, it happens that within-race inequality in personal income is disproportionately small. But this is not the case, as can be seen from tables 6-2 and 6-3. Inequality within each ethnic group is high, with the Chinese showing a consistently higher level than the Malays, who in turn show more inequality than the Indians. (Among recipients of other races, inequality is, not surprisingly, extremely high.) The between-race contribution to personal income inequality does indeed turn out to be smaller than the between-race contribution to per capita household income inequality; this can be verified in the later section "Decomposition by Race and Location."

The Interpretation of Decomposition for Three Inequality Measures

In chapter 3 the decomposition of per capita household income inequality was carried out by means of the Theil entropy index T. This index is decomposable in the weak sense only, however, and not according to my strict definition (see "The Methodology of Inequality Decomposition" in chapter 3). Thus, although the T index can be written as the sum of a between-group component and a within-group component, the within-group component is *not* the value of the T index when all between-group income differences are suppressed. The within-group component for the T index is a weighted average of the T indices for each group where the weights are the income shares of the groups in total income.

The interpretation of decomposition in the weak and strict senses is immediate if one writes out the decomposition formulas for the weakly decomposable Theil T index and the strictly decomposable Theil L measure. Adopting the notation of chapter 3, divide the population into two groups, say, Malays and non-Malays, with mean incomes μ_1, μ_2 and population sizes n_1, n_2, respectively.[16] Let the overall mean income be μ and the overall population size n. Let the subscripts 1, 2 on an inequality index denote the value of the index for groups 1, 2, respectively.

---

16. There is no loss of generality in partitioning the population into two groups only: the extension for more than two groups is obvious and follows by induction.

The Theil T index can be expressed as the sum:

$$T = T_W + T_B$$

where $\qquad T_W = \dfrac{n_1 \mu_1}{n\mu} T_1 + \dfrac{n_2 \mu_2}{n\mu} T_2$

and $\qquad T_B = \dfrac{n_1 \mu_1}{n\mu} \log \dfrac{\mu_1}{\mu} + \dfrac{n_2 \mu_2}{n\mu} \log \dfrac{\mu_2}{\mu}.$

T_B is the between-group component, since it is the value of the T index when all within-group income differences are suppressed. If everyone in group 1 gets income μ_1, and everyone in group 2 gets income μ_2, the T index is easily seen to be equal to T_B. (This follows directly from the definition of the index, or by putting $T_1 = T_2 = 0$ in the above expression.) However, T_W is *not* the value of the T index when all between-group income differences are suppressed but inequality within each group remains constant. If the group mean incomes μ_1, μ_2 are equalized to the overall mean μ by equiproportionate changes in the income of every person within a group, the T index reduces to $(n_1/n) T_1 + (n_2/n) T_2$. (This follows directly from the definition of the index, or by putting $\mu_1 = \mu_2 = \mu$ in the above expression for T.) Because it is mean-independent, the same value of the T index results if the group means are equalized to any level other than μ, for example, μ_2. Thus the elimination of between-group inequality (for example, by multiplying all group 1 or Malay incomes by a factor of μ_2/μ_1) results in a value for the T index which is not $T_W [= (n_1 \mu_1/n\mu) T_1 + (n_2 \mu_2/n\mu) T_2]$. Hence T is not decomposable in the strict sense, and therefore T_B does not measure the reduction in inequality if between-group income differences are eliminated.[17] Of course, T_B does still measure the extent of inequality arising from the between-group (Malay/non-Malay) differences in mean income. This is because T is additively decomposable in the weak sense.

The Theil L measure can be expressed as the sum:

$$L = L_W + L_B$$

where $\qquad L_W = \dfrac{n_1}{n} L_1 + \dfrac{n_2}{n} L_2$

and $\qquad L_B = \dfrac{n_1}{n} \log \dfrac{\mu}{\mu_1} + \dfrac{n_2}{n} \log \dfrac{\mu}{\mu_2}.$

L_B is clearly the between-group component, since it is the value of the L measure when all within-group income differences are suppressed. If

17. The elimination of between-group income differences leads to a reduction in overall inequality of

$$T - (n_1/n)T_1 - (n_2/n)T_2 = T_B + [T_W - (n_1/n)T_1 - (n_2/n)T_2] \neq T_B.$$

everyone in group 1 gets income μ_1, and everyone in group 2 gets income μ_2, the L measure is equal to L_B. (Again, this follows directly from the definition of the L measure, or by putting $L_1 = L_2 = 0$ in the above expression.) Furthermore, L_W is indeed the within-group component according to the strict definition. When all between-group income differences are suppressed by the equalization of group mean incomes, but inequality *within* each group is kept constant, the L measure reduces to $(n_1/n)L_1 + (n_2/n)L_2 = L_W$ (Again, this follows directly from the definition, or by putting $\mu_1 = \mu_2 = \mu$ in the above expression for L.) Since L is the sum of the between-group component, L_B, and the within-group component according to the strict definition, L_W, the measure is additively decomposable in the strict sense. This property allows us to interpret unambiguously the between-group component L_B.

By one interpretation, L_B measures the extent of inequality which arises if between-group differences in mean income are the only source of income variation. In other words, it is the value of the L measure if inequality is eliminated within each group, but the group mean incomes remain constant. By another interpretation, L_B measures the reduction in overall inequality if between-group differences in mean income are eliminated, but inequality within each group remains constant. These two interpretations of the between-group component give the same answer for an inequality index decomposable in the strict sense.

The two interpretations are not consistent for measures that are decomposable in the weak sense only. For these measures the within-group component is defined to be a weighted sum of the inequality indices for each group, where the weights are a function of the population share and income share of the groups. If the weights depend on the population shares alone, then the measure is decomposable in the strict sense, as verified for L above. Otherwise, the two interpretations of the between-group component lead to different answers. The elimination of inequality within each group while holding group mean incomes constant yields the between-group component. But the elimination of between-group differences in mean income while holding inequality within each group constant does *not* yield the within-group component. Although the inequality indices for each group remain constant, the weights on these indices change if group mean incomes are equalized. When the mean income for each group is the same, the income share of a group collapses to its population share, which changes the weight on its inequality index (unless the income and population shares are the same to begin with, in which case there is no between-group inequality).

When the two interpretations lead to the same answer, there is an unambiguous meaning to the between-group contribution to overall inequality. For example, the contribution of between-race differences in mean income to overall inequality can be measured either as the inequality which arises when these differences are the only source of income variation, or as the amount by which inequality falls when these differences are eliminated. While it is convenient to have an index whose between-group component gives the answer to both questions, thereby removing any ambiguity, it is clearly not essential. In fact, either question can be answered using any index, decomposable or not. Decomposability is an attractive property which helps circumvent some of the computations required to answer the different questions, including the extent of inequality within groups.

The variance of log-income is another index which can be built up as the sum of inequality in its constituent parts. Let V be the overall variance of log-income, and V_1, V_2 the variance of log-income for groups 1, 2, respectively. Let $\tilde{\mu}$ be the overall geometric mean income, and $\tilde{\mu}_1$, $\tilde{\mu}_2$ the geometric mean incomes of groups 1, 2, respectively. Then V can be expressed as the sum

$$V = V_W + V_B$$

where
$$V_W = \frac{n_1}{n} V_1 + \frac{n_2}{n} V_2.$$

and
$$V_B = \frac{n_1}{n} (\log \tilde{\mu}_1 - \log \tilde{\mu})^2 + \frac{n_2}{n} (\log \tilde{\mu}_2 - \log \tilde{\mu})^2.$$

V_W is a weighted average of the variance of log-income within each group where the weights are population shares of the groups. However, V_B is *not* the variance of log-income when all within-group income differences are suppressed but group arithmetic mean incomes are held constant. Rather, V_B is the value of V when everyone in group 1 gets the geometric mean $\tilde{\mu}_1$ and everyone in group 2 gets the geometric mean $\tilde{\mu}_2$. Thus V_B measures the inequality which arises from between-group differences in geometric mean income, not in arithmetic mean income.

It is easy to verify that the variance of log-income V is, in fact, decomposable in the strict sense around the group geometric means. But it is not decomposable around the group arithmetic means. The geometric mean income is not equal to the arithmetic mean income, and the equalization of group geometric mean incomes through equiproportionate changes in the income of every person within a group does not lead to the equalization of group arithmetic mean incomes. Nevertheless, the between-group component V_B provides the answer to either question concerning between-group inequality in geometric mean incomes. V_B measures the extent of inequality if the between-group differences in geometric mean income are the only source of income variation and inequality within each group is set to zero. V_B also measures the reduction in overall inequality if inequality within each group is held constant but the between-group differences in geometric mean income are eliminated through equiproportionate changes in the income of every person within a group. This is because the weights on the within-group variances of log-income are population shares, which do not change with changes in group mean incomes.

Decomposition by Race and Location

Personal income inequality in Malaysia has been decomposed by using all three inequality measures discussed in the previous section: Theil's entropy index T, Theil's second measure L, and the variance of log-income V, or varlog. Unlike the per capita household income distribution in chapter 3, the personal income distribution allows all three measures to be computed because it has no zero-income recipients.[18]

Table 6-5 presents a breakdown of the personal income distribution by race as well as location. The between-race contribution to personal income inequality is 9.2 percent by Theil T, 9.6 percent by Theil L, and 7.9 percent by varlog.[19] The fact that Theil L yields a between-race contribution of 9.6 percent implies that if the between-race differences in arithmetic mean income were eliminated, but inequality within each race remained the same, the reduction in overall inequality would be 9.6 percent. The fact that varlog yields a between-race contribution of 7.9 percent implies that if the between-race differences in geometric mean income were eliminated, but inequality within each race remained the same, the reduction in overall inequality would be 7.9 percent.

The NEP's racial balance objective can be taken to imply the elimination of inequality in arithmetic mean incomes between the races, leaving unchanged the inequality within each race (see chapters 1 and 3). The implementation of this objective would therefore bring about a reduction of 9.6 percent in the strictly decomposable Theil L measure.[20] This result supports the conclusion in chapter 3 about the limited effect of racial balance on individual income inequality, especially since policy can influence only the personal income distribution.

18. As noted in chapter 3, the Theil L measure and varlog blow up to infinity when there are zero incomes.

19. For the index $A(\varepsilon)$ based on the Atkinson equally distributed equivalent income (see chapter 3), the between-race contribution to personal income inequality is: 10.1 percent for $\varepsilon = 0.5$; 9.8 percent for $\varepsilon = 0.9$; 9.6 percent for $\varepsilon = 0.99$ (computed from table 6-3).

20. The reduction in varlog and the weakly decomposable Theil T index have to be specially computed; this can be done from the data given in table 6-5.

The Theil entropy index T is a measure which can be used to decompose both personal income inequality and per capita household income inequality whereas PES data make computation of Theil L and varlog impossible for the per capita household income distribution. As predicted earlier, the between-race contribution to personal income inequality is indeed smaller than the between-race contribution to per capita household income inequality: 9.2 percent compared with 13.0 percent according to the Theil T index.[21]

The between-location contribution to personal income inequality in Malaysia is approximately the same as the between-race contribution: 9.5 percent by Theil T, 10.0 percent by Theil L, and 7.3 percent by varlog. Thus if rural-urban inequalities were completely removed, but intrarural and intraurban inequality remained the same, the reduction in overall inequality would be 10 percent. Hence it cannot be claimed that rural-urban differences in income are responsible for more than a small fraction of overall inequality in the country.[22]

The racial disparity ratios for the country as a whole are distinctly larger than those for urban areas. For instance, the Chinese-Malay disparity ratio for Malaysia is 1.77, whereas for metropolitan towns it is 1.05 and for towns 1.26. A disproportionate presence of Malays in rural areas where the average income is relatively low and of Chinese in urban areas where the average income is relatively high, together with a Chinese-Malay disparity ratio of 1.70 for rural areas,[23] accounts for the higher overall disparity ratio of 1.77. To reduce such overall racial income disparities, the government has declared its desire to promote migration flows and urbanization of Malays (MTR, chap. 1).

The smaller disparity ratios for urban areas also bring about low between-race contributions there. Race accounts for less than 2 percent (1.9, 1.8, and 1.5 percent by the three measures, respectively) of income inequality in towns, and less than 5 percent (4.5, 3.6, and 1.7 percent, respectively) of inequality in metropolitan towns. It follows that the elimination of racial disparities within urban areas would by itself have a negligible effect on inequality. The effect should be somewhat larger (8.4 percent) in rural areas, however, since they have higher racial disparity ratios.

A regional decomposition of the personal income distribution was also undertaken, though it is not shown here. There are significant differences in

21. See tables 6-5 and 3-10, respectively.

22. Contrast the views on this subject in Lipton (1968) or (1977).

23. The higher disparity ratio in rural than in urban areas perhaps arises in part from greater racial disparities in asset-holding in rural areas.

Table 6-5. Decomposition by Race and Location of Inequality in the Personal Income Distribution

Racial group	Item	Metropolitan towns	Towns	Rural areas	Peninsular Malaysia	Between-location contribution to inequality (percent)	
Malay	Gini	0.4610	0.4838	0.4509	0.4751		
	Theil T	0.4724	0.4134	0.3800	0.4370	9.4	Theil T
	Theil L	0.3961	0.4583	0.3765	0.4193	8.3	Theil L
	Varlog	0.7418	1.0057	0.7589	0.8293	6.1	Varlog
	Geometric mean	163.4	107.7	71.2	77.7		
	Arithmetic mean	242.8	170.3	103.7	118.2		
	Sample size	1,297	1,711	17,313	20,321		
Chinese	Gini	0.5246	0.4936	0.4487	0.4908		
	Theil T	0.5772	0.4848	0.3945	0.4958	2.7	Theil T
	Theil L	0.5034	0.4527	0.3734	0.4430	3.0	Theil L
	Varlog	0.9213	0.8896	0.7503	0.8428	1.3	Varlog
	Geometric mean	154.7	136.4	121.9	134.3		
	Arithmetic mean	255.8	214.4	177.1	209.1		
	Sample size	4,665	3,194	7,331	15,190		
Indian	Gini	0.5242	0.4481	0.3853	0.4693		
	Theil T	0.6069	0.3506	0.3335	0.4998	11.4	Theil T
	Theil L	0.4943	0.3794	0.2722	0.3925	13.7	Theil L
	Varlog	0.8465	0.8286	0.4812	0.6571	7.5	Varlog
	Geometric mean	173.6	139.5	104.1	121.9		
	Arithmetic mean	284.5	203.9	136.7	180.4		
	Sample size	1,244	514	3,236	4,994		

Other

Gini	0.5858	0.5809	0.7765	0.7048
Theil T	0.6206	0.6242	1.2736	0.9442
Theil L	0.7647	0.6887	1.4578	1.2016
Varlog	1.8184	1.4565	2.3611	2.5426
Geometric mean	432.1	210.5	91.8	172.5
Arithmetic mean	928.3	419.1	394.3	573.5
Sample size	99	44	158	301

Between-race-and-location contribution to inequality (percent)

Theil T	9.3
Theil L	7.0
Varlog	19.4

All racial groups

Gini	0.5259	0.4912	0.4655	0.5063
Theil T	0.5945	0.4642	0.4320	0.5360
Theil L	0.5047	0.4576	0.4035	0.4763
Varlog	0.9041	0.9392	0.7918	0.8967
Geometric mean	161.5	127.4	85.7	101.3
Arithmetic mean	267.5	201.3	128.4	163.0
Sample size	7,305	5,463	28,038	40,806

Between-race-and-location contribution to inequality (percent)

Theil T	9.5
Theil L	10.0
Varlog	7.3

Between-race contribution to inequality (percent)

Theil T	4.5	1.9	8.6	9.2	15.0
Theil L	3.6	1.8	8.4	9.6	15.7
Varlog	1.7	1.5	7.3	7.9	12.2

Note: Metropolitan towns are Johore Bahru, Malacca, Kuala Lumpur, Klang, Ipoh, and Georgetown. Towns are all others of more than 10,000 population (see chapter 2, note 18, for a listing). All other areas are considered rural.

mean income between the states, but these account for only about 8 percent of inequality in the country. Government strategy for regional development, "to reduce the marked economic disparities which currently exist between States" (MTR, p. 18), is thus unlikely to reduce personal income inequality significantly. Development of the rice-growing northern states (Kedah, Kelantan, Perlis, and Trengganu) is likely to reduce poverty, however, which is heavily concentrated there (see chapter 4). It is also likely to reduce racial income disparities because the population of these states is predominantly Malay.[24] The policy of developing these largely Malay backward states is therefore consistent with both prongs of the NEP, provided the gains do in fact accrue uniformly among their populations and are not captured disproportionately by the upper-income groups (such as Chinese traders, millers, and middlemen) at the expense of Malay peasants.

Decomposition by Sex of Income Recipient

A disaggregation of the personal income distribution by sex of income recipient has also been carried out (see table 6-6). It shows that for personal income the male-female disparity ratio in Malaysia is 1.96, which is even higher than the racial disparity ratio of 1.75 between the non-Malays and Malays. The male-female disparity ratio within each racial group is 2.08 among Malays, 1.94 among Chinese, 1.88 among Indians, and 3.66 among other races. Of the total number of income recipients in the sample, only 30.2 percent are females and 69.8 percent males. The male-female breakdown of income recipients within each racial group reveals an interesting pattern: females constitute 28.6 percent of Malay income recipients, 32.9 percent of Chinese, 28.8 percent of Indian, and 20.6 percent of other races. These figures suggest a significant difference in female participation rates between Chinese on the one hand, and Malays and Indians on the other—presumably because of religious and cultural factors.[25]

The between-sex contribution to personal income inequality in the country is 7.2 percent by Theil T, 9.1 percent by Theil L, and 10.4 percent

24. Of the three major ethnic groups, regional disparities are largest among the Malays. The between-state contribution to Malay inequality is about 9 percent, while it is only about 2 percent for the Chinese, and about 4 percent for the Indians.

25. This phenomenon probably helps explain the lower average number of income recipients among Malay and Indian households than among Chinese households (table 6-1), which in turn explains the higher racial disparity ratios for household income than for personal income (table 6-4).

by varlog. Hence the elimination of male-female differences in mean income will bring about a reduction in individual income inequality of about 10 percent. The between-sex contribution to personal income inequality seems to be of the same order of magnitude as the between-race contribution. The combined between-race-and-sex contribution to overall income inequality is 16.8 percent by Theil T, 19.3 percent by Theil L, and 19.3 percent by varlog. This indicates the proportion of inequality attributable to mean income differences among the race-and-sex groups, however these differences may have come about.

Breakdown by Employment Status

As defined earlier, an income recipient is any person who obtains income from one or more of the eleven sources listed in PES. For instance, the person could be an employer receiving profits from his or her enterprise, or an employee receiving a wage or salary, or even an unemployed person receiving a transfer. In this section income recipients are considered according to their employment status. Since income data in PES were not coded by source of income, the employment status breakdown might be used to shed some light on particular factor income distributions.

The PES permits disaggregation into eight categories of employment status (Department of Statistics, 1973). Here the PES categories of unpaid family worker, student, housewife or houseworker, unemployed, and other have been aggregated into a single category called "other." Table 6-7 thus shows four major categories; two of these, employees and own-account workers, account for more than 90 percent of all income recipients.

It seems reasonable to assume that personal income of employees consists largely of wage income, though some investment or interest income may also accrue from accumulated savings; thus the personal income distribution among employees may be a reasonably good surrogate for the wage income distribution. The income of other groups, however, contains significant elements of both labor and property income, though the actual proportion varies according to the activities of the group. In the case of employers, it seems plausible to assume that their income consists mainly of returns to capital invested. But in the case of own-account (that is, self-employed) workers, it is difficult to determine the proportion of income that is a return to capital and the proportion that is a return to labor and other factors. (Even in theory this imputation is difficult if the markets for capital, labor, and other factors are not perfect.) For own-account workers, capital assets typically consist of land (rural smallholders), shop (urban shopkeepers), or transport equipment (transport operators). The

Table 6-6. Decomposition by Race and Sex of Inequality in the Personal Income Distribution

Racial group	Item	Male	Female	All persons	Between-sex contribution to inequality (percent)	
Malay	Gini	0.4393	0.4870	0.4751		
	Theil T	0.3853	0.4424	0.4370	9.7	Theil T
	Theil L	0.3537	0.4128	0.4193	11.6	Theil L
	Varlog	0.6929	0.7229	0.8293	15.4	Varlog
	Geometric mean	97.5	44.2	77.7		
	Arithmetic mean	138.9	66.8	118.2		
	Sample size	14,503	5,818	20,321		
Chinese	Gini	0.4773	0.4470	0.4908		
	Theil T	0.4783	0.3671	0.4958	8.1	Theil T
	Theil L	0.4169	0.3615	0.4430	10.0	Theil L
	Varlog	0.7831	0.7168	0.8428	9.7	Varlog
	Geometric mean	164.0	89.4	134.3		
	Arithmetic mean	248.9	128.3	209.1		
	Sample size	10,187	5,003	15,190		
Indian	Gini	0.4672	0.3874	0.4693		
	Theil T	0.4973	0.3246	0.4998	6.6	Theil T
	Theil L	0.3873	0.2767	0.3925	9.4	Theil L
	Varlog	0.6415	0.5024	0.6571	8.5	Varlog
	Geometric mean	141.5	84.1	121.9		
	Arithmetic mean	208.5	110.9	180.4		
	Sample size	3,558	1,436	4,994		

				Between-race-and-sex contribution to inequality (percent)
Other				
Gini	0.6856	0.6247	0.7048	
Theil T	0.8751	0.7659	0.9442	8.1 Theil T
Theil L	1.1746	0.7953	1.2016	8.8 Theil L
Varlog	2.6326	1.5261	2.5426	5.4 Varlog
Geometric mean	208.4	83.2	172.5	
Arithmetic mean	674.5	184.3	573.5	
Sample size	239	62	301	
All racial groups				
Gini	0.4885	0.4850	0.5063	
Theil T	0.5108	0.4370	0.5360	7.2 Theil T
Theil L	0.4355	0.4270	0.4763	9.1 Theil L
Varlog	0.7969	0.8177	0.8967	10.4 Varlog
Geometric mean	123.8	63.6	101.3	
Arithmetic mean	191.4	97.5	163.0	
Sample size	28,487	12,319	40,806	
Between-race contribution to inequality (percent)				
Theil T	10.3	10.9	9.2	16.8 Theil T
Theil L	11.1	11.5	9.6	19.3 Theil L
Varlog	7.8	14.6	7.9	19.3 Varlog

proportion of income that can be attributed to capital and other factors is likely to be different in each case, and there is little that can be concluded about the nonlabor income distribution in general.

In the case of employers the personal income distribution might give some idea about the capital asset distribution. If it is assumed that employer income consists entirely of returns on capital (or that the proportion of capital income to total income is constant), and also that the rate of return on capital is constant, then the income and wealth distributions for employers will be identical. Generally, however, imperfections of various kinds imply a variable return on wealth. In this situation, mapping the wealth distribution to the income-from-wealth distribution involves the addition of extra variance (or "noise"). If W is wealth, r the rate of return on it, and y the income from wealth, then

$$y = rW \text{ and } \log y = \log r + \log W.$$

Hence, $\text{var}(\log y) = \text{var}(\log W) + \text{var}(\log r) + 2\,\text{cov}(\log W, \log r).$

With a zero or positive correlation between the logarithm of wealth and the logarithm of the rate of return, the income-from-wealth distribution will be more unequal than the wealth distribution. Extra information such as this is needed on the joint distribution of wealth and its rate of return before anything can be inferred about one distribution from a knowledge of the other. (Compare the exactly analogous problem in chapter 3 and appendix F of mapping the household income distribution to the per capita household income distribution.)

The PES data on personal income distribution disaggregated by race and employment status are presented in table 6-7, which shows the standard inequality measures, geometric and arithmetic mean incomes, and sample size. The arithmetic mean income of employers (M\$738.8) is almost four-and-a-half times larger than that of employees (M\$166.6). The mean incomes of the two other groups are closer together and only slightly below the mean income of employees. This last fact, together with there being few employers with high incomes, explains the relatively small contribution of employment status to personal income inequality[26] (11.9 percent by Theil T, 9.0 percent by Theil L, and 6.5 percent by varlog).

By any of the measures computed, employer incomes are distributed more unequally than self-employed incomes, and these are distributed

---

26. The dependence of the between-group contribution to inequality on the mean income and population share of a particular group can be examined from the decomposition formula for the measure given in chapter 3 or appendix C. For example, other things being equal, the higher the mean income of a group whose mean is above the overall mean, the greater the

more unequally than employee incomes. Thus nonlabor incomes seem less equally distributed than labor incomes in Malaysia. To move to the wealth distribution requires making assumptions about the rate of return. If there is relatively small variability in this, and little correlation between it and wealth, the wealth distribution in Malaysia should also be more unequal than the labor income distribution.

The ethnic decompositions of these distributions are more interesting. Racial disparity ratios are largest for own-account workers, and so also is the between-race contribution to inequality (24.3 percent by Theil T, 25.2 percent by Theil L, and 20.5 percent by varlog). This undoubtedly reflects wide disparities among the races in asset ownership, with the Malays, by and large, owning and cultivating paddy and rubber smallholdings in rural areas, and the Chinese owning shops and other sales or service establishments in the urban informal sector.[27]

Among employers, too, the racial disparity ratios are fairly large. The Chinese, who account for 80 percent of employers, receive significantly more than the Malays, who account for only 10 percent of employers. Indian employers, who account for another 10 percent, receive slightly less than the Chinese. These disparities indicate larger average wealth holdings for the Chinese and Indians than for the Malays; the differences in income seem much too large to be explicable by differential rates of return.[28]

Although there are no data on the wealth distribution among individuals in Malaysia, MTR (table 1-4) reports a racial breakdown for the ownership of corporate and noncorporate assets in modern agriculture and industry.

---

between-group contribution to inequality according to the Theil L measure. Adopting the notation of chapter 3, we can partially differentiate (L_B/L) with respect to μ_1 to give

$$\frac{\partial(L_B/L)}{\partial \mu_1} = \frac{L_w}{L^2}\left(\frac{n_1}{n}\right)\left(\frac{1}{\mu}-\frac{1}{\mu_1}\right) > 0 \quad \text{if} \quad \mu_1 > \mu.$$

The dependence of (L_B/L) on the population share (n_1/n) of group 1 can be similarly examined (the answer is somewhat messier to report). The same exercises can also be conducted for the other inequality measures which are decomposable.

27. Most own-account workers in rural areas probably cultivate paddy or rubber smallholdings. As seen in chapter 5, paddy farms are owned mainly by Malays, while rubber smallholdings are distributed more evenly between Malays and non-Malays. Most own-account workers in urban areas probably operate small-scale family enterprises such as retail establishments in the commercial sector and service or trucking businesses in the transport sector. These are owned to a large extent by the Chinese.

28. Some of the differences in rates of return might arise from differences in entrepreneurial ability. More generally, in seeking to explain racial income disparities for own-account workers and employers, factors such as initial endowment, savings propensity, and access to loans are likely to be important.

Table 6-7. Decomposition by Race and Employment Status of Inequality in the Personal Income Distribution

Racial group	Item	Employers	Employees	Own-account workers	Other[a]	All income recipients	Between-employment-status contribution to inequality (percent)	
Malay	Gini	0.6764	0.4788	0.3965	0.5139	0.4751		
	Theil T	1.1274	0.4323	0.2892	0.5005	0.4370	8.0	Theil T
	Theil L	0.9484	0.4371	0.2935	0.4735	0.4193	8.0	Theil L
	Varlog	1.6328	0.9067	0.6064	0.8621	0.8293	5.0	Varlog
	Geometric mean	163.6	92.6	66.5	51.5	77.7		
	Arithmetic mean	422.4	143.4	89.2	82.8	118.2		
	Sample size	68	10,660	7,952	1,639	20,319		
Chinese	Gini	0.4900	0.4537	0.4305	0.4993	0.4908		
	Theil T	0.4966	0.3965	0.3687	0.4553	0.4958	17.9	Theil T
	Theil L	0.4204	0.3729	0.3557	0.4782	0.4430	14.2	Theil L
	Varlog	0.7267	0.7275	0.7488	0.9988	0.8428	10.4	Varlog
	Geometric mean	505.0	123.3	164.6	93.1	134.3		
	Arithmetic mean	768.9	179.0	234.9	150.2	209.1		
	Sample size	548	10,280	3,076	1,286	15,190		
Indian	Gini	0.5617	0.4391	0.5114	0.5175	0.4693		
	Theil T	0.6916	0.4185	0.6444	0.4577	0.4998	7.4	Theil T
	Theil L	0.5568	0.3408	0.4834	0.5298	0.3925	6.5	Theil L
	Varlog	0.8724	0.5781	0.8101	1.1560	0.6573	3.7	Varlog
	Geometric mean	412.7	119.6	138.7	93.9	121.9		
	Arithmetic mean	720.2	168.1	224.9	159.6	180.4		
	Sample size	63	4,180	509	240	4,992		

						Between-race-and-employment-status contribution to inequality (percent)
Other						
Gini	0.3283	0.6276	0.5391	0.6232	0.7048	
Theil T	0.1980	0.7093	0.7330	0.6882	0.9442	Theil T 28.2
Theil L	0.2843	0.9621	0.5199	0.8780	1.2016	Theil L 33.4
Varlog	0.7775	2.3924	0.7105	1.9840	2.5426	Varlog 29.7
Geometric mean	1,333.7	322.1	52.2	150.2	172.5	
Arithmetic mean	1,772.3	843.0	87.8	361.3	573.5	
Sample size	6	169	95	31	301	
All racial groups						
Gini	0.5205	0.4764	0.4821	0.5361	0.5063	
Theil T	0.5612	0.4568	0.4685	0.5352	0.5360	Theil T 11.9
Theil L	0.5024	0.4205	0.4283	0.5389	0.4763	Theil L 9.0
Varlog	0.9537	0.8160	0.8225	1.0434	0.8967	Varlog 6.5
Geometric mean	447.0	109.4	87.1	69.1	101.3	
Arithmetic mean	738.8	166.6	133.6	118.4	163.0	
Sample size	685	25,289	11,632	3,196	40,802	
Between-race contribution to inequality (percent)						Between-race-and-employment-status contribution to inequality (percent)
Theil T	3.1	7.2	24.3	10.6	9.2	Theil T 21.7
Theil L	3.6	5.2	25.2	10.1	9.6	Theil L 19.3
Varlog	12.9	3.3	20.5	9.0	7.9	Varlog 14.8

a. The category of "other" here consists of the five PES categories of unpaid family workers, students, housewives or houseworkers, unemployed persons, and others.

Modern agriculture covers only estates under rubber, oil palm, coconut, and tea, with ownership specified in terms of total planted acreage; industry covers only manufacturing, construction, and mining, with ownership in terms of fixed assets (in millions of Malaysian dollars). (Other branches such as commerce, banking, and transport are not included under industry here.) I have converted the planted acreage figures for modern agriculture into money values at M$1,000 per acre, and added these to the fixed asset figures for industry. Foreign (that is, non-Malaysian) capital, which in fact accounts for 52 percent of estate acreage and for 51 percent of fixed assets in industry, is excluded from the following breakdown of asset ownership in Malaysia:

	Percentage share of assets in modern agriculture and industry	*Percentage share of employer income from all sources (table 6-6)*
Malay	19.4	5.7
Chinese	63.0	83.2
Indian	4.5	9.0
Other	13.1	2.1
Total	100.0	100.0

Employees are the most homogeneous group among the categories considered. Not only is the level of inequality in their incomes smallest, but so also are the racial disparity ratios and the between-race contribution to inequality. Among employees, the Chinese-Malay disparity ratio is only 1.25, and the Indian-Malay ratio is only 1.17. The between-race contribution to inequality among employees is 7.2 percent by Theil T, 5.2 percent by Theil L, and 3.3 percent by varlog. These disparity ratios for employee incomes indicate that only a small part of the overall disparity ratios for personal income are attributable to racial differences in labor income. It is the relatively large differences in nonlabor income and the disproportionate distribution of the races by employment status that account for the higher overall Chinese-Malay disparity ratio of 1.77 and Indian-Malay ratio of 1.53.

It is possible to list various factors that could account for observed disparities in labor income (see Atkinson, 1975). Because of the limitations of PES data, only two factors can be examined to any extent, namely, education and age (or experience). The next chapter contains a detailed analysis of education, age, and employee incomes in urban areas. Here I briefly mention some other explanations that are sometimes advanced for interracial disparities in labor income.

Interracial Earnings Differentials among Rubber Tappers

Apart from differences in education and training generally, earnings differentials could also arise from intergroup differences in ability, opportunities, and tastes. While it is common to observe interpersonal differences in ability, there is no prima facie reason to expect any interracial differences in this attribute. In any case, it seems rather difficult to agree upon an economically relevant and operationally usable definition of ability which can permit empirical testing. The role played by opportunity also raises problems. For example, it is difficult to estimate the extent to which income differences among groups arise from discrimination, if any, in education or employment.

Differences in tastes would appear to relate to differences in one of at least three major characteristics: propensity to save, risk aversion, and leisure preference.[29] The first two characteristics probably affect the incomes of employers and self-employed more than of employees, and are of no concern here.[30] In regard to differences in leisure preference, there are some isolated data which allow a partial test. Thillainathan (1976) has compiled an interesting time series on the daily and monthly earnings of rubber tappers on estates.[31] Since the activity is rather narrowly defined and payment is by piece rate, any differences in monthly earnings can probably be attributed to differences in productivity and in the number of days worked per month, assuming there are no systematic differences in employment practice, estate yields, or work-force composition. The data, covering a fourteen-year period, 1960–73, show a Chinese-Malay disparity

29. Consideration of these factors immediately reminds one of the inadequacy of current income as a measure of welfare, static or dynamic. Current welfare depends on current consumption as well as leisure, among other things. Ignoring leisure generally overstates inequality in current-period utility, unless leisure and income are highly complementary. To compensate for variations in leisure time among individuals and groups, a measure such as Kolm's "leisurely equivalent income" is needed (see Kolm, 1969, pp. 181–82). Lifetime welfare is also not adequately captured by current income: different savings propensities can lead to different amounts accumulated (and bequeathed), and hence to different income and utility profiles over the life cycle.

30. To the extent that employee incomes include returns to capital, however, the propensity to save and risk aversion are indeed relevant factors. But there are not yet reliable data on savings, and testing for differences in risk aversion is likely to be even more difficult.

31. The data have been compiled from the *Annual Reports* and *Handbook of Labour Statistics* of the Ministry of Labour and Manpower, Kuala Lumpur.

ratio in average monthly earnings of 1.25, and an Indian-Malay ratio of 1.14; for average daily earnings, the corresponding disparity ratios are 1.15 and 1.07, respectively (Thillainathan, 1976, pp. 47–48). Thus, in terms of latex output per day, the Chinese appear to be about 15 percent more productive than the Malays, and the Indians about 7 percent more productive than the Malays. When these differences in daily earnings are netted out, the rest of the monthly earnings disparities should be due to differences in the number of days worked per month.[32] On average, therefore, the Chinese would seem to work about 9 percent more days per month than the Malays, and the Indians about 7 percent more than the Malays. This could be some indication of the relative preference between leisure and income among the three ethnic groups, at least in one major industry in the country.[33]

Decomposition by Occupational Category

One of the objectives of NEP Prong 2 is to reduce (and eventually eliminate) the identification of race with economic function. Although economic function could be defined by a variety of characteristics, it has generally been associated with occupation and sometimes sector of employment. This section examines the extent to which the major racial groups are identified with particular occupations, and the effects of this on personal income inequality.

Table 6-8 presents a breakdown of income recipients according to eight broad (one-digit) occupational categories, cross-classified by racial

32. In a quite different context, I have analyzed the effects of differences in leisure preference among workers on the shape of the optimal earnings schedule offered by an employer. These differences give rise to an unequal earnings distribution, which is less or more equal than the leisure preference distribution according to the convexity or concavity of the earnings schedule. See Anand (1970).

33. A body of data for the gravel pump mining industry during 1960–73 (Thillainathan, 1976, pp. 50–52) enables a comparison of the earnings differentials between Chinese and Indian unskilled workers. The jobs performed by the two groups are not specified exactly, and the data seem generally less robust than those for the rubber tappers. Since 1970 there is an average monthly earnings differential of 20 percent between the Chinese and the Indians, and a daily earnings differential of 17 percent. Thus, on average, the Chinese would seem to work 3 percent more days per month than the Indians. The daily earnings differential of 17 percent is likely to be due at least in part to differences in personal characteristics between the groups. The differential could arise from differences in physical productivity as well as in daily overtime, but differences in skill mix between the groups are also possible, as this is an industry with a gradation of skills within the unskilled labor category.

group.[34] It shows the usual statistics for this breakdown, including the four inequality measures (Gini, Theil T, Theil L, and varlog), the geometric and arithmetic mean income, and sample size.

The racial pattern of employment for all occupations shows the Malays accounting for 50 percent, Chinese 37 percent, Indians 12 percent, and others 1 percent (calculated from table 6-8). This pattern is almost identical to that of the racial proportions in the population of the country as a whole. The racial groups, however, are not represented in these proportions *within* the various occupations, and severe imbalances exist in some. For instance, the Malays constitute 85 percent of all farmers but only 28 percent of all sales workers; and in the administrative and managerial, clerical and related, and production worker categories, the Malays account for little more than 30 percent of the work force. In contrast, the Chinese constitute less than 13 percent of farmers but some 60 percent of sales workers and 57 percent of production workers; further, they account for 46 percent of administrative and managerial personnel and also of clerical staff, but for only 25 percent of farm laborers (of whom 55 percent are Malays). Indians are over-represented in the administrative and managerial (21 percent), clerical and related (17 percent), and farm laborer (20 percent) categories, but are markedly underrepresented in the farmer (1 percent) category.

These imbalances in the racial pattern of employment, with the Malays concentrated in the less well-paid occupations and the Chinese in the better-paid ones, account for a large part of the income disparities between the races. Further, within each occupation there are sometimes significant differences in mean income among the races, with the Malays often, but not always, receiving less than the Chinese and Indians. This imbalance, which is examined below, compounds the effect on income disparities of the already uneven occupational distribution among the races. To reduce the wide differentials "generated by existing racial inequalities in the job-hierarchy, especially in the modern sectors of the economy," the government stresses that "increased efforts will be needed to progressively expand the professional, managerial and technical skills of the Malays so that their position in the occupational structure within each of the major sectors of the economy is enhanced" (MTR, p. 80). The labor market policies (such as racial quotas in employment and admission to institutes of higher education) associated with the specified restructuring of high- and middle-level Malay manpower are examined in chapter 8, in the context of a wider discussion of NEP Prong 2.

---

34. The note to table 6-11 at the end of this chapter contains a definition of the one-digit occupational categories. These were regrouped from the more detailed two-digit classification available in PES.

Table 6-8. Decomposition by Race and Occupation of Inequality in the Personal Income Distribution

Racial group	Item	Professional and technical (1)	Administrative and managerial (2)	Clerical and related (3)	Sales workers (4)	Service workers (5)	Farmers (6)	Farm laborers (7)	Production workers (8)	All occupations	Between-occupation contribution to inequality (percent)	
Malay	Gini	0.3445	0.5206	0.3671	0.4747	0.4018	0.3652	0.3680	0.4039	0.4771		
	Theil T	0.2102	0.5962	0.2540	0.4295	0.2961	0.2318	0.2357	0.2782	0.4429	37.0	Theil T
	Theil L	0.2560	0.4715	0.2811	0.4197	0.3435	0.2509	0.2582	0.3392	0.4209	32.0	Theil L
	Varlog	0.6555	0.7543	0.6808	0.8312	0.8211	0.5408	0.5567	0.8099	0.8267	23.2	Varlog
	Geometric mean	246.8	358.5	179.7	77.7	121.8	65.3	56.9	94.3	80.0		
	Arithmetic mean	318.8	574.5	238.0	118.2	171.7	83.9	73.7	132.3	121.9		
	Sample size	1,001	237	682	1,079	1,325	5,791	5,191	2,340	17,646		
Chinese	Gini	0.3808	0.4804	0.3638	0.5074	0.4899	0.4309	0.3070	0.3996	0.4903		
	Theil T	0.2690	0.4211	0.2389	0.5681	0.4890	0.3453	0.1753	0.3227	0.4960	24.7	Theil T
	Theil L	0.2713	0.4041	0.2451	0.4761	0.4359	0.3515	0.1836	0.3113	0.4396	24.9	Theil L
	Varlog	0.5812	0.7628	0.5326	0.8749	0.8065	0.7473	0.4013	0.6651	0.8290	19.7	Varlog
	Geometric mean	349.7	494.0	228.7	166.9	107.9	150.4	89.9	125.0	142.4		
	Arithmetic mean	458.7	740.0	292.2	268.7	166.9	213.7	108.0	170.7	221.0		
	Sample size	797	364	879	2,346	1,458	860	2,341	4,045	13,090		
Indian	Gini	0.4937	0.5006	0.3949	0.5175	0.4331	0.4750	0.2189	0.2972	0.4744		
	Theil T	0.4846	0.4561	0.2616	0.7049	0.3610	0.3870	0.0923	0.1811	0.5142	34.9	Theil T
	Theil L	0.4504	0.4180	0.3086	0.4883	0.3498	0.4353	0.0984	0.1680	0.3963	40.4	Theil L
	Varlog	0.8837	0.7076	0.7469	0.7526	0.7069	0.9490	0.2211	0.3403	0.6425	27.5	Varlog
	Geometric mean	361.4	270.9	212.1	126.6	104.7	103.3	89.5	152.4	125.7		
	Arithmetic mean	567.0	411.5	288.8	206.4	148.5	159.7	98.8	180.3	186.8		
	Sample size	288	177	329	457	501	78	1,885	680	4,395		

										Between-race-and-occupation contribution to inequality (percent)
Other										
Gini	0.5119	0.3088	0.3593	0.7192	0.5243	0.3616	0.3422	0.6195	0.7032	
Theil T	0.4357	0.1830	0.2277	1.0625	0.4818	0.2272	0.2422	0.7631	0.9363	60.0 Theil T
Theil L	0.5819	0.1735	0.3412	1.1401	0.6663	0.2294	0.2119	0.7452	1.2194	63.1 Theil L
Varlog	1.4646	0.3318	0.9996	1.9189	1.6626	0.4502	0.3453	1.1738	2.6269	62.6 Varlog
Geometric mean	573.3	2,235.7	189.1	101.2	341.6	43.7	28.6	220.1	181.4	
Arithmetic mean	1,025.8	2,659.1	265.9	316.4	665.1	54.9	35.3	463.7	613.9	
Sample size	60	21	32	14	23	72	17	23	262	
All racial groups										
Gini	0.4176	0.5291	0.3742	0.5277	0.4590	0.4234	0.3339	0.3979	0.5093	
Theil T	0.3423	0.5363	0.2520	0.6151	0.4118	0.3404	0.2003	0.3104	0.5441	31.8 Theil T
Theil L	0.3366	0.4911	0.2749	0.5216	0.3996	0.3286	0.2233	0.3184	0.4798	31.7 Theil L
Varlog	0.7240	0.8716	0.6415	0.9636	0.8158	0.6513	0.5033	0.7093	0.8953	23.8 Varlog
Geometric mean	302.7	409.1	206.6	130.5	113.7	72.6	69.7	116.3	105.4	
Arithmetic mean	423.8	668.6	271.9	219.9	169.5	100.9	87.2	159.9	170.2	
Sample size	2,146	799	1,922	3,896	3,307	6,801	9,434	7,088	35,393	
Between-race contribution to inequality (percent)										
Theil T	12.8	16.9	1.8	8.1	4.4	22.1	7.8	3.6	9.7	38.5 Theil T
Theil L	11.8	14.3	1.7	11.0	3.1	19.2	7.0	3.2	10.2	38.0 Theil L
Varlog	5.9	15.5	1.9	11.6	1.5	12.4	10.5	3.7	8.6	29.9 Varlog

Note: See note to table 6-11 for the definition of the eight one-digit occupational categories in terms of the two-digit code used in the PES. It can be verified from table 6-11 that there were 5,413 income recipients who were not in the labor force or whose occupation was not available (code numbers 00, 10, and 99)—hence the sample size of 35,393 for all occupations in table 6-8 compared with a sample size of 40,806 for all income recipients in table 6-2, 6-3, 6-5, or 6-6.

An examination of the mean incomes of the major racial groups within each occupation (table 6-8) reveals that the Chinese receive higher incomes on average than the Malays and Indians, and that the Indians receive higher incomes than the Malays. With the exception of farmers and sales workers, racial income disparities within occupations are not as large as overall racial income disparities. There are some notable exceptions to the general ranking of the three racial groups by income level:

—In the professional and technical occupations, the Indians receive the highest mean incomes.

—In the administrative and managerial category, the Malays receive significantly higher incomes than the Indians.

—In the category of service workers, the Malays receive the highest mean incomes, but the difference between the racial groups is not large.

—In the category of production workers, the Indians receive the highest mean incomes, but again the difference between the three racial groups is not very large.

More detailed information on income by racial group and occupation at the two-digit level is contained in table 6-11 at the end of this chapter. The table presents for each subcategory the mean income, standard deviation of income, and sample size.[35] Thus, the disaggregation of the one-digit administrative and managerial category in table 6-8 shows that the Malays receive significantly more than the Chinese in the subcategory of government administrators and legislative officials (two-digit code 20 in table 6-11), but the Chinese receive more than the Malays in the subcategory of managers (two-digit code 21). Higher Malay incomes in the administrative subcategories are probably a reflection of the preferential treatment in hiring and promotion given to Malays in the government sector. In addition, the level of earnings in the public sector is about 50 percent higher than in the private sector (Mazumdar, 1975), so that government's public sector employment policies (four-to-one quotas in favor of Malays at some levels of the hierarchy) should contribute to a narrowing of between-race income differentials. This deployment of the government machine to help the Malays is meant to counterbalance the natural advantage enjoyed by the Chinese in the business sector.

The racial disparity ratios among farmers are greatest, with Chinese farmers receiving more than two-and-a-half times as much as Malay

35. The mean and standard deviation of income immediately allow one to compute a well-known measure of inequality, the coefficient of variation. This is defined as the standard deviation of income divided by the arithmetic mean income.

farmers, and Indian farmers (constituting only 1 percent of the category) receiving almost twice as much as Malay farmers. These differentials strongly suggest that average Chinese landholdings are much larger than average Malay landholdings (see the previous section also), but there are no independent data on land distribution in Malaysia.[36] The disparity ratios among farmers tally with the large between-race contribution to inequality in their incomes (22.1 percent by Theil T, 19.2 percent by Theil L, and 12.4 percent by varlog).

The between-race contribution to inequality within other occupations is not large, except for the administrative and managerial category, where it is about 16 percent. As one might expect, the incomes of clerical, service, and production workers are fairly homogeneous across racial groups, and this is reflected in the small between-race contributions to inequality. These are occupations in which the degree of labor unionization is high and uniform wage contracts are likely to prevail.[37] Higher between-race contributions to inequality within other occupations (table 6-8) probably arise from greater variation in skill levels and wealth owned.

Interoccupation differentials (within each racial group) are much larger than interracial differentials (within each occupational category). The between-occupation contribution to personal income inequality for all racial groups is 31.8 percent by Theil T, 31.7 percent by Theil L, and 23.8 percent by varlog, whereas the between-race contribution is 10.2 percent or less by the three measures.[38] In computing this between-occupation contribution, race was not held constant in any sense, and it might be claimed that some of the between-occupation contribution observed is really the effect of race. As noted earlier in this section, there is indeed some multicollinearity between occupation and race, so that a part of the between-occupation contribution could be a between-race effect.[39] But

36. Some data on rubber smallholdings imply a ratio of 2:1 for Chinese-to-Malay average size of holding. An agricultural census of the country has recently been taken, but the results are not yet available.

37. For sales workers and farm laborers, the between-race contributions are not quite so small. Apart from nonunionization, this might reflect differential ownership of assets (see, for example, occupational code 41, working proprietors, in table 6-11) and preferential hiring within one's own race.

38. As discussed in appendix C, one expects different between-group contributions from different measures of inequality. It is interesting, however, that the differences are not wildly large (as, theoretically, they could be).

39. If, for instance, there were just as many occupations as racial groups, and each racial group were perfectly identified with one occupation, then the between-occupation contribution would be indistinguishable from the between-race contribution. This is obviously not the case in Malaysia, where the racial groups are distributed over every occupation, albeit unevenly (see table 6-8).

from table 6-8, the between-occupation contribution within each racial group is just as high as the between-occupation contribution overall. For Malays this is 37.0 percent by Theil T, 32.0 percent by Theil L, and 23.2 percent by varlog; for Chinese it is 24.7, 24.9, and 19.7 percent, respectively; and for Indians it is 34.9, 40.4, and 27.5 percent, respectively. This suggests that the overall contribution is genuinely one of occupation.

Another way to attempt to disentangle the contributions of the variables is by a two-way decomposition of inequality by race *and* occupation (4 times 8 separate groups). With this finer partition, the between-group contribution becomes 38.5, 38.0, and 29.9 percent according to Theil T, Theil L, and varlog, respectively. It can be shown that any two-way contribution is always greater than or equal to each of the one-way contributions, and less than or equal to their sum. Had the between-race-and-occupation contribution been *equal to* the sum of the between-race and between-occupation contributions, the variables might be called uncorrelated or orthogonal. The divergence of the two-way contribution from the sum of the one-way contributions might then be said to indicate the degree of collinearity. The sum of the between-race and between-occupation contributions is 41.5 percent by Theil T, 41.9 percent by Theil L, and 32.4 percent by varlog, while the between-race-and-occupation contributions are 38.5, 38.0, and 29.9 percent by the three measures, respectively. This indicates only slight dependence between occupation and race in their contributions to overall inequality.

The analogy with regression analysis may be carried further. The between-race contribution to overall income inequality is analogous to the proportion of variance of, say, income (or log-income) explained by race in a simple regression between income (or log-income) as the dependent variable, and race as the explanatory variable. Similarly, the between-occupation contribution to overall income inequality is analogous to the R^2 of a single-variable regression between income (or log-income) and occupation. The between-race-and-occupation contribution to overall income inequality is analogous to the proportion of variance of income (or log-income) explained by both race and occupation in a multiple regression between income (or log-income) as the dependent variable, and race and occupation as the explanatory variables. The R^2 of the multiple regression is greater than or equal to the R^2's of each of the simple regressions, and less than or equal to their sum—just as the two-way between-group contribution is greater than or equal to each of the one-way contributions, and less than or equal to their sum. When the explanatory variables are uncorrelated or orthogonal, the R^2 of the multiple regression is equal to the sum of the R^2's of the simple regressions. Otherwise, with multicollinearity, the proportion of variance of income (or log-income) explained by race *and* occupation cannot be split up into a part explained by race alone and another part explained by occupation alone. In this case, the R^2's (and coefficient estimates) of the simple regressions include the effect of the omitted variable to the extent that it is collinear with the included variable.

The R^2 of a multivariate regression equation is like the between-group contribution of a multivariate partition (that is, a partition defined by multiple variables). Just as the R^2 increases (does not decrease) as variables are added, the between-group contribution increases (does not decrease) as the partition is made finer with additional defining variables. But an a priori comparison of R^2's, or between-group contributions, cannot be made if the variables or the groups are not nested. Thus it cannot be said whether the R^2, or between-group contribution, of an arbitrary set of independent variables, or partition of the population, will be greater or smaller than that of another set of variables or partition—even if one has many more variables or groups than the other.[40] It is only when variables are actually added, or the partition is actually made finer, that the R^2, or between-group contribution, increases. In the limit, however, just as R^2 tends to unity as the number of variables tends to the number of observations (that is, the degrees of freedom shrink to zero), so also does the between-group contribution tend to unity as the number of groups tends to the number of people in the population (that is, the partition becomes so fine that each group contains only one person).

The methodology of inequality decomposition does not allow the measurement of the pure contribution of a factor to overall inequality: the effect of all variables correlated with the factor is also included.[41] Just as the R^2 of a simple regression between income (or log-income) and race does not hold other variables constant, so the between-race contribution to overall income inequality does not hold the effect of other variables constant. The between-race contribution to inequality measures the effect of race both on its own and in association with other factors, such as occupation, education, and so on.[42] Thus 8.6 to 10.2 percent is the total contribution of race to inequality, not the contribution of race with other factors held

40. For example, if each group has the same mean income, then no matter how many groups there are, the between-group contribution will be zero.

41. In linear regression analysis, however, the partial correlation coefficient can be used to measure the correlation between two variables holding the effect of other variables constant, that is, removing their influence. There is no analogy to the partial correlation coefficient in inequality decomposition analysis.

42. Everything that makes the racial income distributions what they are is thus taken into account; the between-race contribution simply measures the fraction of overall inequality attributable to racial differences in mean income, however these came about.

Table 6-9. Decomposition by Race and Employment Sector of Inequality in the Personal Income Distribution

Racial group	Item	Agriculture (1ᵃ)	Agricultural products (2)	Mining and quarrying (3)	Manufacturing (4)	Construction (5)	Public utilities (6)	Commerce (7)	Transport, storage, and communication (8)	Services (9)	All sectors	Between-sector contribution to inequality (percent)
Malay	Gini	0.3937	0.3590	0.3624	0.4906	0.4101	0.2336	0.4717	0.3377	0.4277	0.4709	
	Theil T	0.2749	0.2305	0.3422	0.4454	0.5865	0.1117	0.4130	0.2022	0.3563	0.4313	26.5 Theil T
	Theil L	0.2893	0.2460	0.2607	0.4537	0.3312	0.0945	0.4174	0.2067	0.3730	0.4114	25.7 Theil L
	Varlog	0.6062	0.5294	0.4653	0.9057	0.4674	0.1602	0.8510	0.4365	0.8541	0.8140	20.6 Varlog
	Geometric mean	61.1	63.0	168.9	66.0	143.6	176.3	85.3	150.4	166.7	80.9	
	Arithmetic mean	81.5	80.6	219.3	103.8	200.0	193.7	129.4	184.9	242.0	122.0	
	Sample size	5,458	5,695	183	1,326	343	224	1,301	725	3,045	18,300	
Chinese	Gini	0.4499	0.3787	0.4108	0.5056	0.4069	0.4439	0.5178	0.2982	0.4964	0.4888	
	Theil T	0.3870	0.2928	0.5051	0.5319	0.3799	0.3762	0.5821	0.1614	0.4476	0.4939	6.7 Theil T
	Theil L	0.3806	0.2581	0.3166	0.4768	0.3016	0.3672	0.4934	0.1552	0.4692	0.4365	7.9 Theil L
	Varlog	0.7823	0.4797	0.4660	0.9091	0.5189	0.7510	0.8982	0.3061	0.9934	0.8212	5.7 Varlog
	Geometric mean	111.6	107.6	161.3	118.1	157.1	208.9	177.2	192.8	166.3	141.1	
	Arithmetic mean	163.3	139.2	221.4	190.2	212.5	301.5	290.3	225.1	265.8	218.3	
	Sample size	1,119	2,398	438	2,698	646	77	2,631	601	2,720	13,328	
Indian	Gini	0.4449	0.2969	0.2843	0.3999	0.2534	0.3622	0.5255	0.3150	0.5477	0.4662	
	Theil T	0.3482	0.2312	0.1879	0.3424	0.1174	0.3183	0.6618	0.1728	0.6126	0.5014	14.2 Theil T
	Theil L	0.3743	0.1743	0.1448	0.2982	0.1166	0.2341	0.4981	0.1715	0.5573	0.3844	19.2 Theil L
	Varlog	0.7985	0.2938	0.2210	0.5631	0.2369	0.3467	0.8084	0.3475	1.0444	0.6246	11.2 Varlog
	Geometric mean	85.0	95.9	158.6	132.1	161.1	192.1	140.2	193.9	159.3	124.7	
	Arithmetic mean	123.6	114.2	183.3	178.1	181.1	242.8	230.7	230.2	278.2	183.1	
	Sample size	112	2,062	62	234	145	146	538	287	1,077	4,663	
Other	Gini	0.3826	0.6705	0.2941	0.5735	0.1354	0.2741	0.6834	0.5489	0.5872	0.7037	
	Theil T	0.2674	0.8846	0.2111	0.5730	0.0451	0.2216	0.8780	0.5774	0.6190	0.9387	32.1 Theil T
	Theil L	0.2509	1.3648	0.3166	0.6869	0.0505	0.3461	1.2733	0.5673	0.7692	1.2192	46.3 Theil L
	Varlog	0.4543	3.0720	0.8494	1.4277	0.1108	0.9535	2.8787	1.0279	1.8320	2.6217	44.2 Varlog

Geometric mean	38.5	254.6	1063.6	383.6	184.1	557.0	178.4	290.3	440.8	180.3
Arithmetic mean	49.5	996.6	1459.7	762.3	193.7	787.3	637.4	512.0	951.2	610.3
Sample size	82	19	3	15	3	3	20	15	104	264

All racial groups

Gini	0.4330	0.3802	0.4021	0.5156	0.3918	0.3430	0.5350	0.3301	0.3937	0.5040	
Theil T	0.3540	0.5359	0.4612	0.9727	0.4683	0.3391	0.9867	0.3960	0.9672	0.8773	16.1 Theil T
Theil L	0.3463	0.2770	0.3038	0.5035	0.2877	0.2103	0.5352	0.1950	0.4667	0.4698	19.0 Theil L
Varlog	0.6913	0.3158	0.4615	0.5484	0.4118	0.2694	0.6220	0.2006	0.4785	0.5347	15.6 Varlog
Geometric mean	67.5	78.0	164.4	99.6	153.5	188.0	139.4	173.4	167.8	105.3	
Arithmetic mean	95.4	102.9	222.8	164.8	204.7	232.0	238.1	210.8	267.6	168.4	
Sample size	6,771	10,174	686	4,273	1,137	450	4,490	1,628	6,946	36,555	

Between-race-and-sector contribution to inequality (percent)

Between-race contribution to inequality (percent)

Theil T	12.9	16.9	6.7	8.0	0.3	9.7	8.6	5.9	6.6	9.5	23.5 Theil T
Theil L	11.8	14.6	5.8	8.5	0.5	10.6	11.2	5.2	4.6	10.0	26.8 Theil L
Varlog	7.9	11.4	3.4	8.4	0.4	3.5	10.6	4.5	1.5	8.2	21.7 Varlog

Between-race-and-sector contribution to inequality (percent)

a. The industrial classification used in PES is the standard two-digit code from Department of Statistics, *Malaysian Industrial Classification* (Kuala Lumpur, 1971). The nine one-digit sectors in this table have been regrouped from the two-digit PES code as follows:

Two-digit PES code	One-digit code	Description
00,10.99	—	Not in labor force, or sector not available
01–09	1	Agriculture
11–19	2	Agricultural products
20–29	3	Mining and quarrying
30–49	4	Manufacturing
50–59	5	Construction
60–69	6	Public utilities
70–79	7	Commerce
80–89	8	Transport, storage, and communication
90–98	9	Services

constant.[43] Similarly, 23.8 to 31.8 percent is the total contribution of occupation to inequality. The conclusion from the race-occupation decompositions is that occupational differences contribute much more to personal income inequality than do racial differences.

Decomposition by Sector of Employment

One of the government's aims in restructuring the racial pattern of employment is "to achieve greater equalization of income among the different races in the country" (Robless, 1975a, p. 44). Two factors underlying racial income disparities are seen as: "(i) the concentration of Malays in the agricultural sector where output per worker is the lowest; (ii) the concentration of Chinese in the mining, manufacturing and construction sectors where output per worker is two to three times higher than in agriculture" (Robless, 1975a, p. 42). Imbalances also exist within sectors of employment: within each sector Malays are concentrated in the "lower occupational levels of the job hierarchy, especially in the unskilled and semi-skilled categories" (MTR, p. 9). The sectoral imbalances are confirmed in table 6-9, which also shows a significant concentration of Chinese in commerce.

For the one-digit industrial classification into nine sectors shown in table 6-9, the between-sector contribution to personal income inequality is considerably less than the between-occupation contribution. The between-sector contribution stands at 16.1, 19.0, and 15.6 percent by the three measures, respectively, which is half to two-thirds the between-occupation contribution. Sectoral differences in mean income, therefore, do affect overall inequality, but not by very much. The result casts doubt on the emphasis that planners often place on differences in sectoral productivity in explaining personal income inequality. Since 80 to 85 percent of inequality arises within sectors, it becomes difficult to agree, for example, that "a primary reason for the degree of inequality . . . is the sectoral distribution of employment among income classes and racial groups" (Robless, 1975a, p. 41).

The sectoral distribution of employment contributes a variable amount to income inequality within each racial group. The between-sector contribution to Chinese income inequality is only 6 to 8 percent, to Malay income inequality about 25 percent, and to Indian income inequality about

---

43. If it were possible to hold other factors constant, the extent of inequality attributable to racial discrimination could be measured.

15 percent—while the between-sector contribution to overall income inequality is about 17 percent.

The between-race contribution to overall income inequality is about half as much as the between-sector contribution. Table 6-9 shows the between-race contribution to income inequality in each sector. This is especially small in the construction sector (less than 1 percent), and also fairly small in mining, transport, and services. In general, these sectors use manual and unskilled labor for which the rate of wage payment is fairly uniform. In other sectors, the between-race contribution is higher, which probably reflects differential ownership by racial groups of physical and human capital. For example, in agriculture, agricultural products, and commerce, it is probably the superior possession by Chinese of land and other assets that accounts for the large income disparity ratios. In manufacturing, the relatively large disparity ratios are probably the result of a superior average level of skills among the Chinese. In the next chapter, I examine the extent to which skills acquired through education and experience are associated with the incomes that people receive.

Multivariate Decompositions

With the possible exception of occupation, the decompositions so far have not accounted for much of personal income inequality. These results are of value in a negative sense, for they cast doubt on some current beliefs concerning the factors responsible for income inequality in developing countries. They also suggest that the variables and the degree of disaggregation for which data are commonly available might have limited power to explain personal income inequality.

Some multisector distributional planning models assume an income generation process with a two-way classification of income recipients by sector and skill (or occupation).[44] All workers in each sector-skill group are assumed to receive the same wage, the mean income of the group.[45] Thus income inequality is generated in these models solely by between-group differences in mean income; any within-group inequality is superimposed

44. Some of the better-known models of this type are those of Weisskoff (1973), Morley and Williamson (1973), Thorbecke and Sengupta (1972), and Adelman and Robinson (1977). A more complete bibliography of such models may be found in Chenery and others (1974) or Blitzer, Clark, and Taylor (1975).

45. In some models, this wage is fixed exogenously, but in the more sophisticated general equilibrium models, such as those of Adelman and Robinson (1977) or Adelman and Tyson (1974), the wage for each sector-skill category is determined endogenously.

exogenously. The decompositions for Malaysia suggest that a multisector (input-output) model of this type would explain only about 30 percent of personal income inequality (see table 6-10).[46]

Other models assign "welfare weights" to particular groups of people defined not by income level but by race or region (see, for example, Marglin, 1967). These weights, if based solely on the mean income of the group, can be misleading indicators of the relative social value of income accruing to the group. The reason is that they completely ignore within-

Table 6-10. Multivariate Decomposition
of Personal Income Inequality

Description of multivariate grouping		Number of groups	Between-group contribution to personal income inequality (percent)		
			Theil T	Theil L	Varlog
3 locations (as in table 6-5)	× 9 employment sectors (as in table 6-9)	27	18.8	21.6	17.1
9 employment sectors (as in table 6-9)	× 4 employment-status categories (as in table 6-7)	36	26.0	25.4	19.9
8 occupations (as in table 6-8)	× 9 employment sectors (as in table 6-9)	72	34.5	33.5	26.9
6 educational categories[a]	× 9 employment sectors (as in table 6-9)	54	31.1	31.4	25.9
6 educational categories[a]	× 8 occupations (as in table 6-8)	48	38.1	36.4	29.3
13 age groups[b]	× 8 occupations (as in table 6-8)	104	40.3	40.9	34.1
13 age groups[b]	× 6 educational categories[a]	78	42.2	38.7	35.2
13 age groups[b] × 6 educational categories[a]	× 8 occupations (as in table 6-8)	624	54.1	49.6	44.1

a. The 6 educational categories (as in table 4-3) are: none, some primary, completed primary, lower secondary (forms I–III), some upper secondary (forms IV–V), and school certificate or higher.

b. The 13 age groups (in years) are:

1–14	35–39	60–64
15–19	40–44	65–69
20–24	45–49	70 +
25–29	50–54	
30–34	55–59	

46. This does not detract from the usefulness of multisector models in indicating areas where policy intervention can, in fact, reduce inequality, by however small an amount.

group income inequality, which can be substantial.[47] This is what prompted, in the previous chapter, the detailed cross-classification of certain income groups (the poor) in preference to a broader approach which simply discriminates on the basis of region or race.

In an attempt to explore the sources of inequality and the determinants of income in Malaysia, some further decompositions, based on two-way and three-way partitions by relevant variables, are presented in table 6-10. The multivariate decompositions do not add very much to the single-variable decompositions. For instance, the partition of 8 occupations times 9 employment sectors yields a between-group contribution of 34.5 percent by Theil T, 33.5 percent by Theil L, and 26.9 percent by varlog. This is not much more than the one-way between-occupation contribution of 31.8, 31.7, and 23.8 percent, respectively, by the three measures (table 6-8). The hypothetical distribution which assigns to each person in an industry-occupation cell the mean income of the cell will thus account for only about 30 percent of overall income inequality. This suggests that the existing categories need to be disaggregated or other variables added, or both, to simulate better the personal income distribution.[48]

Other decompositions do yield higher between-group contributions. Interestingly, education, age, and occupation seem to be the most important variables in explaining inequality (table 6-10). The decomposition by education and occupation accounts for 38.1, 36.4, and 29.3 percent of inequality by Theil T, Theil L, and varlog, respectively; the decomposition by age and occupation accounts for 40.3, 40.9, and 34.1 percent of inequality; the decomposition by age and education accounts for 42.2, 38.7, and 35.2 percent of inequality. Finally, when all three variables are combined in a three-way decomposition, the between-group contribution to inequality is 54.1 percent by Theil T, 49.6 percent by Theil L, and 44.1 percent by varlog. In absolute terms, this explanatory power is not huge, but it suggests that life-cycle factors such as age and education should figure prominently in any model seeking to explain personal income inequality. The human capital model in the next chapter uses exactly these variables to explain income inequality.

47. A model which takes some account of within-group income inequality is that of Squire and van der Tak (1975). They estimate welfare weights by assuming a particular distribution for incremental income among the members of a group. In a different context, Sen (1976b) estimates indices of regional welfare by combining the mean income of a region with a measure (the Gini coefficient) of the income inequality within it.

48. Examples of disaggregation for the occupational category are large-, medium-, and small-scale farmers, and skilled and unskilled production workers. Any additional variable which can distinguish asset ownership among individuals is also likely to improve performance. Other variables should incorporate personal characteristics such as age and education.

Table 6-11. Arithmetic Mean Income of Income Recipients
by Two-digit Occupational Category and Race
(M$ per month)

Two-digit occupation code	Item	All racial groups	Malay	Chinese	Indian	Other
01. Physical	Mean income	465	323	375	743	1,615
scientists and	Standard deviation	485	229	250	871	0
related	Sample size	41	10	22	8	1
technicians						
02. Architects	Mean income	1,337	775	1,288	1,394	1,654
and engineers	Standard deviation	713	444	678	667	830
	Sample size	46	4	26	6	10
03. Engineering	Mean income	409	351	473	413	309
assistants,	Standard deviation	260	203	321	206	183
draftsmen, etc.	Sample size	177	72	69	32	4
04. Aircraft	Mean income	1,289	196	343	—	2,353
and ships'	Standard deviation	1,191	66	0	—	595
officers	Sample size	10	4	1	0	5
05. Life scientists	Mean income	608	447	660	1,169	1,369
and related	Standard deviation	690	356	439	815	2,048
technicians	Sample size	39	29	3	4	3
06. Medical	Mean income	821	420	713	1,288	472
doctors,	Standard deviation	1,104	305	802	1,663	150
dentists,	Sample size	123	21	64	35	3
vets, etc.						
07. Nurses	Mean income	260	192	320	256	545
and midwives	Standard deviation	178	163	178	145	0
	Sample size	169	70	76	22	1
08. Statisticians,	Mean income	1,796	—	—	1,796	—
mathema-	Standard deviation	1,701	—	—	1,701	—
ticians, etc.	Sample size	3	0	0	3	0
09. Economists	Mean income	965	818	1,111	1,111	—
	Standard deviation	358	507	0	0	—
	Sample size	6	3	2	1	0
11. Accountants	Mean income	970	980	1,033	479	1,508
	Standard deviation	602	775	506	183	945
	Sample size	24	3	13	5	3
12. Jurists	Mean income	1,431	1,867	986	1,767	—
	Standard deviation	656	0	452	683	—
	Sample size	9	1	4	4	0
13. Teachers	Mean income	365	311	414	422	875
	Standard deviation	256	171	219	366	954
	Sample size	1,275	705	416	135	19
14. Workers in	Mean income	173	212	181	112	147
religion	Standard deviation	197	264	145	94	218
	Sample size	87	33	26	21	7

Two-digit occupation code	Item	All racial groups	Malay	Chinese	Indian	Other
15. Authors and	Mean income	519	544	531	343	—
journalists	Standard deviation	311	315	336	286	—
	Sample size	20	10	8	2	0
16. Commercial	Mean income	197	165	199	343	—
artists and	Standard deviation	173	86	185	0	—
photographers	Sample size	53	8	44	1	0
17. Performing	Mean income	282	259	349	90	—
artists and	Standard deviation	190	121	247	0	—
composers	Sample size	24	12	10	2	0
18. Athletes and	Mean income	303	255	343	115	690
sportsmen	Standard deviation	172	49	0	0	0
	Sample size	8	5	1	1	1
19. Professional	Mean income	544	613	459	618	481
and technical	Standard deviation	354	490	270	268	273
workers n.e.c.	Sample size	32	11	12	6	3
20. Government	Mean income	1,268	1,049	705	1,537	3,628
administrators	Standard deviation	1,753	1,481	604	727	3,187
and legislative officials	Sample size	68	53	6	3	6
21. Managers	Mean income	898	721	897	633	2,191
	Standard deviation	1,097	1,580	1,004	761	832
	Sample size	287	36	217	24	10
30. Clerical	Mean income	723	669	751	711	1,111
supervisors	Standard deviation	394	209	439	454	0
	Sample size	56	14	22	19	1
31. Government	Mean income	513	444	834	402	—
executive	Standard deviation	445	335	708	203	—
officials	Sample size	114	76	22	16	0
32. Stenogra-	Mean income	343	369	334	350	231
phers, typists,	Standard deviation	352	545	275	209	93
and card- punch operators	Sample size	181	45	106	26	4
33. Bookkeepers	Mean income	342	342	324	435	313
and cashiers	Standard deviation	296	211	306	319	304
	Sample size	367	61	254	48	4
34. Computing	Mean income	258	252	203	441	—
machine	Standard deviation	134	95	108	170	—
operators	Sample size	20	8	9	3	0
35. Transport	Mean income	471	351	518	545	—
and communi-	Standard deviation	218	140	264	196	—
cation super- visors	Sample size	36	12	12	12	0

(*Table continues on the following page.*)

Table 6-11 (*continued*).

Two-digit occupation code	Item	All racial groups	Malay	Chinese	Indian	Other
36. Transport	Mean income	181	182	183	128	—
conductors	Standard deviation	88	114	57	88	—
	Sample size	72	34	36	2	0
37. Mail distri-	Mean income	151	151	176	139	217
bution clerks	Standard deviation	71	69	75	66	179
	Sample size	190	117	20	51	2
38. Telephone	Mean income	233	263	210	195	191
and telegraph	Standard deviation	106	107	115	76	141
operators	Sample size	39	20	8	8	3
39. Clerical	Mean income	258	232	275	270	280
and related	Standard deviation	178	163	183	191	173
workers n.e.c.	Sample size	1,017	385	434	179	19
40. Managers	Mean income	700	174	893	424	—
(wholesale and	Standard deviation	730	83	851	217	—
retail trade)	Sample size	22	2	14	6	0
41. Work	Mean income	390	179	503	381	347
proprietors	Standard deviation	721	200	830	885	434
(wholesale and	Sample size	1,206[a]	367	698	135	5
retail trade)						
43. Technical	Mean income	384	366	413	209	—
salesmen and	Standard deviation	283	402	249	263	—
commercial	Sample size	79	13	58	8	0
travellers						
44. Insurance and	Mean income	357	195	401	272	1,144
real estate	Standard deviation	478	109	504	325	1,525
salesmen and	Sample size	67	14	39	12	2
auctioneers						
45. Salesmen and	Mean income	131	79	156	112	58
shop assistants	Standard deviation	111	62	124	77	49
	Sample size	2,410	636	1,491	276	7
49. Sales	Mean income	134	79	121	267	—
workers n.e.c.	Standard deviation	203	38	85	421	—
	Sample size	135	49	60	26	0
50. Managers	Mean income	343	—	438	153	—
(catering and	Standard deviation	224	—	215	53	—
lodging	Sample size	6	0	4	2	0
services)						
51. Work	Mean income	375	185	472	287	1,111
proprietors	Standard deviation	452	227	511	356	0
(catering and	Sample size	298	71	177	49	1
lodging						
services)						

Two-digit occupation code	Item	All racial groups	Malay	Chinese	Indian	Other
52. Housekeeping	Mean income	166	290	155	165	190
supervisors	Standard deviation	128	0	138	0	0
	Sample size	16	1	13	1	1
53. Cooks,	Mean income	116	87	123	115	455
waiters,	Standard deviation	88	68	80	56	578
bartenders, etc.	Sample size	518	110	331	74	3
54. Maids and	Mean income	77	58	90	57	98
housekeeping	Standard deviation	56	53	57	37	29
service	Sample size	1,003	271	590	139	3
workers n.e.c.						
55. Building	Mean income	126	111	136	128	90
caretakers and	Standard deviation	82	60	100	55	0
cleaners	Sample size	96	31	48	16	1
56. Launderers	Mean income	161	111	155	194	—
and dry-	Standard deviation	170	84	181	150	—
cleaners	Sample size	84	5	61	18	0
57. Barbers and	Mean income	173	116	185	226	—
beauticians	Standard deviation	163	47	194	158	—
	Sample size	209	59	112	38	0
58. Protective	Mean income	250	242	266	209	985
service workers	Standard deviation	207	163	228	148	753
	Sample size	847	666	68	101	12
59. Service	Mean income	148	152	159	130	217
workers n.e.c.	Standard deviation	75	62	105	57	179
	Sample size	236	111	58	65	2
60. Farm	Mean income	301	199	272	282	2,763
managers and	Standard deviation	424	77	184	350	1,020
supervisors	Sample size	245	56	78	107	4
61. Farmers	Mean income	101	84	214	160	55
	Standard deviation	108	62	220	158	41
	Sample size	6,801	5,791	860	78	72
62. Agricultural	Mean income	83	70	100	99	35
and animal	Standard deviation	53	51	55	47	31
husbandry	Sample size	8,282[a]	4,453	1,943	1,871	14
workers						
63. Forestry	Mean income	184	175	228	87	—
workers	Standard deviation	148	151	136	101	—
	Sample size	107	71	29	7	0
64. Fishermen,	Mean income	107	87	143	119	37
hunters, and	Standard deviation	83	52	112	50	14
related workers	Sample size	1,046	667	369	7	3

(*Table continues on the following page.*)

Table 6-11 *(continued)*.

Two-digit occupation code	Item	All racial groups	Malay	Chinese	Indian	Other
70. Production	Mean income	322	255	396	199	—
supervisors	Standard deviation	219	117	258	103	—
and general	Sample size	119	37	64	18	0
foremen						
71. Miners and	Mean income	180	160	186	144	1,867
quarrymen	Standard deviation	486	81	576	40	0
	Sample size	411	90	283	37	1
72. Metal	Mean income	162	157	163	171	—
processors	Standard deviation	121	50	137	59	—
	Sample size	46	8	35	3	0
73. Wood and	Mean income	158	130	175	158	—
paper workers	Standard deviation	125	72	141	183	—
	Sample size	271	97	157	17	0
74. Chemical	Mean income	112	111	112	113	78
processors	Standard deviation	61	63	67	45	18
	Sample size	346	113	155	76	2
75. Spinners	Mean income	46	41	68	115	—
and weavers	Standard deviation	37	35	39	0	—
	Sample size	165	140	24	1	0
76. Tanners	Mean income	110	140	102	—	—
and	Standard deviation	78	0	88	—	—
fellmongers	Sample size	5	1	4	0	0
77. Food	Mean income	143	84	174	143	—
and beverage	Standard deviation	255	73	317	74	—
processors	Sample size	375	122	230	23	0
78. Tobacco	Mean income	97	58	166	149	—
preparers and	Standard deviation	113	64	175	69	—
tobacco prod-	Sample size	86	53	21	12	0
uct workers						
79. Tailors and	Mean income	105	64	114	131	—
dressmakers	Standard deviation	132	67	144	94	—
	Sample size	603	122	466	15	0
80. Shoemakers	Mean income	106	107	106	128	—
and leather	Standard deviation	78	34	82	18	—
goods makers	Sample size	85	6	77	2	0
81. Cabinet-	Mean income	158	104	164	343	—
makers and	Standard deviation	137	89	141	0	—
wood workers	Sample size	107	13	93	1	0
82. Stone cutters	Mean income	143	—	143	—	—
and carvers	Standard deviation	90	—	90	—	—
	Sample size	13	0	13	0	0

Two-digit occupation code	Item	All racial groups	Malay	Chinese	Indian	Other
83. Blacksmiths	Mean income	178	126	203	236	65
and machine-	Standard deviation	148	69	173	126	0
tool operators	Sample size	99	52	61	5	1
84. Machinery	Mean income	206	221	192	262	715
fitters and	Standard deviation	169	143	145	194	1,007
machine	Sample size	668	130	484	50	4
assemblers						
85. Electrical	Mean income	221	211	208	242	1,156
fitters and	Standard deviation	182	117	146	136	1,508
workers	Sample size	287	71	164	50	2
86. Broadcasting	Mean income	218	254	189	103	343
station and	Standard deviation	121	121	123	53	0
sound	Sample size	13	6	4	2	1
equipment						
operators						
87. Plumbers,	Mean income	166	195	152	230	233
welders, etc.	Standard deviation	101	110	94	114	0
	Sample size	134	15	103	15	1
88. Jewelry and	Mean income	253	121	271	219	—
precious metal	Standard deviation	357	90	391	250	—
workers	Sample size	86	4	64	18	0
89. Glassformers	Mean income	108	66	157	146	—
and potters	Standard deviation	92	36	121	38	—
	Sample size	60	32	24	4	0
90. Rubber and	Mean income	132	161	128	65	—
plastics	Standard deviation	95	108	94	0	—
products	Sample size	34	6	27	1	0
makers						
91. Paper and	Mean income	46	47	45	—	—
paperboard	Standard deviation	36	25	37	—	—
products	Sample size	42	5	37	0	0
makers						
92. Printers	Mean income	156	128	146	325	—
and related	Standard deviation	205	114	108	577	—
workers	Sample size	143	51	79	13	0
93. Painters	Mean income	164	133	168	165	—
	Standard deviation	92	77	95	43	—
	Sample size	121	12	106	3	0
94. Production	Mean income	55	33	121	121	140
and related	Standard deviation	79	35	128	87	0
workers n.e.c.	Sample size	240	179	56	4	1

(*Table continues on the following page.*)

Table 6-11 (*continued*).

Two-digit occupation code	Item	All racial groups	Malay	Chinese	Indian	Other
95. Bricklayers	Mean income	149	130	154	136	739
and other	Standard deviation	98	74	93	57	882
construction workers	Sample size	783	204	542	35	2
96. Stationary	Mean income	179	167	180	194	—
engine	Standard deviation	72	78	71	61	—
operators	Sample size	116	40	52	24	0
97. Dockers	Mean income	170	172	173	161	146
and freight	Standard deviation	116	82	162	69	24
handlers	Sample size	334	139	123	68	4
98. Transport	Mean income	188	168	213	185	157
equipment	Standard deviation	111	106	120	87	72
operators	Sample size	1,296	612	497	183	4
00. No	Mean income	118	83	150	160	361
occupation	Standard deviation	161	111	182	172	496
	Sample size	3,196	1,639	1,286	240	31
10. Not	Mean income	65	65	—	65	—
applicable	Standard deviation	0	0	—	0	—
	Sample size	2	1	0	1	0
99. Not	Mean income	112	112	112	116	74
available	Standard deviation	61	61	64	54	54
	Sample size	2,215	1,035	814	358	8

— Not applicable.
n.e.c.: Not elsewhere classified.
a. The racial affiliation of one person in this two-digit category was not available.

Note: The occupational classification used in the PES is a standard two-digit code from Department of Statistics, *Index of Occupations* (Kuala Lumpur, January 1971). Its coding scheme is based on the more comprehensive *Dictionary of Occupational Classification* (Kuala Lumpur, 1968). In the present study the two-digit classification of the PES has been recoded into eight broad, one-digit occupational categories as follows:

Two-digit PES code	One-digit code	Description
00, 10, 99	—	Not in labor force, or occupation not available
01–09, 11–19	1	Professional and technical
20–31, 40, 50, 60	2	Administrative and managerial
32–39	3	Clerical and related
41–49	4	Sales workers
51–59	5	Service workers
61	6	Farmers
62–69	7	Farm laborers
70–98	8	Production workers

7

Earnings Functions for
Urban Employees

THE GOVERNMENT OF MALAYSIA regards education as an important policy instrument for redressing income imbalances:

> The lack of education is a major factor adversely affecting the ability of an individual to enhance the quality of his life and to advance his economic position. Consequently, the lack of education becomes both a symptom as well as a significant factor contributing towards poverty. Education is thus a major vehicle for the achievement of the objectives of the New Economic Policy (MTR, p. 189).

Education is an important dimension of the nonhomogeneity of labor, and it is part of the aim of this chapter to examine the relation between education and income, and between educational inequality and income inequality. I shall not present a life-cycle model of education and income distribution, but rather draw upon the existing theory of human capital to explain incomes in terms of education and age (experience). The theory applies only to earnings or labor income, data on which are not available separately in PES. Hence I have restricted the sample to urban employees, whose income may be assumed to derive entirely, or largely, from labor. Rural employees have been excluded because the theory is not directly applicable in the context of rural labor markets, which tend to be imperfect. Also, owing to the nature of work in rural areas, a significant part of the income of rural employees may derive from nonhuman capital, that is, assets such as land.

Earnings functions based on the so-called human capital model have thus been estimated for urban employees in Peninsular Malaysia. But it should be emphasized at the outset that these earnings functions are consistent with other theories of earnings (such as "screening" and "job competition"), although the latter have not been developed to the same extent. In any case, simple reduced-form equations between income and the variables of education and age are consistent with too many different hypotheses to allow for sharp tests between alternative models (see Anand, 1976*b*).

The earnings function estimated here quantifies the response of income to education and experience; the relation has been estimated using the PES cross-sectional data on urban wage earners. Even if one rejects the formal interpretation of the estimated equations in terms of human capital theory, the approach turns out to be useful for a purely descriptive analysis of the data. There is much merit in adopting this framework simply to describe age-income profiles for different levels of education. The estimated equations are a convenient method of summarizing labor market information in terms of earnings differentials for individuals at different age-education levels. Furthermore, the regression equations automatically generate a measure of income inequality used in this study, the variance of log-income, which facilitates inequality comparisons between urban labor and other incomes.

Under restrictive assumptions the earnings functions can also allow rough orders of magnitude to be obtained for what may be called individual or private rates of return to education. The assumptions required to interpret the estimated coefficients as true rates of return are admittedly heroic, but since the main purpose here is to *compare* the returns to education across various groups—occupational, racial, and other—this problem is perhaps less important. The resulting comparisons among groups could be suggestive of the role of educational policy in narrowing racial, occupational, or regional income inequalities—though further information about the demand side of the labor market would be required for any conclusions.[1] For small changes in supply, however, the income differentials for different levels of education and experience can be assumed constant; hence the earnings function analysis can at least guide the choice of educational projects, if not policies.

The Earnings Function

A formal derivation of the human capital earnings function is outside the scope of this chapter. It is in any case unnecessary since a detailed

---

1. For example, a policy of simultaneously upgrading overall skill levels may well affect the income premiums commanded by education. Only if the macrodemand curves for labor of different skill levels are perfectly elastic (that is, only if the different types of labor are perfectly substitutable in production) can conclusions be drawn about educational policy, or large changes in supply, simply on the basis of the estimated earnings equations. For a discussion of the human capital model in the context of the supply of and demand for labor of different types, see Anand (1976*b*).

exposition of the model can be found in any of the standard works on the subject.[2] I will therefore restrict myself to a statement of the estimating form used and will provide only a heuristic justification for it.

The estimating form employed is:

$$\log y = \beta_0 + \beta_1 S + \beta_2 T - \beta_3 T^2 \qquad \beta_i \geqslant 0, i = 0, 1, 2, 3$$

where y = annual income; S = number of years of formal schooling; and T = number of years of labor force experience. Years of labor market experience, T, are assumed to be measured by age A, minus schooling, S, minus 5; that is, $T = A - S - 5$, where six is assumed to be the age at the commencement of schooling. This definition of labor market experience raises obvious problems if employment is not continuous and there are periods of unemployment and job search. It is particularly unsatisfactory for women, because their participation in the labor force is often intermittent for various reasons.

The model of optimal investment in human capital which underlies the earnings function for an individual was initiated by Ben-Porath (1967). It predicts a declining rate of investment in human capital with age. The intuitive reasoning behind this result is that most of the investment is made at younger ages to give individuals a longer period in their finite lifetimes over which they can receive returns. But the entire investment is not made instantaneously (before beginning the working life) because the marginal cost of acquiring human capital rises within each period, so that it pays to spread the investment over time.[3] The investment declines over time both because marginal benefits decline[4] and because the marginal cost curve itself shifts upward with advancing age. There is also the depreciation of human capital with age (owing to obsolescence and physiological factors), which accentuates this decline in investment.

Qualitatively, the Ben-Porath analysis implies three distinct phases of investment in human capital over the life cycle. In the initial phase, all available time is spent acquiring human capital. This period of complete specialization is one of full-time schooling and no earnings, and it can end before the completion of schooling. In the second phase, there is positive but declining investment in human capital. This is a period of on-the-job training and includes part-time schooling, when a declining fraction of

2. See, for example, Mincer (1970) and the references contained therein. The particular estimating form employed here is derived in Chiswick and Mincer (1972) and Mincer (1974, 1976).

3. Attempts to increase investment within a given period run into diminishing returns: costs increase with the speed of production of human capital.

4. The marginal benefit of investment is measured by the discounted present value of increases in earning power over the remaining lifetime.

available labor time is spent on the further acquisition of human capital. In the final phase, all available time is spent earning, and none is spent acquiring additional human capital—indeed, there is a net loss arising from depreciation. These results become clear if a formal optimizing model of investment in human capital is set up with its associated phase diagram (not included here).

These considerations lead to a declining rate of investment in human capital over the life span, which becomes negative in the final phase. The decline itself implies that earnings rise to a peak (at zero net investment) and then begin to fall off. But the exact shape of the earnings function depends on the particular rate of decline assumed, that is, on the shape of the life-cycle investment schedule. A *linear* decline in the postschool investment schedule generates the following quadratic earnings function (shown in figure 7-1 in the appendix to this chapter):[5]

$$\log y = \beta_0 + \beta_1 S + \beta_2 T - \beta_3 T^2 \qquad \beta_i \geqslant 0, i = 0, 1, 2, 3.$$

Apart from those mentioned, the main assumptions subsumed in the derivation of this earnings function are: (1) a constant labor market return (β_1) for every year of schooling, and (2) independence between the return to formal schooling and to postschool investment (that is, no interaction effect between education and on-the-job experience). Furthermore, other relevant determinants of earnings have been omitted, such as ability and the proportion of the year actually spent working (the "weeks worked" variable in Mincer, 1974, 1976).[6]

The simplicity and econometric tractability of this earnings function make it agreeable to work with. As stated above, quite apart·from its interpretation in terms of human capital theory,[7] it furnishes some useful by-products. Since the dependent variable is the logarithm of income, the estimated regression equation explains the variance of log y—a familiar index of inequality. The computed R^2 can then be interpreted as the percentage of inequality (measured by the variance of log-income) that is explained by the model. Further properties of this earnings function, which turn out to be useful in interpreting the regression results, are derived in the

5. An exponentially declining schedule would have generated a different earnings function, namely, the Gompertz curve (see Mincer, 1974).

6. See also Bhalla (1973).

7. For example, a quadratic experience (or age) – log-income profile is also implied by the stochastic model of income determination proposed by Aitchison and Brown (1957); this posits proportionate growth of an individual's income at a rate depending on experience and a (normally and independently distributed) random variable.

appendix to this chapter. Some of these appear to have gone unnoticed by the human capitalists.

The Return to Education

The coefficient β_1 in the earnings function

$$\log y = \beta_0 + \beta_1 S + \beta_2 T - \beta_3 T^2$$

shows the effect of schooling on log-income if experience T is held constant. If, however, age A is held constant, the effect of schooling on log-income is given by differentiating partially with respect to S the expression

$$\log y = \beta_0 + \beta_1 S + \beta_2 (A - S - 5) - \beta_3 (A - S - 5)^2.$$

Hence
$$\left[\frac{\partial \log y}{\partial S} \right]_{A \text{ const}} = \beta_1 - \beta_2 + 2\beta_3 (A - S - 5)$$

$$= \beta_1 - 2\beta_3 \left[\frac{\beta_2}{2\beta_3} - (A - S - 5) \right].$$

Thus if $T = (A - S - 5) < \beta_2/2\beta_3$, the quantity in square brackets is positive, and β_1 overestimates the return to education with age constant. The reason, of course, is that with age held constant, an additional year of schooling is at the expense of a year's experience. The reduction in experience offsets to some extent the effect β_1 of schooling on log-income. The extent to which it offsets β_1 depends on the marginal return to a year's experience,

$$\frac{\partial \log y}{\partial T} = \beta_2 - 2\beta_3 T = \beta_2 - 2\beta_3 (A - S - 5),$$

which is precisely as shown in the equation above.

The coefficient β_1 on S in the earnings function must be interpreted with care. In certain very special circumstances, it can be taken to be the rate of return to education. With T held constant, partial differentiation with respect to S gives $\beta_1 = (1/y)(\Delta y/\Delta S)$. Thus β_1 indicates the percentage increase in annual income $\Delta y/y$ for an additional period of schooling ΔS. For one extra year of schooling, $\Delta S = 1$, and $\beta_1 = \Delta y/y$. Thus β_1 measures the internal rate of return to an investment of y which raises income in perpetuity by Δy. If the investment cost of an extra year's schooling for an individual happens to be exactly y, β_1 measures the rate of return to it.[8]

8. Strictly speaking, β_1 is the internal rate of return if the investment of y yields the flow of Δy *forever*. With a finite working life, the rate of return will be less than β_1, but the difference will be negligible provided the working life is of normal duration (say, thirty years).

To an individual, the investment cost of a year's schooling is the sum of the opportunity cost and the direct (or out-of-pocket) cost, which includes tuition fees (if applicable), books, and so forth. The opportunity cost is the earnings forgone while at school; the direct cost is additional, but possibly small in relation to earnings forgone. In any event, if the total cost is some factor k times y, the rate of return to education is given by deflating β_1 by k. With detailed information on k, therefore, the earnings functions can be used to assess the private return to education.[9] To calculate the social return to education, further information and assumptions are necessary about government subsidies to education, wages' reflection of the marginal productivity of labor, and so on.[10]

Important caveats attach to estimates of the private or social return to education derived from a single year's cross-sectional data. There is the usual problem of drawing time series inferences from cross-sectional regression results. Apart from that, it is questionable how long values measured for a particular year will retain their validity. This may be because technical progress affects the productivity of different types of labor differently or because supplies of different types of labor change rapidly.[11] Thus, even if the first problem is ignored, the return estimated from a cross-sectional earnings function will be valid only for a marginal expansion of education, which does not disturb the general equilibrium of skilled wage rates very much. Otherwise, with downward sloping demand curves for skilled labor, a large expansion in the supply of educated manpower could reduce wage rates significantly. Even though education commands a large income premium when it is scarce, it will not necessarily continue to do so when it has become much more plentiful. If, however, the macrodemand curves for skilled labor are perfectly elastic (reflecting infinite substitutability in production between different types of labor), the calculated returns will prevail even for large educational programs or policies (see Anand, 1976b).

9. It may happen that direct costs roughly match student vacation earnings, in which case $k = 1$ approximately. For example, if the earnings forgone are those for the academic year of, say, nine months (as opposed to the whole year), and if direct costs match earnings during the remaining two or three months, then $k = 1$.

10. PES incomes are already pre- rather than posttax (see chapter 2), so no adjustment is required on the benefit side to calculate the social return. See Hoerr (1973) for estimates of educational costs in Malaysia and a social cost-benefit analysis of education based on the 1967–68 Malaysian Socio-Economic Sample Survey of Households.

11. In view of the government's policy of employment restructuring, supplies of different types of educated labor are indeed likely to change rapidly during the period of the Outline Perspective Plan, 1970–90 (see the sections "The New Economic Policy" in chapter 1 and "Some Implications of Employment Restructuring" in chapter 8).

Two further points need to be noted in discussing rates of return to education. First, if education is used merely as a screening device and does not contribute to the productivity of labor, the calculation of the private return is unaffected, but that of the social return will have to be based on factors such as the value of the information obtained through screening.[12] Second, since the possibility of unemployment has not been taken into account, the expected (in the statistical sense) rate of return should be considered. Thus, if the alternative to schooling is unemployment, the opportunity cost or earnings forgone will be zero. Therefore the return to education for an unemployed person will be higher than that for an employed person contemplating the same increment in schooling. Similarly, the return expected from schooling at a particular level will be affected by unemployment at the next level. In other words, k will vary according to the individual's actual and prospective employment status. If the probability of unemployment decreases with education, the unadjusted regression estimate β_1 will underestimate the expected rate of return. For in that case the ratio between expected income gained and expected income forgone will be larger than the ratio between actual income gained and actual income forgone.

Although the coefficient β_1 is only a crude version of rate of return, for convenience I shall hereafter call β_1 the "return" (*not* rate of return) to schooling: remember that β_1 does at least measure the proportionate income increase associated with schooling. For policy purposes it is sometimes useful to consider the absolute income increase, in which case β_1 needs to be multiplied by the appropriate base income level y.

Some Problems of PES Data

Since income data in PES are not coded by source, it is not possible here to distinguish earned income from other types such as income from business or property (see the subsection "Definition of PES Income" in chapter 2). In order to fit the earnings function, therefore, it was necessary to choose a subset of income recipients for whom earned or labor income was believed a priori to be coterminous with total income. Thus the sample was narrowed down to employees in the urban sector only, a subsample of 8,263 individuals (5,843 males and 2,420 females).[13]

---

12. See Stiglitz (1975) for a discussion of the theory and social benefits of screening.

13. The returns to education for this subsample of individuals may yet be overestimated owing to the likelihood of higher-income (and older) employees' deriving a larger share of their income from nonhuman capital (property and accumulated saving). In the regressions that follow, the income interval means assigned to these individuals are the same as those assigned to income recipients in general (see table 2-1).

Table 7-1. Earnings Functions for Urban Male Employees by Occupation and Race

Estimated regression equation	R^2 and standard error of estimate	F-ratio and degrees of freedom	Mean and variance of log y, S, T, and y			

Occupation 1: Professional and technical

$\log y_M = 6.74401 + 0.08705S + 0.05511T - 0.00072T^2$
$(0.00934)\ (0.00950)\ (0.00019)$
$R^2 = 0.324$, SEE $= 0.454$; $F = 31.64$, DF $= 198$
$\overline{\log y} = 8.435$, var$(\log y) = 0.301$; $\overline{S} = 12.027$, var$(S) = 19.279$; $\overline{T} = 17.394$, var$(T) = 134.647$; $\overline{y} = 5,340$, var$(y) = 9.856\ 10^6$

$\log y_C = 6.35481 + 0.12691S + 0.04895T - 0.00066T^2$
$(0.00815)\ (0.01022)\ (0.00024)$
$R^2 = 0.469$, SEE $= 0.539$; $F = 82.67$, DF $= 281$
$\overline{\log y} = 8.512$, var$(\log y) = 0.542$; $\overline{S} = 13.170$, var$(S) = 19.919$; $\overline{T} = 14.202$, var$(T) = 115.629$; $\overline{y} = 6,372$, var$(y) = 24.404\ 10^6$

$\log y_I = 5.89927 + 0.14896S + 0.07980T - 0.00129T^2$
$(0.01331)\ (0.01297)\ (0.00023)$
$R^2 = 0.670$, SEE $= 0.545$; $F = 72.26$, DF $= 107$
$\overline{\log y} = 8.612$, var$(\log y) = 0.875$; $\overline{S} = 12.820$, var$(S) = 28.749$; $\overline{T} = 18.550$, var$(T) = 181.159$; $\overline{y} = 8,190$, var$(y) = 69.739\ 10^6$

$\log y_O = 6.81433 + 0.11814S + 0.08517T - 0.00197T^2$
$(0.05662)\ (0.04993)\ (0.00135)$
$R^2 = 0.280$, SEE $= 0.860$; $F = 2.85$, DF $= 22$
$\overline{\log y} = 9.196$, var$(\log y) = 0.904$; $\overline{S} = 15.422$, var$(S) = 11.667$; var$(T) = 13.519$, var$(T) = 124.110$; $\overline{y} = 14,379$, var$(y) = 140.682\ 10^6$

$\log y_{TOT} = 6.30867 + 0.12408S + 0.06305T - 0.00096T^2$
$(0.00579)\ (0.00602)\ (0.00013)$
$R^2 = 0.461$, SEE $= 0.549$; $F = 176.81$, DF $= 620$
$\overline{\log y} = 8.534$, var$(\log y) = 0.557$; $\overline{S} = 12.833$, var$(S) = 21.391$; $\overline{T} = 15.980$, var$(T) = 136.642$; $\overline{y} = 6,695$, var$(y) = 35.767\ 10^6$

Occupation 2: Administrative and managerial

$\log y_M = 6.09361 + 0.12568S + 0.08452T - 0.00088T^2$
$(0.01956)\ (0.01630)\ (0.00032)$
$R^2 = 0.464$, SEE $= 0.646$; $F = 22.21$, DF $= 77$
$\overline{\log y} = 8.749$, var$(\log y) = 0.750$; $\overline{S} = 11.710$, var$(S) = 20.018$; $T = 20.068$, var$(T) = 179.973$; $\overline{y} = 9,610$, var$(y) = 192.918\ 10^6$

$\log y_C = 6.03720 + 0.14174S + 0.08995T - 0.00098T^2$
$(0.01477)\ (0.01583)\ (0.00030)$
$R^2 = 0.485$, SEE $= 0.607$; $F = 38.65$, DF $= 123$
$\overline{\log y} = 8.933$, var$(\log y) = 0.699$; $\overline{S} = 10.496$, var$(S) = 19.625$; $\overline{T} = 23.543$, var$(T) = 171.290$; $\overline{y} = 10,455$, var$(y) = 74.512\ 10^6$

$\log y_I = 5.95274 + 0.15920S + 0.06370T - 0.00081T^2$
$(0.02779)\ (0.02468)\ (0.00044)$
$R^2 = 0.464$, SEE $= 0.558$; $F = 12.99$, DF $= 45$
$\overline{\log y} = 8.494$, var$(\log y) = 0.545$; $\overline{S} = 10.122$, var$(S) = 11.453$; $\overline{T} = 25.551$, var$(T) = 207.450$; $\overline{y} = 6,611$, var$(y) = 41.999\ 10^6$

$\log y_O = 6.98792 + 0.16349S + 0.06891T - 0.00102T^2$
$(0.11222)\ (0.13823)$
$R^2 = 0.371$, SEE $= 0.752$; $F = 0.79$, DF $= 4$
$\overline{\log y} = 10.274$, var$(\log y) = 0.514$; $\overline{S} = 14.125$, var$(S) = 10.125$; $\overline{T} = 25.250$, var$(T) = 126.786$; $\overline{y} = 37,470$, var$(y) = 1,154.248\ 10^6$

$\log y_{TOT} = 5.96794 + 0.14145S + 0.09120T - 0.00108T^2$
$(0.01115)\ (0.01072)\ (0.00020)$
$R^2 = 0.453$, SEE $= 0.650$; $F = 72.19$, DF $= 261$
$\overline{\log y} = 8.836$, var$(\log y) = 0.765$; $\overline{S} = 10.908$, var$(S) = 18.490$; $\overline{T} = 22.904$, var$(T) = 181.501$; $\overline{y} = 10,302$, var$(y) = 157.318\ 10^6$

Occupation 3: Clerical and related

$\log y_M = 6.00163 + 0.10015S + 0.08555T - 0.00116T^2$
$(0.01320)\ (0.01042)\ (0.00023)$
$R^2 = 0.341$, SEE $= 0.617$; $F = 42.70$, DF $= 248$
$\overline{\log y} = 7.818$, var$(\log y) = 0.570$; $\overline{S} = 9.502$, var$(S) = 10.724$; $\overline{T} = 14.808$, var$(T) = 126.649$; $\overline{y} = 3,212$, var$(y) = 10.475\ 10^6$

$\log y_C = 5.96774 + 0.09660S + 0.09828T - 0.00139T^2$
$(0.00949)\ (0.00730)\ (0.00014)$
$R^2 = 0.368$, SEE $= 0.580$; $F = 80.34$, DF $= 414$
$\overline{\log y} = 8.052$, var$(\log y) = 0.528$; $\overline{S} = 10.078$, var$(S) = 14.050$; $\overline{T} = 19.195$, var$(T) = 190.459$; $\overline{y} = 4,027$, var$(y) = 11.885\ 10^6$

Occupation (continued)

$\log y_I = 5.43999 + 0.11824S + 0.11640T - 0.00165T^2$
$\quad\quad\quad\;(0.01316)\;\;(0.01160)\;\;(0.00025)$

$\log y_O = 3.89049 - 0.09287S + 0.29097T - 0.00505T^2$
$\quad\quad\quad\;(0.08029)\;\;(0.05657)\;\;(0.00108)$

$\log y_{TOT} = 5.79988 + 0.10511S + 0.10116T - 0.00141T^2$
$\quad\quad\quad\quad\;(0.00655)\;\;(0.00525)\;\;(0.00011)$

Dep.	R^2	SEE	F	DF	$\overline{\log y}$	var(log y)	$\bar{S}$	var(S)	$\bar{T}$	var(T)	$\bar{y}$	var(y)
y_I	0.516	0.620	71.49	201	7.858	0.783	9.766	12.072	17.239	154.349	3,613	8.926×10^6
y_O	0.657	0.649	9.56	15	7.776	1.022	9.184	4.950	19.132	142.968	3,321	4.497×10^6
y_{TOT}	0.407	0.607	203.26	890	7.935	0.618	9.825	12.502	17.508	166.140	3,688	10.746×10^6

Occupation 4: Sales[a]

$\log y_M = 5.23758 + 0.10067S + 0.11222T - 0.00147T^2$
$\quad\quad\quad\;(0.03176)\;\;(0.02774)\;\;(0.00057)$

$\log y_C = 5.14879 + 0.13317S + 0.12290T - 0.00168T^2$
$\quad\quad\quad\;(0.00887)\;\;(0.00638)\;\;(0.00012)$

$\log y_I = 5.73251 + 0.08007S + 0.07022T - 0.00088T^2$
$\quad\quad\quad\;(0.01765)\;\;(0.01395)\;\;(0.00026)$

$\log y_{TOT} = 5.21236 + 0.12212S + 0.11912T - 0.00166T^2$
$\quad\quad\quad\quad\;(0.00787)\;\;(0.00583)\;\;(0.00011)$

Dep.	R^2	SEE	F	DF	$\overline{\log y}$	var(log y)	$\bar{S}$	var(S)	$\bar{T}$	var(T)	$\bar{y}$	var(y)
y_M	0.330	0.755	9.69	59	6.898	0.810	7.079	12.486	11.841	121.660	1,581	5.477×10^6
y_C	0.502	0.598	185.42	552	7.339	0.714	6.430	10.727	17.187	168.235	2,180	5.944×10^6
y_I	0.377	0.569	20.36	101	7.073	0.504	6.210	11.436	20.714	267.571	1,521	1.920×10^6
y_{TOT}	0.466	0.626	210.22	724	7.260	0.730	6.466	10.995	17.202	182.112	2,059	6.197×10^6

Occupation 5: Service

$\log y_M = 5.34974 + 0.13303S + 0.10608T - 0.00142T^2$
$\quad\quad\quad\;(0.01034)\;\;(0.00940)\;\;(0.00020)$

$\log y_C = 6.08223 + 0.07743S + 0.06183T - 0.00076T^2$
$\quad\quad\quad\;(0.01329)\;\;(0.00741)\;\;(0.00011)$

$\log y_I = 6.28622 + 0.08078S + 0.03476T - 0.00032T^2$
$\quad\quad\quad\;(0.01518)\;\;(0.00803)\;\;(0.00011)$

$\log y_O = 3.07565 + 0.40362S + 0.13175T - 0.00172T^2$
$\quad\quad\quad\;(0.15973)\;\;(0.14114)\;\;(0.00299)$

$\log y_{TOT} = 5.82197 + 0.11204S + 0.06981T - 0.00082T^2$
$\quad\quad\quad\quad\;(0.00747)\;\;(0.00419)\;\;(0.00007)$

Dep.	R^2	SEE	F	DF	$\overline{\log y}$	var(log y)	$\bar{S}$	var(S)	$\bar{T}$	var(T)	$\bar{y}$	var(y)
y_M	0.465	0.488	103.82	358	7.717	0.441	6.844	9.216	21.924	131.243	2,753	4.537×10^6
y_C	0.233	0.615	27.87	276	7.257	0.488	5.137	12.518	24.623	374.735	1,780	2.028×10^6
y_I	0.177	0.557	12.52	175	7.355	0.370	5.168	11.621	29.117	281.079	1,881	1.971×10^6
y_O	0.520	1.308	2.17	6	8.408	2.379	9.800	11.733	15.900	181.878	8,762	49.673×10^6
y_{TOT}	0.325	0.591	132.67	827	7.492	0.516	5.943	11.717	24.310	253.652	2,310	4.338×10^6

Occupation 7: Farm laborers[a]

$\log y_M = 6.18609 + 0.05126S + 0.04171T - 0.00055T^2$
$\quad\quad\quad\;(0.02377)\;\;(0.01634)\;\;(0.00028)$

$\log y_C = 5.33538 + 0.09833S + 0.11264T - 0.00149T^2$
$\quad\quad\quad\;(0.02632)\;\;(0.01443)\;\;(0.00020)$

$\log y_I = 6.29225 + 0.05935S + 0.04978T - 0.00077T^2$
$\quad\quad\quad\;(0.04321)\;\;(0.02904)\;\;(0.00043)$

$\log y_{TOT} = 5.95603 + 0.06063S + 0.06386T - 0.00088T^2$
$\quad\quad\quad\quad\;(0.01674)\;\;(0.00977)\;\;(0.00015)$

Dep.	R^2	SEE	F	DF	$\overline{\log y}$	var(log y)	$\bar{S}$	var(S)	$\bar{T}$	var(T)	$\bar{y}$	var(y)
y_M	0.073	0.692	3.38	128	7.027	0.505	5.023	8.049	23.659	173.940	1,385	0.684×10^6
y_C	0.458	0.608	20.53	73	7.148	0.655	4.649	12.382	25.273	367.392	1,728	2.350×10^6
y_I	0.107	0.690	1.68	42	7.148	0.498	3.609	8.410	31.565	210.729	1,649	3.465×10^6
y_{TOT}	0.154	0.684	15.28	252	7.086	0.546	4.648	9.588	25.621	245.046	1,536	1.689×10^6

245

Table 7.1 (continued).

Estimated regression equation	R^2 and standard error of estimate	F-ratio and degrees of freedom	Mean and variance of log y, S, T, and y
Occupation 8: Production workers			
$\log y_M = 5.79966 + 0.08216S + 0.09019T - 0.001237T^2$ (0.01022) (0.00812) (0.00015)	$R^2 = 0.326$ SEE = 0.523	$F = 60.89$ DF = 377	$\overline{\log y} = 7.504$ var($\log y$) = 0.403 $\overline{S} = 5.938$ var(S) = 9.203 $\overline{T} = 22.413$ var(T) = 151.710 $\bar{y} = 2{,}174$ var(y) = 1.807 10^6
$\log y_C = 5.60324 + 0.08086S + 0.11354T - 0.001557T^2$ (0.00569) (0.00357) (0.00006)	$R^2 = 0.447$ SEE = 0.545	$F = 422.44$ DF = 1,569	$\overline{\log y} = 7.396$ var($\log y$) = 0.535 $\overline{S} = 5.120$ var(S) = 9.191 $\overline{T} = 20.402$ var(T) = 189.250 $\bar{y} = 2{,}040$ var(y) = 1.845 10^6
$\log y_I = 6.52732 + 0.06709S + 0.04647T - 0.000537T^2$ (0.00683) (0.00688) (0.00012)	$R^2 = 0.315$ SEE = 0.400	$F = 68.09$ DF = 275	$\overline{\log y} = 7.644$ var($\log y$) = 0.231 $\overline{S} = 5.731$ var(S) = 17.086 $\overline{T} = 25.262$ var(T) = 188.176 $\bar{y} = 2{,}351$ var(y) = 1.780 10^6
$\log y_O = 6.89637 + 0.16673S + 0.06364T - 0.002017T^2$ (0.08402) (0.07988) (0.00181)	$R^2 = 0.503$ SEE = 0.919	$F = 2.70$ DF = 8	$\overline{\log y} = 8.281$ var($\log y$) = 1.236 $\overline{S} = 9.625$ var(S) = 27.278 $\overline{T} = 15.458$ var(T) = 154.112 $\bar{y} = 7.574$ var(y) = 96.127 10^6
$\log y_{TOT} = 5.73677 + 0.07933S + 0.10148T - 0.001377T^2$ (0.00423) (0.00298)	$R^2 = 0.403$ SEE = 0.541	$F = 503.27$ DF = 2,241	$\overline{\log y} = 7.450$ var($\log y$) = 0.489 $\overline{S} = 5.359$ var(S) = 10.459 $\overline{T} = 21.321$ var(T) = 185.244 $\bar{y} = 2{,}131$ var(y) = 2.461 10^6
All occupations together			
$\log y_M = 5.42422 + 0.14240S + 0.09301T - 0.001207T^2$ (0.00451) (0.00445) (0.00009)	$R^2 = 0.451$ SEE = 0.613	$F = 402.64$ DF = 1,469	$\overline{\log y} = 7.738$ var($\log y$) = 0.684 $\overline{S} = 7.890$ var(S) = 17.044 $\overline{T} = 19.834$ var(T) = 153.706 $\bar{y} = 3{,}241$ var(y) = 19.104 10^6
$\log y_C = 5.32333 + 0.13874S + 0.11040T - 0.001437T^2$ (0.00283) (0.00246) (0.00004)	$R^2 = 0.521$ SEE = 0.612	$F = 1,199.62$ DF = 3,312	$\overline{\log y} = 7.606$ var($\log y$) = 0.780 $\overline{S} = 6.853$ var(S) = 18.779 $\overline{T} = 19.768$ var(T) = 205.500 $\bar{y} = 2{,}979$ var(y) = 12.466 10^6
$\log y_I = 5.69940 + 0.13495S + 0.07047T - 0.000847T^2$ (0.00486) (0.00441) (0.00007)	$R^2 = 0.476$ SEE = 0.612	$F = 293.74$ DF = 970	$\overline{\log y} = 7.704$ var($\log y$) = 0.712 $\overline{S} = 7.457$ var(S) = 22.413 $\overline{T} = 23.339$ var(T) = 228.454 $\bar{y} = 3{,}287$ var(y) = 17.462 10^6
$\log y_O = 4.68325 + 0.23471S + 0.10384T - 0.001387T^2$ (0.02701) (0.03273) (0.00075)	$R^2 = 0.520$ SEE = 0.989	$F = 27.43$ DF = 76	$\overline{\log y} = 8.590$ var($\log y$) = 1.961 $\overline{S} = 11.744$ var(S) = 20.525 $\overline{T} = 16.819$ var(T) = 150.128 $\bar{y} = 11{,}804$ var(y) = 266.112 10^6
$\log y_{TOT} = 5.41823 + 0.14005S + 0.09793T - 0.001257T^2$ (0.00215) (0.00193) (0.00003)	$R^2 = 0.492$ SEE = 0.628	$F = 1,881.79$ DF = 5,839	$\overline{\log y} = 7.669$ var($\log y$) = 0.775 $\overline{S} = 7.282$ var(S) = 19.437 $\overline{T} = 20.339$ var(T) = 197.338 $\bar{y} = 3{,}217$ var(y) = 19.437 10^6

Note: The subscripts M, C, I, O, and TOT refer to Malay, Chinese, Indian, other, and total, respectively. Numbers in parentheses are the standard error of the estimated coefficient. The variables S and T are measured in years, and the variable y in Malaysian dollars per year.

a. The lack of observations on "others" in this occupation prevented the estimation of a regression equation for them.

Workers in the rural sector were excluded for two reasons. First, it is likely that a significant fraction of their income takes the form of returns to nonhuman capital, in particular, land and other physical assets. Second, the earnings model as developed may not apply equally well to farm labor for various institutional reasons, such as capital and labor market imperfections and the nature of rural work. If it were possible to hold constant the ownership of assets other than human capital, an analysis of the effects of education on agricultural productivity and income would be particularly important, given the objective of raising smallholder productivities analyzed in chapter 5. This points urgently to the need to collect data on physical assets such as land, livestock, and houses in future income and expenditure surveys in the country.

Estimates by Race, Occupation, and Sex

Table 7-1 shows estimates of the earnings function for a sample restricted to urban male employees; there is also a breakdown by broad occupational category and racial group.[14] Table 7-6 in the appendix to this chapter shows estimates of the earnings function for urban female employees. The last panel of table 7-1 (and the penultimate panel of table 7-6) shows the estimates for all occupations together, fitted separately by racial group. The last panel of table 7-6 provides earnings function estimates for *all* urban employees, male and female, disaggregated by race.

In the tables the subscripts M, C, I, O, or TOT on the dependent variable $\log y$ indicate the particular subsample of Malays, Chinese, Indians, others, or total, respectively, for which the equation has been estimated. The numbers in parentheses below each estimated coefficient (except the constant) of the regression equation give the standard error of the coefficient.[15] SEE and F refer to the standard error of estimate and F-ratio, respectively, and DF denotes degrees of freedom. The next four columns in the panel show the mean and variance of $\log y$, S, T, and y, respectively (y is here measured in Malaysian dollars per year). The mean of $\log y$ is the

---

14. The same definition of broad occupational categories is used here as in earlier chapters (see note to table 6-11). There were no observations for occupation 6 (farmers) in the sample of urban employees, farmers being either self-employed or employers. But there was a small number of employees (256 males and 217 females) in occupation 7 (farm, forestry, and fishing workers).

15. The computer program used to estimate the regression equations unfortunately does not provide standard errors for the constant term.

logarithm of the geometric mean income, and the variance of $\log y$ is a familiar measure of inequality (the variance of log-income).[16]

For regressions on microdata such as the PES sample, the overall fits obtained are rather good. They are certainly comparable to fits of the same equation estimated for developed countries (see Chiswick and Mincer, 1972; Mincer, 1974; and Psacharapoulos, 1973). Almost all the equations and almost all the coefficients of independent variables are significant at the 1 percent level. The variables S and T possess positive coefficients, and the coefficient of T^2 has the expected negative sign. In general, the results are fairly encouraging.

The goodness-of-fit of the equation is shown by an R^2 of 0.492. This means that age and education by themselves explain about half the observed inequality in earnings, as measured by the variance of log-income. This level of explanation is really quite impressive in light of the many important income-determining variables that have been omitted, such as the number of weeks in the year actually worked, ability differences, and the quality of schooling received.[17]

The parabolic age–log-income profile is confirmed for each level of education by the negative and significant coefficient on T^2.[18] The coefficient on S substantiates a positive association between education and income. There is a 14.01 percent coefficient on education for all males in the urban sector, with a t-ratio of more than 65.[19]

The arithmetic mean income of the 5,843 ($= DF + 4$) urban male employees in the sample is M\$3,217 per year (or M\$268 per month), and the variance of log-income is 0.775.[20] Their average level of schooling is 7.282 years and of experience, 20.339 years. Hence, the average age of males in the sample is 32.621 years (since $\overline{A} = \overline{T} + \overline{S} + 5 = 20.339 + 7.282 + 5.000$). As

16. Note also that the square root of variance, divided by the mean, of S and T furnishes measures of inequality (the coefficient of variation) for schooling S and experience T (see chapter 3 and appendix A).

17. The omitted variables are on the so-called supply side; variables on the demand side have been ignored altogether.

18. The equation for the racial group "others" in some occupations is not significant, and neither are the t-ratios of some coefficients. In general there are very few degrees of freedom for regression equations for this group (see table 7-1).

19. The coefficients β_1, β_2, and β_3 will be unbiased if the omitted variables are uncorrelated with the included ones of education, experience, and experience squared. This may not be a good assumption for the omitted variable of ability (or father's income), which might well be correlated with education. In that case, the estimated coefficient β_1 will be biased upward.

20. This degree of inequality is smaller than that among all employees in Malaysia. From table 6-6, the variance of log-income for the latter group is 0.816. But all urban employees, male and female, display a larger degree of inequality in their incomes (0.868, from the last panel of table 7-6) than this.

shown in the appendix to this chapter, the peak of the experience-income profile occurs at an experience level of $\beta_2/2\beta_3 = 0.09793/2(0.00125)$, or 39.172 years. For the average level of schooling (7.282), therefore, the age-income profile peaks at 51.454 years. It peaks later for those with more schooling and earlier for those with less, and the later peak occurs at a higher level of income (see the appendix to this chapter).

Racial Differences

Of the three major racial groups in Malaysia, the Malays obtain the highest return to education. Each additional year of schooling (holding experience constant) raises the annual income of a Malay by 14.24 percent, of a Chinese by 13.87 percent, and of an Indian by 13.50 percent.[21] (The following discussion of racial differences excludes consideration of the other races.) Although each of these coefficients has extremely high t-ratios, paired t-tests suggest that they are not significantly different. The overall return of 14.01 percent falls within the confidence interval of the three separate coefficients.[22] At the 95 percent significance level one cannot reject $\beta_1 = 0.1401$ for any racial group.[23] The higher coefficient for Malays is consistent with education's giving them a better entry into occupations with high incomes, such as government jobs.

The arithmetic mean income of Indian male employees (M\$3,287) is higher than that of Malays (M\$3,241), which in turn is higher than that of Chinese (M\$2,979). The Indian:Malay:Chinese labor income disparities for males stand at 1.10:1.09:1.00.[24] Since the returns to education between the groups are highly similar, differences in mean income should be associated with differences in levels of schooling and experience.[25] This is

21. Every additional year of schooling raises the income of a member of the other races by 23.47 percent.

22. The 95 percent confidence interval is the coefficient value, plus or minus approximately two standard errors.

23. At any rate, differences between occupations within a race seem to compensate for between-race differences within an occupation, so that when all occupations are considered together, no racial differences seem to emerge.

24. The sample excludes rural workers, and urban workers are relatively highly represented in government.

25. Since, however, the experience-income profiles are different for the three groups (significantly different β_2 and β_3), so also are the age-income profiles. Corresponding to the average level of schooling for each group, the age-income profile peaks at 51.64 years for the Malays, at 50.45 years for the Chinese, and at 54.41 years for the Indians. The profile is most sharply peaked for the Chinese, as measured by the size of the coefficient β_3 (see the appendix to this chapter).

indeed borne out. Since $\overline{A} = \overline{T} + \overline{S} + 5$, the combination of average schooling and experience levels for a group implies the average age level. In the sample, the average age of Indians is 35.80 years, of Malays 32.72 years, and of Chinese 31.62 years. This is the same as the relative income position of the three communities. The ranking of communities according to average schooling levels, however, is different: the Malays have the highest average level of education (7.89 years), followed by the Indians (7.46 years), and then the Chinese (6.85 years).

Inequality in earnings, as measured by the variance of log-income, is smallest for the Malays at 0.684; the Indians are next with an inequality level of 0.712, and the Chinese have the highest inequality of earnings at 0.780. This inequality in earnings is associated exactly with inequality in education and experience for the races. The Malays have the smallest inequality in years of schooling as measured by the coefficient of variation, $(\text{var } S)^{1/2}/\overline{S}$. The coefficients of variation of schooling for Malays, Indians, and Chinese are 0.52, 0.63, and 0.63, respectively. Inequality in years of experience displays the same ranking, indicated by a coefficient of variation of 0.63 for Malays, 0.65 for Indians, and 0.73 for Chinese.[26]

Two further questions concerning these findings are of some policy interest. First, how does preferential government policy toward the Malays in employment, promotions, and university quotas bear on these results?[27] Second, what part of the inequality between Malays and non-Malays can be explained by differences in educational attainment?

Some observers claim that the higher Malay returns are linked to the government's discrimination in employment and promotion policies. But it is difficult to quantify the extent to which the application of pro-Malay policies might have affected the above results. Nevertheless, certain occupations, in which the application of pro-Malay policies is likely to have been most intense, do display higher returns and average incomes for the Malays (see, for example, occupation 20, government administrators and legislative officials, in table 6-11). A countervailing factor, however, may be operating in the case of the Chinese. They control a large share of private business and probably practice preferential hiring of other Chinese in their businesses (for reasons of language or clan). This fact is consistent with the lower average levels of schooling among Chinese employees but com-

26. It can be shown that inequality in earnings is affected not only by inequality in S and T (and their covariance), but also by the average levels of S and T. To demonstrate this, simply take the variance of both sides of the earnings function.

27. There is, for example, a guarantee of places and jobs for the Malays in the public sector. See article 157 of the constitution of Malaysia.

parably high rates of return.[28] On balance, it is not possible to deduce a bias in any particular direction.

The second question presents a larger set of issues, which requires a comparison of labor and nonlabor incomes between the races. This was done in the previous chapter by use of the surrogate variable, employment status. In regard to labor incomes, it is not unreasonable to assert that differences in educational attainment do account for much of the difference in earnings. This follows from the statistically insignificant difference in returns to education among the major racial groups. Other things being equal, it would seem that labor income differences are associated with differences in education received. If causation can be attributed, and there is high substitutability in production between labor of different levels of skill or education, these findings suggest that education could be an instrument of mobility for Malays in the category of employees. (But see the caveats on drawing time series inferences from cross-sectional estimates of the earnings function in the earlier section "The Return to Education.")

Occupational Differences

Substantial differences exist in income inequality for urban male employees across occupations. The degree of inequality in income is fairly small among production workers [$\text{var}(\log y) = 0.489$], service workers (0.516), and professional and technical staff (0.557). The highest degree of inequality is found among administrative and managerial personnel (0.765). These results are again explained by differences in the level and inequality of schooling and experience.

One of the main findings is that returns to education are generally high in modern sector occupations and generally low in the traditional sector. From table 7-1, it is seen that high returns obtain in the administrative and managerial (14.15 percent), professional and technical (12.41 percent), and sales (12.21 percent) occupations; and low returns obtain among farm laborers (6.06 percent) and production workers (7.93 percent). As expected, the return to formal schooling is highest in white-collar activities and relatively low in blue-collar (production worker) and traditional sector (farm laborer) jobs. Schooling seems to suit better the job requirements of modern sector (tertiary) occupations.

It is also the case that the (human capital) earnings model performs least well in explaining the incomes of traditional sector employees (see the

---

28. Many Chinese start work in business (a family-owned shop or commercial establishment) straight after primary school.

earlier section "Some Problems of PES Data"). It explains only ($R^2 =$) 15.4 percent of the variance of log-income of farm laborers. At the other end, the best explanations of inequality by the model are for the sales (R^2 of 0.466), professional and technical (R^2 of 0.461), and administrative and managerial (R^2 of 0.453) categories.[29]

The average levels of schooling are also lower in the traditional than in the modern sector occupations. The average level of schooling for farm laborers is only 4.65 years, which is lower than that in any other occupation. For professional and technical personnel the average level of schooling is as high as 12.83 years, and for administrative and managerial personnel it is 10.91 years, but these job classifications undoubtedly require more education. Average income levels across occupations are positively correlated with average schooling levels. Mean incomes for the administrative and managerial and the professional and technical categories are at the top of the scale—while an average monthly income of only M$128 puts farm laborers at the bottom of the scale.

These results are consistent with another explanation. It could be that certain occupations have higher rewards associated with them purely for institutional or class reasons. Entrants into these occupations might be screened by means of educational qualifications. Then higher schooling levels would be associated with the higher paid occupations. Thus, even if its relation with productivity is tenuous, it may be that education is deployed as a screening device for certain high-income occupations, which would explain the observed positive relation between income and education.[30]

The ethnic breakdown within each occupation shows that Indians seem to benefit more than other groups from schooling in occupations 1–3 (professional and technical, administrative and managerial, clerical and related). The explanation for this is probably sociocultural (see Sandhu, 1967 and 1969). At the same time, the Malays display lower returns than other racial groups in the professional and technical and the administrative and managerial occupations. As service workers, however, they obtain the highest return to schooling.

The relation between starting salary and overall lifetime income in an occupation can be illustrated by the separate age-income profiles for

29. Of course, the amount of variation in log y is itself different for each occupational category, so the R^2's would be different even with the same standard error of estimate. But the R^2's still represent the proportion of inequality explained by education and experience in each occupational category.

30. It is not clear how the effects of experience can be explained in these terms—by gerontocratic principles, perhaps, or a "first in last out" system for nontransferable skills.

occupations. If lifetime income (undiscounted) in an occupation is approximated by the mean income of employees belonging in it (at different stages of their life cycle), it can be seen that starting salary is imperfectly correlated with expected total income.[31] Administrative and managerial personnel, for instance, have a lower starting salary but 50 percent more lifetime income than professional and technical persons. The former's earnings peak at a later age and a higher income level than the latter's (the earnings peak is given by an income level of $\exp[\beta_0 + \beta_1 \overline{S} + (\beta_2^2/4\beta_3)]$; see the appendix to this chapter). At the other end, production workers and farm laborers have a low earnings peak—which also occurs at an earlier stage in their life cycle.

These results shed some light on an interesting question concerning urban unemployment in Peninsular Malaysia. There is currently substantial unemployment among secondary school-leavers in the country (see Mazumdar, 1975), who are said to be queuing up for white-collar jobs in clerical and related occupations. It is suggested that starting pay scales in government create unrealistically high earnings expectations in such jobs, and this has caused an oversupply of, and unemployment among, secondary school-leavers. It turns out, however, that clerical and related occupations have not only relatively high initial salaries, but also high lifetime incomes (in relation, for example, to comparable occupations such as sales and services). Thus it is not clear that starting salary rather than lifetime income has influenced people's job choice in this case.

Male-Female Differences

Regression equations parallel to those in table 7-1 have been estimated for female employees in the urban sector and are included as table 7-6. In the last panel of this table male and female employees in all occupations are pooled.

As in the case of males, the earnings function for females is highly significant and displays the predicted signs on S, T, and T^2. The return to schooling is slightly lower for females (13.77 percent) than for males (14.01 percent), but a paired t-test shows the difference to be not statistically significant. The earnings model explains a smaller fraction of income inequality among females than among males (R^2 of 0.430 compared with 0.492). A major reason is probably that T is an inaccurate measure of labor

---

31. Starting salaries are the anti-log of the term $\beta_0 + \beta_1 S$ in the earnings function. The estimate obtained thereby will be biased, though consistent; the earnings function will give an unbiased estimate only of the logarithm of the starting salary.

market experience for women (see the earlier section entitled "The Earnings Function").[32]

Females generally obtain a lower return to schooling within each occupation than males.[33] A notable exception is the case of occupation 3, clerical and related workers, in which females obtain a higher return (13.25 percent) than males (10.51 percent). This is perhaps due to their superior skills in this occupation and the lack of opportunities for employment in others. Women in clerical and related occupations have an average of 12.11 years of schooling compared with 9.83 years for men.

The average levels of experience (17.35 years), schooling (6.59 years), and therefore age (28.94 years) are all lower for females than for males. The age-income profile is flatter for females than for males, as measured by the size of the coefficient β_3,[34] which is 0.00073 for females compared with 0.00125 for males. This may reflect the fact that women have more limited opportunities for promotion than do men. The female experience-income profile peaks at an experience level of 43.62 years, which exceeds the level at which the male experience-income profile peaks (39.17 years). It should be reiterated, however, that the measure T of labor market experience is not satisfactory for women.

Female mean incomes are lower than male mean incomes within every occupation; overall, the mean income of females is slightly more than half that of males (M$1,784 per year compared with M$3,217). Within each occupation, income inequality among females is lower than among males, but overall it is higher (varlog of 0.837 compared with 0.775). This reflects greater between-occupation differentials for women.

For all 8,263 urban employees together, male and female, there is a 14.77 percent return to schooling. Their mean income is M$2,798 per year, and variance of log-income is 0.868. Their average level of schooling is 7.08 years; of experience, 19.46 years; and of age, 31.54 years. The age-income profile corresponding to the average level of schooling for all urban employees peaks at 52.41 years. The coefficient of variation of schooling is 0.677 and of experience 0.734. The variables S, T, T^2 explain 48.5 percent of the inequality in income among urban employees.

---

32. Perhaps T is a better measure of labor market experience in developing than in developed countries. The institution of the joint family may allow working women to leave children at home to be looked after by relatives, so that women employees need not withdraw from the labor force for very long in Malaysia.

33. The equation for occupation 2, administrative and managerial personnel, does not have enough degrees of freedom to allow valid statistical inference.

34. See property (6) and figure 7-2 in the appendix to this chapter.

Estimates by Age Cohort

The sample of urban male employees is disaggregated into three successive age cohorts (table 7-2) to study their separate earnings functions. The three groups consist of those under 30 years, those between 30 and 49 years, and those over 50 years. The motivation for this disaggregation is to identify possible differences in the return to education among cohorts.

The regression results indicate significantly different returns for the three groups. The youngest age group obtains the highest return to schooling of 18.10 percent. This is followed by the middle age group (30–49 years), which obtains a return of 11.91 percent, while the oldest age group (50+ years) obtains a return of only 6.94 percent. A possible explanation for these findings is that there is a "vintage" or "obsolescence" effect in education. In other words, the quality of schooling has improved over time or previously acquired education has become less relevant or effective for present day (1970) job requirements.[35] It is clear that significant changes have indeed taken place in the level and nature of education in Malaysia. For example, there is a markedly higher average level of schooling among the younger age groups (approximately eight and seven years, respectively) than among the oldest group (five years). Another explanation for the findings is that the independence assumption between the return to formal schooling and to experience is not valid (see the earlier section "The Earnings Function"). For example, if older people earn higher incomes because of their experience, an extra year of schooling may yield a lower return as a proportion of their present income.

The fraction of inequality explained by the model (R^2) is largest for the under 30 age group. Significantly weaker fits are associated with the older age groups, possibly because they derive larger fractions of their income in the form of returns to accumulated savings, that is, from nonhuman capital.[36]

The level of inequality in income is smallest for the middle group, with var(log y) = 0.519. Part of the reason for this may be the greater homogeneity of this group (the size of its defining interval, 30–49 years, is relatively small).

---

35. Another explanation could be that older people just happen to occupy jobs for which education is less important, or that education has been increasingly used as screening for jobs.

36. In fact, this would be a reason for observing higher returns to education in the estimates for the older age groups. The fact that returns are actually lower seems to reinforce the explanation offered above.

Table 7-2. Earnings Functions for Urban Male Employees by Age Cohort

Age: Under 30 years

$$\log y_{\text{TOT}} = 4.74180 + 0.18102S + 0.14101T - 0.00158T^2$$
$$(0.00378)\quad(0.00804)\quad(0.00037)$$

$R^2 = 0.470$	$F = 813.11$	$\overline{\log y} = 7.301$	$\bar{S} = 7.977$	$\bar{T} = 9.153$	$\bar{y} = 2{,}115$
$\text{SEE} = 0.619$	$\text{DF} = 2{,}749$	$\text{var}(\log y) = 0.723$	$\text{var}(S) = 15.422$	$\text{var}(T) = 27.303$	$\text{var}(y) = 5.396\ 10^6$

Age: 30–49 years

$$\log y_{\text{TOT}} = 6.44727 + 0.11910S + 0.03987T - 0.00038T^2$$
$$(0.00367)\quad(0.00907)\quad(0.00016)$$

$R^2 = 0.390$	$F = 513.23$	$\overline{\log y} = 8.041$	$\bar{S} = 7.083$	$\bar{T} = 25.759$	$\bar{y} = 4{,}235$
$\text{SEE} = 0.563$	$\text{DF} = 2{,}408$	$\text{var}(\log y) = 0.519$	$\text{var}(S) = 21.939$	$\text{var}(T) = 62.786$	$\text{var}(y) = 28.869\ 10^6$

Age: 50–98 years

$$\log y_{\text{TOT}} = 10.72164 + 0.06939S - 0.10498T + 0.00073T^2$$
$$(0.01000)\quad(0.02800)\quad(0.00026)$$

$R^2 = 0.393$	$F = 145.40$	$\overline{\log y} = 7.840$	$\bar{S} = 5.166$	$\bar{T} = 46.480$	$\bar{y} = 4{,}072$
$\text{SEE} = 0.710$	$\text{DF} = 674$	$\text{var}(\log y) = 0.826$	$\text{var}(S) = 20.312$	$\text{var}(T) = 70.431$	$\text{var}(y) = 33.619\ 10^6$

All ages

$$\log y_{\text{TOT}} = 5.41823 + 0.14005S + 0.09793T - 0.00125T^2$$
$$(0.00215)\quad(0.00193)\quad(0.00003)$$

$R^2 = 0.492$	$F = 1{,}881.79$	$\overline{\log y} = 7.669$	$\bar{S} = 7.282$	$\bar{T} = 20.339$	$\bar{y} = 3{,}217$
$\text{SEE} = 0.628$	$\text{DF} = 5{,}839$	$\text{var}(\log y) = 0.775$	$\text{var}(S) = 19.437$	$\text{var}(T) = 197.388$	$\text{var}(y) = 19.437\ 10^6$

Note: See note to table 7-1.

256

The average age of persons in the under 30 age group is 22.13 years, and in the middle and older groups it is 37.84 years and 56.65 years, respectively. The mean income level is highest for the middle age group (M\$4,235 per year), a reflection of the fact that this group is closer to its earnings peak than are other groups. Predicted peaks in the age–log-income (or age-income) profile differ among the three groups. A peak at 57.60 years is forecast for the under 30 group, and at 64.54 years for the 30–49 age group. Most employees in the 50+ age group are past their true income peak, and their earnings function is estimated mainly from incomes to the right of this point. The function fitted for this group turns out to be convex with a trough at 82.07 years, suggesting that a more gradual decline in income may occur than is indicated by the original concave functional form. But the function is obviously not valid over the entire range beyond the turning point, for instance after a person's withdrawal from the labor force. Not much significance should therefore be attached to the convex shape of the age–log-income profile for this group.

For female employees, much the same results are in evidence (not shown here). The smaller return to schooling acquired earlier is less marked, however, and the explanatory power of the function is rather weak for the oldest age group of females ($R^2 = 0.198$).

Language of Instruction

Returns to education are highest for males who have attended English-language schools (the category of "other" languages of instruction is excluded).[37] For males who have been to such schools, the return to schooling is 16.38 percent (table 7-3). Average levels of income and schooling are also highest for these persons. The inequality in their incomes is largest, and the variables S, T, and T^2 account for 59.4 percent of it.

An education in the Tamil language receives the lowest return of only 6.71 percent. (The average level of schooling is also smallest for people who have attended Tamil schools.) Returns to education in the Chinese or Malay language are significantly higher (table 7-3).[38] One explanation for these findings is the possibility that Tamil school qualifications are

37. After the "other" races, the Chinese obtain the highest return (not shown here) of 17.33 percent to schooling in the English language of instruction, followed by the Indians (15.18 percent), and the Malays (14.12 percent).

38. In the sample, Tamil-language schools were attended only by Indians, Chinese-language schools only by Chinese (except for one non-Chinese), and Malay-language schools mainly by Malays (847 out of 875).

Table 7-3. Earnings Functions for Urban Male Employees by Language of Instruction

English

$$\log y_{\text{TOT}} = 5.08280 + 0.16376S + 0.12000T - 0.00167T^2$$
$$(0.00368) \quad (0.00402) \quad (0.00010)$$

$\overline{S} = 10.569$ $\overline{T} = 13.888$
var$(S) = 14.592$ var$(T) = 117.017$

$\overline{\log y} = 7.964$ $\overline{y} = 4{,}671$
var$(\log y) = 0.999$ var$(y) = 39.442 \times 10^6$

$R^2 = 0.594$ $F = 1{,}068.62$
SEE $= 0.637$ DF $= 2{,}188$

Malay

$$\log y_{\text{TOT}} = 5.33086 + 0.12168S + 0.10433T - 0.00137T^2$$
$$(0.00635) \quad (0.00558) \quad (0.00011)$$

$\overline{S} = 6.346$ $\overline{T} = 21.537$
var$(S) = 10.631$ var$(T) = 146.532$

$\overline{\log y} = 7.511$ $\overline{y} = 2{,}364$
var$(\log y) = 0.571$ var$(y) = 4.695 \times 10^6$

$R^2 = 0.469$ $F = 256.46$
SEE $= 0.552$ DF $= 871$

Chinese

$$\log y_{\text{TOT}} = 5.45793 + 0.10707S + 0.11395T - 0.00161T^2$$
$$(0.00446) \quad (0.00338) \quad (0.00006)$$

$\overline{S} = 5.587$ $\overline{T} = 21.164$
var$(S) = 9.092$ var$(T) = 167.278$

$\overline{\log y} = 7.479$ $\overline{y} = 2{,}298$
var$(\log y) = 0.572$ var$(y) = 4.140 \times 10^6$

$R^2 = 0.452$ $F = 549.61$
SEE $= 0.560$ DF $= 1{,}998$

Tamil

$$\log y_{\text{TOT}} = 6.14768 + 0.06711S + 0.06504T - 0.00092T^2$$
$$(0.00989) \quad (0.00801) \quad (0.00013)$$

$\overline{S} = 4.981$ $\overline{T} = 29.978$
var$(S) = 7.529$ var$(T) = 173.724$

$\overline{\log y} = 7.446$ $\overline{y} = 1{,}977$
var$(\log y) = 0.308$ var$(y) = 1.334 \times 10^6$

$R^2 = 0.250$ $F = 36.77$
SEE $= 0.483$ DF $= 330$

Other

$$\log y_{\text{TOT}} = 6.07881 + 0.19314S + 0.01496T - 0.00012T^2$$
$$(0.02381) \quad (0.02795) \quad (0.00048)$$

$\overline{S} = 9.616$ $\overline{T} = 27.616$
var$(S) = 33.418$ var$(T) = 185.564$

$\overline{\log y} = 8.236$ $\overline{y} = 7{,}490$
var$(\log y) = 1.562$ var$(y) = 80.467 \times 10^6$

$R^2 = 0.691$ $F = 38.71$
SEE $= 0.715$ DF $= 52$

Note: Owing to 384 individuals for whom the language of instruction was not available, the total number of observations here (5,459) does not tally with that in table 7-1 (5,843). See also the note to table 7-1.

insufficiently recognized. In Malaysia, Tamil is neither an official working language nor a business language (unlike English, Malay, or Chinese). Another is that the effective demand for Tamil-educated workers is low, and many are employed in occupations (such as farm laborers and production workers) which show low rates of return to schooling.

The high returns realized in English-language schools could be the result of two factors. First, it is likely that the quality of instruction in the English schools is superior to that in the vernacular schools—as manifested by higher teacher-student ratios and better facilities such as books and libraries. Second, the higher returns in the English schools might reflect a screening effect. A knowledge of the language is a definite advantage in many of the more highly paid occupations in government and business (for example, in multinational firms); in some, it might even be a prerequisite.[39]

Type of Degree

In commenting on the age-income profiles of persons at the highest level of education, those who hold a degree or diploma, I consider first the shape of the income profile for males with the same degree and thus the same level of schooling. Then I look into the differences between such profiles for different degrees. The S term is absent from these equations because for each one the number of years of schooling is the same.

The starting salary, that is, the salary with no experience ($T = 0$), is indicated by the size of the constant term in the regressions.[40] It is evident from table 7-4 that the starting salary is highest for engineers and is closely followed by that for doctors; for teachers (those with an education degree or diploma), it is about two-thirds the level for doctors. The average lifetime income (again undiscounted) is highest for doctors, not engineers. So the earnings of medical degree holders rise faster and overtake those of engineers after starting at a lower level.

---

39. The average level of schooling is highest for those who have attended English-language schools, at approximately ten years. Similarly high average levels of schooling prevail in the professional and technical and the administrative and managerial occupations—which is consistent with people in these occupations having been to English-language schools.

40. Unfortunately, the computer program used for estimation does not calculate the standard error for the constant term in the regression. Thus tests of statistical significance of differences between intercepts cannot be made. Note that the intercept in any case provides an unbiased estimate only of the logarithm of the starting salary.

Table 7-4. Earnings Functions for Urban Male Employees by Type of Degree or Diploma

Education degree or diploma

$$\log y_{\text{TOT}} = 8.34768 + 0.03216T - 0.00043T^2$$
$$(0.01185) \quad (0.00038)$$

$\log y = 8.636$	$\bar{S} = 16.000$	$\bar{T} = 11.480$	$\bar{y} = 6{,}151$
$\text{var}(\log y) = 0.153$	$\text{var}(S) = 0.000$	$\text{var}(T) = 55.004$	$\text{var}(y) = 10.729\ 10^6$

$R^2 = 0.141 \qquad F = 14.47$
$\text{SEE} = 0.365 \qquad \text{DF} = 176$

Medical degree or diploma

$$\log y_{\text{TOT}} = 8.81623 + 0.04690T + 0.00050T^2$$
$$(0.03570) \quad (0.00137)$$

$\overline{\log y} = 9.313$	$\bar{S} = 19.000$	$\bar{T} = 8.913$	$\bar{y} = 14.406$
$\text{var}(\log y) = 0.541$	$\text{var}(S) = 0.000$	$\text{var}(T) = 82.538$	$\text{var}(y) = 128.270\ 10^6$

$R^2 = 0.537 \qquad F = 11.59$
$\text{SEE} = 0.525 \qquad \text{DF} = 20$

Engineering degree or diploma

$$\log y_{\text{TOT}} = 8.88111 + 0.07041T - 0.00152T^2$$
$$(0.02128) \quad (0.00061)$$

$\log y = 9.306$	$\bar{S} = 17.500$	$\bar{T} = 9.500$	$\bar{y} = 12{,}935$
$\text{var}(\log y) = 0.313$	$\text{var}(S) = 0.000$	$\text{var}(T) = 71.742$	$\text{var}(y) = 65.622\ 10^6$

$R^2 = 0.185 \qquad F = 6.82$
$\text{SEE} = 0.513 \qquad \text{DF} = 60$

Other degrees or diplomas[a]

$$\log y_{\text{TOT}} = 7.79079 + 0.10650T - 0.00185T^2$$
$$(0.01204) \quad (0.00036)$$

$\overline{\log y} = 8.533$	$\bar{S} = 17.000$	$\bar{T} = 10.776$	$\bar{y} = 3{,}601$
$\text{var}(\log y) = 0.957$	$\text{var}(S) = 0.000$	$\text{var}(T) = 102.784$	$\text{var}(y) = 14.427\ 10^6$

$R^2 = 0.313 \qquad F = 76.66$
$\text{SEE} = 0.813 \qquad \text{DF} = 336$

Note: Although a breakdown by racial group was effected within each degree type, frequently there were not enough degrees of freedom to warrant it. The breakdown is not reported here. See also the note to table 7-1.

a. Agriculture, pure and natural science, government and political science, management and administration, economics and commerce, and others.

Inequality in the income of teachers is very small indeed, with a variance of log-income of just 0.153. This largely reflects pay scales in state schools where, for example, the rate of annual pay increases is constrained to about 3 percent. The degree of inequality in the earnings of engineers is also fairly low, with var(log y) = 0.313. Again, this is probably explained by the absorption of a majority of engineers into government departments at predetermined salary scales (which are more equal than in the private sector).

Doctors' incomes are more unequal. An important reason for this is probably the variation among doctors in private practice in the number of hours worked, which depends partly on different choices between income and leisure. Unit rates also vary, of course, owing to such factors as skill and reputation. Interestingly, concavity is not verified in the age–log-income profile for doctors (the coefficients on T and T^2 not being significant). This may be due to labor-supply effects over the life cycle or the absence of institutionally determined salary scales. The main point is that the profession allows considerable flexibility in the number of hours worked.

Female employees with equivalent qualifications have somewhat lower starting salaries both as teachers and as doctors—a reflection of possible discrimination against women. They also have significantly lower average income levels, possibly because of lower average levels of experience or because of part-time work, that is, differences in the "weeks worked" variable. Even with the same measured T, interruptions in post-training work experience could reduce average incomes.[41]

Breakdown by Region

The earnings functions were estimated separately for each state in Peninsular Malaysia (table 7-5).[42] This allows an examination of inter-regional differences in education and incomes and may also shed some light on the extent to which regional inequality can be explained by differences in schooling and experience.[43]

41. The male-female difference in annual teacher salaries is not very large (M$6,151 compared with M$4,563), nor is the difference in their average experience levels (11.48 years compared with 10.16 years).

42. Since, as noted in the appendix to chapter 5, there is no urban population for Perlis state, the estimates here refer to ten Peninsular Malaysian states only.

43. Interregional analyses using this framework are reported for the United States in Chiswick (1975). There are too few observations here (ten states) to explain regional inequality in terms of the means, variances, and covariances of schooling, experience, and experience squared.

Table 7-5. Earnings Functions for Urban Male Employees by State

Johore

$$\log y_{\text{TOT}} = 5.28116 + 0.14021S + 0.10718T - 0.00146T^2$$
$$\phantom{\log y_{\text{TOT}} = 5.28116 +\ } (0.00638)\quad (0.00574)\quad (0.00011)$$

$R^2 = 0.474$ $F = 222.09$ $\overline{\log y} = 7.562$ $\bar{S} = 7.562$ $\bar{T} = 19.561$ $\bar{y} = 2{,}774$
$\text{SEE} = 0.634$ $\text{DF} = 739$ $\text{var}(\log y) = 0.761$ $\text{var}(S) = 18.096$ $\text{var}(T) = 188.762$ $\text{var}(y) = 8.517\ 10^6$

Kedah

$$\log y_{\text{TOT}} = 5.19841 + 0.13604S + 0.10467T - 0.00132T^2$$
$$\phantom{\log y_{\text{TOT}} = 5.19841 +\ } (0.01174)\quad (0.00952)\quad (0.00017)$$

$R^2 = 0.433$ $F = 73.14$ $\overline{\log y} = 7.517$ $\bar{S} = 7.242$ $\bar{T} = 21.095$ $\bar{y} = 2{,}770$
$\text{SEE} = 0.697$ $\text{DF} = 287$ $\text{var}(\log y) = 0.848$ $\text{var}(S) = 16.761$ $\text{var}(T) = 218.025$ $\text{var}(y) = 10.720\ 10^6$

Kelantan

$$\log y_{\text{TOT}} = 4.78393 + 0.17886S + 0.09575T - 0.00107T^2$$
$$\phantom{\log y_{\text{TOT}} = 4.78393 +\ } (0.01545)\quad (0.01516)\quad (0.00027)$$

$R^2 = 0.481$ $F = 48.88$ $\overline{\log y} = 7.433$ $\bar{S} = 7.225$ $\bar{T} = 21.410$ $\bar{y} = 2{,}992$
$\text{SEE} = 0.781$ $\text{DF} = 158$ $\text{var}(\log y) = 1.153$ $\text{var}(S) = 21.478$ $\text{var}(T) = 191.615$ $\text{var}(y) = 13.966\ 10^6$

Malacca

$$\log y_{\text{TOT}} = 4.87935 + 0.16398S + 0.11803T - 0.00152T^2$$
$$\phantom{\log y_{\text{TOT}} = 4.87935 +\ } (0.01225)\quad (0.01028)\quad (0.00019)$$

$R^2 = 0.560$ $F = 84.16$ $\overline{\log y} = 7.513$ $\bar{S} = 7.235$ $\bar{T} = 20.270$ $\bar{y} = 2{,}835$
$\text{SEE} = 0.636$ $\text{DF} = 198$ $\text{var}(\log y) = 0.906$ $\text{var}(S) = 17.834$ $\text{var}(T) = 214.125$ $\text{var}(y) = 10.787\ 10^6$

Negri Sembilan

$$\log y_{\text{TOT}} = 5.79133 + 0.14144S + 0.07413T - 0.00116T^2$$
$$\phantom{\log y_{\text{TOT}} = 5.79133 +\ } (0.01278)\quad (0.01254)\quad (0.00023)$$

$R^2 = 0.522$ $F = 53.84$ $\overline{\log y} = 7.721$ $\bar{S} = 7.970$ $\bar{T} = 20.503$ $\bar{y} = 3{,}365$
$\text{SEE} = 0.616$ $\text{DF} = 148$ $\text{var}(\log y) = 0.778$ $\text{var}(S) = 20.991$ $\text{var}(T) = 201.392$ $\text{var}(y) = 14.876\ 10^6$

Pahang

$$\log y_{\text{TOT}} = 5.76133 + 0.12102S + 0.09174T - 0.00123T^2$$
$$\phantom{\log y_{\text{TOT}} = 5.76133 +\ } (0.00938)\quad (0.00785)\quad (0.00014)$$

$R^2 = 0.475$	$F = 81.41$	$\overline{\log y} = 7.740$	$\overline{S} = 7.443$	$\overline{T} = 19.513$	$\overline{y} = 2{,}941$
$\text{SEE} = 0.542$	$\text{DF} = 270$	$\text{var}(\log y) = 0.554$	$\text{var}(S) = 16.952$	$\text{var}(T) = 198.567$	$\text{var}(y) = 4.541 \; 10^6$

Penang

$$\log y_{\text{TOT}} = \underset{}{5.38412} + \underset{(0.00543)}{0.12682S} + \underset{(0.00507)}{0.10299T} - \underset{(0.00009)}{0.00138T^2}$$

$R^2 = 0.501$	$F = 274.84$	$\overline{\log y} = 7.578$	$\overline{S} = 7.066$	$\overline{T} = 21.455$	$\overline{y} = 2{,}858$
$\text{SEE} = 0.583$	$\text{DF} = 822$	$\text{var}(\log y) = 0.678$	$\text{var}(S) = 17.720$	$\text{var}(T) = 202.397$	$\text{var}(y) = 13.027 \; 10^6$

Perak

$$\log y_{\text{TOT}} = 5.39270 + \underset{(0.00500)}{0.12466S} + \underset{(0.00438)}{0.10675T} - \underset{(0.00008)}{0.00139T^2}$$

$R^2 = 0.499$	$F = 330.00$	$\overline{\log y} = 7.623$	$\overline{S} = 7.012$	$\overline{T} = 21.343$	$\overline{y} = 2{,}868$
$\text{SEE} = 0.605$	$\text{DF} = 993$	$\text{var}(\log y) = 0.729$	$\text{var}(S) = 19.592$	$\text{var}(T) = 206.390$	$\text{var}(y) = 7.494 \; 10^6$

Selangor

$$\log y_{\text{TOT}} = 5.53159 + \underset{(0.00321)}{0.14742S} + \underset{(0.00291)}{0.09323T} - \underset{(0.00005)}{0.00110T^2}$$

$R^2 = 0.566$	$F = 879.22$	$\overline{\log y} = 7.819$	$\overline{S} = 7.374$	$\overline{T} = 19.745$	$\overline{y} = 3{,}863$
$\text{SEE} = 0.578$	$\text{DF} = 2{,}024$	$\text{var}(\log y) = 0.768$	$\text{var}(S) = 21.019$	$\text{var}(T) = 190.495$	$\text{var}(y) = 36.804 \; 10^6$

Trengganu

$$\log y_{\text{TOT}} = 5.31429 + \underset{(0.01599)}{0.16569S} + \underset{(0.01711)}{0.07339T} - \underset{(0.00033)}{0.00091T^2}$$

$R^2 = 0.396$	$F = 35.795$	$\overline{\log y} = 7.573$	$\overline{S} = 8.241$	$\overline{T} = 18.461$	$\overline{y} = 2{,}997$
$\text{SEE} = 0.752$	$\text{DF} = 164$	$\text{var}(\log y) = 0.918$	$\text{var}(S) = 19.886$	$\text{var}(T) = 167.904$	$\text{var}(y) = 12.324 \; 10^6$

Peninsular Malaysia

$$\log y_{\text{TOT}} = 5.41823 + \underset{(0.00215)}{0.14005S} + \underset{(0.00193)}{0.09793T} - \underset{(0.00003)}{0.00125T^2}$$

$R^2 = 0.492$	$F = 1{,}881.79$	$\overline{\log y} = 7.669$	$\overline{S} = 7.282$	$\overline{T} = 20.339$	$\overline{y} = 3{,}217$
$\text{SEE} = 0.628$	$\text{DF} = 5{,}839$	$\text{var}(\log y) = 0.775$	$\text{var}(S) = 19.437$	$\text{var}(T) = 197.338$	$\text{var}(y) = 19.437 \; 10^6$

Note: Perlis is omitted from the table since it has no urban population. See also the note to table 7-1.

There are fairly wide interstate disparities in the average level of income and education for urban male employees (table 7-5). Mean incomes are lowest in Kedah (M$2,770 per year) and highest in Selangor (M$3,863 per year), the disparity ratio being 1.0:1.4.[44] Inequality in income, however, is relatively low in Selangor, but high in Kedah. In general, there appears to be a negative correlation across states between the level and inequality of urban employees' incomes. (This contrasts with the result in chapter 3 on the positive association across states between the level and inequality of individual per capita incomes.)

The differences among states in returns to schooling are also fairly wide. They vary from 12.10 percent in Pahang to 17.89 percent in Kelantan,[45] and there is a further negative association between the income level of a state and the return to schooling in it. The generally higher returns in poorer states can probably be explained by the fact that high-wage (skilled) labor has greater mobility nationally than does low-wage (unskilled) labor.[46] This leads to a wider income gap in the poorer states than in the richer ones. It is also consistent with the negative correlation observed earlier between the level and inequality of income across states.

The earnings functions fit best in the most developed state, Selangor, where they explain 56.6 percent of the inequality in incomes. The coefficient of determination (R^2) is in fact more than 40 percent in every state except Trengganu (where it is 39.6 percent).

Appendix: Some Properties of the Earnings Function

The earnings function used in this chapter,

$$\log y = \beta_0 + \beta_1 S + \beta_2 T - \beta_3 T^2,$$

generates many of the observed characteristics of individual earnings profiles.[47] These characteristics are depicted by a life cycle that begins with a period of no earnings, followed by a period in which earnings rise and then eventually fall off. Earnings are also observed to be a roughly concave

44. These interstate differences in the incomes of urban male employees are much smaller than the interstate differences in incomes of all employees (see chapter 6).

45. A paired *t*-test shows that the two coefficients are significantly different from one another at the 99.5 percent level of confidence.

46. In other words, it is posited that there is a greater degree of equilibrium geographically in the market for skilled labor than for unskilled labor.

47. The properties of individual earnings profiles were originally derived in Anand (1974*b*, pp. 10–14) in the section "Implications of the Human Capital Model of Earnings."

function of age, especially in the neighborhood of the peak. As a function of the level of schooling, earnings peak at a later age for those with more schooling, and the peak itself occurs at a higher level of income.

This earnings function, borrowed from the theory of optimal investment in human capital, turns out to fit the above characteristics rather well. This is demonstrated here, and some further properties of the earnings function are derived which prove useful in interpreting the regression results in this chapter. These properties appear to have gone largely unnoticed by the human capitalists.

1. Income begins to be earned only upon the completion of schooling at age $A = S + 5$, and the starting log-income level is $\beta_0 + \beta_1 S$.

2. The maximum of the age–log-income (or age-income) profile occurs when the slope $\partial \log y/\partial A = (1/y)(\partial y/\partial A) = 0$, that is, when $\beta_2 - 2\beta_3(A - S - 5) = 0$. Hence the age at which the age–log-income (or age-income) profile peaks, for schooling level S, is $A = S + 5 + (\beta_2/2\beta_3)$. It follows, therefore, that the profile corresponding to a higher S peaks at a later age A. In other words, the age-income curve turns down later in life for those with more schooling.

3. The log-income corresponding to the peak of the S profile is obtained by substituting $T = (A - S - 5) = (\beta_2/2\beta_3)$ into the earnings function. This gives

$$\log y = \beta_0 + \beta_1 S + (\beta_2^2/2\beta_3) - \beta_3(\beta_2^2/4\beta_3^2)$$
$$= \beta_0 + \beta_1 S + (\beta_2^2/4\beta_3).$$

This is also evident from rewriting the earnings function as

$$\log y = [\beta_0 + \beta_1 S + (\beta_2^2/4\beta_3)] - \beta_3[T - (\beta_2/2\beta_3)]^2.$$

For a given S, the second term of this expression is always nonpositive, so the maximum of $\log y$ must occur when it is zero (that is, when $T = \beta_2/2\beta_3$). The maximum value is then given by the first term, as in the previous expression. Hence log-income, and therefore income, peaks at a higher level for the profile corresponding to a higher S.

4. For any S, the age–log-income profile is concave because

$$\partial^2 \log y/\partial A^2 = -2\beta_3 < 0.$$

In fact its shape is an inverted parabola since $\log y$ is a quadratic function of A.

Conclusions (1) to (4) can be illustrated diagrammatically. Figure 7-1 depicts the age–log-income profiles for three different levels of schooling. Some further properties of the earnings function are given below.

5. The experience (T)–log-income profile is also concave and parabolic in shape.

Figure 7-1. *Age–Log-income Profiles for Three Levels of Schooling*

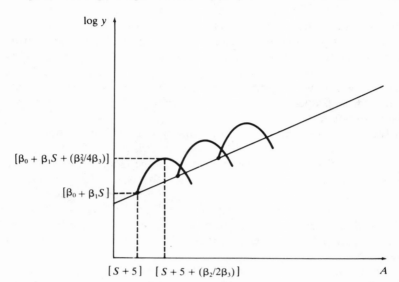

6. The flatness of the age–log-income (or age-income) profile is indicated by the magnitude of the coefficient β_3 in the quadratic earnings function. A small coefficient (in absolute terms) indicates a flat profile, whereas a large coefficient indicates a peaked profile.[48] Thus, a glance at the estimated coefficients of T^2 in the various subsamples considered will establish the relative peakedness of their earnings profiles. (For example, the age-income profiles of males can be compared with those of females.)

7. In contrast to the age–log-income profile (which is parabolic), the age-income profile is not everywhere concave. By differentiation,

$$\partial^2 \log y/\partial A^2 = -(\partial \log y/\partial A)^2 + [(1/y)(\partial^2 y/\partial A^2)].$$

Hence
$$(1/y)(\partial^2 y/\partial A^2) = -2\beta_3 + (\beta_2 - 2\beta_3 T)^2$$

and thus $\partial^2 y/\partial A^2 < 0$ only in a neighborhood around the peak at age $A = S + 5 + (\beta_2/2\beta_3)$ given by $[\beta_2 - 2\beta_3(A - S - 5)]^2 < 2\beta_3$.[49] Outside this neighborhood, that is, for values of A more than $(2\beta_3)^{-1/2}$ away from the peak at $S + 5 + (\beta_2/2\beta_3)$, the age-income profile is convex.

---

48. This is clear from the expression for the earnings function in (3) above, in which the square has been completed on T.

49. Note that at the peak itself, $(1/y)(\partial^2 y/\partial A^2) = -2\beta_3 < 0$; that is, the age-income profile is locally concave at the peak.

Figure 7-2. *Age-Income Profile for a Given Level of Schooling*

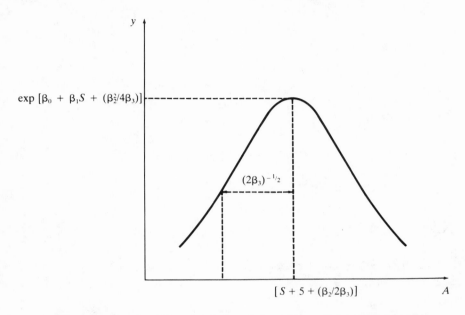

8. The latter implications also follow by rewriting the earnings function as:

$$y = \exp\left\{ \left[\beta_0 + \beta_1 S + (\beta_2^2/4\beta_3) \right] - \beta_3 \left[T - (\beta_2/2\beta_3) \right]^2 \right\}$$

$$= \exp\left\{ \left[\beta_0 + \beta_1 S + (\beta_2^2/4\beta_3) \right] - \beta_3 \left[A - \left[S + 5 + (\beta_2/2\beta_3) \right] \right]^2 \right\}$$

This is the expression for a normal (or Gaussian) distribution in T, or A, given S.[50] Therefore, the experience-income and age-income profiles are bell-shaped, like the curves of a normal distribution.

Properties (6), (7), and (8) of the earnings function are illustrated in figure 7-2, which shows the age-income profile for a given level of schooling.

50. The modal value for the T distribution is $\beta_2/2\beta_3$, while that for the A distribution is $S + 5 + (\beta_2/2\beta_3)$.

Table 7-6. Earnings Functions for Urban Female Employees by Occupation and Race and for Total of Male and Female Employees in All Occupations by Race

Occupation 1: Professional and technical

$\log y_M = 6.79243 + 0.06841S + 0.04536T - 0.00103T^2$
$\quad(0.01428)\ (0.01867)\quad(0.00048)$
$R^2 = 0.237$; $SEE = 0.567$; $F = 9.73$; $DF = 94$; $\bar{S} = 12.245$; $\text{var}(S) = 24.553$; $\bar{T} = 13.051$; $\text{var}(T) = 99.724$; $\overline{\log y} = 7.946$; $\text{var}(\log y)) = 0.408$; $\bar{y} = 3,296$; $\text{var}(y) = 2.835\ 10^6$

$\log y_C = 6.52519 + 0.09312S + 0.04671T - 0.00067T^2$
$\quad(0.00895)\ (0.00827)\quad(0.00019)$
$R^2 = 0.341$; $SEE = 0.462$; $F = 39.10$; $DF = 227$; $\bar{S} = 14.143$; $\text{var}(S) = 16.136$; $\bar{T} = 11.316$; $\text{var}(T) = 89.717$; $\overline{\log y} = 8.225$; $\text{var}(\log y)) = 0.320$; $\bar{y} = 4,319$; $\text{var}(y) = 5.524\ 10^6$

$\log y_I = 5.86618 + 0.12938S + 0.06874T - 0.00120T^2$
$\quad(0.02286)\ (0.01819)\quad(0.00035)$
$R^2 = 0.527$; $SEE = 0.544$; $F = 20.79$; $DF = 56$; $\bar{S} = 14.025$; $\text{var}(S) = 13.478$; $\bar{T} = 11.925$; $\text{var}(T) = 99.914$; $\overline{\log y} = 8.211$; $\text{var}(\log y)) = 0.594$; $\bar{y} = 4,918$; $\text{var}(y) = 21.160\ 10^6$

$\log y_O = 6.99854 + 0.07143S + 0.02866T - 0.00218T^2$
$\quad(0.06546)\ (0.04181)\quad(0.00120)$
$R^2 = 0.705$; $SEE = 0.536$; $F = 5.57$; $DF = 7$; $\bar{S} = 16.091$; $\text{var}(S) = 7.291$; $\bar{T} = 10.727$; $\text{var}(T) = 151.018$; $\overline{\log y} = 8.390$; $\text{var}(\log y)) = 0.682$; $\bar{y} = 6,303$; $\text{var}(y) = 50.709\ 10^6$

$\log y_{TOT} = 6.43237 + 0.09597S + 0.05217T - 0.00088T^2$
$\quad(0.00706)\ (0.00680)\quad(0.00016)$
$R^2 = 0.351$; $SEE = 0.514$; $F = 71.51$; $DF = 396$; $\bar{S} = 13.714$; $\text{var}(S) = 18.253$; $\bar{\bar{T}} = 11.816$; $\text{var}(\bar{T}) = 95.073$; $\overline{\log y} = 8.159$; $\text{var}(\log y)) = 0.404$; $\bar{y} = 4,213$; $\text{var}(y) = 8.681\ 10^6$

Occupation 2: Administrative and managerial[a]

$\log y_{TOT} = 5.62930 + 0.18664S + 0.01965T + 0.00004T^2$
$\quad(0.03844)\ (0.06899)\quad(0.00162)$
$R^2 = 0.899$; $SEE = 0.478$; $F = 8.888$; $DF = 3$; $\bar{S} = 9.500$; $\text{var}(S) = 35.083$; $\bar{T} = 13.357$; $\text{var}(T) = 157.560$; $\overline{\log y} = 7.676$; $\text{var}(\log y)) = 1.130$; $\bar{y} = 3,706$; $\text{var}(y) = 18.919\ 10^6$

Occupation 3: Clerical and related

$\log y_M = 5.40377 + 0.11547S + 0.16802T - 0.00367T^2$
$\quad(0.03244)\ (0.03290)\quad(0.00110)$
$R^2 = 0.288$; $SEE = 0.689$; $F = 10.63$; $DF = 79$; $\bar{S} = 12.295$; $\text{var}(S) = 9.439$; $\bar{T} = 6.572$; $\text{var}(T) = 33.562$; $\overline{\log y} = 7.648$; $\text{var}(\log y)) = 0.641$; $\bar{y} = 2,661$; $\text{var}(y) = 2.666\ 10^6$

$\log y_C = 5.22096 + 0.13773S + 0.12617T - 0.00202T^2$
$\quad(0.01391)\ (0.01418)\quad(0.00042)$
$R^2 = 0.431$; $SEE = 0.561$; $F = 53.28$; $DF = 211$; $\bar{S} = 12.130$; $\text{var}(S) = 12.275$; $\bar{T} = 8.163$; $\text{var}(T) = 62.915$; $\overline{\log y} = 7.661$; $\text{var}(\log y)) = 0.546$; $\bar{y} = 2,701$; $\text{var}(y) = 3.979\ 10^6$

$\log y_I = 5.30169 + 0.12446S + 0.13428T - 0.00204T^2$
$\quad(0.03570)\ (0.03853)\quad(0.00119)$
$R^2 = 0.443$; $SEE = 0.645$; $F = 10.09$; $DF = 38$; $\bar{S} = 11.905$; $\text{var}(S) = 9.344$; $\bar{T} = 10.048$; $\text{var}(T) = 54.839$; $\overline{\log y} = 7.817$; $\text{var}(\log y)) = 0.693$; $\bar{y} = 3,185$; $\text{var}(y) = 4.116\ 10^6$

$\log y_O = 1.96313 + 0.38153S + 0.87138T - 0.02662T^2$
$\quad(0.24565)\ (0.49161)\quad(0.01556)$
$R^2 = 0.537$; $SEE = 1.147$; $F = 1.160$; $DF = 3$; $\bar{S} = 10.571$; $\text{var}(S) = 9.619$; $\bar{T} = 12.714$; $\text{var}(T) = 73.905$; $\overline{\log y} = 7.160$; $\text{var}(\log y)) = 1.421$; $\bar{y} = 1,978$; $\text{var}(y) = 2.067\ 10^6$

$\log y_{TOT} = 5.26085 + 0.13250S + 0.13360T - 0.00232T^2$
$\quad(0.01249)\ (0.01269)\quad(0.00038)$
$R^2 = 0.364$; $SEE = 0.623$; $F = 65.49$; $DF = 343$; $\bar{S} = 12.111$; $\text{var}(S) = 11.165$; $\bar{T} = 8.102$; $\text{var}(T) = 56.100$; $\overline{\log y} = 7.666$; $\text{var}(\log y)) = 0.605$; $\bar{y} = 2,735$; $\text{var}(y) = 3.655\ 10^6$

Occupation 4: Sales[a]

$\log y_M = 5.49770 + 0.14356S + 0.03071T - 0.00044T^2$
$\quad(0.03194)\ (0.02562)\quad(0.00048)$
$R^2 = 0.764$; $SEE = 0.273$; $F = 8.635$; $DF = 8$; $\bar{S} = 6.958$; $\text{var}(S)\ 13.021$; $\bar{T} = 17.625$; $\text{var}(T) = 417.142$; $\overline{\log y} = 6.734$; $\text{var}(\log y)) = 0.230$; $\bar{y} = 915$; $\text{var}(y) = 0.110\ 10^6$

$\log y_C = 5.75586 + 0.07619S + 0.06944T - 0.00121T^2$
$\quad(0.01950)\ (0.01748)\quad(0.00034)$
$R^2 = 0.160$; $SEE = 0.548$; $F = 6.79$; $DF = 107$; $\bar{S} = 7.450$; $\text{var}(S) = 14.454$; $\bar{T} = 11.748$; $\text{var}(T) = 111.431$; $\overline{\log y} = 6.840$; $\text{var}(\log y)) = 0.347$; $\bar{y} = 1,104$; $\text{var}(y) = 0.496\ 10^6$

$\log y_{TOT} = 5.79335 + 0.07767S + 0.06469T - 0.00114T^2$
$\quad(0.01742)\ (0.01535)\quad(0.00029)$
$R^2 = 0.177$; $SEE = 0.527$; $F = 8.75$; $DF = 122$; $\bar{S} = 7.313$; $\text{var}(S) = 14.475$; $\bar{T} = 12.313$; $\text{var}(T) = 138.931$; $\overline{\log y} = 6.827$; $\text{var}(\log y)) = 0.330$; $\bar{y} = 1,081$; $\text{var}(y) = 0.451\ 10^6$

Occupation 5: Service [a]

$\log y_{\mathrm{M}} = 5.31354 + 0.05898S + 0.08771T - 0.00147T^2$ $R^2 = 0.139$ $F = 9.07$ $\bar{S} = 3.956$ $\bar{T} = 20.392$ $\overline{\log y} = 6.502$ $\bar{y} = 908$
           (0.02084) (0.01873) (0.00038) $\mathrm{SEE} = 0.761$ $\mathrm{DF} = 168$ $\mathrm{var}(S) = 10.318$ $\mathrm{var}(T) = 152.978$ $\mathrm{var}(\log y) = 0.661$ $\mathrm{var}(y) = 0.517\ 10^6$

$\log y_{\mathrm{C}} = 6.41334 + 0.02881S + 0.02207T - 0.00021T^2$ $R^2 = 0.041$ $F = 7.49$ $\bar{S} = 2.744$ $\bar{T} = 25.656$ $\overline{\log y} = 6.853$ $\bar{y} = 1{,}150$
           (0.01326) (0.00690) (0.00010) $\mathrm{SEE} = 0.652$ $\mathrm{DF} = 520$ $\mathrm{var}(S) = 8.693$ $\mathrm{var}(T) = 324.460$ $\mathrm{var}(\log y) = 0.441$ $\mathrm{var}(y) = 0.530\ 10^6$

$\log y_{\mathrm{I}} = 5.41470 + 0.12619S + 0.05089T - 0.00063T^2$ $R^2 = 0.169$ $F = 6.09$ $\bar{S} = 2.920$ $\bar{T} = 21.771$ $\overline{\log y} = 6.465$ $\bar{y} = 863$
           (0.03623) (0.02022) (0.00038) $\mathrm{SEE} = 0.745$ $\mathrm{DF} = 90$ $\mathrm{var}(S) = 5.727$ $\mathrm{var}(T) = 198.907$ $\mathrm{var}(\log y) = 0.646$ $\mathrm{var}(y) = 0.398\ 10^6$

$\log y_{\mathrm{TOT}} = 6.14464 + 0.04448S + 0.02786T - 0.00025T^2$ $R^2 = 0.059$ $F = 16.61$ $\bar{S} = 3.059$ $\bar{T} = 24.023$ $\overline{\log y} = 6.734$ $\bar{y} = 1{,}069$
           (0.01069) (0.00601) (0.00009) $\mathrm{SEE} = 0.716$ $\mathrm{DF} = 790$ $\mathrm{var}(S) = 9.073$ $\mathrm{var}(T) = 276.397$ $\mathrm{var}(\log y) = 0.544$ $\mathrm{var}(y) = 0.536\ 10^6$

Occupation 7: Farm laborers [a]

$\log y_{\mathrm{M}} = 5.15026 + 0.00781S + 0.03564T - 0.00053T^2$ $R^2 = 0.074$ $F = 0.56$ $\bar{S} = 2.520$ $\bar{T} = 29.520$ $\overline{\log y} = 5.640$ $\bar{y} = 307$
           (0.02335) (0.02902) (0.00044) $\mathrm{SEE} = 0.391$ $\mathrm{DF} = 21$ $\mathrm{var}(S) = 13.260$ $\mathrm{var}(T) = 173.510$ $\mathrm{var}(\log y) = 0.144$ $\mathrm{var}(y) = 0.027\ 10^6$

$\log y_{\mathrm{C}} = 6.09509 + 0.04606S + 0.04083T - 0.00044T^2$ $R^2 = 0.147$ $F = 10.06$ $\bar{S} = 2.246$ $\bar{T} = 23.581$ $\overline{\log y} = 6.833$ $\bar{y} = 1{,}030$
           (0.01754) (0.00987) (0.00015) $\mathrm{SEE} = 0.464$ $\mathrm{DF} = 175$ $\mathrm{var}(S) = 8.015$ $\mathrm{var}(T) = 197.326$ $\mathrm{var}(\log y) = 0.248$ $\mathrm{var}(y) = 0.190\ 10^6$

$\log y_{\mathrm{I}} = 6.84629 + 0.09683S + 0.00018T - 0.00005T^2$ $R^2 = 0.246$ $F = 0.98$ $\bar{S} = 1.615$ $\bar{T} = 32.615$ $\overline{\log y} = 7.049$ $\bar{y} = 1{,}223$
           (0.06195) (0.14970) (0.00232) $\mathrm{SEE} = 0.372$ $\mathrm{DF} = 9$ $\mathrm{var}(S) = 3.923$ $\mathrm{var}(T) = 51.090$ $\mathrm{var}(\log y) = 0.138$ $\mathrm{var}(y) = 0.182\ 10^6$

$\log y_{\mathrm{TOT}} = 6.37131 + 0.00566S + 0.02121T - 0.00025T^2$ $R^2 = 0.031$ $F = 2.27$ $\bar{S} = 2.240$ $\bar{T} = 24.806$ $\overline{\log y} = 6.709$ $\bar{y} = 959$
           (0.01859) (0.01135) (0.00018) $\mathrm{SEE} = 0.611$ $\mathrm{DF} = 213$ $\mathrm{var}(S) = 8.329$ $\mathrm{var}(T) = 192.215$ $\mathrm{var}(\log y) = 0.380$ $\mathrm{var}(y) = 0.228\ 10^6$

Occupation 8: Production workers [a]

$\log y_{\mathrm{M}} = 5.44079 + 0.09078S + 0.04434T - 0.00073T^2$ $R^2 = 0.185$ $F = 5.23$ $\bar{S} = 4.740$ $\bar{T} = 19.192$ $\overline{\log y} = 6.269$ $\bar{y} = 700$
           (0.03518) (0.02168) (0.00031) $\mathrm{SEE} = 0.692$ $\mathrm{DF} = 69$ $\mathrm{var}(S) = 14.404$ $\mathrm{var}(T) = 252.310$ $\mathrm{var}(\log y) = 0.564$ $\mathrm{var}(y) = 0.327\ 10^6$

$\log y_{\mathrm{C}} = 5.68518 + 0.05878S + 0.06278T - 0.00077T^2$ $R^2 = 0.138$ $F = 23.62$ $\bar{S} = 4.412$ $\bar{T} = 15.063$ $\overline{\log y} = 6.602$ $\bar{y} = 902$
           (0.01206) (0.00831) (0.00013) $\mathrm{SEE} = 0.591$ $\mathrm{DF} = 443$ $\mathrm{var}(S) = 10.506$ $\mathrm{var}(T) = 144.804$ $\mathrm{var}(\log y) = 0.402$ $\mathrm{var}(y) = 0.553\ 10^6$

$\log y_{\mathrm{I}} = 4.73171 + 0.15598S + 0.08263T - 0.00065T^2$ $R^2 = 0.488$ $F = 1.59$ $\bar{S} = 3.944$ $\bar{T} = 23.278$ $\overline{\log y} = 6.774$ $\bar{y} = 1{,}020$
           (0.08311) (0.11877) (0.00221) $\mathrm{SEE} = 0.561$ $\mathrm{DF} = 5$ $\mathrm{var}(S) = 22.278$ $\mathrm{var}(T) = 255.694$ $\mathrm{var}(\log y) = 0.384$ $\mathrm{var}(y) = 0.343\ 10^6$

$\log y_{\mathrm{TOT}} = 5.69058 + 0.05973S + 0.05973T - 0.00082T^2$ $R^2 = 0.101$ $F = 19.55$ $\bar{S} = 4.449$ $\bar{T} = 15.772$ $\overline{\log y} = 6.559$ $\bar{y} = 876$
           (0.01163) (0.00794) (0.00013) $\mathrm{SEE} = 0.628$ $\mathrm{DF} = 525$ $\mathrm{var}(S) = 11.193$ $\mathrm{var}(T) = 163.592$ $\mathrm{var}(\log y) = 0.436$ $\mathrm{var}(y) = 0.522\ 10^6$

269

Table 7-6 (continued).

All occupations together

$$\log y_M = 5.20134 + 0.14738S + 0.07082T - 0.001157T^2$$
$$(0.00895)\quad(0.00962)\quad(0.00018)$$

$R^2 = 0.421$ $F = 111.46$ $\overline{\log y} = 6.935$ $\overline{S} = 7.329$ $\overline{T} = 16.593$ $\bar{y} = 1{,}663$
$\mathrm{SEE} = 0.795$ $\mathrm{DF} = 459$ $\mathrm{var}(\log y) = 1.085$ $\mathrm{var}(S) = 29.999$ $\mathrm{var}(T) = 177.996$ $\mathrm{var}(y) = 2.532\ 10^6$

$$\log y_C = 5.46229 + 0.13305S + 0.06785T - 0.00075T^2$$
$$(0.00366)\quad(0.00372)\quad(0.00006)$$

$R^2 = 0.437$ $F = 442.23$ $\overline{\log y} = 7.073$ $\overline{S} = 6.167$ $\overline{T} = 17.602$ $\bar{y} = 1{,}697$
$\mathrm{SEE} = 0.631$ $\mathrm{DF} = 1{,}709$ $\mathrm{var}(\log y) = 0.706$ $\mathrm{var}(S) = 30.110$ $\mathrm{var}(T) = 229.071$ $\mathrm{var}(y) = 3.007\ 10^6$

$$\log y_I = 5.12670 + 0.16787S + 0.07747T - 0.00106T^2$$
$$(0.00924)\quad(0.01212)\quad(0.00024)$$

$R^2 = 0.628$ $F = 122.17$ $\overline{\log y} = 7.261$ $\overline{S} = 7.695$ $\overline{T} = 17.400$ $\bar{y} = 2{,}482$
$\mathrm{SEE} = 0.670$ $\mathrm{DF} = 217$ $\mathrm{var}(\log y) = 1.191$ $\mathrm{var}(S) = 36.107$ $\mathrm{var}(T) = 176.026$ $\mathrm{var}(y) = 10.014\ 10^6$

$$\log y_O = 5.73004 + 0.14582S + 0.00674T - 0.00103T^2$$
$$(0.04283)\quad(0.05851)\quad(0.00159)$$

$R^2 = 0.476$ $F = 5.76$ $\overline{\log y} = 7.767$ $\overline{S} = 12.478$ $\overline{T} = 13.217$ $\bar{y} = 4{,}012$
$\mathrm{SEE} = 0.850$ $\mathrm{DF} = 19$ $\mathrm{var}(\log y) = 1.191$ $\mathrm{var}(S) = 23.715$ $\mathrm{var}(T) = 127.632$ $\mathrm{var}(y) = 29.029\ 10^6$

$$\log y_{TOT} = 5.43235 + 0.13772S + 0.06369T - 0.00073T^2$$
$$(0.00326)\quad(0.00341)\quad(0.00006)$$

$R^2 = 0.430$ $F = 608.28$ $\overline{\log y} = 7.070$ $\overline{S} = 6.589$ $\overline{T} = 17.349$ $\bar{y} = 1{,}784$
$\mathrm{SEE} = 0.691$ $\mathrm{DF} = 2{,}416$ $\mathrm{var}(\log y) = 0.837$ $\mathrm{var}(S) = 31.212$ $\mathrm{var}(T) = 213.603$ $\mathrm{var}(y) = 3.886\ 10^6$

All occupations together, male and female

$$\log y_M = 5.13026 + 0.15751S + 0.10063T - 0.00138T^2$$
$$(0.00426)\quad(0.00430)\quad(0.00008)$$

$R^2 = 0.442$ $F = 509.57$ $\overline{\log y} = 7.546$ $\overline{S} = 7.756$ $\overline{T} = 19.059$ $\bar{y} = 2{,}864$
$\mathrm{SEE} = 0.708$ $\mathrm{DF} = 1{,}932$ $\mathrm{var}(\log y) = 0.897$ $\mathrm{var}(S) = 20.186$ $\mathrm{var}(T) = 161.338$ $\mathrm{var}(y) = 15.591\ 10^6$

$$\log y_C = 5.25608 + 0.14504S + 0.10183T - 0.00126T^2$$
$$(0.00226)\quad(0.00208)\quad(0.00004)$$

$R^2 = 0.501$ $F = 1{,}679.81$ $\overline{\log y} = 7.425$ $\overline{S} = 6.619$ $\overline{T} = 19.030$ $\bar{y} = 2{,}542$
$\mathrm{SEE} = 0.639$ $\mathrm{DF} = 5{,}025$ $\mathrm{var}(\log y) = 0.818$ $\mathrm{var}(S) = 22.739$ $\mathrm{var}(T) = 214.539$ $\mathrm{var}(y) = 9.612\ 10^6$

$$\log y_I = 5.51637 + 0.14685S + 0.07240T - 0.00084T^2$$
$$(0.00436)\quad(0.00422)\quad(0.00007)$$

$R^2 = 0.510$ $F = 412.52$ $\overline{\log y} = 7.622$ $\overline{S} = 7.501$ $\overline{T} = 22.241$ $\bar{y} = 3{,}138$
$\mathrm{SEE} = 0.639$ $\mathrm{DF} = 1{,}191$ $\mathrm{var}(\log y) = 0.829$ $\mathrm{var}(S) = 24.926$ $\mathrm{var}(T) = 223.923$ $\mathrm{var}(y) = 16.173\ 10^6$

$$\log y_O = 4.82882 + 0.21605S + 0.91007T - 0.00113T^2$$
$$(0.02391)\quad(0.02913)\quad(0.00069)$$

$R^2 = 0.465$ $F = 28.70$ $\overline{\log y} = 8.406$ $\overline{S} = 11.908$ $\overline{T} = 16.015$ $\bar{y} = 10{,}064$
$\mathrm{SEE} = 1.022$ $\mathrm{DF} = 99$ $\mathrm{var}(\log y) = 1.894$ $\mathrm{var}(S) = 21.107$ $\mathrm{var}(T) = 146.076$ $\mathrm{var}(y) = 222.999\ 10^6$

$$\log y_{TOT} = 5.29352 + 0.14772S + 0.09437T - 0.00117T^2$$
$$(0.00181)\quad(0.00171)\quad(0.00003)$$

$R^2 = 0.485$ $F = 2{,}592.85$ $\overline{\log y} = 7.494$ $\overline{S} = 7.079$ $\overline{T} = 19.463$ $\bar{y} = 2{,}798$
$\mathrm{SEE} = 0.669$ $\mathrm{DF} = 8{,}259$ $\mathrm{var}(\log y) = 0.868$ $\mathrm{var}(S) = 22.981$ $\mathrm{var}(T) = 203.929$ $\mathrm{var}(y) = 15.307\ 10^6$

a. The lack of observations on particular racial groups in this occupation prevented the estimation of regression equations for them. See also the note to table 7-1.

8

Conclusions
and Some Notes on Policy

THIS STUDY HAS EXAMINED PATTERNS of income inequality in Malaysia from the data generated by the 1970 Post-Enumeration Survey. It has described a large number of results on income distribution and hinted at the broad policy implications that follow from such a diagnostic analysis. Income data from the Post-Enumeration Survey have not yet been analyzed or even tabulated, and a major purpose of this study has been to document the state of income inequality in the country. Naturally, I have attempted to go beyond this to suggest the sources of income inequality and of poverty. In fact, I have tried to build up an anatomy of income distribution for Malaysia. In an area where the quality of the data is notoriously poor, it is hoped that this study will contribute a benchmark for comparative studies elsewhere, as better income data begin to be collected and analyzed systematically.

The chapter begins with a brief reappraisal of PES data and a summary of the main findings on income distribution in the country. There is a review of the methodology, the major results on inequality decomposition, and the main findings on poverty. The rest of the chapter is concerned with a more general policy analysis of Prongs 1 and 2 of the NEP. Policies to reduce poverty in Malaysia are surveyed, and four broad types are identified that seem especially relevant: direct income transfers, fiscal policies, intervention in commodity markets, and rural development. These policies are discussed and evaluated in the light of knowledge about the poor derived from the detailed poverty maps in chapters 4 and 5. There is next a brief review of the employment restructuring targets to achieve racial economic balance, and some implications and costs of implementing them are noted. The chapter concludes with a cursory discussion of the underlying aims and mutual consistency of Prongs 1 and 2 of the NEP.

Summary and Conclusions

The most frequently used variable in this study has been race. Chapter 1, which contains a general introduction to and perspective on Malaysia, traces the development and importance of ethnic pluralism in the country. This pluralism has led the government to show special concern for racial income distribution and, more generally, for racial economic disparities. Thus the New Economic Policy of 1971 proclaimed the major objective of "restructuring Malaysian society to correct racial economic imbalances." It is in the context of this historical and economic situation that I have disaggregated by race in most of the analyses in this study.

The two prongs of the NEP have been examined in chapter 1 in relation to income distribution among individuals. The study of individual income distribution, which forms the central framework of this book, has permitted a detailed analysis of poverty and racial income distribution. The two prongs of the NEP have been characterized by their separate effects on the individual income distribution (figure 1-1). Prong 1 implies drawing a poverty line and moving all the poor above it, irrespective of race. Prong 2 corresponds to a proportionate rise in all Malay incomes which keeps within-race inequality constant but eliminates between-race inequality completely.

The income distribution data used in this study were collected through the Post-Enumeration Survey of 1970. Since no official report on the survey has been prepared, chapter 2 presents a detailed description and evaluation of the PES, including its survey design, sampling procedure, and income definition. A comparison with two previous surveys conducted in Malaysia shows that the PES, while by no means perfect, is the best source of income data to date on household and individual incomes in Malaysia. The principal sources of error are likely to have been the usual ones of response associated with the collection of income data, rather than sampling errors arising from survey design and sample size (which was approximately 135,000 individuals). Although it was not primarily an income survey, an elaborate system of probing, prompting, and other checks was followed to obtain satisfactory income data. The definition used for income also appears to have been fairly comprehensive, including income received in both cash and kind. A very rough guide to the quality of PES income data is suggested by a comparison with estimates of aggregate personal income based on the national accounts. Average household income shown in the PES was approximately 75 percent of that estimated via the 1970 national accounts data. This degree of understatement is not particularly large, even by the standards of household income surveys in developed countries (such as France, Germany, and the United Kingdom). At any rate, it cannot be taken as a reason for dismissing the PES data as unsuitable for analysis.

The broad features of the PES household income distribution show overall inequality in Malaysia to be fairly high (Gini coefficient of 0.5129), especially in comparison with other economies, such as Taiwan and the Republic of Korea, at similar stages of development. But the careful examination required of these different data sources to establish full comparability is outside the scope of this study, and reliable international comparisons of inequality must await detailed empirical research. More important, however, are intertemporal comparisons of inequality in Malaysia itself, since other researchers have concluded from a superficial examination of the earlier Household Budget Survey (HBS, 1957–58) that inequality in the country has sharply worsened. Because the published report on the HBS is deficient in information on income definition, sample coverage, and so on, I have attempted to reconstruct an account of this survey, along the lines of that given for PES, from unpublished records and files in the Malaysian Department of Statistics and conversations with persons responsible for conducting it. This account is documented in detail and used to demonstrate that the 1957 survey is simply not comparable with the 1970 survey, and that no conclusions can be reached from these surveys about intertemporal changes in inequality. The exercise is valuable both for researchers hoping to use the HBS, 1957–58, and as an illustration of the dangers in making inequality comparisons without first establishing comparability.

A detailed examination of PES income data that uses different population units and income concepts shows overall inequality in Malaysia to be high (tables 3-7 and 3-8). The distribution of individuals by per capita household income reveals that the poorest 40 percent of the people in Malaysia get only 12.3 percent of total income while the richest 5 percent get 28.5 percent, and the ratio of income shares between the highest quintile and lowest quintile is almost 13 to 1. The Gini coefficient and Theil T index for this distribution are 0.4980 and 0.5161, respectively. The distribution of income recipients by personal income (that is, the personal income distribution) shows that the poorest 40 percent of income recipients obtain 11.3 percent of total income while the richest 5 percent obtain 28.5 percent, and the ratio of income shares between the highest quintile and the lowest quintile is almost 16 to 1. The Gini coefficient, Theil T index, Theil L measure, and variance of log-income (varlog) for this distribution are 0.5063, 0.5360, 0.4763, and 0.8967, respectively (table 6-5).

Racial income disparities have traditionally been measured in terms of the ratios between the mean income of one racial group to that of another.

Again, these vary according to the distribution considered, that is, the population unit and income concept used. For the distribution of households by household income, the racial disparity ratios are 2.29 Chinese : Malay and 1.77 Indian : Malay. But for the distribution of individuals by per capita household income, the disparity ratios are 2.00 Chinese : Malay and 1.65 Indian : Malay. These ratios are lower than those often bandied in public, which neglect racial differences in average household size (Chinese, 5.839 members; Indians, 5.453 members; Malays, 5.084 members). For the distribution of income recipients by personal income, the disparity ratios are even smaller: 1.77 Chinese : Malay and 1.53 Indian : Malay. The reason is that the Chinese and Indians have higher average participation rates (strictly, average number of income recipients divided by average household size) than the Malays (table 6-1). Hence, in terms of incomes that can be directly influenced by economic policy, the racial disparity ratios are a good deal smaller than is popularly believed.

The individual income distributions show large inequalities within the racial groups. Ranked by per capita household income, Malay and Chinese individuals are distributed very similarly about their respective means (although it is sometimes suggested that Malay incomes are less dispersed). The corresponding fractile shares are close to one another, as corroborated by various relative inequality measures (including the Atkinson index when this is computable; see table 3-9). The Gini coefficient for the Malays and Chinese is 0.4553 and 0.4542, respectively, and the Theil T index is 0.4114 and 0.4228, respectively. Indian incomes are distributed somewhat more unequally, with a Gini coefficient of 0.5003 and a Theil T index of 0.5448. The incomes of "other" races are distributed extremely unequally (Gini coefficient of 0.7071 and Theil T index of 0.9371), which is not surprising given the heterogeneity of this group (rich Europeans and very poor Thais and other Asians). For the personal income distribution, the Gini coefficient, Theil T index, Theil L measure, and varlog, respectively, are: 0.4751, 0.4370, 0.4193, and 0.8293 for the Malays; 0.4908, 0.4958, 0.4430, and 0.8428 for the Chinese; 0.4693, 0.4998, 0.3925, and 0.6571 for the Indians; and 0.7048, 0.9442, 1.2016, and 2.5426 for the others.

These large income inequalities within racial groups suggest that racial income disparities may be only part of a much wider problem of income inequality in the country. It is thus interesting to ask how much of overall inequality is explained by such racial income disparities. To do this in an unambiguous manner involves using an index which is decomposable in the strict sense defined in chapter 3: an index is strictly decomposable if the amount by which inequality reduces when mean income differences between the groups are eliminated (keeping within-group inequality constant) is the same as the amount of inequality which arises when each member of a group gets the mean income of that group and within-group inequality is eliminated. Of the inequality indices used in this study, two are thus decomposable: the Theil *L* measure and varlog (the latter only around group geometric mean incomes).

These two measures are computable for the personal income distribution: the between-race contribution to inequality is 9.6 percent according to the Theil *L* measure and 7.9 percent according to varlog. In other words, the Prong 2 policies designed to achieve racial balance (keeping within-race inequality unchanged but eliminating between-race inequality altogether) will reduce overall income inequality by less than 10 percent. This result contradicts the claim that racial disparities explain much of the income inequality in Malaysia: more than 90 percent of it arises from the large income disparities *within* each racial group. Thus it is somewhat misleading to quote racial disparity ratios in the context of the redress of individual income inequality, although this is often done in public debate.

Taking the redress of individual income inequality as the objective of policy, I have derived the redress of poverty rule (filling in the poverty gap from the bottom up) as the most "efficient" rule for distributing incremental income (chapter 3 and appendix E). This rule yields a distribution which Lorenz-dominates the distribution of any other rule and hence shows less inequality for any index which is mean-independent, is population-size independent, and satisfies the principle of transfers. The best strategy to redress inequality turns out to be to redress poverty irrespective of race, which is in fact the aim of Prong 1 of the NEP. Chapters 4 and 5 explore the extent and nature of poverty in Malaysia, so that policy measures for its alleviation can be better informed.

After consideration of both the absolute and the relative approaches to the definition of a poverty line, a poverty line for Malaysia is set at a per capita household income level of M$25 per month. Some 36.5 percent of households and 40.2 percent of individuals fall below this level of per capita household income (as the poor have larger than average size households). Other indices of poverty are also examined, which incorporate the income gap of the poor, normalized by some measure of aggregate income available for redistribution. A recent index proposed by Sen uses rank-order weights on the income gaps of the poor. This index turns out to be the same as computing the difference between the poverty line and the equally distributed equivalent income of the poor with the use of a rank-order welfare function. The aggregate poverty gap in Malaysia stands at 7.3 percent of total personal income, and a transfer to the poor of 8.3 percent of the income of the nonpoor (or 12.7 percent of their income in excess of the poverty line) is required to close the gap. Estimates of other measures are also presented (table 4-2), but the simple incidence-of-poverty measure is adopted for the decomposition of poverty.

A profile of poverty in Malaysia is constructed, which identifies the poor in terms of socioeconomic variables such as race, location, employment status, occupation, and education (table 4-3). Such information is useful not only in understanding better the correlates and circumstances of poverty, but also in identifying areas of government intervention for the redress of poverty. One-way classifications reveal that 87.7 percent of poor households are in rural areas; 78.1 percent are Malay; 41.5 percent are concentrated in the four northern states of Kedah, Kelantan, Perlis, and Trengganu; 93.5 percent are headed by employees or own-account workers; 77.4 percent are headed by farmers or farm laborers; 75.1 percent are headed by workers in agriculture or the agricultural products sector; and 97.2 percent of poor household heads have not gone beyond primary school. Groups which suffer particularly high rates of poverty (above the average of 36.5 percent) are households in rural areas (44.6 percent); Malays (51.4 percent) and "other" races (40.3 percent); households in Kedah (48.6 percent), Kelantan (65.2 percent), Perlis (58.9 percent), and Trengganu (54.6 percent); households whose heads are own-account workers (50.1 percent) and unemployed (38.0 percent); households whose heads are farmers (61.9 percent) and farm laborers (48.6 percent); households whose heads are in agriculture (61.5 percent) and agricultural products (46.2 percent); households whose heads have no education (49.0 percent) or only some primary education (39.1 percent); and households headed by females (44.9 percent), households with more than five members (40.0 percent or more), households with three or more children under the age of 15 (41.5 percent or more), and households with fewer than two income recipients (41.9 percent or more); see table 4-3.

When several of the characteristics associated with high rates of poverty are taken together, the chances of being poor can become extremely high. To design minimum leakage policies and projects to redress poverty, it is necessary to zero in on high-risk subgroups which are homogeneous but nevertheless account for a significant fraction of overall poverty. This has been done in chapter 5 by increasing the selected level of detail of relevant variables and cross-classifying them to obtain a multidimensional profile. From the two-digit matrix thus generated, five subgroups of rural poor are isolated, which account for 79 percent of total rural poverty (table 5-1). These subgroups are then further disaggregated regionally to identify special pockets of poverty (table 5-2). The five subgroups (with their poverty incidences in parentheses) are households headed by: paddy farmers (65.8 percent); rubber smallholders (55.6 percent); laborers on paddy and mixed-agriculture farms (63.9 percent); workers on rubber estates and smallholdings (47.5 percent); and fishermen (50.9 percent). The economic problems of these homogeneous subgroups, and measures to raise their productivity and incomes, are examined individually (double-cropping of paddy, land settlement and consolidation, revision of the export duty on rubber, rubber replanting with high-yielding stock, and other programs to assist traditional smallholders). The regional disaggregation also allows identification of special (regional) components of rural development policies which, as argued later in this chapter, are a major means for raising the income levels of the rural poor in Malaysia.

Whereas such variables as race, region, location, employment status, and industrial sector are fairly good guides for identifying poverty in Malaysia, they turn out to be relatively poor at explaining overall income inequality. Chapter 6 decomposes personal income inequality in terms of these variables, in an attempt to explore the sources of inequality. The purpose here is to describe the contribution of particular variables to inequality, but there is no attempt at an explicit model or theory of income determination. For example, there is no explanation of *why* the Chinese mean income is 1.77 times the Malay mean income, but merely a description of the effect of this on overall inequality. When it is found that the between-race contribution to personal income inequality is less than 10 percent, variables such as assets, educational level, and occupation are not being held constant in the decomposition.[1] The decomposition analysis simply amounts to an ex post accounting of the sources of inequality which does, however, yield some important insights; it also throws light on hypotheses and perceptions of inequality which have a bearing on policymaking.

One of the significant sources of inequality in developing countries generally is alleged to be the large rural-urban differences in mean income (Lipton, 1968 or 1977). But in Malaysia rural-urban differences explain only 10.0 percent of personal income inequality by the Theil L measure and 7.3 percent by varlog; most of the inequality arises *within* rural and *within* urban areas.

Higher stages of urbanization appear to be associated with higher levels of inequality (table 6-5). And a regional decomposition shows that between-state differences in income (which are quite large) account for only 8 percent of inequality in the country. Racial disparity ratios in the country as a whole are higher than those in any of the three locations (metropolitan towns, towns, and rural areas) because of the disproportionate presence of Chinese and Indians in urban areas and of Malays in rural areas. Thus the NEP perception of racial economic imbalances owing to the "identification

---

1. We cannot, therefore, infer that this gives some idea of the inequality attributable to racial discrimination, which, if anything, is likely to be overestimated because other variables are not held constant.

of race with geographical location" seems largely valid; however, its removal is unlikely to reduce personal income inequality very much.

An obvious determinant of personal income inequality is inequality in the distribution of assets, both physical and human. Although there are no data on the distribution of physical wealth among individuals in Malaysia, the breakdown of the personal income distribution by employment status does shed some light on the distribution of capital assets. Employers' incomes are distributed more unequally than own-account workers' incomes, which are in turn distributed more unequally than employees' incomes. There are also very large disparities between the mean income of employers and that of other groups (which are fairly close to the overall mean), but the contribution of employment status to income inequality is relatively small (9.0 percent by the Theil L measure and 6.5 percent by varlog) because, in fact, there are few employers with high incomes.[2] The racial disaggregation for employers and own-account workers, employment categories in which capital or property income is likely to be significant, reveals large disparities between the races (especially among own-account workers, for whom the between-race contribution to inequality is more than 20 percent by both measures). This undoubtedly reflects wide disparities between the racial groups in asset ownership. Employees form the most homogeneous category, with racial income disparity ratios of only 1.25 Chinese:Malay and 1.17 Indian:Malay. (These differentials could arise from between-group differences in skill level and, possibly, leisure preference.)

The decomposition by occupational category also suggests that average wealth among the Chinese is greater than that among the Malays. For

---

2. By the way it is defined, the between-group component of inequality depends only on the population share and mean income of each group (see also the formulas in chapter 3 or appendix C). Other things being equal, the higher the mean income of the richest group, the greater the between-group component (this follows by direct manipulation of the formula or by applying corollary 1 in appendix E); further, the lower the population share of the richest group, the smaller the between-group component provided its population share is not "too large" initially. For the Theil L measure, for example, if there are only two groups, with $\mu_1 > \mu_2$, we have

$$\frac{\partial L_B}{\partial(n_1/n)} = \frac{1}{(n_1/n_2) + \dfrac{1}{(\mu_1/\mu_2) - 1}} - \log(\mu_1/\mu_2).$$

Hence $\dfrac{\partial L_B}{\partial(n_1/n)} > 0$ provided the initial population share (n_1/n) is less than

$$\left[\frac{1}{\log(\mu_1/\mu_2)} - \frac{1}{(\mu_1/\mu_2) - 1}\right].$$

instance, the racial disparity ratios and between-race contribution to income inequality among farmers is largest of the eight one-digit occupational categories (19.2 percent by Theil L and 12.4 percent by varlog). Table 6-8 also shows that the major racial groups are not proportionately distributed across the occupations, with the Chinese usually overrepresented in the better-paid occupations and the Malays overrepresented in the less well-paid ones. Mean incomes within occupations are generally highest for Chinese and lowest for Malays, with the Indians occupying a middle position. There are some significant exceptions to this ranking at the two-digit level of disaggregation (table 6-11) where, for example, Malay government administrators and legislative officials receive more than Chinese, possibly reflecting the preferential treatment in hiring and promotion given to Malays in the public sector.

The between-occupation contribution to overall income inequality in Malaysia is greater than that of any other single variable examined: 31.7 percent by the Theil L measure and 23.8 percent by varlog. Thus the personal income distribution is more closely related to major categories of occupation than to any other variable including industrial sector, whose contribution is 19.0 percent and 15.6 percent, respectively (by the two measures).[3] Furthermore, multivariate decompositions by the variables so far considered do not add very much to the single-variable decomposition by occupation. For instance, the two-way decomposition by eight occupational categories and nine industrial sectors yields a between-group contribution of 33.5 percent by the Theil L measure and 26.9 percent by varlog. These results suggest that the standard categories of sector, occupation, and employment status may be too broad for the purposes of simulating personal income distribution. Other combinations of variables which include personal characteristics such as age and education perform significantly better (see table 6-10), and if personal wealth data were available the performance would improve even more.

Given these decomposition results, I have attempted to explain income inequality in terms of age and education in chapter 7. This has been done by means of earnings function regressions for urban employees, whose income

---

3. Given the large intrasectoral variation in incomes (80 to 85 percent of overall inequality), the government's policy of specifying Malay employment quotas within broadly defined industrial sectors may not be very effective in rectifying even the racial disparity ratios. The large intrasectoral income differences arise from the dualism which prevails *within* sectors (such as formal-informal subsector variations in productivity and other forms of regional-occupational dualism). However, if employment quotas were imposed within subsectors such as modern manufacturing, they would probably be even more disruptive than sectoral quotas because the Malay base is likely to be smaller there.

may be assumed to accrue mostly as wages or labor earnings. Although the particular estimating form used for the earnings function has some basis in the so-called human capital model, the purpose is not to test this model but to use it to describe age-income profiles at different levels of education. The estimated equations are a convenient way of summarizing labor market information in terms of earnings differentials for individuals at different age-education levels, and the regressions automatically generate a measure of income inequality used in this study, the variance of log-income, or varlog. The life-cycle factors of experience and education explain (in the R^2 sense) almost 50 percent of the income inequality among urban employees as measured by varlog. This level of explanation is quite impressive in light of the omission of many important variables for individuals (such as ability, time worked, and proportion of unearned income in total income) on which there are no data. The private rate of return to education (coefficient on the schooling term in the log-income regression) is 14.01 percent for all urban male employees, and there are no significant differences in this between the races. Differences in urban male employee incomes between the races stand at 1.10:1.09:1.00 for Indian:Malay:Chinese, and these are matched by differences in their average levels of education and experience. Interpersonal inequality in urban male employee incomes is also highly correlated with inequality in education and experience, but policy implications about the role of education in reducing income inequality cannot be deduced without further stringent assumptions, for example, about the demand side of the labor market and the validity of the cross-sectional estimates for time series inferences. Returns to education are higher in modern sector (tertiary) occupations and for those educated in English, possibly because of screening. The return to schooling for all urban female employees is 13.77 percent, and females generally obtain a lower return to education within each occupation than males, and their age–log income profiles are flatter. A disaggregation by age cohort shows significantly higher returns for the younger age groups, which perhaps reflects an obsolescence effect in education.

Policies to Reduce Poverty in Malaysia

The first prong of the New Economic Policy seeks to eradicate poverty in Malaysia. In the light of the detailed information about poverty generated from the PES (see chapters 4 and 5), it is possible to speculate on policies that could be used to influence the welfare levels of the poor. These vary from direct income maintenance to indirect taxation and fiscal policies, including state provision of public goods and services. A survey of the typical areas of intervention and instruments of policy may be found in Ahluwalia (1974*b*). In this section four broad types of policy are briefly reviewed which seem particularly relevant in the Malaysian context: direct income transfers, fiscal policies, intervention in commodity markets, and rural development policies.

Direct Income Transfers

Implicit in the poverty indices estimated in chapter 4 is the idea of closing the poverty gap by means of direct transfers from the nonpoor to the poor. The poverty gap of 7.3 percent of total personal income in Malaysia could be eliminated by a transfer of 8.3 percent of the income of the nonpoor.[4] Such a proportional income transfer from all the nonpoor would place a heavy burden on those just above the poverty line (and those not very much above it). It is perhaps more meaningful to consider transfer schemes whereby the entire burden is borne by the rich (top 5 percent or some other appropriately chosen upper-income class). As a fraction of the income of the top 5 percent, the poverty gap is 25.6 percent; of the top 10 percent, it is 18.7 percent; of the top 20 percent, it is 13.3 percent; and of the top 40 percent, it is 9.8 percent. These figures give some idea of the scale of the problem if direct income transfers were used to eliminate poverty.[5]

The Ministry of Welfare Services in Malaysia is currently considering a public assistance program "to provide financial assistance to those with little or no income so that they can enjoy a minimum level of living" (Department of Social Welfare, 1976, p. 1). The idea of social security is not new in Malaysia, and in the past the social welfare departments of states have allocated small amounts for general welfare (including natural disaster relief, school aid, and relief for the needy, the destitute, and the elderly).[6] The government also seems to recognize the responsibility of the state to assure a minimum income level for all its citizens: "The national interest requires that all people have sufficient income to maintain a living conducive to health and well-being. Today this philosophy has added significance when it is borne in mind that the twin objectives of the S.M.P. are the eradication of poverty and the restructuring of society" (Department of Social Welfare, 1976, p. 1).

4. If the extreme poverty line of M$15 per month were adopted, it would require a transfer of only 1.8 percent of the income of the nonpoor to eradicate poverty.

5. These figures do not indicate the total cost of implementing such transfers.

6. The allocation for welfare services in the Second Malaysia Plan (SMP), 1971–75, was M$13.47 million, or 0.2 percent of the total plan allocation. Of this, M$4.36 million was actually spent between 1971 and 1973 (MTR, p. 101).

Table 8-1. Taxes Paid by Households below the Poverty Line.

Tax	Taxes paid by all households (M$ thousand)	Percentage of total federal taxes	Taxes (M$ thousand) paid by			Percentage of tax borne by poor households
			All poor households	Rural poor households	Urban poor households	
Export taxes	250,320	13.9	4,876	4,876	...	1.9
Rubber	76,190	4.2	4,876	4,876	...	6.4
Tin	129,712	7.2	...	...	...	...
Other	44,418	2.5	...	...	...	...
Import duties, excises, licenses[a]	884,662	49.3	75,463	66,310	9,153	8.5
Food[b]	51,316	2.9	7,605	6,870	735	14.8
Beverages and tobacco	213,626	11.9	27,985	25,360	2,625	13.1
Textiles	33,139	1.8	2,293	2,091	202	6.9
Rent, fuel, and power	74,209	4.1	8,334	7,217	1,117	11.2
Transport	310,658	17.4	14,072	12,382	1,690	4.5
Other	201,714	11.2	15,174	12,390	2,784	7.5
Inland Revenue	661,889	36.8	...	...	...	...
Income tax[c]	560,997	31.2	...	...	...	...
Other	100,892	5.6	...	...	...	...
Total federal taxes	1,796,871	100.0	80,339	71,186	9,153	4.5
Land taxes[d]	n.a.	—	n.a.	3,247	n.a.	n.a.
Zakat	n.a.	—	556	556	...	n.a.
Total plus land taxes and zakat			84,142	74,989		

— Not applicable.   . . . Zero or negligible.   n.a. Not available.

a. Based on Alternative 1 in Andic (1975), which allocated import duties, excise taxes, and licenses according to the expenditure pattern of poor households in relation to that of all households in each one-digit category of goods and services of the HES sample.

b. Sugar represents 94 percent (import duty M$29,803 thousand, excise tax M$18,372 thousand of the total tax of M$51,316 thousand collected on food (Andic, 1975, table 12).

c. Corporate taxes represent nearly 75 percent of income tax collections.

d. Does not include land taxes paid by coconut smallholders. There is also insufficient information to estimate any land taxes paid by or shifted to urban poor households.

Sources: Andic (1975), tables 12, 14, 16; EPU (1975), table 9; and Government of Malaysia (1974).

The question therefore arises whether full income maintenance is a feasible policy in Malaysia. There are two obvious constraints to consider. First, does the administrative machinery exist to implement a very large cash transfer scheme (even if the government could afford it)? Second, can the public exchequer raise the resources to finance this scheme? It is also necessary to ask whether income maintenance, even if feasible, would necessarily be optimal as a long-run policy.

Given the size of the state government machinery which runs the current (inadequate) public assistance program, it is doubtful if it could handle anything approaching a full income maintenance program.[7] A register does not exist of the economically active, nor is it easy to devise one with the present extremely limited coverage of the income tax net (a complete register does not exist even for the unemployed). Further, since such a large proportion of heads of households (39.3 percent), and an even larger proportion of heads of poor households (55.3 percent), are self-employed (see table 4-3), verification of income to determine the magnitude of assistance to be given becomes an extremely difficult task. In addition, vested interests and power realities at the local level could prevent the funds from reaching the intended beneficiaries.[8] These problems are not insurmountable, but they do imply heavy additional expenditures for training and administration if an effective social assistance program is to be mounted.

The financial commitment by the government, solely for transfers to fill the income gap of the poor, works out to approximately M$401 million in 1970.[9] This takes no account of the sums required to administer the program, nor of the additional commitment resulting from the reduction in work effort and earnings by those faced with such a negative income-tax schedule. (For instance, if all the poor were to earn zero incomes, the poverty gap would rise from M$401 million to M$1,107 million!)

The federal tax revenue in 1970 has been estimated at M$1,797 million from all sources (table 8-1). The income gap of the poor therefore amounts to some 22.3 percent of total tax revenue. This figure seems very high inasmuch as it excludes administrative costs, disincentive effects on labor

---

7. The size of the government machinery may also be a constraint for other types of policies, such as rural development (see the later subsection "Rural Development Policies").

8. The transfer process could be largely thwarted by those who wield power or who can exert influence on those who wield power. The poor, as is well known, exert a political influence that is woefully incommensurate with their number.

9. From table 4-2, the average poverty gap is M$9.05 per month or M$108.6 per year, and approximately 3.69 million people $(0.402 \times 9.182$ million) are in poverty in Peninsular Malaysia.

supply, and leakages to the nonpoor.[10] The burden on the public exchequer of a full income support program would appear prohibitive if these costs were to be included.

On the other side of the public ledger, could tax revenue be increased substantially to finance even a watered-down income maintenance scheme? Such a scheme might involve negative income taxation with marginal tax rates somewhat less than 100 percent at the poverty line. In the next subsection there is discussion of the limited ability to redistribute via the fiscal system in Malaysia; here it is merely noted that the direct tax base in the country appears to be fairly small, as is the case in most developing countries. Out of a labor force in 1970 of 3.768 million, for instance, there were only 0.201 million income tax payers.[11] The revenue from personal income taxes cannot be increased substantially simply by making the structure more progressive.[12] The base itself has to broaden, but this is difficult to achieve in a country where income levels are low and implementation is difficult owing to the own-account nature of employment.

Indirect taxes, which represent 63 percent of total revenue, could probably be raised somewhat, but the poor are likely to end up bearing much of the burden. A careful study of the structure of optimal commodity taxes in Malaysia is needed, which takes account of distributional

10. Leakages to the nonpoor in the income maintenance programs of advanced industrial countries have been documented in OECD (1976). This study suggests that perhaps only a third of income maintenance expenditure actually reaches the poor in the average OECD country.

11. In 1970 there were 200,983 resident individuals in Malaysia who paid total taxes worth M$123 million. According to Department of Inland Revenue (1974, p. 30), the racial breakdown was:

	Number of persons assessed	Income assessed (M$ million)	Income tax charged (M$ million)
Malay	40,628	283.8	12.2
Chinese	130,997	945.7	77.8
Indian	24,430	201.7	12.6
Other	4,928	116.3	20.6
Total	200,983	1,547.5	123.2

The personal income tax base was thus rather small, with less than 30 percent of total personal income (PES estimate, M$5,400 million) actually assessed. This corresponds to the top 5 percent of personal income recipients being assessed (see table 6-2). "Other" races pay the highest proportion of their income in tax (17.7 percent), the Chinese are next (8.2 percent), and the Indians, who have a smaller assessed income than the Malays, pay a larger proportion of it in tax (6.2 percent compared with 4.3 percent).

12. Increased progressivity might lead to greater evasion while impinging even more heavily on the small base where implementation is easy, namely, the modern corporate and government sectors.

concerns. On the basis of a tax incidence study (reviewed in the next subsection), it appears that greater progressivity in the tax system is possible, but is likely to conflict with revenue collection after a point. There might be some scope for heavier taxation of foreign enterprises and for taxation of new sources, such as oil production and urban property.[13] By the standards of developing countries, however, Malaysia already collects a relatively high proportion of its GDP (23 percent in 1970) in government revenue.

A full income support program can probably be ruled out in the present institutional setting. For the government to operate such a program, a substantial mobilization of resources would be required, as well as a reallocation of current public expenditure. While both may be possible to some extent (and should be pursued), it is reasonable to ask whether full income maintenance is the best way of eradicating poverty in Malaysia. The important distinction here is between the static and the dynamic effects of alternative policies, which must be compared over a longer period than a single year. On this basis, a policy that might easily dominate the static income maintenance program is a transfer of the same capitalized value of resources to the poor for investment rather than consumption.[14] An investment redistribution policy (in such forms as land improvement, drainage, and the provision of fertilizers and complementary inputs) would increase the productivity of the poor and thus be capable of generating higher income streams in the future.[15] Dynamically, therefore, it would appear to be preferable to a consumption transfer or income maintenance policy.[16] Such productivity-augmenting policies will have to be identified case by case and tailored to the needs of particular poverty subgroups; they are discussed in the later subsection on rural development.

13. The possibly adverse effects of increased taxation on private foreign investment need not be important, since Malaysia is already committed to reducing the share of foreign interests in the ownership of corporate assets (see chapter 1, the section "The New Economic Policy").

14. It is assumed that the income transferred under an income maintenance program would be mostly consumed.

15. To the extent that there is a connection between consumption and productivity (see Bliss and Stern, 1976), even direct income transfers may help improve individual productivity.

16. Obviously it is necessary to take account of time preference (via a discount rate) if one policy does not dominate the other period by period. Although the benefits of investment redistribution policies might accrue slightly later, with "reasonable" discount rates they would still seem preferable since they make possible larger income gains in the future. People in extreme poverty might then be dealt with through direct income transfers, for not only is their discount rate likely to be very high but their capacity to generate increased income streams from investment transfers is probably quite low.

Fiscal Policies

A second way to improve the welfare of the poor is through fiscal policies that alter the distribution of the tax burden or the benefits of public spending. Ideally, tax policy recommendations should be based on a full-fledged study of optimal taxation and public expenditure. In the absence of such a study for Malaysia, I consider taxation separately from expenditure and review in particular the estimates of taxes paid by the poor. Tax policies to benefit the poor can be better established if it is known which taxes are borne by them and to what extent. A special study was commissioned by the Economic Planning Unit (EPU) on tax incidence (Andic, 1975), the results of which are briefly described here. Little work, however, has so far been done on the incidence of public spending.[17]

The methodology of the EPU tax incidence study is fairly standard and consists of allocating the total revenue from each tax between poor and nonpoor households. It assumes that personal income taxes and land taxes are borne entirely by the payer, export taxes are shifted fully backward (to labor and owners of capital),[18] and import duties and excise taxes are shifted fully forward (to consumers). Import duties, excise taxes, and licenses have been allocated on the basis of preliminary information from the 1973 Household Expenditure Survey (HES).[19] Export taxes are assumed either not to fall on the poor (as in the case of tin, timber, or palm oil) or, as in the case of rubber, to fall on smallholders in proportion to their production.[20] The incidence of state land taxes and zakat (a religious tax levied on Muslim paddy growers)[21] has been calculated in a rough-and-ready manner by applying the average of state rates to an estimate of the

---

17. The Distributive Effects of Public Spending (DEPS) survey was, however, conducted by Jacob Meerman during 1974–75. But its results became available only after this study had been completed.

18. The assumption here is that of perfectly elastic world demand for Malaysian exports.

19. See Andic (1975), tables 7, 8, and 9. The preliminary HES data indicate the rough pattern of expenditure by household expenditure class according to eight broad categories of goods and services. A poverty line of M$150 household expenditure per month was adopted to define the poor in Andic (1975).

20. Production has been assumed proportional to acreage. All figures on acreage and production are taken from Department of Statistics (1972).

21. The rates of zakat vary from state to state: a certain minimum production is exempted from the tax and the remainder is taxed ad valorem. In the case of another religious tax, fitrah, levied on Muslims, insufficient information prevented its allocation between the poor and the nonpoor.

land cultivated by poor farmers.[22] Taxes within the purview of the Inland Revenue, namely, personal and corporate income taxes,[23] are reckoned not to affect poor households because of the high exemption limit for personal income tax (M$2,000 a year for residents) and the judgment that corporate taxes are not shifted to an extent which affects the poor. The results of the tax incidence calculations are summarized in table 8-1.[24]

Of total federal taxes, export taxes represent 13.9 percent, import duties 26.4 percent, excises 13.8 percent, licenses 9.1 percent, and Inland Revenue 36.8 percent (table 8-1 and Andic, 1975, table 11). Accordingly, indirect taxes (foreign trade and excise) account for almost two-thirds of tax revenue whereas income tax accounts for about one-third. And of the income tax collected, nearly 75 percent is corporate and only 25 percent personal.

Table 8-1 shows that the poor bear a disproportionate burden of the import duties and excise taxes on food (94 percent of food revenue derives from sugar), beverages, and tobacco—items that make up a relatively large proportion of their budget. While their share of income is 10.2 percent (Andic, 1975, table 3A), they pay 14.8 percent of the total taxes on food, 13.1 percent of the taxes on beverages and tobacco, and 11.2 percent of the taxes on rent, fuel, and power. Import duties and excises as a whole, however, are moderately progressive: the poor pay 8.5 percent of the revenues collected from such taxes.[25] Categories which account for large tax collections from the poor are beverages and tobacco; transport (bus and taxi services); rent, fuel, and power; and the miscellaneous category "other."

Export taxes are borne only to a small extent by the poor (1.9 percent), owing to the negligible impact of tin, timber, and palm oil duties on them. But the rubber export tax does fall significantly on rubber smallholders in

---

22. The average annual tax rate on rubber land was estimated at M$6 per acre, on paddy land M$2 per acre, and on coconut land M$5 per acre (Andic, 1975, table 13). A paddy farmer was assumed to be in poverty if he held less than five acres, and a rubber smallholder if he held less than eight acres. On this basis, 78 percent of paddy farmers (holding an average of 3.1 acres) and 13 percent of rubber smallholders were estimated as poor in 1970. No information was available on landholding and poverty among coconut smallholders.

23. The Inland Revenue also collects the tax on tin and timber profits and development taxes (Department of Inland Revenue, 1974).

24. These results are subject to the usual caveats, such as the partial equilibrium nature of the analysis; see de Wulf (1975) for a detailed critique of incidence studies.

25. To determine the progressivity of the tax system, one should also estimate how prices of nontaxed items are affected; for example, protective tariffs might raise the price of other, domestically produced goods which are substitutes. Such general equilibrium effects should be included in comparing the burden with and without the tax system.

poverty, who end up paying 6.4 percent of the tax revenue collected from this duty and surcharge (Government of Malaysia, 1974). As long as world demand for Malaysian rubber remains elastic, the tax will be shifted backward and act as a direct levy on producers. The estates may be able partly to shift it further backward to their employees, but smallholders cannot escape the brunt because they supply land and labor inelastically.

The only other taxes borne by the poor are state land taxes and zakat, which is paid by Muslim paddy farmers. Together, these account for about 5 percent of the total taxes paid by poor households. Direct taxes in Malaysia are judged not to fall on households below the poverty line.

The results of this fiscal incidence study suggest that the federal tax system is reasonably progressive: poor households pay 4.5 percent of all federal taxes, but they receive 10.2 percent of total household income. The scope for redistribution via the tax system is therefore limited, even though particular taxes might be reduced to improve the relative position of the poor (with offsetting increases elsewhere to restore revenue). By far the greatest burden of taxation on the poor stems from import duties, excises, and licenses. Two-thirds of the taxes paid by the poor under this heading are accounted for by beverages and tobacco, petroleum products, and vehicles. These items, however, also account for three-quarters of the total revenue from this source, and for as much as a third of total federal tax revenue. A reduction in tax rate for these items thus seems unlikely since the revenue loss would be substantial: its social cost would probably be judged to exceed the welfare gain to the poor (and nonpoor).

Items for which a tax reduction is likely to be socially beneficial are goods that are consumed wholly or largely by the poor. A price reduction on such goods is an effective means of improving their welfare levels.[26] For example, an exemption of duties on coarse cotton fabrics might be of considerable benefit, since the taxes on this commodity are likely to be regressive and to fall particularly heavily on the poor. But before specific changes in the tax system can be recommended, it is necessary to identify with greater precision the demand patterns of poor households.[27]

An obvious candidate for tax revision is the rubber export duty.[28] Smallholders bear their share of the burden of this tax, and its alleviation

---

26. The instrument is somewhat blunted if demand from the nonpoor increases more than proportionately as a result of the price reduction.

27. This should be possible through a detailed analysis of the HES 1973 data.

28. The standard rationale for an export tax is the "optimal-tariff" argument in international trade theory: if a country can exercise monopoly power in world trade, it can improve social welfare over the free-trade situation by levying an export tax (which improves its terms of trade) and redistributing the tax revenue to citizens in a nondistortionary way.

should significantly (and quickly) improve the welfare of a sizable subgroup among the rural poor. Since it is a product tax, however, it will not be easy to discriminate in favor of the poorer producers. The size of holding seems the natural distinguishing variable, and one approach would be to adopt a rough rebate system for smallholders with less than some given acreage, say, ten acres.[29] Another approach would be to revise the basis for the rubber tax and shift it from the export to the production stage. A progressive special revenue or production tax on rubber land would enable the entire tax burden to be shifted to nonpoor smallholders and to estates.[30]

The state land taxes also ought to be reconsidered. At present the states levy the land tax at a flat rate, although they differentiate according to land use in agriculture. They should be persuaded to introduce progressivity into the system and to exempt owner-cultivated holdings below a certain acreage. The land tax offers substantial scope for increasing government revenues and is an efficient instrument that can be levied in a progressive manner. Since people cannot easily pass it on or avoid it by a change in behavior, the tax creates minimal distortions (deadweight loss). It should be exploited much more as a revenue source than it has been in the past. Although a restructured land tax would have only a small effect in relieving the present burden on the rural poor (since the present tax base and rates are small), it would boost the tax yield significantly owing to much higher average rates through progressivity.

The general conclusion emerging from this investigation of the distribution of the tax burden is that since the poor pay a relatively small fraction of total taxes, the benefits to them from tax relief are likely to be limited.[31] This does not, however, detract from the need for revision of the tax system to reduce the incidence on the poor still further and to introduce greater progressivity to maintain or increase tax revenues. Raising the posttax incomes of the poor by even a few percentage points generates a large increase in social welfare. The other aspect of fiscal policy, the distribution

---

Malaysia cannot exert monopoly power in the world rubber market, however, because it faces a highly elastic demand curve for the product (since other countries supply large quantities of synthetic rubber, which is a near-perfect substitute for natural rubber). The argument for the rubber export duty in Malaysia, therefore, is not an optimal-tariff argument, and its revision will not affect the country's terms of trade.

29. The rebate might be given, for example, in the form of subsidized inputs or higher replanting grants. The rubber replanting cess might also be reconsidered at the same time.

30. The imposition of such a tax requires a cadastral survey to bring land records up to date.

31. According to Andic (1975), removal of *all* taxes would increase the incomes of the poor by only about 16 percent.

of public expenditure benefits financed by taxation, is likely to be a more powerful instrument for benefiting the poor. Unlike taxation relief, expenditure programs are not limited to the amount of revenue collected from the poor; they are also easier to focus on beneficiaries below the poverty line.

Intervention in Commodity Markets

Closely related to indirect tax policies are government policies that intervene in commodity markets through price or quantity controls. For instance, price support policies seek to establish a floor price for a commodity, with the government undertaking to buy from producers at the guaranteed minimum price. The stocks purchased are subsequently sold by the government through ("fair price") ration shops or in international markets. The government thus supports the producer price of a commodity by intervening in the domestic market as a buyer, a move which in turn supports producer incomes. In Malaysia compensatory price policies need to be considered for two commodities: paddy and rubber. As seen from table 5-2, paddy and rubber smallholders account for more than half the rural poor.

There is already a guaranteed minimum price (GMP) for paddy in Malaysia, which was M$16 per picul in 1970.[32] The government finances the GMP by exercising a quantitative control over imported rice, which is cheaper than local rice and constitutes about 10 percent of domestic consumption. Rice may be imported only by means of a license, which is granted on condition that the importer purchase a certain fixed ratio of the higher-priced local rice from the government stockpile (see Grant, 1970). The ratio is regulated in accordance with government policy on the optimal size of the stockpile. The objectives of the price support program are not only to raise the incomes of paddy planters and assure them of a ready market, but also to "encourage the cultivation of food, as this is part of the agricultural diversification programme" (Selvadurai, 1972*a*, p. 8). Programs to improve yields per acre and reduce unit production costs are being implemented, but it is recognized that Malaysia will remain a relatively high-cost producer of rice for some time (Selvadurai, 1972*a*, p. 5).

The government's policy of price support coupled with import controls raises both domestic producer and consumer prices above the international price. This policy avoids the problem of budgetary finance for the subsidy

---

32. See Selvadurai (1972*a*), pp. 70-71. The conversion factor for piculs into pounds (avoirdupois) is: 1 picul = 133.3 pounds.

to producers (via the GMP) since it is largely self-financing. It does imply, however, that the consumer bears the cost of the subsidy to domestic producers.[33] Unfortunately, many of the poor, who are net buyers of rice, therefore end up paying for the price support program—including those in the poverty subgroups of rubber smallholders, agricultural workers, fishermen, and urban poor. One subgroup of the poor is thus taxed to support another subgroup, the paddy farmers, and it is not at all clear that the net social benefits of this policy are positive. Without a careful quantification of the welfare gains to paddy farmers and the welfare losses to other consumers, it is difficult to comment on the desirability of the government's price support program (see Goldman, 1975).

The government's price support scheme appears to have similar effects to those of an import tariff. An import tariff, however, is equivalent to a production subsidy and consumption tax at the *same* rate (see Corden, 1971), whereas the rice price support scheme implies a production subsidy at a *higher* rate than the consumption tax.[34] Both policies subsidize domestic production but both create a distortion on the consumption side.[35] The welfare loss inflicted by a consumption tax is especially high since rice constitutes a large fraction of the typical poor household's budget. To minimize the burden on the nonpaddy poor it would be preferable to finance the production subsidy by some means other than a consumption tax on rice. Funding the subsidy from general government taxation is likely to create a much smaller burden (see table 8-1).

In the previous section, the case for price intervention in the market for rubber was considered to some extent. Since 93.6 percent of the benefits of a rubber price increase are likely to accrue to nonpoor households (see table 8-1), price support for rubber is clearly an inefficient income transfer policy. There is, however, some point in the government's attempting to *stabilize* the price received by producers. This varies significantly with changes in demand for Malaysian rubber as a result of booms and recessions in the automobile industry, changes in the price of synthetic rubber, and so on. A more stable price for rubber seems especially important for poorer smallholders, who are likely to find it difficult to withstand periods of abnormally low income. The government might consider a buffer-stock scheme to iron out some of the short-term fluctuations in price, accumulat-

33. This is not shown in the tax incidence estimates in table 8-1.
34. Under an import tariff, the implicit consumption tax goes partly to finance the production subsidy and partly to increase net government revenue; under the price support scheme, the implicit consumption tax is used entirely to finance the production subsidy.
35. The same effect on domestic production and farm incomes could be achieved by subsidizing input use, but this policy would distort input prices.

ing surpluses in years when the international price is low and disposing of them in years when it is high.[36] Another approach might be to negotiate longer-term commodity agreements with importing countries.

Rural Development Policies

Rural development policies attack poverty through various measures which help to raise the productivity of specific subgroups in the population. A rural development package might include improvements in irrigation facilities, provision of credit and input subsidies, marketing improvements, land development, and education and extension services.[37] These agricultural supports will vary with the particular subgroup for which they are intended, and individual packages can be designed to suit each project.

Two prominent features of rural development policies distinguish them from other policies to redress poverty. First, unlike fiscal and agricultural price policies, they appear easier to direct toward the poor. Many public expenditure policies can be aimed explicitly at low-income groups—for example, the selection of settlers for new land development schemes, or an irrigation scheme to permit double-cropping in a poor paddy-farming region. In contrast, population-wide policies can result in substantial leakages to the nonpoor. Even policies oriented toward specific target groups are unlikely to be completely efficient, however, and actual implementation is bound to result in leakages. For instance, middlemen and administrators may take illegal cuts in administering them and thus prevent the benefits from reaching only the intended subgroups.

Second, rural development policies are distinguished by their effects on output growth. If it is decided for equity reasons to transfer a fixed amount of income from nonpoor to poor, is it better to do so through tax-price (or income maintenance) policies or through development expenditure policies

36. Although rubber producers acting on their own are capable of operating this policy, they cannot be expected to do so for a variety of reasons. Chief among these are an inability to borrow when the price is low (because of imperfect capital markets), lack of information about market trends, and incapacity to bear risk. Government intervention is socially desirable since it reduces price and therefore income uncertainty for individual smallholders.

37. A useful survey of rural development policies is provided in World Bank (1975). In a speech to the World Bank's Board of Governors, Robert McNamara (1973, p. 17) identified the following essential elements of a strategy to increase smallholder productivities: "acceleration in the rate of land and tenancy reform, better access to credit, assured availability of water, expanded extension facilities backed by intensified agricultural research, greater access to public services, new forms of rural institutions and organizations that will give as much attention to promoting the inherent potential and productivity of the poor as is generally given to protecting the power of the privileged."

which raise the productive capacity of the poor? In the former case the budgetary transfer is akin to a straight redistribution of income, whereas in the latter case the transfer should yield a permanent gain in output and income for the poor. A dynamic comparison between the two types of policy is possible only if additional assumptions are made about the productivity of poverty-oriented investment (rural development) in relation to investment by the nonpoor, and about the effects of the transfer on aggregate saving and investment.

Suppose that the productivity of poverty-oriented investment is the same as that of investment by the nonpoor. Then rural development is dynamically superior if the transfer increases the aggregate volume of investment. Obversely, suppose that the budgetary transfer leaves aggregate saving and investment unaffected. Then rural development is again a dynamically superior policy if its rate of return exceeds the rate of return on the displaced investment. Otherwise, it is better to let the higher return obtain on investment by the nonpoor and to transfer a proportion of this to the poor every year. On both counts, there are reasons to suppose that rural development might be more efficient. First, the increase in productivity of the poor may itself be sufficiently high (because of double-cropping, improved fertilizers, and the like) to raise the average rate of return on aggregate investment. Second, a rural development policy should imply a higher aggregate level of saving and investment than a straight income transfer policy, since the former redirects the entire transfer to investment whereas the latter allows consumption out of the transfer.[38]

Taken together the two counts do suggest that rural development may be more efficient than other policies to redress poverty. Moreover, such policies, if properly designed, can be the most effective means of zeroing in on the poor. By an appropriate matching of target groups and project packages, the leakage of benefits can be minimized. For these reasons I attempted to identify homogeneous subgroups of rural poor in chapter 5. The components of direct-benefit productivity-raising programs can be put together for such subgroups with relative ease, but actual projects may be selected only after in-depth cost-benefit studies.[39]

38. Indeed, unless the marginal propensity to save of the nonpoor is unity, a rural development policy should imply a higher overall level of investment than would occur in the absence of transfers. By contrast, since the nonpoor are likely to have a higher savings propensity than the poor, a straight income transfer policy should imply a lower overall level of investment than would occur without any transfers.

39. Income distribution weights should be incorporated into such cost-benefit analyses. In an appraisal of a Malaysian highway project (Anand, 1976a) before this study was complete, it was not possible to incorporate distributional weights because of difficulties in identifying the ultimate beneficiaries of the project, but these problems do not arise for the typical rural development project.

Some Implications of Employment Restructuring

The second prong of the New Economic Policy seeks to ensure that employment in the various sectors of the economy and employment by occupational levels will reflect the racial composition of the population. The Outline Perspective Plan (OPP) in the *Mid-Term Review of the Second Malaysia Plan* (MTR) specifies targets for employment by racial group which are to be achieved by 1990 (see the section "The New Economic Policy" in chapter 1).[40]

Various instruments in both the public and private sectors are used to achieve these targets. Direct hiring in the public sector, including criteria that favor the selection of Malays in government schemes—for example, in land settlement, timber concessions, licensing, and government tenders—helps ensure the fulfillment of racial employment targets for the public sector. In the private sector, a combination of instruments seems to be used to regulate employment and asset ownership. Permits and licenses to operate certain businesses and trades—such as bus, taxi, and trucking operations—are granted on an ethnic basis.[41] The licensing of industries through such legislation as the Industrial Coordination Act provides control over racial employment in the manufacturing sector.[42] Employment restructuring is also implemented through ad hoc checks, controls, and moral suasion whenever government permission or approval of any kind is needed. There is also a directive to the banks that 20 percent of all credit be given to Malays. Finally, admission quotas are applied in universities and other training institutes to increase the supply of qualified Malays.[43]

The sectoral employment targets for the Malay share of employment in 1990 have been set at approximately 50 percent plus or minus 3 percent (see

40. The OPP contains racial employment targets by sector only, but the Third Malaysia Plan (TMP) also specifies the targets by occupational category.

41. This has led to the so-called Ali-Baba phenomenon, in which a Malay lends his name to a Chinese to obtain the business permit and is then treated as a sleeping partner in the firm. Ali is a common Muslim name among Malays; Baba is another name for the Chinese.

42. The Industrial Coordination Act of 1975 is designed to ensure "the orderly development of industries and to facilitate the collection of industrial information." The act makes a license mandatory for manufacturing firms employing twenty-five or more workers and having share capital of more than M$250,000. It thus allows a close check on the racial pattern of employment in manufacturing enterprises.

43. The special provisions for Malays are set out in Articles 3, 38, 89, 152, and 153 of the constitution.

MTR, table 4-5). The exception is agriculture, for which the Malay share in the terminal year is 60 percent. The 1990 racial employment targets for Malays:Chinese:Indians are 60:29:11 in agriculture, 50:40:10 in manufacturing and construction, 50:39:11 in mining, and 48:40:12 in commerce. Sizable intersectoral labor movements will be needed to achieve these targets, with Malay employment in the modern sectors having to grow much faster than average. Particularly interesting are the implications of the targets for Malay employment in the manufacturing and construction sectors, and for Chinese employment in the agricultural and mining sectors. During 1970–90 Malay employment will have to grow at an average rate of 10.5 percent a year in manufacturing and 9.5 percent a year in construction. Both requirements will be difficult to achieve. At the same time, the growth of Malay employment in agriculture is to be kept down to a mere 0.6 percent a year, while Chinese employment in agriculture has to expand at 2.7 percent a year. The growth of Chinese employment in agriculture is at more than twice the sectoral rate, which implies that nearly 60 percent of all new agricultural jobs in this period will have to be taken up by the Chinese. In the mining sector, Chinese employment will have to fall at 1.5 percent a year.

The OPP does not specify how this intersectoral and geographic mobility is to be brought about. For example, the targets for the agricultural sector necessitate a significant amount of reverse, or urban-rural, migration by the Chinese. But because of the substantial urban-rural differences in incomes and other amenities, such migration is unlikely to take place. Most new agricultural jobs are likely to arise on the land development schemes for rubber and palm oil, and to increase the participation of the Chinese in these schemes, land would have to be reserved for them and sufficiently attractive bonuses and subsidies offered. Such discrimination in favor of non-Malays would be difficult to defend when poverty criteria clearly favor resettlement by Malays, who account for 83.9 percent of rural households in poverty.

The unequal racial allocation of new job opportunities by sector is likely to affect the new generation of non-Malays disproportionately and lead to a sense of deprivation. It has therefore been suggested that the racial employment targets might be implemented in relation to flows rather than stocks (Thillainathan, 1970, 1975a; and Moore, 1975). In other words, the racial allocation of *new* labor force entrants should be in proportion to the population ratios of the racial groups. Ultimately, of course, this policy would also achieve the stock target, but the time span would be stretched out over a period considerably longer than twenty years.

Employment restructuring by sector alone will help to narrow income differences between the races but not to eliminate them. As shown in chapter 6, there are large intrasectoral differences in output and income per worker. If the occupational structure of employment within each sector is also balanced racially, the income differences between the races will be reduced more effectively.

The racial employment targets by occupational level in the Third Malaysia Plan (TMP) imply that Malays are particularly underrepresented in the professional and technical and in the administrative and managerial occupations (see also chapter 6). Simple calculations show that achieving proportional racial representation within each occupation by 1990 will call for even greater redirection of manpower than the sectoral composition targets.[44]

The government, of course, recognizes the crucial role of expanding the supply of skilled manpower: "The current stock of qualified Malays at the managerial, professional, and technical levels requires substantial expansion and this will necessitate increasing the proportion of Malays pursuing courses in science, technology, economics, and business administration and other professional courses" (MTR, p. 13). Some progress has already been made in this direction by vigorously expanding vocational education, by accelerating the training of skilled workers, by constructing special secondary schools for rural areas, by placing increased emphasis on science and technology at the university level, and by expanding the MARA Institute of Technology which provides technical and vocational training to Malays. Programs are also being designed to provide Malays with basic knowledge of business management and administration. Methods other than formal training in institutes are also envisaged, particularly for the development of Malay managerial and entrepreneurial talent. Malay participation in business and commerce is to be supported by government finance, technical assistance, and other facilities. Non-Malay and foreign enterprises are being encouraged to participate in the development of Malay and other indigenous executives, managers, and entrepreneurs. Such on-the-job training is to be supplemented by having the government set up enterprises and train Malays to take them over in due course.

What are the difficulties with the NEP's targets for employment restructuring? Some commentators feel that Malay managerial talent cannot be created as rapidly as the NEP implies and that excessively speedy implementation of the policy may be a mistake (Rafferty, 1975a, b). It is

44. Under one set of assumptions, Moore (1975) estimates that during the 1970–90 period 63.3 percent of all new jobs in four leading occupations (professional and technical, administrative and managerial, clerical, and sales) will have to be reserved for Malays, and 57 percent of all new Malay entrants to the labor force will have to be directed to these four occupations.

probable that pursuing the racial participation ratios for skilled occupations will require increasing the percentage of Malays in many training and educational institutes well beyond their share in the population. This may imply a lowering of standards and the admission of underqualified Malays into institutions of higher education (Moore, 1975). But this is likely to be a temporary cost, borne only during the transition period until the system adjusts to its new equilibrium. Questions have been raised, however, as to whether even the overall output of Malaysian vocational training institutes and universities will be sufficient to meet the manpower needs of the OPP, and whether the present flow (and past stock) of technologically skilled Malays will be adequate to fill the Malay quotas.[45]

It is also possible that efficiency could be jeopardized by excessively rapid employment restructuring. Given the present lack of trained Malays, some authors believe there will be "unfilled slots" in the higher occupational levels or "slots which can at best be filled by underqualified persons" (Thillainathan, 1975a; Moore, 1975). This outcome could itself constrain growth of overall output and employment because of the long lags associated with training high- and middle-level manpower and providing appropriate educational and training facilities. Yet the rapid growth of output is a necessary condition for the success of the NEP, for it is "only through such growth that the objectives of the NEP can be achieved without any particular group in Malaysian society experiencing any loss or feeling any sense of deprivation" (MTR, p. 63).

The potential for the medium-term growth of output and employment could be affected by the emigration of skilled manpower if racial employment quotas are rigidly enforced. Some highly skilled non-Malays might choose to emigrate if faced with limited opportunities for promotion and career advancement.[46] Given the scarcity of high-level manpower in Malaysia, growth prospects could be adversely affected by unforeseen reductions in supply. In addition, growth prospects could be dampened by a reluctance of the business community to invest if quotas make investment less profitable at the margin.

Thus rigid enforcement of the restructuring targets could entail tradeoffs with medium-term output and employment growth; such growth would itself be instrumental in any effort to restructure and to eradicate poverty.

45. According to von der Mehden (1975), the difficulties of developing Malay managerial pools in the private sector arise out of cultural and educational factors which may take more than two decades to reverse. From interviews conducted in 1973, he concludes that trained Malays have traditionally found the civil service and politics more attractive fields of endeavor than commerce and industry—but this may be changing.

46. Indeed, Shaplen (1977) claims that some Chinese professionals are already emigrating.

While it is not easy to quantify the tradeoffs, one would expect some cost in output and efficiency if employment quotas impose a constraint on economic activity.[47] But such losses may be interpreted as short- and medium-term adjustment costs, which could be offset partially or even outweighed by longer-term gains. Once the stock of skilled Malay manpower has been increased in line with the Malay population ratio, improved long-run efficiency could ensue from the wider pool of talent.

The New Economic Policy: Concluding Comments

The reduction of individual income inequality is an objective of considerable importance in most developing countries, and is one about which the government of Malaysia has itself expressed concern (see MTR, p. 62, and TMP, p. 51). But it is not an explicit objective of the New Economic Policy. The eradication of poverty and the correction of racial imbalances are the NEP's twin objectives.

It has been shown in chapter 3 and appendix E that the redress of poverty is the most efficient method of redressing individual income inequality. More precisely, if decreases in individual incomes are ruled out, the maximum reduction in inequality is obtained through a policy of distributing incremental income to fill the poverty gap from the bottom upward. Hence reducing racial income imbalance—by increasing Malay incomes so that the Malay distribution is scaled up toward the non-Malay distribution—will be less efficient in redressing individual income inequality. In fact, as seen in chapters 3 and 6, the complete elimination of racial income imbalance will reduce individual income inequality by only about 10 percent; at the same time, it will entail a far greater expenditure than that required for the eradication of poverty.[48]

It is useful to compare the reduction in inequality for the same expenditure on the two prongs. Since a smaller amount is required to eradicate poverty than to eliminate racial income imbalance, let us assume that the expenditure on each prong is the total income gap of the poor. This

47. Quotas in proportion to population ratios can produce economic inefficiencies of various kinds. These inefficiencies could turn out to be particularly acute when quotas are applied in favor of a majority community such as the Malays in Malaysia—in contrast with a minority community, such as the blacks in the United States or the scheduled castes and tribes in India.

48. In terms of the PES distribution of individuals by per capita household income, the poverty gap works out to M$401 million a year in 1970, while M$1,879 million a year is required to raise all Malay incomes by a factor of 1.96 to eliminate the racial disparity ratio between the Malays and non-Malays.

amount allows all poor individuals to be brought up to the poverty line and allows all Malay incomes to be raised by a factor of 1.20 (Malay incomes need to be raised by a factor of 1.96 to eliminate racial income imbalance completely). The expenditure on the first or poverty prong achieves a reduction in individual income inequality of 17.1 percent as measured by the Gini coefficient and of 20.5 percent as measured by the Theil T index.[49] The same amount spent on the second or racial balance prong achieves a reduction in individual income inequality of 2.5 percent as measured by the Gini coefficient and of 4.5 percent as measured by the Theil T index.[50] As an instrument for individual inequality reduction, therefore, the first prong is much more efficient than the second.

Despite the differences between the two prongs of the NEP, there turns out to be a common area of policy in which the two are mutually consistent. The first prong seeks to help the poor irrespective of race; the second prong seeks to help Malays, including middle- and upper-income Malays. As it happens, the intersection of the two target groups is rather large, with almost four-fifths (78.1 percent) of poor households Malay, and just over half (51.4 percent) of Malay households poor (see table 4-3). Hence policies that raise the incomes of poor Malays will help promote both prongs.

This interdependence can be explored further. Suppose that M$1 is spent on each prong at the margin; what is the indirect effect on the other prong? Clearly this effect will depend on the particular way the M$1 is distributed over the target population. For example, if M$1 is spent on the first prong, the amount accruing to Malays will depend on whether it is spent on redressing poverty from the bottom upward or on alleviating poverty close to the poverty line. Similarly, if M$1 is spent on the second prong, the amount accruing to the poor will depend on how it is distributed over different parts of the Malay income distribution. It is assumed that the marginal M$1 is spent on each prong just as the average M$1 would be spent. In other words, the marginal M$1 is distributed over the poor so that

---

49. Owing to zero-income individuals, varlog and the Theil L measure are not computable for the distribution of individuals by per capita household income. After all poor individuals have been brought up to the poverty line, inequality in this distribution would be given by:

	Malay	Chinese	Indian	Other	Total
Gini coefficient	0.3023	0.4325	0.4463	0.6681	0.4126
Theil T index	0.2493	0.3971	0.4799	0.8411	0.4104
Mean income (M$ per month)	39.42	68.95	58.33	189.51	53.08

50. When all Malay incomes are raised by a factor of 1.20, the new Gini coefficient is 0.4857 and the new Theil T index is 0.4929. (See the section "Policy Considerations" in chapter 3 for the results when all Malay incomes are raised by a factor of 1.96.)

the poverty gap of each individual is reduced equiproportionately, and the marginal M$1 is distributed over Malays so that all Malay incomes are raised equiproportionately.

Under these assumptions, the indirect effect on Prong 2 of M$1 spent on Prong 1 is M$0.79 (see chapter 4); that is, 79 cents of every dollar spent at the margin on reducing poverty serve also to reduce racial income imbalance. The indirect effect on Prong 1 of M$1 spent on Prong 2 is M$0.25; that is, 25 cents of every dollar spent at the margin on reducing racial income imbalance serve also to reduce poverty. Thus the indirect effect of focusing on poverty is greater than the indirect effect of focusing on racial imbalance.[51]

Ultimately, however, the indirect effects of one prong on the other may be of limited consequence. The two are not only logically independent, but also defensible in and of themselves. In addition, the two prongs have their basis in considerations that go beyond the narrowly economic ones.

Prong 1 can be justified in terms of two moral principles. The first is humanitarian: people's basic needs should be satisfied. The second is egalitarian: income inequality should be reduced.[52] Under certain conditions, both principles can be derived from utilitarianism; both can also be defended as nonutilitarian principles of distributive justice.

Prong 2 raises other moral issues. One is equality of opportunity. The association of race with economic function may be seen as evidence of unequal opportunities in the past. Although formal equality of opportunity may now be said to exist, the perceptions and aspirations of Malays may still be constrained by historical and social tradition. Quota systems that place Malays in jobs hitherto unfilled by them may help to provide role models and widen the perception of choices available to them.[53] Another moral issue is compensatory justice. For example, if there have been past injustices against the Malay community, there is a prima facie case for compensation. Such arguments for compensatory justice have recently

51. The indirect effect of focusing on rural poverty would be even greater: if the marginal M$1 on Prong 1 were distributed only among the rural poor, Malay incomes would be raised by more than 79 cents.

52. This defense of Prong 1 in terms of egalitarianism is contingent on the fact (established in appendix E) that the redress of poverty leads efficiently to the redress of inequality.

53. They may also enhance the self-esteem of younger generations of Malays (although in the short run they could have the opposite effect psychologically). Malays might thus be encouraged to aim for positions they previously ruled out, and this would help create real equality of opportunity. Once equal access has been achieved, however, discrimination on grounds of race becomes difficult to defend.

been advanced to defend policies of reverse discrimination or affirmative action in favor of blacks and women in the United States.[54]

Political considerations also need to be taken into account. If racial imbalances persist and race is seen to be associated with economic function, tensions could develop between the racial groups which might threaten the country's stability—a danger highlighted by the 1969 riots. It is thus possible to adduce strong prudential reasons in support of the government's policy of restructuring. The NEP has been justified in terms of the "overriding objective to promote national unity in the country." The government recognizes that national unity has several facets, and indeed stresses "there must be no delusion that national unity can be achieved by purely economic means." Nevertheless, the redress of racial economic imbalances is a necessary condition for maintaining harmony in this multiracial society. The redress of poverty, which cuts across ethnic lines, is also a necessary condition for maintaining national unity. The ultimate success of the NEP will depend on the achievement of an equitable balance between the two prongs.

54. See Cohen, Nagel, and Scanlon (1977) for discussions of the philosophical basis of such policies. Some people reject reverse discrimination on the ground that liability for the actions of past generations cannot be located within the present generation. Even if liability could be so located, reverse discrimination may be thought unfair because a few individuals end up bearing the costs of compensation, which should properly be borne by the community as a whole. In the case of Malaysia, there are further complications. First, it might be argued that the economic backwardness of Malays is not itself proof of past injustices. Second, even if there were such proof, the problem of locating liability would be compounded by the former presence of a colonial power in the country. To the extent that non-Malays have been the beneficiaries of colonial policy, however, it might be held appropriate that they should bear some of the costs of compensation.

Appendixes

The Measurement
of Income Inequality

THE FOLLOWING SIX APPENDIXES present some recent results on the measurement of income inequality. In part they are a selective survey of work in the area, which has been adapted to shed light on problems that concern us in the text. In part they also present some new results (see appendixes B, E, and F) which have arisen out of measurement problems encountered in the empirical analysis of the Malaysian data. For excellent surveys of the literature on inequality measurement in general, see Theil (1967, chapter 4), Atkinson (1970), and Sen (1973a).

A

A Brief Review

MOST OF THE IMPORTANT RESULTS in inequality measurement, and many inequality indices themselves, are based on the Lorenz curve for an income distribution. This brief review begins with a definition of the Lorenz curve for a continuous income distribution specified as an income density function $f(y)$;[1] the definition for a discrete distribution is provided later (see appendix D). Let

$$F(x) = \int_0^x f(y) \mathrm{d}y$$

be the cumulative population share corresponding to income level x, so that $F(x)$ is the proportion of the population that receives income less than or equal to x. Let

$$\Phi(x) = (1/\mu) \int_0^x y f(y) \mathrm{d}y$$

be the cumulative income share corresponding to income level x, where $\mu = \int_0^\infty y f(y) \mathrm{d}y$ is the mean of the distribution. This defines an implicit relation between F and Φ in terms of the parameter x. The graph $F(x), \Phi(x)$ is said to be the Lorenz curve of the income distribution $f(y)$.

Alternatively, starting with the pth percentile in the income distribution, we can define x as the income level which cuts off the bottom p percent, that is, $p = F(x)$ or $x = F^{-1}(p)$. The income share of the bottom p percent in the distribution is then $\Phi[F^{-1}(p)]$. This function gives the Lorenz curve of the distribution, $L(p)$, which shows the cumulative income share corresponding to percentile $p (0 \leqslant p \leqslant 1)$. Thus $L(p) = \Phi[F^{-1}(p)]$ on the support of $F(x)$. It is easy to check the following propositions, which are illustrated in figure A-1.

1. $0 \leqslant F \leqslant 1, 0 \leqslant \Phi \leqslant 1$; $F(0) = \Phi(0) = 0$, $F(\infty) = \Phi(\infty) = 1$.
2. The Lorenz curve $L(p)$ $(0 \leqslant p \leqslant 1)$ is *convex*, and its derivative $L'(p)$ is given by

$$L'(p) = \frac{F^{-1}(p)}{\mu} = \frac{x}{\mu}$$

---

1. As $f(y)$ is a density function for income, $y \geqslant 0, f(y) \geqslant 0$, and $\int_0^\infty f(y) \mathrm{d}y = 1$.

Figure A-1. *The Lorenz Diagram*

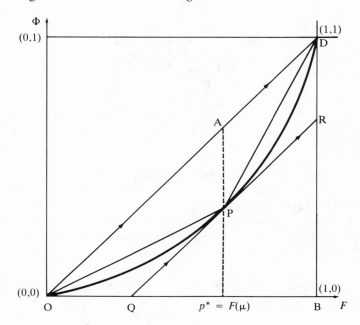

where $x = F^{-1}(p)$ is the income level which cuts off the bottom p percent.

3. The slope of the Lorenz curve equals unity at the percentile $p^* = F(\mu)$, so that the fraction of the population receiving income less than or equal to the mean μ can be read off immediately.

Indices Based Directly on the Lorenz Diagram

The Lorenz curve corresponding to the distribution in which everyone receives the same income is the line OD in figure A-1;[2] this is referred to as the line (or diagonal) of perfect equality. There are several inequality indices which attempt to measure the divergence between the Lorenz curve for a given income distribution and the line of perfect equality. The best known and most widely used among these is the Gini coefficient. It is described below together with some other indices based on the Lorenz diagram.

2. This distribution has a point-mass income density function.

The Gini coefficient G is defined as the area between the Lorenz curve and the line of equality divided by the area of the triangle OBD below this line. The Gini coefficient varies between the limits of 0 (perfect equality) and 1 (perfect inequality), and the greater the departure of the Lorenz curve from the diagonal, the larger is the value of the Gini coefficient.

An alternative definition for the Gini coefficient can be specified in algebraic terms as

$$G = \tfrac{1}{2}(\Delta/\mu)$$

where $\Delta = \int_0^\infty \int_0^\infty |x - y| f(x) f(y) \, dx \, dy$ is the absolute mean difference (see Kendall and Stuart, 1963). Thus G can also be defined as one-half the relative mean difference. In appendix B these two definitions are shown to be equivalent.

Another measure of inequality based on the Lorenz diagram is the value of the maximum discrepancy between the line of perfect equality and the Lorenz curve (see Schutz, 1951). The distance between the diagonal and the Lorenz curve is evidently maximized at the point p^* in figure A-1 where the slope of the Lorenz curve is equal to unity; hence the value of the maximum discrepancy is AP or $[p^* - L(p^*)]$.

The value of the maximum discrepancy turns out to be equal to one-half the relative mean deviation M, which is another measure of inequality (see Sen, 1973a). It is not difficult to prove that

$$[p^* - L(p^*)] = M/2 = \tfrac{1}{2}(\delta/\mu)$$

where $\delta = \int_0^\infty |y - \mu| f(y) \, dy$ is the absolute mean deviation.

Yet another measure has been proposed which tries to capture the divergence between the Lorenz curve and the line of perfect equality. This is defined as the area of the largest triangle that can be inscribed between the Lorenz curve and the line of equality, divided by the area of the triangle OBD below this line. As shown below, this measure reduces to the value of the maximum discrepancy, or $M/2$!

The triangle with the largest area that can be inscribed in the convex set defined by the Lorenz curve and the line of equality is OPD. This is seen by constructing the quadrilateral OQRD which contains the convex set; OQRD has OD as base and opposite side QR parallel to OD and tangential to the Lorenz curve. Now OPD is clearly a triangle of maximal area that can be inscribed in the larger set OQRD. A fortiori, it is a triangle of maximal area that can be inscribed in the required subset. The area of triangle OPD is $(1/2)(\mathrm{OD})(\mathrm{AP}/\sqrt{2}) = [p^* - L(p^*)]/2$, while that of triangle OBD is $1/2$. Hence the value of the inequality measure is $[p^* - L(p^*)]$, or $M/2$.

Other Indices

There are three basic properties that one would like an inequality index to satisfy: (1) mean or scale independence, that is, the index remains invariant if everyone's income is changed by the same proportion; (2) population-size independence, that is, the index remains invariant if the number of people at each income level is changed by the same proportion;[3] and (3) the Pigou-Dalton condition, that is, any transfer from a richer to a poorer person that does not reverse their relative ranks reduces the value of the index (Sen, 1973a, p. 27).

The properties of mean independence and population-size independence together imply that the index can be computed directly from the Lorenz curve of the income distribution: knowledge of mean income and total population size are unnecessary (see appendix D). Conversely, an index that can be computed directly from the Lorenz curve obviously satisfies the properties of mean independence and population-size independence.

The inequality indices in the previous section are defined in terms of the Lorenz diagram and thus satisfy the properties of mean independence and population-size independence. The Gini coefficient satisfies the Pigou-Dalton condition also,[4] but the other indices, which are equivalent to the relative mean deviation up to a scalar multiple, do not. From the definition of the relative mean deviation, it is clear that it is insensitive to income transfers between people on the same side of the mean.[5]

There are two common statistical measures of dispersion for a distribution: the range and the variance. The range can be defined as the absolute difference between the highest and lowest income levels divided by the mean income. Since it ignores the distribution *inside* the extremes, the range obviously violates the Pigou-Dalton condition. The variance, however, does satisfy this property—but it violates mean independence. A way around this deficiency is to deflate the variance by the square of the mean. This gives the squared coefficient of variation, which satisfies all three

3. With this property, the index depends only on the relative population frequencies at each income level, not the absolute population frequencies. In the continuous case this is equivalent to the index being computable from the income density function alone.

4. This is plain from the geometrical definition of the Gini coefficient. A transfer of income from a richer to a poorer person raises the entire Lorenz curve between the corresponding percentiles; hence it reduces the Gini coefficient.

5. Again this is evident from the geometrical representation of the relative mean deviation. In figure A-1, the length of AP is unaltered by income transfers on one side only of $p^* = F(\mu)$ (see also Atkinson, 1970).

properties. In addition, the squared coefficient of variation satisfies a (weak) decomposability property (see chapter 3, the section "The Methodology of Inequality Decomposition").

The other inequality indices considered are defined in terms of a discrete income distribution. Let the vector $\mathbf{y} = (y_1, y_2, \ldots, y_n)$ denote an income distribution among n persons, where $y_i \geq 0$ is the income of person $i(i = 1, 2, \ldots, n)$. Let the arithmetic mean income of the distribution be μ, so that

$$\mu = \frac{1}{n} \sum_{i=1}^{n} y_i.$$

The variance of income var(y) can then be written as

$$\mathrm{var}(y) = \frac{1}{n} \sum_{i=1}^{n} (y_i - \mu)^2.$$

If all incomes are multiplied by the factor λ, the variance of income changes by the factor λ^2. It is easily checked that for a positive scalar λ

$$\mathrm{var}(\lambda y) = \lambda^2 \mathrm{var}(y).$$

Unlike the variance of income, the variance of the *logarithm* of income var$(\log y)$ is a mean-independent measure of inequality. Let $\tilde{\mu}$ be the geometric mean income of the distribution, so that by definition

$$\log \tilde{\mu} = \frac{1}{n} \sum_{i=1}^{n} \log y_i.$$

Then the variance of log-income or var$(\log y)$ can be written as

$$\mathrm{var}(\log y) = \frac{1}{n} \sum_{i=1}^{n} (\log y_i - \log \tilde{\mu})^2.$$

Now if all incomes are multiplied by the positive factor λ, the variance of log-income does not change at all. It is easily checked that for a scalar $\lambda > 0$,

$$\mathrm{var}(\log \lambda y) = \mathrm{var}(\log y).$$

The variance of log-income also obviously satisfies the property of population-size independence. However, it does not satisfy the Pigou-Dalton condition for the entire range of incomes.[6]

The deviation of the logarithms of income is sometimes taken from the logarithm of the arithmetic mean $\log \mu$ rather than the logarithm of the

---

6. The Pigou-Dalton condition is not satisfied for incomes above $\tilde{\mu}e$, where e is the base of the natural logarithms.

geometric mean $\log \tilde{\mu}$ (see Sen, 1973a). This yields a slightly different measure which is also mean-independent:

$$v = \frac{1}{n} \sum_{i=1}^{n} (\log y_i - \log \mu)^2.$$

It can easily be verified that

$$v = \text{var}(\log y) + (\log \mu - \log \tilde{\mu})^2.$$

But $(\log \mu - \log \tilde{\mu})$ is itself a measure of inequality, namely, Theil's second measure L (see below). Thus v is really the sum of two distinct inequality measures, $\text{var}(\log y)$ and the square of the Theil L measure.

Both $\text{var}(\log y)$ and v suffer from a rather serious practical defect. The measures are *not* defined if there is a person in the distribution with zero income. Unfortunately, this happens to be the case with some of the Malaysian distributions considered. To overcome this problem, some have suggested that the zero-income recipients be assigned a small positive income (such as 1). But the choice of the amount assigned makes all the difference to the value of the measure. The sensitivity of the measure to this arbitrary procedure, and the inability to defend the particular amount assigned, render the measure unusable in such situations. One attractive feature of the variance of log-income, however, is that it is decomposable around group geometric mean incomes (see chapters 3 and 6 and appendix C). Another derives from its relation to the lognormal distribution (see Aitchison and Brown, 1957) and to the estimating form of the human capital model (see chapter 7).

Finally, two inequality measures of Theil (1967) are considered. The first is Theil's entropy index T based on the notion of entropy in information theory. It is defined as

$$T = \frac{1}{n} \sum_{i=1}^{n} \frac{y_i}{\mu} \log \frac{y_i}{\mu}$$

where $n\mu = \sum_{i=1}^{n} y_i = Y$ is the total income. Note that (y_i/μ) is simply the slope of the Lorenz curve at the percentile corresponding to income level y_i. Hence T, like the measures in the previous section, can be computed directly from the Lorenz curve of the income distribution. The motivation for T, however, derives from the "entropy" $H(\mathbf{y})$ associated with the income shares $(y_1/Y), \ldots, (y_n/Y)$:

$$H(\mathbf{y}) = \sum_{i=1}^{n} (y_i/Y) \log \frac{1}{(y_i/Y)}.$$

The closer are the income shares (y_i/Y) to the population shares $(1/n)$, the greater is $H(\mathbf{y})$; and when each (y_i/Y) equals $(1/n)$, $H(\mathbf{y})$ attains its maximum value of $\log n$. On the other hand, if one income share tends to unity and all the others tend to zero, $H(\mathbf{y})$ tends to its minimum value of zero. Thus the entropy $H(\mathbf{y})$ of an income distribution can be regarded as a measure of income *equality*. Theil obtains a measure of income *inequality* by subtracting $H(\mathbf{y})$ from its maximum value, $\log n$.[7] This inequality measure is T, which can be written as

$$T = \log n - H(\mathbf{y})$$
$$= \sum_{i=1}^{n} (y_i/Y)\log\frac{(y_i/Y)}{(1/n)}.$$

As $(1/n)$ is the population share and (y_i/Y) the income share of person i, Theil interprets T as "the expected information of a message which transforms population shares into income shares" (1967, p. 95). When there is perfect equality, each person's income share (y_i/Y) and population share $(1/n)$ are equal, and T assumes the value zero.[8] When there is perfect inequality, however, a single person receives all the income and everyone else receives zero income: one of the y_i's is then equal to Y, and all other y_i's are equal to zero. In this case, T assumes its maximum value of $\log n$; all terms with a zero income share tend to zero, since $x \log x \to 0$ as $x \to 0$.

The Theil entropy index T fulfills most of the desirable properties specified for a measure of inequality. It is mean-independent and population-size-independent; it satisfies the Pigou-Dalton condition; it is defined for distributions with zero-income recipients; and, finally, it is additively decomposable in the weak sense, with income-share weights for the within-group component—which sum to unity (see chapters 3 and 6 and appendix C).

Another inequality index of Theil (1967) I call Theil's second measure L. It is analogous to the entropy index T except that it reverses the roles of income share (y_i/Y) and population share $(1/n)$ in the formula for T. Thus Theil's second measure can be written as

$$L = \sum_{i=1}^{n} (1/n)\log\frac{(1/n)}{(y_i/Y)}.$$

Theil interprets L as "the expected information content of the indirect message which transforms the income shares as prior probabilities into the population shares as posterior probabilities" (1967, p. 125). Like T, the index L attempts to measure the divergence between income shares and

---

7. The difference between the maximum entropy value, $\log n$, and the actual entropy value, $H(\mathbf{y})$, is called redundancy in communication theory.

8. T may be thought of as a general distance function which measures the divergence between income shares and population shares.

population shares, but it uses a somewhat different distance function. Since $Y = n\mu$, Theil's second measure L can also be written as

$$L = \frac{1}{n} \sum_{i=1}^{n} \log \frac{\mu}{y_i}.$$

As (y_i/μ) is the slope of the Lorenz curve at the percentile corresponding to income level y_i, the measure L can be computed directly from the Lorenz curve of the income distribution. Rewriting the expression for L,

$$\begin{aligned} L &= \log \mu - \frac{1}{n} \sum_{i=1}^{n} \log y_i \\ &= \log \mu - \log \tilde{\mu} \\ &= \log \frac{\mu}{\tilde{\mu}} \end{aligned}$$

where $\tilde{\mu}$ is the geometric mean income of the distribution. In other words, L is the logarithm of the ratio of the arithmetic mean income of the distribution to the geometric mean income.[9]

Theil's second measure L obviously satisfies the properties of mean independence and population-size independence; it also satisfies the Pigou-Dalton condition. Moreover, L is additively decomposable in the strict sense, with population-share weights for the within-group component—which sum to unity (see chapters 3 and 6 and appendix C). One disadvantage, however, is that it is not defined for distributions with zero incomes, since $\log x \to -\infty$ as $x \to 0$.

---

9. L is also a simple monotonic increasing transform of Atkinson's (1970) index I when the inequality aversion parameter ε is equal to unity. In this case, the Atkinson equally distributed equivalent income is just the geometric mean income $\tilde{\mu}$ of the distribution, and $I = 1 - (\tilde{\mu}/\mu)$. Hence, $L = -\log(1 - I)$.

B

The Gini Coefficient

THE MOST COMMON DEFINITION of the Gini coefficient is in terms of the Lorenz diagram—as the ratio of the area between the Lorenz curve and the line of equality, to the area of the triangle below this line (see appendix A). Various other definitions have also been discussed in the literature and are useful for different purposes. Here several definitions of the Gini coefficient are reviewed, and their equivalence is demonstrated.

Suppose there are n individuals (or households) who are labeled in nondescending order of income as: $y_1 \leqslant y_2 \leqslant \ldots \leqslant y_n$. Denote this (ordered) income distribution by the vector $\mathbf{y} = (y_1, y_2, \ldots, y_n)$, and let μ be its mean. Let F_i be the cumulative population share and Φ_i the cumulative income share corresponding to individual $i (i = 1, 2, \ldots n)$. Define $F_0 = \Phi_0 = 0$. Thus

$$F_i = \frac{i}{n} \quad \text{and} \quad \Phi_i = \frac{1}{n\mu} \sum_{k=1}^{i} y_k \quad \text{for } i = 0, 1, \ldots, n.$$

The first definition is the one used in this study to estimate Gini coefficients for Malaysia.

Definition 1 (Geometric)

$$G_1 = 1 - \sum_{i=0}^{n-1} (F_{i+1} - F_i)(\Phi_{i+1} + \Phi_i).$$

It is shown that G_1 is equivalent to the geometric definition of the Gini coefficient given above. Figure B-1 illustrates the Lorenz curve for the discrete income distribution $\mathbf{y} = (y_1, y_2, \ldots, y_n)$ where $y_1 \leqslant y_2 \leqslant \ldots \leqslant y_n$. The shaded part shows a typical segment of the area below the Lorenz curve. The total area below the Lorenz curve

$$= \frac{1}{2} \sum_{i=0}^{n-1} (F_{i+1} - F_i)(\Phi_{i+1} + \Phi_i).$$

Figure B-1. *The Lorenz Curve for a Discrete Income Distribution*

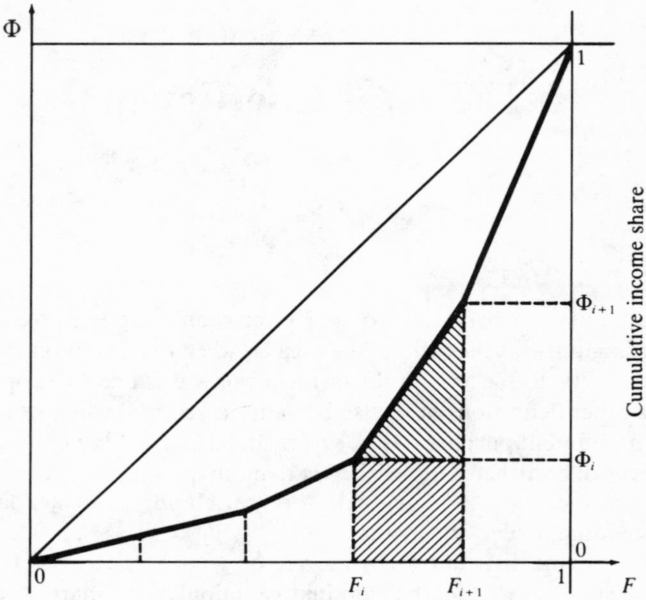

Therefore the Gini coefficient

$$
\begin{aligned}
&= \frac{1}{1/2}\left[\frac{1}{2} - \frac{1}{2}\sum_{i=0}^{n-1}(F_{i+1} - F_i)(\Phi_{i+1} + \Phi_i)\right] \\
&= 1 - \sum_{i=0}^{n-1}(F_{i+1} - F_i)(\Phi_{i+1} + \Phi_i) \\
&= G_1.\,\|
\end{aligned}
$$

Definition 2 (Rao, 1969)

$$
G_2 = \sum_{i=1}^{n-1}(F_i\Phi_{i+1} - F_{i+1}\Phi_i).
$$

It is shown that $G_1 = G_2$.

$$
\begin{aligned}
G_1 &= 1 - \sum_{i=0}^{n-1}(F_{i+1} - F_i)(\Phi_{i+1} + \Phi_i) \\
&= 1 + \sum_{i=0}^{n-1}(F_i\Phi_{i+1} - F_{i+1}\Phi_i) - \sum_{i=0}^{n-1}(F_{i+1}\Phi_{i+1} - F_i\Phi_i).
\end{aligned}
$$

But
$$\sum_{i=0}^{n-1} (F_{i+1}\Phi_{i+1} - F_i\Phi_i) = F_n\Phi_n - F_0\Phi_0 = 1,$$

since $F_n = \Phi_n = 1$, and $F_0 = \Phi_0 = 0$. Therefore

$$G_1 = \sum_{i=1}^{n-1} (F_i\Phi_{i+1} - F_{i+1}\Phi_i)$$
$$= G_2. \|$$

Definition 3 (Kendall and Stuart, 1963)

Kendall and Stuart define the Gini coefficient as one-half the relative mean difference, that is, one-half the average value of absolute differences between *all* pairs of incomes divided by the mean income. Thus,

$$G_3 = \frac{1}{2n^2\mu} \sum_{i=1}^{n} \sum_{j=1}^{n} |y_i - y_j|.$$

This definition implies that $2n^2\mu G_3$ is the sum of every element of the symmetrical $n \times n$ matrix whose (i,j)th element is $|y_i - y_j|$. It is shown that $G_3 = G_2$. Since individuals are labeled in nondescending order of income

$$y_1 \leqslant y_2 \leqslant \ldots \leqslant y_n,$$

G_3 can be written as:

$$G_3 = \frac{1}{2n^2\mu} \left[2 \sum_{i=1}^{n} \sum_{j \leqslant i} (y_i - y_j) \right]$$

$$= \frac{1}{n^2\mu} \sum_{i=1}^{n} \left[iy_i - \sum_{j=1}^{i} y_j \right] = \frac{1}{n^2\mu} \sum_{i=1}^{n} [iy_i - n\mu\Phi_i].$$

Substituting $\dfrac{y_i}{n\mu} = (\Phi_i - \Phi_{i-1})$ and $\dfrac{i}{n} = F_i$,

one has $G_3 = \sum_{i=1}^{n} \left[F_i(\Phi_i - \Phi_{i-1}) - \frac{1}{n}\Phi_i \right] = \sum_{i=1}^{n} \left[\left(F_i - \frac{1}{n} \right)\Phi_i - F_i\Phi_{i-1} \right]$

$$= \sum_{i=1}^{n} (F_{i-1}\Phi_i - F_i\Phi_{i-1}) \qquad \text{since } F_i - F_{i-1} = \frac{1}{n}$$

$$= \sum_{i=1}^{n-1} (F_i\Phi_{i+1} - F_{i+1}\Phi_i)$$

$$= G_2. \|$$

Definition 4 (Sen, 1973*a*)

With individuals labeled in nondescending order of income so that $y_1 \leqslant y_2 \leqslant \ldots \leqslant y_n$, Sen defines the Gini coefficient as

$$G_4 = 1 + \frac{1}{n} - \frac{2}{n^2 \mu}[ny_1 + (n-1)y_2 + \ldots + 2y_{n-1} + y_n]$$

$$= \frac{n+1}{n} - \frac{2}{n^2 \mu} \sum_{i=1}^{n} (n+1-i)y_i.$$

This form makes clear the income-weighting scheme in the welfare function behind the Gini coefficient. Rank-order weights are applied to different people's income levels so that the poorest person receives a weight of n, the ith poorest person a weight of $(n+1-i)$, and the richest (or n^{th} poorest) person a weight of unity. It is shown that $G_3 = G_4$. As before, G_3 can be written as

$$G_3 = \frac{1}{n^2 \mu} \sum_{i=1}^{n} \sum_{j \leqslant i} (y_i - y_j),$$

which is the sum of all the elements of the lower triangular matrix:

$$\begin{bmatrix} (y_1 - y_1) & 0 & \ldots & 0 \\ (y_2 - y_1)(y_2 - y_2) & \ldots & & 0 \\ . & . & & . \\ . & . & & . \\ . & . & & 0 \\ (y_n - y_1)(y_n - y_2) & \ldots & (y_n - y_n) \end{bmatrix}$$

Summing the first element in each bracket horizontally by row gives $\sum_{i=1}^{n} iy_i$; summing the second element in each bracket vertically by column gives $-\sum_{j=1}^{n} (n+1-j)y_j$.

Hence

$$G_3 = \frac{1}{n^2 \mu} \left[\sum_{i=1}^{n} iy_i - \sum_{i=1}^{n} (n+1-i)y_i \right]$$

$$= \frac{1}{n^2 \mu} \left[\sum_{i=1}^{n} (n+1)y_i - 2 \sum_{i=1}^{n} (n+1-i)y_i \right]$$

$$= \frac{n+1}{n} - \frac{2}{n^2 \mu} \sum_{i=1}^{n} (n+1-i)y_i$$

$$= G_4. \parallel$$

Definition 5 (Fei and Ranis, 1974)

Fei and Ranis express the Gini coefficient as a linear transform of the rank index of the income distribution. The rank index R is defined as a weighted average of the *ranks* of persons in the income distribution, where the weights are their income shares. With individuals labeled in non-descending order of income as $y_1 \leqslant y_2 \leqslant \ldots \leqslant y_n$, the rank index R can be written:

$$R = \sum_{i=1}^{n} i y_i \Big/ \sum_{i=1}^{n} y_i.$$

The Gini coefficient G_5 is then defined as

$$G_5 = \frac{2}{n} R - \frac{n+1}{n}$$

$$= \frac{2}{n^2 \mu} [1 y_1 + 2 y_2 + \ldots + n y_n] - \frac{n+1}{n}.$$

It is shown that $G_4 = G_5$.

$$G_4 = \frac{n+1}{n} - \frac{2}{n^2 \mu} \sum_{i=1}^{n} (n+1-i) y_i$$

$$= \frac{n+1}{n} - \frac{2}{n^2 \mu} \left[\sum_{i=1}^{n} (n+1) y_i - \sum_{i=1}^{n} i y_i \right]$$

$$= \frac{2}{n^2 \mu} \sum_{i=1}^{n} i y_i - \left(\frac{n+1}{n} \right)$$

$$= G_5 . \|$$

Up to a multiplicative constant, G_5 can also be expressed as the *covariance* of income and its rank:

$$G_5 = \frac{2}{n \mu} \text{cov}(i, y_i).$$

This is easily checked as follows. By definition of covariance,

$$\text{cov}(i, y_i) = \frac{1}{n} \sum_{i=1}^{n} (i - \bar{i})(y_i - \bar{y})$$

$$= \frac{1}{n} \sum_{i=1}^{n} i y_i - \bar{i}\bar{y},$$

where a bar above a variable denotes its mean. But since

$$\bar{i} = \frac{1}{n} \sum_{i=1}^{n} i = \frac{(n+1)}{2}, \quad \text{and} \quad \bar{y} = \mu,$$

$$\text{cov}(i, y_i) = \frac{1}{n} \sum_{i=1}^{n} iy_i - \frac{(n+1)}{2}\mu.$$

Therefore

$$\frac{2}{n\mu} \text{cov}(i, y_i) = \frac{2}{n^2 \mu} \sum_{i=1}^{n} iy_i - \frac{(n+1)}{n}$$

$$= G_5. \|$$

The equivalence of five alternative definitions of the Gini coefficient has thus been demonstrated.

The Effect of Changes in Certain Incomes

It is often useful to predict the effect on inequality of changes in certain incomes in the distribution. In appendix E general results on this question are proved in terms of Lorenz dominance, but here attention is restricted to the Gini coefficient.

It is clear that if the income of every individual is raised by the same proportionate amount, the Gini coefficient, being mean-independent, will remain unchanged. But if the income of everyone is raised by the same *absolute* amount, say $\varepsilon > 0$, the Gini coefficient will decrease as a straightforward function of ε. This is easily seen. Starting with the distribution $\mathbf{y} = (y_1, y_2, \ldots, y_n)$, let $\mathbf{x} = (x_1, x_2, \ldots, x_n)$ be the distribution with $x_i = (y_i + \varepsilon), i = 1, 2, \ldots, n$. Then if the mean of distribution $\mathbf{y}$ is μ, the mean of distribution $\mathbf{x}$ is $(\mu + \varepsilon)$. Using definition 3 of the Gini coefficient, one has

$$G(\mathbf{x}) = \frac{1}{2n^2(\mu + \varepsilon)} \sum_{i, j} |x_i - x_j|$$

$$= \frac{1}{2n^2(\mu + \varepsilon)} \sum_{i, j} |y_i - y_j|$$

$$= \frac{\mu}{(\mu + \varepsilon)} G(\mathbf{y})$$

$$< G(\mathbf{y}).$$

Indeed the Lorenz curve for distribution $\mathbf{x}$ lies above that for distribution $\mathbf{y}$ (see corollary 3 in appendix E). Distribution $\mathbf{x}$ evidently tends to perfect equality as the absolute amount ε by which everyone's income is raised becomes indefinitely large. From the expression for $G(\mathbf{x})$, it follows that $G(\mathbf{x}) \to 0$ as $\varepsilon \to \infty$.

Now suppose the income of only certain individuals in the distribution is changed. For example, suppose the income of the richest person is raised and the income of the poorest person is reduced. In this case, the ranks of these two persons in the distribution are unaltered and, from the rank index definition, the Gini coefficient can be seen to increase. Indeed the new distribution will show more inequality in the Lorenz sense (see corollary 1 in appendix E). In the general case, let the income of the jth poorest person in the distribution be changed *without* altering this person's rank; the effect on the Gini coefficient can then be measured by using the rank index definition. By definition 5 of the Gini coefficient,

$$G = \frac{2}{n} R - \frac{n+1}{n}$$

where

$$R = \sum_{i=1}^{n} i y_i \Big/ \sum_{i=1}^{n} y_i$$

is the rank index of the income distribution. Differentiating G partially with respect to y_j, one has

$$\frac{\partial G}{\partial y_j} = \frac{2}{n} \left(\frac{\partial R}{\partial y_j} \right)$$

$$= \frac{2}{n} (j - R) \Big/ \sum_{i=1}^{n} y_i$$

which is $\lessgtr 0$ as $j \lessgtr R$. Hence if the jth poorest person's income is raised without altering the rank order of individuals, G falls if $j < R$ and G rises if $j > R$. If the jth poorest person's income is reduced without altering the rank order, then G rises if $j < R$ and G falls if $j > R$.

It can be shown that $(n+1)/2 \leqslant R \leqslant n$.[1] Hence if the income of anyone below the median income level[2] is raised (reduced) without altering the rank order of individuals, the Gini coefficient will fall (rise).

---

1. Since it is always the case that $G \geqslant 0$ (see definition 3 of the Gini coefficient),

$$G = (2/n)R - (n+1)/n \geqslant 0, \quad \text{or} \quad R \geqslant (n+1)/2.$$

And since $i \leqslant n$, it follows that

$$R = \sum_{i=1}^{n} i y_i \Big/ \sum_{i=1}^{n} y_i \leqslant \sum_{i=1}^{n} n y_i \Big/ \sum_{i=1}^{n} y_i = n.$$

Therefore, $(n+1)/2 \leqslant R \leqslant n$.

2. The median income level may be defined as $y_{n/2}$ or $y_{(n+1)/2}$ depending on whether n is even or odd.

The Disaggregation of Income by Factor Components

The personal income of an income recipient is typically the sum of income from several sources (see, for example, the definition of PES income in chapter 2). For simplicity, suppose that personal income is made up of two factor income components only, corresponding to labor and capital in functional income terms. Thus, let personal income y_i be the sum of wage income w_i and property income r_i; that is, $y_i = w_i + r_i$, for $i = 1, \ldots, n$.

What is the relation between the Gini coefficient $G(\mathbf{y})$ for total personal income and the Gini coefficients $G(\mathbf{w})$ and $G(\mathbf{r})$ for wage income and property income, respectively? Let a bar above a variable denote its mean over the population, so that

$$\bar{y} = \frac{1}{n}\sum_{i=1}^{n} y_i, \quad \bar{w} = \frac{1}{n}\sum_{i=1}^{n} w_i, \quad \bar{r} = \frac{1}{n}\sum_{i=1}^{n} r_i; \quad \text{and } \bar{y} = \bar{w} + \bar{r}.$$

Then the following result of Rao (1969) can be stated:

$$G(\mathbf{y}) \leqslant \frac{\bar{w}}{\bar{y}} G(\mathbf{w}) + \frac{\bar{r}}{\bar{y}} G(\mathbf{r}).$$

Definition 3 of the Gini coefficient turns out to be the most convenient one for proving this result. (The proof given by Rao is a little complicated because he uses definition 2.) Thus,

$$2n^2 \bar{y} G(\mathbf{y}) = \sum_{i,j} |y_i - y_j|$$

$$= \sum_{i,j} |w_i - w_j + r_i - r_j|$$

$$\leqslant \sum_{i,j} |w_i - w_j| + \sum_{i,j} |r_i - r_j|$$

with equality if and only if $w_i \lesseqgtr w_j$ whenever $r_i \lesseqgtr r_j$ for all i, j, that is, if and only if the rank order of individuals by wage income is *identical* to their rank order by property income. Applying the definitions of $G(\mathbf{w})$ and $G(\mathbf{r})$, it follows that

$$2n^2 \bar{y} G(\mathbf{y}) \leqslant 2n^2 \bar{w} G(\mathbf{w}) + 2n^2 \bar{r} G(\mathbf{r}).$$

Hence
$$G(\mathbf{y}) \leqslant \frac{\bar{w}}{\bar{y}} G(\mathbf{w}) + \frac{\bar{r}}{\bar{y}} G(\mathbf{r}). \;\|$$

Thus the Gini coefficient for total income is less than or equal to a weighted average of the Gini coefficients for wage income and property income, where the weights are the *shares* of wage and property income in total income, respectively. The result obviously generalizes to more than two factor income components. Information on the distribution of factor income components therefore allows an upper bound to be placed on the distribution of total personal income. It can be shown that the larger the rank correlations between factor income components and total income, the closer is the overall Gini to the weighted average of factor income Ginis. Equality obtains if and only if the rank ordering of individuals is the same by *every* component of income.

On the Decomposition of the Gini Coefficient

An inequality index is defined to be additively decomposable in the weak sense (see chapter 3) if it can be written as the sum of a between-group component and a within-group component where (1) the between-group component is the value of the inequality index when each member of a group receives the mean income of the group; and (2) the within-group component is a weighted sum of the inequality indices for each group where the weights depend only on the population or income shares of the group, or both. It is shown that, in general, the Gini coefficient is *not* decomposable according to this definition.

Divide the population into two subgroups, labeled x and y, respectively.[3] Let there be n_x individuals in the x subgroup with incomes $x_i(i = 1, \ldots, n_x)$ and mean income μ_x; let there be n_y individuals in the y subgroup with incomes $y_j(j = 1, \ldots, n_y)$ and mean income μ_y. Further, let n be the size of the whole population and μ its mean income. Then

$$\mu_x = \frac{1}{n_x} \sum_{i=1}^{n_x} x_i, \quad \mu_y = \frac{1}{n_y} \sum_{j=1}^{n_y} y_j, \quad n = n_x + n_y, \quad \text{and } n\mu = n_x\mu_x + n_y\mu_y.$$

What is the relation between the Gini coefficient G for the whole population and the Gini coefficients G_x and G_y for the two subgroups? To study this, definition 3 of the Gini coefficient is most useful:

$$G_y = \frac{1}{2n_y^2\mu_y} \sum_{j=1}^{n_y} \sum_{j'=1}^{n_y} |y_j - y_{j'}|.$$

It is convenient to think of the absolute values $|y_j - y_{j'}|$ as the elements of a symmetrical matrix. For the whole population of $n = (n_x + n_y)$ individuals,

---

3. Results for partitions of the population into more than two subgroups follow by induction.

this matrix can be written in an obvious notation as follows:

	$x_{i'}$	$y_{j'}$
x_i	$\lvert x_i - x_{i'} \rvert$	$\lvert x_i - y_{j'} \rvert$
y_j	$\lvert y_j - x_{i'} \rvert$	$\lvert y_j - y_{j'} \rvert$

The expression $2n^2\mu G$ for the whole population is the sum of all the elements of this matrix. This sum can be disaggregated as follows:

$2n^2\mu G$ = Sum of absolute differences between *all* pairs of incomes

$$= \sum_{i,\,i'} \lvert x_i - x_{i'} \rvert + \sum_{j,\,j'} \lvert y_j - y_{j'} \rvert + 2\sum_{i,\,j} \lvert x_i - y_j \rvert$$

$$= 2n_x^2 \mu_x G_x + 2n_y^2 \mu_y G_y + 2\sum_{i,\,j} \lvert x_i - y_j \rvert.$$

Thus, $$G = \left(\frac{n_x}{n}\right)\left(\frac{n_x \mu_x}{n\mu}\right) G_x + \left(\frac{n_y}{n}\right)\left(\frac{n_y \mu_y}{n\mu}\right) G_y + \frac{1}{n^2 \mu} \sum_{i,\,j} \lvert x_i - y_j \rvert. \quad (B.1)$$

The first two terms in this disaggregation of the Gini coefficient can indeed be taken to represent the within-group component: they are a weighted sum of the subgroup Gini coefficients, where the weights are the subgroup population share times income share.[4] But it is by no means clear that the third term measures the between-group component. By definition, the between-group component G_0 is the value of the Gini coefficient for the distribution in which n_x individuals receive income μ_x and n_y individuals receive income μ_y. It is easily verified that

$$G_0 = \frac{n_x n_y}{n^2 \mu} \lvert \mu_x - \mu_y \rvert.$$

---

4. Thus the weights on the subgroup Gini coefficients sum to a number *less* than unity; the definition of weak decomposability does not require the subgroup weights to sum to unity.

The third term in the disaggregation (B.1) is in general greater than G_0:

$$\sum_{i=1}^{n_x} \sum_{j=1}^{n_y} |x_i - y_j| \geq \sum_{i=1}^{n_x} \left| \sum_{j=1}^{n_y} (x_i - y_j) \right|$$

with equality if and only if each x_i is either larger or smaller than *all* the y_j's

$$= \sum_{i=1}^{n_x} |n_y x_i - n_y \mu_y| \quad \text{since} \quad \sum_{j=1}^{n_y} y_j = n_y \mu_y$$

$$= n_y \sum_{i=1}^{n_x} |x_i - \mu_y|$$

$$\geq n_y \left| \sum_{i=1}^{n_x} (x_i - \mu_y) \right|$$

with equality if and only if *all* the x_i's are either larger or smaller than μ_y

$$= n_y |n_x \mu_x - n_x \mu_y| \quad \text{since} \quad \sum_{i=1}^{n_x} x_i = n_x \mu_x$$

$$= n_x n_y |\mu_x - \mu_y|.$$

Thus
$$\sum_{i=1}^{n_x} \sum_{j=1}^{n_y} |x_i - y_j| \geq n_x n_y |\mu_x - \mu_y|$$

and equality obtains if and only if *all* the x_i's are either larger or smaller than *all* the y_j's. Therefore,

$$\frac{1}{n^2 \mu} \sum_{i,j} |x_i - y_j| \geq \frac{n_x n_y}{n^2 \mu} |\mu_x - \mu_y| = G_0.$$

Hence the third term in the disaggregation of the Gini coefficient is generally greater than the between-group component G_0. Only in very special circumstances is it actually equal to G_0, namely, when all $x_i (i = 1, \ldots, n_x)$ are either larger or smaller than all $y_j (j = 1, \ldots, n_y)$. In other words, the x and y subgroups must be *nonoverlapping* for the third term in the Gini disaggregation (B.1) to measure the between-group component of inequality. When the subgroup distributions do *not* overlap, the Gini coefficient can indeed be decomposed into the sum of a within-group component and a between-group component.[5] But in general all that

5. An obvious example of *nonoverlapping* subgroup distributions occurs when the population is divided into the two subgroups of the *poor* and *nonpoor* by means of a poverty line (see "The Sen Poverty Measure" in chapter 4). In this case, the overall Gini G can be built up from the subgroup Ginis G_p and G_{np} for the poor and nonpoor, respectively, and the subgroup population and income shares. Using the notation of chapter 4, we can substitute

can be asserted is that

$$G \geqslant \left(\frac{n_x}{n}\right)\left(\frac{n_x \mu_x}{n\mu}\right) G_x + \left(\frac{n_y}{n}\right)\left(\frac{n_y \mu_y}{n\mu}\right) G_y + \frac{n_x n_y}{n^2 \mu}\left|\mu_x - \mu_y\right|. \qquad \text{(B.2)}$$

It has been shown that the Gini coefficient is not additively decomposable in the weak sense. Hence it is also not decomposable with the within-group component defined as a population or income-weighted *average* (not just *sum*) of the inequality indices for each group—unlike the two Theil measures (see appendix C). But can a lower bound at least be placed on the overall Gini in terms of a population or income weighted *average* of subgroup Ginis? In other words, is it the case that

$$G \geqslant \left(\frac{n_x}{n}\right) G_x + \left(\frac{n_y}{n}\right) G_y \qquad \text{(B.3)}$$

or

$$G \geqslant \left(\frac{n_x \mu_x}{n\mu}\right) G_x + \left(\frac{n_y \mu_y}{n\mu}\right) G_y. \qquad \text{(B.4)}$$

These lower bounds for G can be better than that in (B.2). For instance, when $\mu_x = \mu_y$ and all inequality arises from inequality within subgroups, the right-hand side of (B.2) is clearly smaller than the right-hand side of either (B.3) or (B.4). Since the weights in (B.2) are population share *times* income share, which is less than either population share or income share by itself, the lower bounds in (B.3) and (B.4) will be better than the lower bound in (B.2) when $\mu_x = \mu_y$. The bound in (B.2) will be better, however, when $G_x = G_y = 0$, and all inequality arises from between-group differences in income. In this case, the right-hand side of (B.2) gives the correct value for the Gini coefficient, that is,

$$G = \frac{n_x n_y}{n^2 \mu}\left|\mu_x - \mu_y\right|,$$

while the right-hand sides of (B.3) and (B.4) both give something worse, namely zero.

To prove the inequalities (B.3) and (B.4), definition 3 of the Gini

---

$n_x = q$, $\mu_x = v$, $G_x = G_p$; $n_y = (n-q)$, $\mu_y = (n\mu - qv)/(n-q)$, $G_y = G_{np}$. Hence,

$$G = \left(\frac{q}{n}\right)\left(\frac{qv}{n\mu}\right) G_p + \left(\frac{n-q}{n}\right)\left(\frac{n\mu - qv}{n\mu}\right) G_{np} + \left(\frac{q}{n}\right) - \left(\frac{qv}{n\mu}\right).$$

From this decomposition, the Gini coefficient for a particular subgroup (for example, G_{np}) can be inferred from the overall Gini (G), the other subgroup Ginis (here simply G_p), and the subgroup population and income shares. Thus the Gini coefficient for the nonpoor in Peninsular Malaysia can be computed from the information in tables 3-8 and 4-2.

coefficient is used together with the identity

$$|y_j - y_{j'}| \equiv y_j + y_{j'} - 2\min(y_j, y_{j'}).$$

Thus

$$G_y = \frac{1}{2n_y^2 \mu_y} \sum_{j=1}^{n_y} \sum_{j'=1}^{n_y} |y_j - y_{j'}|$$

$$= \frac{1}{2n_y^2 \mu_y} \sum_{j, j'} [y_j + y_{j'} - 2\min(y_j, y_{j'})]$$

$$= 1 - \frac{1}{n_y^2 \mu_y} \sum_{j, j'} \min(y_j, y_{j'}).$$

It follows that $\quad \sum\limits_{j, j'} \min(y_j, y_{j'}) = n_y^2 \mu_y (1 - G_y).$ (B.5)

Similarly, $\qquad \sum\limits_{i, i'} \min(x_i, x_{i'}) = n_x^2 \mu_x (1 - G_x).$ (B.6)

Again the terms $\min(y_j, y_{j'})$ can be thought of as the elements of a symmetrical matrix. For the whole population of $n = (n_x + n_y)$ individuals this matrix can be represented as:

	$x_{i'}$	$y_{j'}$
x_i	$\min(x_i, x_{i'})$	$\min(x_i, y_{j'})$
y_j	$\min(y_j, x_{i'})$	$\min(y_j, y_{j'})$

The sum of the minima over *all* pairs of incomes in the population is just the sum of the elements of this matrix. Thus

$$n^2 \mu (1 - G) = \sum_{i, i'} \min(x_i, x_{i'}) + \sum_{j, j'} \min(y_j, y_{j'})$$

$$+ \sum_{i, j} \min(x_i, y_{j'}) + \sum_{i', j} \min(x_{i'}, y_j)$$

$$= n_x^2 \mu_x (1 - G_x) + n_y^2 \mu_y (1 - G_y) + 2\sum_{i, j} \min(x_i, y_j).$$ (B.7)

Hence, $2\sum_{i,j} \min(x_i, y_j) = n^2 \mu(1 - G) - n_x^2 \mu_x(1 - G_x) - n_y^2 \mu_y(1 - G_y)$.

To prove the inequalities (B.3) and (B.4), I make use of the following general result (Zagier, 1977):

Lemma: $2\alpha\beta \sum_{i,j} \min(x_i, y_j) \leqslant \alpha^2 \sum_{i,i'} \min(x_i, x_{i'}) + \beta^2 \sum_{j,j'} \min(y_j, y_{j'})$ for any real numbers α, β.

Proof: For $t \geqslant 0$, define the characteristic functions $\gamma_i(t)$ and $\delta_j(t)$ corresponding to each income level x_i in the x subgroup and each income level y_j in the y subgroup as follows:

$$\gamma_i(t) = \chi_{[0, x_i]}(t) = \begin{cases} 1 & \text{if } t \leqslant x_i \\ 0 & \text{if } t > x_i \end{cases} \text{ for } i = 1, \ldots, n_x$$

$$\delta_j(t) = \chi_{[0, y_j]}(t) = \begin{cases} 1 & \text{if } t \leqslant y_j \\ 0 & \text{if } t > y_j \end{cases} \text{ for } j = 1, \ldots, n_y.$$

Let $\xi(t) = \sum_{i=1}^{n_x} \gamma_i(t)$

and $\eta(t) = \sum_{j=1}^{n_y} \delta_j(t)$.

Thus $\xi(t)$ is the number of individuals in the x subgroup with income greater than or equal to t, and $\eta(t)$ is the number of individuals in the y subgroup with income greater than or equal to t.

It is now shown that

$$\int_0^\infty \xi(t)\eta(t)dt = \sum_{i,j} \min(x_i, y_j).$$

By definition, $\xi(t)\eta(t) = \sum_{i,j} \gamma_i(t)\delta_j(t)$

and $\gamma_i(t)\delta_j(t) = \begin{cases} 1 \text{ if } t \leqslant x_i \text{ and } t \leqslant y_j, \text{ that is, if } t \leqslant \min(x_i, y_j) \\ 0 \text{ otherwise.} \end{cases}$

Thus $\int_0^\infty \xi(t)\eta(t)dt = \int_0^\infty \left[\sum_{i,j} \gamma_i(t)\delta_j(t) \right] dt$

$= \sum_{i,j} \int_0^\infty \gamma_i(t)\delta_j(t)dt$,   reversing the operations of integration and summation,

$= \sum_{i,j} \min(x_i, y_j)$.

Similarly, it follows that

$$\int_0^\infty \xi(t)^2 dt = \sum_{i,\,i'} \min(x_i, x_{i'})$$

and

$$\int_0^\infty \eta(t)^2 dt = \sum_{j,\,j'} \min(y_j, y_{j'}).$$

Therefore, $\alpha^2 \sum_{i,\,i'} \min(x_i, x_{i'}) + \beta^2 \sum_{j,\,j'} \min(y_j, y_{j'}) - 2\alpha\beta \sum_{i,\,j} \min(x_i, y_j)$

$$= \int_0^\infty [\alpha\xi(t) - \beta\eta(t)]^2 dt$$

$$\geqslant 0. \|$$

Note that the value of the integral is zero if and only if $\xi(t)/\eta(t) = \beta/\alpha$ for $t \geqslant 0$. This happens if and only if at each income level the number of individuals in the x subgroup is a constant multiple (β/α) of the number of individuals in the y subgroup. Hence the integral is zero if and only if one subgroup distribution is a replica of the other and, apart from total population size, the two are identical.

Substituting the expressions (B.5), (B.6), and (B.7) in the statement of the lemma, the inequality becomes:

$$\alpha^2 n_x^2 \mu_x(1 - G_x) + \beta^2 n_y^2 \mu_y(1 - G_y) \geqslant \alpha\beta[n^2\mu(1 - G) - n_x^2\mu_x(1 - G_x) - n_y^2\mu_y(1 - G_y)]$$

or $\alpha(\alpha + \beta)n_x^2 \mu_x(1 - G_x) + \beta(\alpha + \beta)n_y^2 \mu_y(1 - G_y) \geqslant \alpha\beta n^2\mu(1 - G)$

and hence, $\alpha n_x^2 \mu_x(1 - G_x) + \beta n_y^2 \mu_y(1 - G_y) \geqslant \dfrac{1}{(1/\alpha) + (1/\beta)} n^2\mu(1 - G).$

This general inequality relating subgroup Gini coefficients and the overall Gini coefficient is valid for *all* real numbers α and β. Substituting

$$\alpha = \frac{1}{n_x\mu_x} \quad \text{and} \quad \beta = \frac{1}{n_y\mu_y},$$

one gets $n_x(1 - G_x) + n_y(1 - G_y) \geqslant n(1 - G),$

that is,

$$G \geqslant \left(\frac{n_x}{n}\right) G_x + \left(\frac{n_y}{n}\right) G_y. \tag{B.3}$$

Substituting $\alpha = \dfrac{1}{n_x}$ and $\beta = \dfrac{1}{n_y}$, one gets

$$n_x\mu_x(1 - G_x) + n_y\mu_y(1 - G_y) \geqslant n\mu(1 - G),$$

that is,
$$G \geqslant \left(\frac{n_x \mu_x}{n\mu}\right) G_x + \left(\frac{n_y \mu_y}{n\mu}\right) G_y. \tag{B.4}$$

Hence it has been shown that the overall Gini is greater than or equal to both a population-weighted average of subgroup Ginis and an income-weighted average of subgroup Ginis.[6] Strict equality obtains in these Gini inequalities only if the subgroup distributions are identical. Otherwise, even with $\mu_x = \mu_y$, that is, with between-group inequality zero, the overall Gini will be strictly greater than the population- or income-weighted average of subgroup Ginis.

6. Zagier (1977) provides various other bounds for the Gini coefficient and a characterization of the class of decomposable inequality indices.

C

The Decomposition of Three Inequality Measures

IN THIS APPENDIX the decomposition of three inequality measures is considered: the Theil entropy index T, the Theil second measure L, and the variance of log-income V. Empirical decompositions have been performed for these three measures in the main text. The exposition here is based on the PES data format actually used in the computations. The basic data array is in the form of a table (similar to table 3-2) showing the joint distribution of individuals by income and some other variable (such as race) according to which the decomposition is desired. In other words, there is a matrix which shows the absolute frequencies n_{ij} of individuals in each cell (i, j). Let the columns j of the matrix refer to different income classes, and the rows i to different values of the decomposition variable (such as race). Assume that each individual in the jth income class (column) receives the mean income y_j of that class (this is the standard assumption in all the tables of the text).

The Theil Entropy Index T

The Theil entropy index T can be defined in terms of this data matrix and notation. Since there are n_{ij} persons in cell (i, j), each assumed to be receiving income y_j (the mean of the jth income class), total income y_{ij} in cell (i, j) is $n_{ij}y_j$. Hence the total income of all persons is

$$Y = \sum_i \sum_j n_{ij} y_j$$
$$= \sum_i Y_i$$

where $Y_i = \Sigma_j \, n_{ij} y_j$ is the total income of the ith group. The total population

327

size n is given by

$$n = \sum_i \sum_j n_{ij}$$

$$= \sum_i n_i$$

where $n_i = \Sigma_j \, n_{ij}$ is the population size of the ith group. The Theil index T for this distribution is then given by (see appendix A)

$$T = \sum_i \sum_j \frac{y_{ij}}{Y} \log \frac{y_{ij}/Y}{n_{ij}/n}$$

where y_{ij}/Y is the income share of cell (i, j), and n_{ij}/n the population share.

Consider the decomposition of the Theil index T into between-group i and within-group i components:

$$T = \sum_i \sum_j \frac{y_{ij}}{Y} \log \frac{y_{ij}/Y}{n_{ij}/n}$$

$$= \sum_i \frac{Y_i}{Y} \sum_j \frac{y_{ij}}{Y_i} \left[\log \frac{y_{ij}/Y_i}{n_{ij}/n_i} + \log \frac{Y_i/n_i}{Y/n} \right]$$

$$= \sum_i \frac{Y_i}{Y} \left[\sum_j \frac{y_{ij}}{Y_i} \log \frac{y_{ij}/Y_i}{n_{ij}/n_i} \right] + \sum_i \frac{Y_i}{Y} \log \frac{Y_i/Y}{n_i/n}$$

since $\sum_j \dfrac{y_{ij}}{Y_i} = 1$ for each i.

Hence, $$T = \sum_i \left[\frac{Y_i}{Y} \right] T_i + \sum_i \frac{Y_i}{Y} \log \frac{Y_i/Y}{n_i/n} \tag{C.1}$$

where $$T_i = \sum_j \frac{y_{ij}}{Y_i} \log \frac{y_{ij}/Y_i}{n_{ij}/n_i}.$$

Equation (C.1) says that the Theil entropy index T can be decomposed into two terms:

$$T = T_W + T_B$$

where $$T_W = \sum_i \left[\frac{Y_i}{Y} \right] T_i$$

is a weighted average of *within-group* i Theil indices T_i, the weights being equal to the *income shares* Y_i/Y of the groups, and

$$T_B = \sum_i \frac{Y_i}{Y} \log \frac{Y_i/Y}{n_i/n}$$

is the *between-group i* Theil index of group income and population shares Y_i/Y and n_i/n, respectively. T_W is called the within-group component, and T_B is called the between-group component.

The between-group contribution is then defined as the ratio of the between-group component T_B to the overall Theil index T. The within-group contribution is defined as (T_W/T).

The Theil Second Measure L

Theil's second measure L simply reverses the roles of population share and income share in the formula for the entropy index T (see appendix A). Using the same notation as for T, the formula for L can be written as

$$L = \sum_i \sum_j \frac{n_{ij}}{n} \log \frac{n_{ij}/n}{y_{ij}/Y}.$$

This reduces to

$$L = \log \frac{Y}{n} - \sum_i \sum_j \frac{n_{ij}}{n} \log y_j,$$

which is the logarithm of the arithmetic mean income minus the logarithm of the geometric mean income.

Now consider the decomposition of the Theil measure L into between-group i and within-group i components:

$$L = \sum_i \frac{n_i}{n} \sum_j \frac{n_{ij}}{n_i} \left[\log \frac{n_{ij}/n_i}{y_{ij}/Y_i} + \log \frac{n_i/n}{Y_i/Y} \right]$$

$$= \sum_i \frac{n_i}{n} \left[\sum_j \frac{n_{ij}}{n_i} \log \frac{n_{ij}/n_i}{y_{ij}/Y_i} \right] + \sum_i \frac{n_i}{n} \log \frac{n_i/n}{Y_i/Y},$$

since $\sum_j \frac{n_{ij}}{n_i} = 1$ for each i.

Hence,
$$L = \sum_i \left[\frac{n_i}{n} \right] L_i + \sum_i \frac{n_i}{n} \log \frac{n_i/n}{Y_i/Y} \tag{C.2}$$

where
$$L_i = \sum_j \frac{n_{ij}}{n_i} \log \frac{n_{ij}/n_i}{y_{ij}/Y_i}.$$

Equation (C.2) says that the Theil second measure L can be decomposed into two terms:

$$L = L_W + L_B$$

where
$$L_W = \sum_i \left[\frac{n_i}{n}\right] L_i$$

is a weighted average of *within-group i* Theil measures L_i, the weights being equal to the *population shares* n_i/n of the groups, and

$$L_B = \sum_i \frac{n_i}{n} \log \frac{n_i/n}{Y_i/Y}$$

is the *between-group i* Theil measure of group population and income shares n_i/n and Y_i/Y, respectively. L_W is called the within-group component, and L_B is called the between-group component.

The between-group contribution is then defined as the ratio of the between-group component L_B to the overall Theil measure L. The within-group contribution is defined as (L_W/L).

The Variance of Log-Income *V*

The variance of the logarithm of income, just like the variance of any variable, can be decomposed into the sum of a between-group and a within-group component. Defining $x_{ij} = \log y_j$ (the same for all i), the total variance of x_{ij} can be written as

$$V = \frac{1}{n} \sum_i \sum_j n_{ij}(x_{ij} - x_{..})^2$$

where $x_{..} = \frac{1}{n}\Sigma_i\Sigma_j n_{ij}x_{ij}$ is the mean of x_{ij} over i and j.

Let $x_{i.} = \Sigma_j n_{ij}x_{ij}/\Sigma_j n_{ij}$ be the mean of x_{ij} over j, and rewrite the expression for V as

$$V = \frac{1}{n} \sum_i \sum_j n_{ij}[(x_{ij} - x_{i.}) + (x_{i.} - x_{..})]^2$$

$$= \frac{1}{n} \sum_i \sum_j [n_{ij}(x_{ij} - x_{i.})^2 + n_{ij}(x_{i.} - x_{..})^2 + 2n_{ij}(x_{ij} - x_{i.})(x_{i.} - x_{..})]$$

$$= \sum_i \frac{n_i}{n} \left[\sum_j \frac{n_{ij}}{n_i}(x_{ij} - x_{i.})^2\right] + \sum_i \frac{n_i}{n}(x_{i.} - x_{..})^2$$

$$= \sum_i \left[\frac{n_i}{n}\right] V_i + \sum_i \frac{n_i}{n}(x_{i.} - x_{..})^2 \tag{C.3}$$

where $V_i = \Sigma_j (n_{ij}/n_i)(x_{ij} - x_{i.})^2$.

The cross-product term in the expansion vanishes because $(x_{i.} - x_{..})$ is constant in the j summation, and $\Sigma_j n_{ij}(x_{ij} - x_{i.}) = 0$ for each i by definition of the mean $x_{i.}$.

Equation (C.3) says that the variance V can be decomposed into two terms:

$$V = V_W + V_B$$

where

$$V_W = \sum_i \left[\frac{n_i}{n}\right] V_i$$

is a weighted average of *within-group i* variances V_i, the weights being equal to the *population shares* n_i/n of the groups, and $V_B = \Sigma_i (n_i/n)(x_{i.} - x_{..})^2$ is the *between-group i* variance of group means $x_{i.}$.[1] V_W is called the within-group component, and V_B is called the between-group component.

The between-group contribution is then defined as the ratio of the between-group component V_B to the total variance V. The within-group contribution is defined as V_W/V.

The variance decomposition (C.3) holds for *any* variable x whether or not this is equal to log-income. The reason for choosing $x = \log y$ was to obtain a mean-independent measure of inequality. Another transformation of y which gives a mean-independent measure is $x = y/\mu$, where μ is the overall arithmetic mean. The variance of (y/μ) is known as the squared coefficient of variation, and its decomposition formula can be obtained from (C.3) (see also chapter 3). The between-group component is the squared coefficient of variation of the group arithmetic means, and the within-group component is a weighted sum of squared within-group coefficients of variation—but the weights, which depend on group population *and* income shares, no longer add up to unity.

Comparison of the Decompositions

In the foregoing it was seen that the two Theil measures and the variance of log-income are nicely decomposable into between- and within-group components. But the between-group contributions are generally different according to the three measures. The measures emphasize different aspects of the distribution, and there is no reason to expect the contribution by one measure to be the same as that by another measure. The Theil L measure, for instance, is very sensitive to changes at low income levels, whereas the Theil T index is not. Thus the within-group component according to the

1. Note that when $x_{ij} = \log y_j$, $x_{i.}$ is the logarithm of the *geometric* (not arithmetic) mean income of group i.

Theil L measure can be made indefinitely large relative to the between-group component by redistributing income *within* a group so that one person's income tends to zero.[2] Hence the between-group contribution by the Theil L measure can be made as small as one likes by letting the income of one person in a multiperson group tend to zero.

There is a further point concerning the decompositions. As derived, the contributions are purely *descriptive*. There is no attempt to base the decompositions on statistical theory. Nor is it easily possible to do so for the two Theil measures, since they do not follow known statistical distributions. By contrast, the decomposition of the variance of log-income can be based on standard analysis of variance, since the ratio of the between-group to the within-group variance is known to follow an F *distribution*. Instead of merely quantifying the between-group contribution, therefore, it is also possible to test it for statistical significance. (With the large number of degrees of freedom in the empirical decompositions in the text, however, all the between-group contributions turn out to be statistically significant.)

---

2. This transfer from poor to rich within a group leaves the between-group component constant, while increasing the within-group component and the overall value of the measure.

D

Lorenz Dominance
and Inequality

IN THIS APPENDIX I first prove Atkinson's celebrated theorem about the ranking of income distributions in terms of welfare, Lorenz dominance, and the principle of transfers. Using Atkinson's theorem, I then go on to show that Lorenz dominance is a useful property to establish even when welfare comparisons are not possible between the underlying distributions— but the purpose is purely a positive or descriptive comparison of inequality.[1]

It is easier here to deal with discrete distributions, so let the vector $\mathbf{y} = (y_1, y_2, \ldots, y_n)$ denote the ordered income distribution $\mathbf{y}: 0 \leqslant y_1 \leqslant y_2 \leqslant \ldots \leqslant y_n$ among n individuals (or households). The Lorenz curve $L_y(.)$ of this distribution can be defined at the discrete points (i/n), for $i = 0, 1, \ldots, n$, as follows:

$$L_y(0) = 0$$

$$L_y(i/n) = \sum_{k=1}^{i} y_k \bigg/ \sum_{k=1}^{n} y_k \qquad \text{for } i = 1, 2, \ldots, n.$$

For all other points p in the interval $[0, 1]$, $L_y(p)$ is defined by linear interpolation.

Now suppose $\mathbf{x}$ and $\mathbf{y}$ are two ordered distributions with the same number of individuals n and the same total income

$$\sum_{k=1}^{n} x_k = \sum_{k=1}^{n} y_k.$$

1. See Sen (1973a) for a distinction between positive and normative comparisons and measures of inequality.

Consider three criteria for ranking these income distributions:
(i) $\mathbf{x} \succeq_L \mathbf{y}$, that is, $\mathbf{x}$ Lorenz-dominates $\mathbf{y}$, which means that

$$L_x(i/n) \geqslant L_y(i/n) \qquad \text{for } i = 0, 1, \ldots, n.$$

(ii) $\mathbf{x} \succeq_T \mathbf{y}$, which means that distribution $\mathbf{x}$ can be obtained from distribution $\mathbf{y}$ by a finite sequence of income transfers from richer to poorer individuals, where each transfer preserves the relative ranks of the two individuals affected. This criterion is the ranking of distributions $\mathbf{x}$ and $\mathbf{y}$ according to the *principle of transfers*. Given an ordered distribution $\mathbf{y}$, a *single* progressive transfer d from a richer individual j to a poorer individual $i (y_i < y_j)$ which preserves their relative ranks leads to a new distribution $\mathbf{x}$ defined as:

$$\begin{aligned}
x_k &= y_k \qquad k \neq i, j \\
x_i &= y_i + d \\
x_j &= y_j - d
\end{aligned}$$

where $x_i \leqslant x_j$, that is, $d \leqslant (y_j - y_i)/2$.[2]
(iii) $\mathbf{x} \succeq_U \mathbf{y}$, which means that $\Sigma_{k=1}^n U(x_k) \geqslant \Sigma_{k=1}^n U(y_k)$ for *all* nondecreasing concave functions $U(y)$. This criterion says that distribution $\mathbf{x}$ yields at least as much welfare as distribution $\mathbf{y}$ for any additively separable, symmetric, nondecreasing, concave social welfare function $\Sigma U(y)$.

It may not always be possible to rank two arbitrary distributions $\mathbf{x}$ and $\mathbf{y}$ by criterion (i), (ii), or (iii).[3] However, when it *is* possible to rank them by one criterion, it will also be possible to rank them by the other criteria, and in that case all three criteria will give the *same* ranking. This is Atkinson's theorem.

Theorem (Atkinson, 1970): The ranking of income distributions $\mathbf{x}$ and $\mathbf{y}$ by criteria (i), (ii), and (iii) is *identical*. Formally, the following statements are equivalent:

(i) $\mathbf{x} \succeq_L \mathbf{y}$
(ii) $\mathbf{x} \succeq_T \mathbf{y}$
(iii) $\mathbf{x} \succeq_U \mathbf{y}$.

---

2. Given symmetry, nothing would be altered if, instead of imposing the condition that the income transfer preserves the relative ranks of individuals i and j, that is, $d \leqslant (y_j - y_i)/2$, the size of the transfer was limited to their income difference, that is, $d \leqslant (y_j - y_i)$. This is the more usual way of defining $\mathbf{x} \succeq_T \mathbf{y}$ (see Atkinson, 1970; Sen, 1973a; and Dasgupta, Sen, and Starrett, 1973).

3. In other words, the criteria $\succeq_L$, $\succeq_U$, and $\succeq_T$ provide only a *partial* ordering among distributions with the same number of people and the same total income.

Proof: It is shown that (i) $\Rightarrow$ (ii) $\Rightarrow$ (iii) $\Rightarrow$ (i). The proof given here is adapted from Rothschild and Stiglitz (1973).

$$\frac{\text{(i)} \Rightarrow \text{(ii)}}{\mathbf{x} \succsim_L \mathbf{y} \Rightarrow \mathbf{x} \succsim_T \mathbf{y}}$$

Since $\mathbf{x}$ and $\mathbf{y}$ have the same total income, $\mathbf{x} \succsim_L \mathbf{y}$ implies that

$$\sum_{k=1}^{i} x_k \geq \sum_{k=1}^{i} y_k \qquad \text{for } i = 1, 2, \ldots, n.$$

Let i be the *first* integer for which $x_i > y_i$, so that $x_k = y_k$ for $k \leq (i-1)$. Define a new distribution $\mathbf{x}(i)$ from $\mathbf{x}$ as follows. Transfer an amount $(x_i - y_i)$ from individual i to individual $(i+1)$; this lowers i's income to y_i and raises $(i+1)$'s income to $x_{i+1} + (x_i - y_i)$. Then the new distribution $\mathbf{x}(i)$ has the properties:

$$\begin{aligned}
x_k(i) &= x_k = y_k & \text{for} \quad k \leq (i-1) \\
x_i(i) &= x_i - (x_i - y_i) = y_i \\
x_{i+1}(i) &= x_{i+1} + (x_i - y_i) \\
x_k(i) &= x_k & \text{for} \quad k > (i+1).
\end{aligned}$$

Thus $\mathbf{x}(i)$ agrees with $\mathbf{y}$ in one more place than $\mathbf{x}$—the first i places instead of the first $(i-1)$ places—and it is still true that $\mathbf{x}(i) \succsim_L \mathbf{y}$ since

$$\sum_{k=1}^{i+1} x_k(i) = \sum_{k=1}^{i+1} x_k.$$

The same procedure may be applied to $\mathbf{x}(i)$ to find an income transfer from poor to rich which produces a new distribution which agrees with $\mathbf{y}$ in at least one more place than $\mathbf{x}(i)$ and still Lorenz-dominates $\mathbf{y}$. Continuing in this manner, the distribution $\mathbf{y}$ is eventually obtained from $\mathbf{x}$ by a sequence of at most $(n-1)$ transfers from poor individuals to rich. Hence $\mathbf{x} \succsim_T \mathbf{y}$.

$$\frac{\text{(ii)} \Rightarrow \text{(iii)}}{\mathbf{x} \succsim_T \mathbf{y} \Rightarrow \mathbf{x} \succsim_U \mathbf{y}}$$

Since $\mathbf{x} \succsim_T \mathbf{y}$ means that $\mathbf{x}$ can be obtained from $\mathbf{y}$ by a finite sequence of income transfers from rich individuals to poor, it will suffice to show that a single transfer from rich to poor does not lower welfare. Without loss of generality, suppose that $\mathbf{x}$ is obtained from $\mathbf{y}$ by a single transfer d from individual 2 to individual 1, where $d \leq (y_2 - y_1)/2$. Then,

$$\begin{aligned}
x_1 &= y_1 + d \\
x_2 &= y_2 - d \\
x_k &= y_k & \text{for} \quad k \geq 3.
\end{aligned}$$

Let $U(y)$ be any nondecreasing concave function, as shown in figure D-1.

Figure D-1. *The Concave Function $U(y)$*

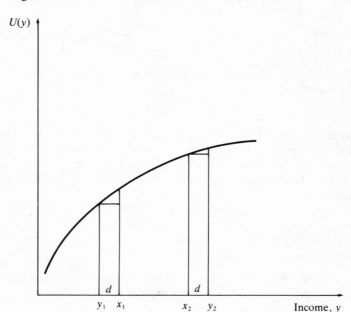

Given the relation between x_1, x_2 and y_1, y_2, it is obvious from the concavity of $U(y)$ that $[U(x_1) - U(y_1)] \geqslant [U(y_2) - U(x_2)]$. Thus

$$[U(x_1) + U(x_2)] \geqslant [U(y_1) + U(y_2)],$$

and therefore

$$\sum_{i=1}^{n} U(x_i) \geqslant \sum_{i=1}^{n} U(y_i).$$

Hence $\mathbf{x} \succsim_U \mathbf{y}$.

$$\underline{\text{(iii)} \Rightarrow \text{(i)}}$$

$$\mathbf{x} \succsim_U \mathbf{y} \Rightarrow \mathbf{x} \succsim_L \mathbf{y}$$

$\mathbf{x} \succsim_U \mathbf{y}$ implies that $\Sigma_{k=1}^{n} U(x_k) \geqslant \Sigma_{k=1}^{n} U(y_k)$ for any nondecreasing concave function $U(y)$. Consider the function: $m_z(y) = \min(y - z, 0)$. For each z, $m_z(y)$ is a nondecreasing concave function of y, as shown in figure D-2. Hence

$$\sum_{k=1}^{n} m_z(x_k) \geqslant \sum_{k=1}^{n} m_z(y_k) \qquad \text{for each } z.$$

That is,

$$\sum_{x_k \leqslant z} (x_k - z) \geqslant \sum_{y_k \leqslant z} (y_k - z). \qquad (\text{D.1})$$

Figure D-2. *The Concave Function $m_z(y)$*

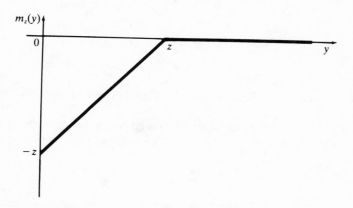

Now suppose that $\mathbf{x} \succeq_L \mathbf{y}$ is *not* true. Then it is not the case that

$$\sum_{k=1}^{i} x_k \geq \sum_{k=1}^{i} y_k \qquad \text{for each } i = 1, 2, \ldots, n.$$

Let i be the *first* integer such that

$$\sum_{k=1}^{i} x_k < \sum_{k=1}^{i} y_k. \tag{D.2}$$

Since

$$\sum_{k=1}^{i-1} x_k \geq \sum_{k=1}^{i-1} y_k,$$

it follows that $x_i < y_i$. Putting $z = y_i$ in (D.1) gives

$$\sum_{x_k \leq y_i} (x_k - y_i) \geq \sum_{y_k \leq y_i} (y_k - y_i)$$

$$= \sum_{k=1}^{i} (y_k - y_i). \tag{D.3}$$

Now

$$\sum_{x_k \leq y_i} (x_k - y_i) = \sum_{x_k \leq x_i} (x_k - y_i) + \sum_{x_i < x_k \leq y_i} (x_k - y_i)$$

$$\text{since } x_i < y_i$$

$$\leq \sum_{x_k \leq x_i} (x_k - y_i) \qquad \text{since the second term is}$$
$$\text{negative}$$

$$= \sum_{k=1}^{i} (x_k - y_i). \tag{D.4}$$

Stringing together (D.4) with (D.3), it follows that

$$\sum_{k=1}^{i} (x_k - y_i) \geq \sum_{k=1}^{i} (y_k - y_i)$$

or

$$\sum_{k=1}^{i} x_k \geq \sum_{k=1}^{i} y_k,$$

which contradicts (D.2). So it must be true that $x \succsim_L y$, and the proof is complete. ||

In fact, a stronger theorem than this can be proved by adopting a weaker criterion for the welfare ranking (iii). The welfare function

$$\sum_{i=1}^{n} U(y_i)$$

can be replaced by a symmetric nondecreasing quasi-concave function of individual incomes $W(y_1, y_2, \ldots, y_n)$ (see Dasgupta, Sen, and Starrett, 1973). Defining the criterion $\succsim_W$ as $x \succsim_W y$ if $W(x) \geq W(y)$ for all symmetric nondecreasing quasi-concave functions W, the theorem can also be proved with $\succsim_U$ replaced by $\succsim_W$ in (iii).

The quasi-concavity restriction on the welfare function can be weakened still further. For the theorem to go through, it is clear that the *weakest* requirement on the function is that welfare does *not decrease* by a transfer of income from a richer to a poorer individual, where the size of transfer is less than or equal to their income difference. I call a function $E(y_1, y_2, \ldots, y_n)$ which satisfies this property "egalitarian"; it is called "locally equality preferring" by Rothschild and Stiglitz (1973). Defining the criterion $\succsim_E$ as $x \succsim_E y$ if $E(x) \geq E(y)$ for all symmetric nondecreasing egalitarian functions E, the theorem is also valid with $\succsim_U$ replaced by $\succsim_E$ in (iii).

Since the class of additively separable concave functions is contained in the class of quasi-concave functions, which in turn is contained in the class of egalitarian (or locally equality preferring) functions, it follows that $x \succsim_E y \Rightarrow x \succsim_W y \Rightarrow x \succsim_U y$. But by the very definition of $\succsim_E$, $x \succsim_T y \Rightarrow x \succsim_E y$, and from Atkinson's theorem, $x \succsim_U y \Rightarrow x \succsim_T y$; therefore, $x \succsim_U y \Rightarrow x \succsim_E y$. The chain of implications is complete and

$$x \succsim_E y \Rightarrow x \succsim_W y \Rightarrow x \succsim_U y \Rightarrow x \succsim_E y.$$

Thus the rankings of distributions by the three criteria $\succsim_U$, $\succsim_W$, and $\succsim_E$ are equivalent, and each is equivalent to $\succsim_L$ and $\succsim_T$.

Given two distributions with the same number of individuals and the same mean income, Atkinson uses Lorenz dominance to establish an unambiguous welfare ranking between them in terms of *all* welfare functions from a wide class. But in any actual comparison of income distributions (for example, between countries or over time), the population size and mean income are likely to be different. With different population sizes but the same mean income, a simple extension of Atkinson's theorem shows that Lorenz dominance still gives an unambiguous ranking between the distributions in terms of per capita welfare.[4] With different mean incomes, the unambiguous welfare ranking survives only when it is the Lorenz-dominant distribution that has the higher mean income. Thus Lorenz dominance cannot always be used for normative comparisons of inequality between two distributions.

I put the Lorenz ranking to a somewhat different use in this study. Even if normative comparisons are not possible, for example, because the underlying distributions refer to different population units or income concepts, the Lorenz ordering can still reveal a good deal about inequality in a positive or descriptive sense. The next result shows that Lorenz dominance provides an unambiguous ranking of distributions by *all* positive inequality indices from a wide class.

Proposition: Let **L** be the class of inequality indices that satisfy three basic properties: mean independence, population-size independence, and the Pigou-Dalton condition. If the Lorenz curve of a distribution $\mathbf{x}(\mu_x, n_x)$ with mean μ_x and population size n_x dominates the Lorenz curve of another distribution $\mathbf{y}(\mu_y, n_y)$ with mean μ_y and population size n_y, then *all* indices from the class **L** will show less inequality for $\mathbf{x}(\mu_x, n_x)$ than for $\mathbf{y}(\mu_y, n_y)$.

Proof: Let I be a typical inequality index from the class **L** of inequality indices. Replicate n_y times the number of people at each income level in $\mathbf{x}(\mu_x, n_x)$, and replicate n_x times the number of people at each income level in $\mathbf{y}(\mu_y, n_y)$. Then multiply each person's income in $\mathbf{x}(\mu_x, n_x n_y)$ by μ_y, and each person's income in $\mathbf{y}(\mu_y, n_x n_y)$ by μ_x. Then the new distributions $\mathbf{x}(\mu_x \mu_y, n_x n_y)$ and $\mathbf{y}(\mu_x \mu_y, n_x n_y)$ have the same population size $n = n_x n_y$ and the same mean $\mu = \mu_x \mu_y$; hence the hypotheses of Atkinson's theorem hold for them. Furthermore, $\mathbf{x}(\mu, n)$ Lorenz-dominates $\mathbf{y}(\mu, n)$ because the Lorenz curve of $\mathbf{x}(\mu, n)$ is identical to the Lorenz curve of $\mathbf{x}(\mu_x, n_x)$, and the Lorenz curve of $\mathbf{y}(\mu, n)$ is identical to the Lorenz curve of $\mathbf{y}(\mu_y, n_y)$. Therefore, by Atkinson's theorem, $\mathbf{x}(\mu, n)$ can be obtained from $\mathbf{y}(\mu, n)$ by a sequence of transfers from rich individuals to poor. Now as the index I satisfies the Pigou-Dalton condition, it will show less inequality for $\mathbf{x}(\mu, n)$ than for $\mathbf{y}(\mu, n)$. (A transfer from rich to poor decreases the value of such an

---

4. If the criterion $\succeq_W$ or $\succeq_E$ is being used instead of Atkinson's $\succeq_U$, then a "symmetry axiom for population" is needed (see Sen, 1973a).

index.) But since the index I is also mean-independent and population-size-independent, its values for $x(\mu_x, n_x)$ and $y(\mu_y, n_y)$ are identical to its values for $x(\mu, n)$ and $y(\mu, n)$, respectively. Hence the index I shows less inequality for $x(\mu_x, n_x)$ than for $y(\mu_y, n_y)$. ‖

All the positive indices considered in this study belong to the class **L**, except for the variance of log-income (at high levels of income). Thus Lorenz dominance automatically implies less inequality according to such indices as the Gini coefficient, the two Theil measures, and the squared coefficient of variation. It also implies less inequality according to so-called normative indices belonging to this class, such as Atkinson's index, which may be used in a positive or descriptive sense. I call the class **L** the Lorenz class of inequality indices.

E

Lemmas on Lorenz Dominance

IN THIS APPENDIX conditions are sought under which one distribution will be Lorenz-preferred to another. Lorenz preference implies an unambiguous ranking of inequality according to *any* index which satisfies mean independence, population-size independence, and the Pigou-Dalton condition. In other words, if one distribution Lorenz-dominates another, then it will show less inequality for any measure from the Lorenz class. Also explored here are the effects on inequality of certain transformations to the underlying distribution, including the under- or overestimation of incomes. The results allow unambiguous comparisons of inequality in terms of the Lorenz partial ordering.

Suppose there are two ordered distributions $\mathbf{x}$ and $\mathbf{y}$ with the same number n of population units.[1] The following lemma provides a sufficiency condition for $\mathbf{x}$ to Lorenz-dominate $\mathbf{y}$.

Lemma 1: Let $\mathbf{x}$ be the ordered income distribution

$$\mathbf{x}:0 \leqslant x_1 \leqslant x_2 \leqslant \ldots \leqslant x_n,$$

and let $\mathbf{y}$ be the ordered income distribution

$$\mathbf{y}:0 \leqslant y_1 \leqslant y_2 \leqslant \ldots \leqslant y_n.$$

If $x_1/y_1 \geqslant x_2/y_2 \geqslant \ldots \geqslant x_n/y_n$, then $\mathbf{x} \succsim_L \mathbf{y}$.

Proof: Since $x_1/y_1 \geqslant x_2/y_2$,

$$\frac{x_1}{y_1} \geqslant \frac{x_1 + x_2}{y_1 + y_2} \geqslant \frac{x_2}{y_2} \qquad (\geqslant \frac{x_3}{y_3}, \text{ by hypothesis}).$$

Therefore $\qquad \dfrac{x_1 + x_2}{y_1 + y_2} \geqslant \dfrac{x_1 + x_2 + x_3}{y_1 + y_2 + y_3} \geqslant \dfrac{x_3}{y_3} (\geqslant \dfrac{x_4}{y_4}, \text{ by hypothesis}).$

---

1. The population unit itself need not be the same for the two distributions; for example, it could be individuals in one distribution and households in the other.

Proceeding in this way, the hypothesis of the lemma implies the following sequence of inequalities:

$$\frac{x_1}{y_1} \geqslant \frac{x_1+x_2}{y_1+y_2} \geqslant \ldots \geqslant \frac{x_1+x_2+\ldots+x_{n-1}}{y_1+y_2+\ldots+y_{n-1}} \geqslant \frac{x_1+x_2+\ldots+x_n}{y_1+y_2+\ldots+y_n} \geqslant \frac{x_n}{y_n}.$$

Hence, $\dfrac{x_1+x_2+\ldots+x_i}{x_1+x_2+\ldots+x_n} \geqslant \dfrac{y_1+y_2+\ldots+y_i}{y_1+y_2+\ldots+y_n}$ for $i = 1, \ldots, n$.

In other words, $\mathbf{x} \succeq_L \mathbf{y}$. ‖ The converse of lemma 1 is obviously not true.

Corollary 1: Let $\mathbf{x}$ be an ordered income distribution. Increase the income of the richest person (n) by an amount $\varepsilon \geqslant 0$, and reduce the income of the poorest person (1) by $\delta \geqslant 0$, and call the new distribution $\mathbf{y}$. Then $\mathbf{x}$ Lorenz-dominates $\mathbf{y}$. Formally, let

$$\mathbf{x}: 0 \leqslant x_1 \leqslant x_2 \leqslant \ldots \leqslant x_{n-1} \leqslant x_n$$
and
$$\mathbf{y}: 0 \leqslant (x_1 - \delta) \leqslant x_2 \leqslant \ldots \leqslant x_{n-1} \leqslant (x_n + \varepsilon)$$

where $\varepsilon, \delta \geqslant 0$. Then $\mathbf{x} \succeq_L \mathbf{y}$. The proof of this result is a simple application of lemma 1, since

$$\frac{x_1}{x_1-\delta} \geqslant \frac{x_2}{x_2} \geqslant \ldots \geqslant \frac{x_{n-1}}{x_{n-1}} \geqslant \frac{x_n}{x_n+\varepsilon}. ‖$$

The result says that if the income of the richest person is underestimated, or the income of the poorest person is overestimated (or both), then inequality is unambiguously underestimated. This conclusion does *not* necessarily follow if incomes at more than one income level are changed at the top and bottom ends of the distribution. It is easy to construct counterexamples to the corollary when such changes are permitted. With certain restrictions on these changes, however, Lorenz comparability is indeed possible. For example, the following result can be proved.

Corollary 2: If *proportional* underestimation *increases* with income, then inequality is unambiguously underestimated. Formally, let

$$\mathbf{x}: 0 \leqslant x_1 \leqslant x_2 \leqslant \ldots \leqslant x_n$$
and
$$\mathbf{y}: 0 \leqslant x_1(1+\varepsilon_1) \leqslant x_2(1+\varepsilon_2) \leqslant \ldots \leqslant x_n(1+\varepsilon_n)$$

where $\varepsilon_1 \leqslant \varepsilon_2 \leqslant \ldots \leqslant \varepsilon_n$. Then $\mathbf{x} \succeq_L \mathbf{y}$. This result is again an easy application of lemma 1, since for $\varepsilon_i \leqslant \varepsilon_{i+1}$,

$$\frac{x_i}{x_i(1+\varepsilon_i)} \geqslant \frac{x_{i+1}}{x_{i+1}(1+\varepsilon_{i+1})} \qquad i = 1, \ldots, (n-1). ‖$$

For *absolute* underestimation of incomes, there is the following result.

Corollary 3: Let **y** be an ordered income distribution. Increase the income of every person in **y** by the same absolute amount $\varepsilon > 0$, and call the new distribution **x**. Then **x** Lorenz-dominates **y**. Formally, let

$$\mathbf{y}: 0 \leqslant y_1 \leqslant y_2 \leqslant \ldots \leqslant y_n$$

and

$$\mathbf{x}: 0 \leqslant (y_1 + \varepsilon) \leqslant (y_2 + \varepsilon) \leqslant \ldots \leqslant (y_n + \varepsilon)$$

where $\varepsilon > 0$. Then $\mathbf{x} \succsim_L \mathbf{y}$. This follows from lemma 1, since for $y_i \leqslant y_{i+1}$,

$$\frac{y_i + \varepsilon}{y_i} \geqslant \frac{y_{i+1} + \varepsilon}{y_{i+1}} \qquad i = 1, \ldots, (n-1). \; \|$$

Therefore increasing everyone's income by the same absolute amount reduces inequality. Put another way, an equal absolute underestimation of incomes leads to an unambiguous overestimation of inequality. It is obvious that the distribution **x** tends to perfect equality when the absolute amount ε by which everyone's income is increased becomes indefinitely large. (As shown in "The Effect of Changes in Certain Incomes" in appendix B, the Gini coefficient $G(\mathbf{x}) \to 0$ as $\varepsilon \to \infty$.)

The effects on inequality of underestimating or overestimating the incomes of particular persons have been discussed. Can anything be said now about the effects on measured inequality of undersampling or oversampling persons at particular income levels? In other words, how does the Lorenz curve shift if persons are added to the existing distribution at various income levels? The general answer to this question is quite unilluminating, but for certain frequently encountered types of undersampling Lorenz dominance can be demonstrated.

Lemma 2: Let $\mathbf{x}(r)$ be an ordered income distribution among r people. Add on a number q of persons at income level zero to $\mathbf{x}(r)$, and call the new distribution among the $q + r = n$ people $\mathbf{y}(n)$. Then $\mathbf{x}(r) \succsim_L \mathbf{y}(n)$.

Proof: Let

$$\mathbf{x}(r): 0 \leqslant x_1 \leqslant x_2 \leqslant \ldots \leqslant x_r.$$

Then $\mathbf{y}(n): 0 = y_1 = y_2 = \ldots = y_q \leqslant y_{q+1} \leqslant y_{q+2} \leqslant \ldots \leqslant y_{q+r}$

$$\text{where } y_{q+i} = x_i \quad \text{for} \quad i = 1, 2, \ldots, r.$$

Now from the definition of the Lorenz curve,

$$L_y\left(\frac{k}{q+r}\right) = 0 \qquad \qquad \text{for } k = 1, 2, \ldots, q$$

and

$$L_y\left(\frac{q+i}{q+r}\right) = \sum_{k=1}^{q+i} y_k \Big/ \sum_{k=1}^{q+r} y_k \quad \text{for } i = 1, 2, \ldots, r$$

$$= \sum_{k=1}^{i} x_k \Big/ \sum_{k=1}^{r} x_k$$

$$= L_x\left(\frac{i}{r}\right) \quad \text{for } i = 1, 2, \ldots, r.$$

But

$$\frac{q+i}{q+r} \geqslant \frac{i}{r} \qquad (\textit{strict for } i \neq r).$$

Thus for each cumulative income share, the cumulative population share for distribution $y(n)$ is greater than for distribution $x(r)$; hence the Lorenz curve $L_y(.)$ lies horizontally to the right of the Lorenz curve $L_x(.)$.[2] Therefore $L_x(.)$ lies above $L_y(.)$; that is, $x(r) \succeq_L y(n)$. ‖

With the addition of persons with *positive* income at the bottom end of the distribution x (or indeed anywhere along x), Lorenz dominance cannot be established, despite the fact that when an increasing number of persons (each with the same positive income) is added, the Lorenz curve tends to the diagonal of perfect equality.

Lemma 3: The distribution of individuals according to per capita household income $z(n)$ Lorenz-dominates their distribution according to personal income $y(n)$.

Proof: $z(n)$ and $y(n)$ have the same number n of individuals. The distribution $z(n)$ can be obtained from the distribution $y(n)$ by a series of rich to poor transfers: redistribute income within each household from members receiving more than its per capita income to members receiving less (which includes members who are zero-income recipients). These are a series of transfers from rich individuals to poor, and hence by Atkinson's theorem $z(n)$ Lorenz-dominates $y(n)$. ‖

The Redress of Poverty Rule

Given an ordered income distribution y, if an additional amount of income Δ becomes available for distribution among the population but the existing

2. The previous results which established Lorenz dominance concern a *vertical* movement of the Lorenz curve. Here, instead of holding the points i/n (the population shares) fixed, I have held the ordinates (income shares) fixed and considered horizontal movements of the abscissas (population shares). It is difficult to prove results about Lorenz dominance when the movement is different from one of these two types.

income of any person cannot be reduced, how should Δ be distributed to maximize social welfare? For an egalitarian social welfare function, the answer is obvious:[3] *Give Δ to the poorest person 1 until his or her income reaches that of person 2. Distribute the remainder equally between them until their incomes reach that of person 3. And so on.* Label the resulting distribution **x**. This distribution policy, with incomes raised from the bottom upward, is called the redress of poverty rule.

The question arises whether the distribution **x** Lorenz-dominates the original distribution **y**. This is immediate from the extension of Atkinson's theorem for egalitarian social welfare functions (see appendix D). It can also be shown by the following two-stage procedure. First, increase each person's income by the same absolute amount $\varepsilon = \Delta/n$. The resulting distribution Lorenz-dominates **y**, by corollary 3. Then obtain the distribution **x** from this by a sequence of transfers of the ε's from rich persons to poor. By Atkinson's theorem (the principle of transfers), **x** Lorenz-dominates this distribution, which in turn has been shown to Lorenz-dominate **y**; hence, by transitivity, $\mathbf{x} \succeq_L \mathbf{y}$. ‖

The redress of poverty rule is most "efficient" for the redress of inequality too. That is to say, if redistribution is permitted only out of the additional income Δ, then the maximum reduction in inequality (for any index from the Lorenz class) is secured by the redress of poverty rule. Any other distribution of the incremental income can always be improved upon in the Lorenz sense (as long as it is not **x** already) by a transfer from rich to poor. Thus **x** Lorenz-dominates all other distributions of the incremental income Δ; hence it yields the maximum reduction in inequality for any index from the Lorenz class. ‖

---

3. A social welfare function is egalitarian (see appendix D) if a transfer of income from rich to poor, which does not reverse their relative ranks, leads to an increase in welfare.

F

Mapping the Household to the per Capita Household Income Distribution

IN THIS APPENDIX, I attempt to show how the distribution of individuals by per capita household income can be obtained from the joint (bivariate) distribution of households by household income and size. The general mathematical mapping between the household and the per capita household income distributions is derived here. Furthermore, for certain special joint distributions of households by household income and size, I obtain analytical expressions for the distribution of individuals by per capita household income.

To simplify the analysis, consider first a *constant* household size within each income class, but allow the size to be different across income classes. This in itself causes the per capita household income distribution to diverge from the household income distribution. I shall later allow a non-zero variance of household size within each income class,[1] and show that even if average household size is constant across income classes there will be a divergence between the household and the per capita household income distributions. I shall also show that the direction of divergence in terms of inequality cannot generally be predicted, except in some very special cases.

If household size is constant within each income class, the following statement is obviously true:

If household size is constant across income classes, then the household and per capita household income distributions are identical.

The next statement is intuitively plausible, and a variant of it is often invoked in empirical work on income distribution. It is, however, false:

---

1. That is, a positive variance in the household size distribution conditional on each income level.

If household size is positively correlated with household income, then the distribution of individuals by per capita household income is more equal than the distribution of households by household income.

The falseness of the second statement is readily demonstrated by counter-example. Let the joint distribution of households by household income and size be as follows:

	Household size	
Household income (M$ per month)	*1*	*4*
200	1	0
300	0	1
Number of households	1	1
Number of individuals	1	4
Per capita household income (M$ per month)	200	75

Household size is positively correlated with household income, but the distribution of households by household income Lorenz-dominates the distribution of individuals by per capita household income; hence it will show less inequality for *any* index from the Lorenz class.[2] The Lorenz curves for the two distributions are shown in figure F-1.

The reason the second statement fails in this example is that the *ranking* of households is reversed in going from household income to per capita household income. If the ranking is preserved under this transformation, it is possible to prove some general results by comparing the two distributions. I first compare the two distributions when the household is maintained as the population unit in both.

Proposition 1: Suppose there are H households with incomes y_h, for $h = 1, \ldots, H$. Let $\mathbf{y}(H)$ be the ordered distribution of households by household income; that is,

$$\mathbf{y}(H): 0 \leqslant y_1 \leqslant y_2 \leqslant \ldots \leqslant y_H.$$

Let m_h be the size of household h, and $z_h = y_h/m_h$ its per capita household income. Let household size m_h *increase* with household income y_h, but at a rate no faster than income y_h. Call $\mathbf{z}(H)$ the distribution of *households* by

---

2. A slight modification of the above example reverses the Lorenz-dominance relation between the two distributions. Let the household with income M$200 be of size 2, and the household with income M$300 of size 3. Then the distribution of individuals by per capita household income will be perfectly equal with the five individuals each receiving M$100, while the distribution of households by household income will be unequal as shown.

Figure F-1. *Individual and Household Lorenz Curves for the Hypothetical Joint Distribution*

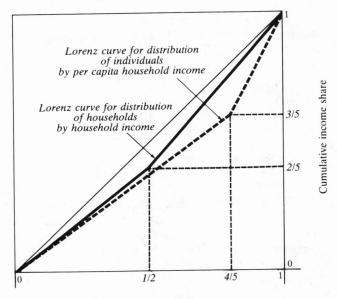

Cumulative population share

per capita household income. Then,

$$\mathbf{z}(H) \succsim {}_L\mathbf{y}(H).$$

Proof: It is given that $m_1 \leqslant m_2 \leqslant \ldots \leqslant m_H$. The fact that m_h increases no faster than y_h means that

$$m_{h+1}/m_h \leqslant y_{h+1}/y_h \qquad \text{for } h = 1, \ldots, (H-1).$$

Therefore $\qquad y_h/m_h \leqslant y_{h+1}/m_{h+1} \qquad \text{for } h = 1, \ldots, (H-1),$

and hence the ordering of households by $z_h = y_h/m_h$ is the same as by y_h. Thus $\mathbf{z}(H)$ is the ordered distribution

$$\mathbf{z}(H) : 0 \leqslant z_1 \leqslant z_2 \leqslant \ldots \leqslant z_H.$$

The result now follows as an easy application of lemma 1 (appendix E),

since $\dfrac{z_1}{y_1} = \dfrac{1}{m_1} \geqslant \dfrac{z_2}{y_2} = \dfrac{1}{m_2} \geqslant \ldots \geqslant \dfrac{z_H}{y_H} = \dfrac{1}{m_H}$ (because m_h is increasing. ‖

For welfare comparisons in the population (chapter 3), it is the distribution of individuals (not households) by per capita household income that is of interest. I prove that this distribution, subject to the same conditions as in proposition 1, Lorenz-dominates the distribution of households by household income.[3]

Proposition 2: Let the ordered distribution of households by household income be

$$\mathbf{y}(H): 0 \leqslant y_1 \leqslant y_2 \leqslant \ldots \leqslant y_H.$$

Let household size m_h increase with household income y_h at such a rate that the ordering of households by $z_h = y_h/m_h$ is the same as by y_h. Assign to each person his or her per capita household income, and call $\mathbf{z}(n)$ the distribution of *individuals* by per capita household income, where

$$n = \sum_{h=1}^{H} m_h$$

is the total number of individuals. Then,

$$\mathbf{z}(n) \succeq {}_L \mathbf{y}(H).$$

Proof: It is given that

$$m_1 \leqslant m_2 \leqslant \ldots \leqslant m_H$$

and that

$$\frac{y_1}{m_1} \leqslant \frac{y_2}{m_2} \leqslant \ldots \leqslant \frac{y_H}{m_H}.$$

I prove the result by showing that the Lorenz curve for $\mathbf{z}(n)$ is a horizontal translation leftward of the Lorenz curve for $\mathbf{y}(H)$. The distribution $\mathbf{z}(n)$ has m_1 persons at y_1/m_1; m_2 persons at y_2/m_2; $\ldots$; m_H persons at y_H/m_H; and by hypothesis these persons are in nondescending order of per capita household income. Thus the Lorenz curve for $\mathbf{z}(n)$ is given by:

$$L_{z(n)}\left(\frac{m_1 + m_2 + \ldots + m_h}{n}\right) = \frac{y_1 + y_2 + \ldots + y_h}{y_1 + y_2 + \ldots + y_H}$$

$$= L_y\left(\frac{h}{H}\right) \qquad \text{for } h = 1, \ldots, H.$$

3. This result was conjectured in Anand (1973), p. 115: "We conjecture that if household size (constant *within* each income class) *increases* but at a rate *no faster than* income, then the individual income distribution will be more equal in the Lorenz sense than the household income distribution."

I show that $\left(\dfrac{m_1 + m_2 + \ldots + m_h}{n}\right) \leqslant \left(\dfrac{h}{H}\right)$ for $h = 1, \ldots, H$.

This means the same income share is received by a smaller population share in $z(n)$ than in $y(H)$. Since $m_1 \leqslant m_2 \leqslant \ldots \leqslant m_H$, we have

$$m_1 \leqslant (m_1 + m_2)/2 \leqslant m_2 \quad (\leqslant m_3).$$

Therefore $(m_1 + m_2)/2 \leqslant (m_1 + m_2 + m_3)/3 \leqslant m_3 \quad (\leqslant m_4)$.
Continuing in this manner,

$$m_1 \leqslant (m_1 + m_2)/2 \leqslant \ldots \leqslant (m_1 + m_2 + \ldots + m_H)/H = n/H.$$

Thus $(m_1 + m_2 + \ldots + m_h)/h \leqslant n/H$ for all $h = 1, \ldots, H$.

So $\left(\dfrac{m_1 + m_2 + \ldots + m_h}{n}\right) \leqslant \left(\dfrac{h}{H}\right)$ for all $h = 1, \ldots, H$.

This proves that the Lorenz curve for $z(n)$ is a horizontal shift leftward of the Lorenz curve for $y(H)$, and hence $z(n) \succsim _L y(H)$.‖

Now consider the more general situation in which household size *varies* within each income class. The relation between the household and per capita household income distributions then becomes more complex. Before examining this in any detail, compare relative inequality in the two distributions with the variance of log-income measure. Using the previous notation of y for household income, m for household size, and z for per capita household income, $z = y/m$. Therefore

$$\log z = \log y - \log m.$$

Hence, $\operatorname{var}(\log z) = \operatorname{var}(\log y) + \operatorname{var}(\log m) - 2\operatorname{cov}(\log y, \log m)$.
Now if $\operatorname{cov}(\log y, \log m) < \frac{1}{2}\operatorname{var}(\log m)$,
then $\operatorname{var}(\log z) > \operatorname{var}(\log y)$.

Thus a positive correlation between $\log y$ and $\log m$ is not enough to ensure that inequality in z is smaller than inequality in y (measured by the variance of log-income). For this result to follow, the covariance between them must be sufficiently large $[> \frac{1}{2}\operatorname{var}(\log m)]$. If in fact $\log y$ and $\log m$ are uncorrelated, z will be distributed more unequally than y. In this case, deflation of household income by household size is like adding extra variance (or noise).[4]

---

4. For instance, a distribution of households according to household income can be made as unequal as one likes according to per capita household income by increasing the variance of household size around a fixed average.

Note, however, that var(log z) refers to the variance of log-per-capita-household-income across the population of *households*, not individuals. Since the variance operator above has been applied over the population of households, the results concern inequality in the distribution of households by per capita household income. In fact, it is the distribution of *individuals* by per capita household income that is of interest. This distribution needs to be derived rather carefully from the joint distribution of households by household income and size.

Let $f(y, m)$ be the joint density function of households with household income y and household size m. Then $g(y) = \int f(y, m)dm$ is the (marginal) density function of households with household income y, and $h(m) = \int f(y, m)dy$ is the (marginal) density function of households with household size m. Hence the total number of *individuals* in the population is $\int mh(m)dm$.

Assuming that household income is equally divided among the members of a household, how is per capita household income $z = y/m$ distributed, where y and m range over all possible values? Let $\phi(z)$ be the density function of individuals according to per capita household income z, so that $\phi(z)dz$ represents the number of individuals with income in the interval $[z, z + dz]$. Evidently, $\phi(z) = \int mf(mz, m)dm \cdot m$. Note that $dm \cdot m$ represents the inverse of the Jacobian of $z = y/m$, the transformation used to change variables from y to z. Further, $f(mz, m)$ gives the number of households with characteristics (mz, m), and $mf(mz, m)$ gives the number of individuals with these characteristics. Multiplying $f(mz, m)$ by m thus represents the step in going from the distribution of *households* according to per capita household income z to the distribution of *individuals* according to per capita household income z.[5]

From the distribution $\phi(z)$, the total number of individuals in the population is

$$\int \phi(z)dz = \int\int m^2 f(mz, m)dm \cdot dz.$$

5. If $f(mz, m)$ had not been multiplied by m, the household (rather than individual) distribution of z would have been obtained. The distribution of households by per capita household income z is given by the density function $\psi(z)$ where

$$\psi(z) = \int f(mz, m)dm \cdot m.$$

The total number of households according to the distribution $\psi(z)$ is

$$\int \psi(z)dz = \int\int f(mz, m)dm \cdot mdz.$$

But from the original bivariate distribution $f(y, m)$, the total number of households is

$$\int\int f(y, m)dy \cdot dm = \int\int f(mz, m)dm \cdot mdz,$$

using $y = mz$. This is consistent with the total number of households according to the distribution $\psi(z)$.

But, from before, $\int mh(m)dm$ should also equal the total number of individuals in the population. By definition,

$$h(m) = \int f(y, m)dy.$$

Put $y = mz$, so that $dy = mdz$ (for a given value of m). Then

$$h(m) = \int mf(mz, m)dz.$$

Hence, $\int mh(m)dm = \int \int m^2 f(mz, m)dz \cdot dm$
$$= \int \phi(z)dz.$$

The derivation of $\phi(z)$ is therefore consistent! The process of deriving $\phi(z)$ from $f(y, m)$ is illustrated geometrically in figure F-2.

I now derive the distribution of individuals by per capita household income in three cases for which the mapping $\phi(z)$ yields an analytical solution.

Figure F-2. *The Derivation of $\phi(z)$ from $f(y,m)$*

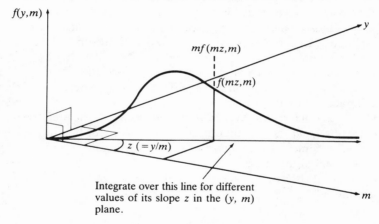

Integrate over this line for different values of its slope z in the (y, m) plane.

Case 1: Suppose the household income and size distributions are *independent*, that is, $f(y, m) = g(y) \cdot h(m)$. Then

$$\phi(z) = \int m^2 g(mz) \cdot h(m)dm.$$

Under what conditions is $\phi(z)$ the same distribution as $g(y) = \int f(y, m)dm$, the distribution of households by household income. If $g(mz)$ is multiplicatively separable as $g(mz) = \sigma(m) \cdot g(z)$, then

$$\phi(z) = g(z)\int m^2 \sigma(m) \cdot h(m)dm$$
$$= g(z) \qquad \text{up to a scalar multiple.[6]}$$

6. In this case, the distribution of *households* by per capita household income z also has density function $g(z)$, up to some other scalar multiple.

For example, if $g(y)$ is a Pareto distribution with coefficient α,

$$g(y) = Ay^{-\alpha}$$

where A is a constant. Then,

$$
\begin{aligned}
g(mz) &= A(mz)^{-\alpha} \\
&= m^{-\alpha}Az^{-\alpha} \\
&= \sigma(m) \cdot g(z),
\end{aligned}
$$

and in this case $g(mz)$ *is* multiplicatively separable. Therefore, if the household income and size distributions are *independent*, and the household income distribution $g(y)$ is a Pareto distribution with coefficient α, then the distribution of individuals by per capita household income $\phi(z)$ is also a Pareto distribution, with the same coefficient α.

Case 2: Still assuming that the household income and size distributions are independent, that is, $f(y, m) = g(y) \cdot h(m)$, suppose $g(y)$ is a negative exponential instead of a Pareto distribution, that is, $g(y) = \lambda e^{-\lambda y}$. Then

$$\phi(z) = \int_a^b \lambda m^2 e^{-\lambda mz} h(m)dm,$$

where the limits of integration a and b represent the minimum and maximum household sizes, respectively. If $h(m) = m^{-k}$, and k is an integer, we can integrate by parts to obtain an explicit expression for $\phi(z)$. In the special case when $k = 2$,

$$\phi(z) = \frac{1}{z}[e^{-\lambda az} - e^{-\lambda bz}].$$

For other values of k the expression for $\phi(z)$ is more complicated, but it is never a negative exponential distribution. Hence, in this case, the distribution of individuals by per capita household income is different from the distribution of households by household income.

Case 3: Suppose now that the household income and size distributions are *not* independent. For instance, let $f(y, m) = Ay^{-m\alpha}h(m)$. Then

$$
\begin{aligned}
\phi(z) &= A \int m^2 (mz)^{-m\alpha} h(m)dm \\
&= A \int m^{2-m\alpha} h(m) \cdot e^{-m\alpha \log z} \cdot dm.
\end{aligned}
$$

The value of this integral depends on the form of the function $h(m)$. If $h(m)$ happens to be $h(m) = 1/(m^{2-m\alpha})$, then

$$
\begin{aligned}
\phi(z) &= A \frac{(-1)}{\alpha \log z} [e^{-m\alpha \log z}]_a^b \\
&= \frac{A}{\alpha \log z} (z^{-a\alpha} - z^{-b\alpha}),
\end{aligned}
$$

where a and b are the minimum and maximum household sizes, respectively. The distribution of households by household income, $g(y)$, is in this case given by

$$g(y) = \int_a^b f(y, m)\,dm$$

$$= A \int_a^b y^{-m\alpha} \frac{1}{m^{2-m\alpha}}\,dm,$$

which, although difficult to integrate, is easily seen to be different from the above distribution $\phi(z)$.

I have tried to illustrate in this appendix the mapping from the household to the per capita household income distribution. Starting with a joint distribution of households by household income and size, I have shown that quite different distributions of individuals by per capita household income may be obtained depending on the nature of interaction between household income and size. In particular, distributions of individuals by per capita household income can be derived which are more *or* less equal than the underlying distribution of households by household income.

References

Adelman, Irma, and C. T. Morris. 1973. *Economic Growth and Social Equity in Developing Countries*. Stanford, Calif.: Stanford University Press.

Adelman, Irma, and Laura D. Tyson. 1974. "A Regional Microeconomic Model of Yugoslavia—Factors Affecting the Distribution of Income in the Short Run." Development Research Center, World Bank, Washington, D.C.

Adelman, Irma, and Sherman Robinson. 1977. *Income Distribution Policy in Developing Countries: A Case Study of Korea*. Stanford, Calif.: Stanford University Press.

Ahluwalia, Montek S. 1974a. "Income Inequality: Some Dimensions of the Problem." In Chenery and others (1974).

————. 1974b. "The Scope for Policy Intervention." In Chenery and others (1974).

————. 1976. "Inequality, Poverty and Development." *Journal of Development Economics*, vol. 3, pp. 307–42.

————. 1977. "Rural Poverty and Agricultural Performance in India." *Journal of Development Studies*, pp. 298–323.

Ahluwalia, Montek S., and others. 1976. "A Social Accounting Matrix for Malaysia." Development Research Center, World Bank, Washington, D.C.

Aitchison, J., and J. A. C. Brown. 1957. *The Lognormal Distribution*. Cambridge, Eng.: Cambridge University Press.

Alatas, Syed Hussein. 1977. *The Myth of the Lazy Native*. London: Frank Cass.

Anand, Sudhir. 1970. "An Optimal Earnings Schedule." Paper presented to the Second World Congress of the Econometric Society, Cambridge, England.

————. 1971. "Rural-Urban Migration in India: An Econometric Study." Harvard University, Cambridge, Mass.

————. 1973. "The Size Distribution of Income in Malaysia, Part I." Development Research Center, World Bank, Washington, D.C.

————. 1974a. "Addendum to the Size Distribution of Income in Malaysia, Part I." Development Research Center, World Bank, Washington, D.C.

————. 1974b. "The Size Distribution of Income in Malaysia, Part II." Oxford: St. Catherine's College.

————. 1975. "Aspects of Poverty in Malaysia." Paper presented to the Fourteenth General Conference of the International Association for Research in Income and Wealth, Aulanko, Finland.

————. 1976*a*. "The Little-Mirrlees Appraisal of a Highway Project in Malaysia." *Journal of Transport Economics and Policy*, vol. 10, no. 3, September.

————. 1976*b*. "Discussion on 'Personal Characteristics and Income' by J. Tinbergen." In *The Personal Distribution of Incomes*. Anthony B. Atkinson, ed. London: Allen and Unwin.

Anand, Sudhir, and S. M. Kanbur. 1978. "Inequality and Development: A Reconsideration." Oxford: St. Catherine's College.

Andic, F. M. 1975. "The Impact of the Tax System on the Poor: With Special Reference to Rural Poor." Kuala Lumpur: Economic Planning Unit.

Arlès, J-P. 1971. "Ethnic and Socio-Economic Patterns in Malaysia." *International Labour Review*, vol. 104, no. 6, December.

Atkinson, Anthony B. 1970. "On the Measurement of Inequality." *Journal of Economic Theory*, vol. 2. no. 3, September.

————. 1975. *The Economics of Inequality*. Oxford: Clarendon Press.

Awang Had Salleh. 1975. "Translation of National Agenda into Educational Strategies: A Proposal for Malaysia." Paper presented at the Second Malaysian Economic Convention, Kuala Lumpur.

Aziz, Ungku A. 1964. "Poverty and Rural Development in Malaysia." *Kajian Ekonomi Malaysia*, vol. 1, no. 1, June.

————. 1965. "Poverty, Proteins and Disguised Starvation." *Kajian Ekonomi Malaysia*, vol. 1, no. 1, June.

————. 1975*a*. "Footprints on the Sands of Time: The Malay Poverty Concept over Fifty Years from Za'ba to Aziz and the Second Malaysia Five Year Plan." In Chee and Khoo (1975).

————. 1975*b*. "Recent Thoughts on Poverty." Paper presented at the Second Malaysian Economic Convention, Kuala Lumpur.

Balassa, Bela. 1977. "The Income Distribution Parameter in Project Appraisal." In *Economic Progress, Private Values, and Public Policy*. B. Balassa and R. Nelson, eds. Amsterdam: North-Holland.

Barlow, C., and C-K. Chan. 1968. "Towards an Optimum Size of Rubber Holding." Paper presented to National Rubber Conference, Kuala Lumpur.

Ben-Porath, Y. 1967. "The Production of Human Capital and the Life-Cycle of Earnings." *Journal of Political Economy*, vol. 75, no. 4, pt. 1, August.

Bhalla, Surjit S. 1973. "The Education-Income Connection—An Investigative Report." Research Program in Economic Development Discussion Paper no. 38. Princeton University, Princeton, N. J.

Bliss, Christopher J., and Nicholas H. Stern. 1976. "Economic Aspects of the Connection between Productivity and Consumption." University of Essex, Discussion Paper no. 67.

Blitzer, Charles R., Peter B. Clark, and Lance Taylor, eds. 1975. *Economy-Wide Models and Development Planning*. New York: Oxford University Press.

Brown, C. 1973. "Rice Price Stabilization and Support in Malaysia." *Developing Economies*, vol. 11, no. 2, June.

Bruno, Michael. 1977. "Distributional Issues in Development Planning—Some Reflections on the State of the Art." Paper presented at the Workshop on Analysis of Distributional Issues in Development Planning, Bellagio, Italy.

Cham, B. N. 1975. "Class and Communal Conflict in Malaysia." *Journal of Contemporary Asia*, vol. 5, no. 4.

Chandra Muzaffar. 1977. "Some Political Perspectives on the New Economic Policy." Paper presented at the Fourth Malaysian Economic Convention, Kuala Lumpur.

Chee, S., and S. M. Khoo, eds. 1975. *Malaysian Economic Development and Policies*. Kuala Lumpur: Malaysian Economic Association.

Chenery, Hollis B., Montek S. Ahluwalia, C. L. G. Bell, John H. Duloy, and Richard Jolly. 1974. *Redistribution with Growth*. London: Oxford University Press.

Chew, A. F. Y. 1968. "Index Numbers in West Malaysia." M. A. thesis, Division of Statistics, Faculty of Economics and Administration, University of Malaya.

Chiswick, B. R. 1975. *Income Inequality: Regional Analyses within a Human Capital Framework*. New York: National Bureau of Economic Research.

Chiswick, B. R., and J. Mincer. 1972. "Time-Series Changes in Personal Income Inequality in the United States from 1939, with Projections to 1985." *Journal of Political Economy*, vol. 80, supplement, May/June.

Cohen, M., T. Nagel, and T. Scanlon, eds. 1977. *Equality and Preferential Treatment*. Princeton, N. J.: Princeton University Press.

Corden, W. M. 1971. *The Theory of Protection*. Oxford: Clarendon Press.

Dandekar, V. M., and N. Rath. 1971. *Poverty in India*. Poona: Indian School of Political Economy.

Dasgupta, Partha S., Amartya K. Sen, and David Starrett. 1973. "Notes on the Measurement of Inequality." *Journal of Economic Theory*, vol. 6, no. 2, April.

Department of Inland Revenue. 1974. *Annual Report of the Department of Inland Revenue, 1970*. Kuala Lumpur: Government Press.

Department of Social Welfare. 1975. "A Joint State and Federal Government Public Assistance Programme." Kuala Lumpur: Ministry of Welfare Services.

———. 1976. "Public Assistance as a State/Federal Government Responsibility." Kuala Lumpur: Ministry of Welfare Services.

Department of Statistics. [1957?]. "Course of Lectures for Training Investigators" [for the Household Budget Survey]. Kuala Lumpur, undated. Cited in text as *Course of Lectures*.

———. [1961?]. *Household Budget Survey of the Federation of Malaya 1957/58: Report*. Kuala Lumpur, undated. Cited in text as *HBS Report*.

———. 1968. *Dictionary of Occupational Classification*. Kuala Lumpur.

———. 1970a. *PES 1970 Instructions to Field Enumerators (Re-listing of Households—PES Form 2)*. Instruction Booklet 2. Kuala Lumpur.

———. 1970b. *PES 1970 Instructions to Field Interviewers (Demographic, Family*

Planning and Income Particulars—PES Form 3). Instruction Booklet 3. Kuala Lumpur.

―――. 1970*c. PES 1970 Instructions to Field Supervisors*. Instruction Booklet 4. Kuala Lumpur.

―――. 1970*d. PES 1970 General Instructions (Including Financial Instructions) to Field Enumerators and Interviewers*. Instruction Booklet 5. Kuala Lumpur.

―――. 1970*e. PES 1970 Sampling Instructions*. Instruction Booklet 6. Kuala Lumpur.

―――. 1970*f. PES Form 3* (Post-Enumeration Survey Questionnaire Booklet). Kuala Lumpur.

―――. 1970*g. Socio-Economic Sample Survey of Households—Malaysia 1967/68*. Kuala Lumpur.

―――. 1971*a. Index of Occupations*. Kuala Lumpur.

―――. 1971*b. Malaysian Industrial Classification*. Kuala Lumpur.

―――. 1972. *Rubber Statistics Handbook 1970*. Kuala Lumpur.

―――. 1973. *PES Coding Manual* (Post-Enumeration Survey 1970–71 "Code Book"). Kuala Lumpur.

de Wulf, L. 1975. "Fiscal Incidence Studies in Developing Countries: Survey and Critique." *IMF Staff Papers*, vol. 22, no. 1, March.

Economic Planning Unit (EPU). 1975. "Survey of Rural Poverty." Kuala Lumpur.

Food and Agriculture Organization (FAO)/World Bank. 1975. "Problems of Rural Poverty in Malaysia." World Bank Report no. 838-MA. Washington, D.C. Restricted circulation

Fei, John C. H., and Gustav Ranis. 1974. "Income Inequality by Additive Factor Components." Economic Growth Center, Yale University.

Fell, H. A., and others. 1959. *Report on Proposals for New Retail Price Indices*. Kuala Lumpur: Special Advisory Committee on Cost of Living Indices, Government Press.

Fisheries Division. 1971. "An Economic Survey of the Fishing Communities on the East Coast of Malaysia." Kuala Lumpur: Ministry of Agriculture and Lands.

Fishlow, Albert. 1972. "Brazilian Size Distribution of Income." *American Economic Review*, vol. 62, May.

―――. 1973. "Brazilian Income Size Distribution—Another Look." Berkeley: University of California.

Goldman, R. 1975. "Staple Food Self-Sufficiency and the Distributive Impact of Malaysian Rice Policy." *Food Research Institute Studies* (Stanford, Calif.), vol. 14, no. 3.

Government of Malaysia. 1971. *Second Malaysia Plan 1971–1975*. Kuala Lumpur: Government Press. Referred to as SMP in the text.

―――. 1972. *Parliamentary Debates on the Constitution Amendment Bill, 1971*. Kuala Lumpur: Government Press.

————. 1973. *Mid-Term Review of the Second Malaysia Plan, 1971–1975*. Kuala Lumpur: Government Press. Referred to as MTR in the text.

————. 1974. *Estimates of Federal Revenue and Expenditure, 1972*. Kuala Lumpur.

————. 1976. *Third Malaysia Plan, 1976–1980*. Kuala Lumpur: Government Press. Referred to as TMP in the text.

Grant, W. R. 1970. "Application of an Economic Model for Evaluating Government Program Cost for Rice." *American Journal of Agricultural Economics*, vol. 52, no. 2, May.

Harris, J. R., and M. P. Todaro. 1970. "Migration, Unemployment and Development: A Two-Sector Analysis." *American Economic Review*, vol. 60, March.

Hirschman, Charles 1972. "Ethnic Stratification in West Malaysia." Ph.D. dissertation, Department of Sociology, University of Wisconsin. Ann Arbor, Mich. University Microfilms, Inc.

————. 1973. "The Determinants of Ethnic Inequality in Peninsular Malaysia." Paper presented at the annual meeting of the Rural Sociological Society, College Park, Maryland.

————. 1974. "Economic Progress in Malaysia: How Widely Has It Been Shared?" *UMBC Economic Review* (Kuala Lumpur), vol. 10.

Hoerr, O. D. 1973. "Education, Income and Equity in Malaysia." *Economic Development and Cultural Change*, vol. 21, no. 2, January. Reprinted in Lim (1975).

Huang, Y. 1975. "Tenancy Patterns, Productivity, and Rentals in Malaysia." *Economic Development and Cultural Change*, vol. 23, no. 4, July.

Jackson, R. M. 1961. *Immigrant Labour and the Development of Malaya: 1786–1920*. Kuala Lumpur: Government Printer.

Jain, Shail. 1975. *Size Distribution of Income: A Compilation of Data*. Baltimore, Md.: Johns Hopkins University Press.

Kakwani, N. C., and N. Podder. 1973. "On the Estimation of Lorenz Curves from Grouped Observations." *International Economic Review*, vol. 14, no. 2, June.

————. 1976. "Efficient Estimation of the Lorenz Curve and Associated Inequality Measures from Grouped Observations." *Econometrica*, vol. 44, no. 1, January.

Kamal, Salih. 1975. "Urban Strategy, Regional Development, and the New Economic Policy." Paper presented at the Second Malaysian Economic Convention, Kuala Lumpur.

Kendall, M. G., and A. Stuart. 1963. *The Advanced Theory of Statistics*. Vol. 1, *Distribution Theory*. 2d ed. London: Griffin.

Khoo, Khay Huat. 1976. "Optimal Utilization and Management of Fishery Resources." *Kajian Ekonomi Malaysia*, vol. 13, nos. 1 and 2, June/December.

Kolm, S. Ch. 1969. "The Optimal Production of Social Justice." In *Public*

Economics. J. Margolis and H. Guitton, eds. London: Macmillan.

Kuznets, Simon. 1955. "Economic Growth and Income Inequality." *American Economic Review*, vol. 45, no. 1, March.

———. 1963. "Quantitative Aspects of Economic Growth of Nations: Distribution of Income by Size." *Economic Development and Cultural Change*, vol. 11, no. 2, pt. 2, January.

———. 1976. "Demographic Aspects of the Size Distribution of Income: An Exploratory Essay." *Economic Development and Cultural Change*, vol. 25, no. 1, October.

Lamb, A. 1964. "Early History." In *Malaysia: A Survey*. Wang Gangwu, ed. London: Pall Mall Press.

Lee, E. L. H. 1975. "Income Distribution in a Developing Economy: A Case Study of West Malaysia." D.Phil. dissertation, Oxford University.

Lim, D., ed. 1975. *Readings on Malaysian Economic Development*. Kuala Lumpur: Oxford University Press.

Lim, Lin Lean. 1974. *The Pattern of Income Distribution in West Malaysia, 1957–1970.* ILO Working Paper. Geneva: International Labour Office.

Lipton, M. 1968. "Strategy for Agriculture: Urban Bias and Rural Planning." In *The Crisis of Indian Planning*. P. P. Streeten and M. Lipton, eds. London: Oxford University Press.

———. 1977. *Why Poor People Stay Poor: Urban Bias in World Development*. London: Temple Smith.

Low, P., ed. 1971. *Trends in Southeast Asia*. No. 2. Proceedings and Background Paper of Seminar on Trends in Malaysia. Singapore: Institute of Southeast Asian Studies.

Marglin, S. A. 1967. *Public Investment Criteria*. London: Allen and Unwin.

Mazumdar, Dipak, assisted by P. Videt-Yontrakich. 1975. "Education and Employment in Urban Malaysia." Development Economics Department, World Bank, Washington, D.C.

McNamara, Robert S. 1972. *Address to the Board of Governors*. Washington, D.C.: World Bank. Reprinted in *The McNamara Years at the World Bank: Major Policy Addresses of Robert S. McNamara, 1968–1981*. Baltimore, Md.: Johns Hopkins University Press, 1981.

——— 1973. *Address to the Board of Governors*. Washington, D.C.: World Bank. Reprinted in *The McNamara Years at the World Bank: Major Policy Addresses of Robert S. McNamara, 1968–1981*. Baltimore, Md.: Johns Hopkins University Press, 1981.

———. 1975. *Address to the Board of Governors*. Washington, D.C.: World Bank. Reprinted in *The McNamara Years at the World Bank: Major Policy Addresses of Robert S. McNamara, 1968–1981*. Baltimore, Md.: Johns Hopkins University Press, 1981.

Milne, R. S. 1976. "The Politics of Malaysia's New Economic Policy." *Pacific Affairs*, vol. 49, no. 2, Summer.

Mincer, J. 1970. "The Distribution of Labor Incomes: A Survey with Special Reference to the Human Capital Approach." *Journal of Economic Literature*, vol. 8, no. 1, March.

———. 1974. *Schooling, Experience and Earnings*. New York: National Bureau of Economic Research.

———. 1976. "Progress in Human Capital Analyses of the Distribution of Earnings." In *The Personal Distribution of Incomes*. Anthony B. Atkinson, ed. London: Allen and Unwin.

Ministry of Labour and Manpower. 1972. *Handbook of Labour Statistics*. Kuala Lumpur.

Mirrlees, James A. 1971. "An Exploration in the Theory of Optimum Income Taxation." *Review of Economic Studies*, vol. 38, April.

Moore, Basil J. 1975. "Restructuring Society." School of Comparative Social Sciences, Universiti Sains Malaysia, Penang.

Morley, S. A., and J. G. Williamson. 1973. "The Impact of Demand on Labor Absorption and the Distribution of Earnings: The Case of Brazil." Paper no. 39. Program of Development Studies, Rice University.

Morrison, I. 1949. "Aspects of the Racial Problem in Malaya." *Pacific Affairs*, no. 22, September.

Muellbauer, John 1976. "Can We Base Comparisons of Welfare between Households on Behaviour?" Birkbeck College, London.

Narkswasdi, U., and S. Selvadurai. 1968. *Economic Survey of Padi Production in West Malaysia*. Kuala Lumpur: Ministry of Agriculture and Co-Operatives.

Organisation for Economic Co-operation and Development (OECD). 1976. *Public Expenditure on Income Maintenance Programmes*. Paris.

Orshansky, M. 1965. "Counting the Poor: Another Look at the Poverty Profile." *Social Security Bulletin*, vol. 28.

Oshima, Harry T. 1970. "Income Inequality and Economic Growth: The Postwar Experience of Asian Countries."*Malayan Economic Review*, vol. 15, no. 12, October.

Palan, V. T. 1968. "Problems of Questionnaire-Design with Particular Reference to Household Surveys." *Kajian Ekonomi Malaysia*, vol. 5, no. 1, June.

Paukert, Felix. 1973. "Income Distribution at Different Levels of Development: A Survey of Evidence." *International Labour Review*, vol. 108, nos. 2–3, August–September.

Peiris, Denzil. 1975. "The Emerging Rural Revolution." *Far Eastern Economic Review* (Hong Kong), January 10, 1975.

Psacharapoulos, G. 1973. *Returns to Education—An International Comparison*. San Francisco: Jossey-Bass/Elsevier International Series.

Purcal, J. T. 1971. *Rice Economy: A Case Study of Four Villages in West Malaysia*. Kuala Lumpur: University of Malaya Press.

Purcell, V. 1967. *The Chinese in Malaya*. Kuala Lumpur: Oxford University Press. 1st ed., 1948.

Puthucheary, J. 1977. "Changes in Ownership and Control in Malaysia." Paper presented at the Fourth Malaysian Economic Convention, Kuala Lumpur.

Pyatt, Graham. 1976. "On the Interpretation and Disaggregation of Gini Coefficients." *Economic Journal*, vol. 86, no. 342, June.

Pyatt, Graham, and Jeffrey I. Round, assisted by Jane Denes. 1977. "The Distribution of Income and Social Accounts: A Study of Malaysia in 1970." Development Research Center, World Bank, Washington, D.C.

Rafferty, Kevin. 1975a. "Clouds Over Eden's Horizon." *Financial Times* (London), February 24, 1975.

———. 1975b. "Pitfalls of the New Economic Policy." *Financial Times* (London), February 24, 1975.

Rajakumar, M. K. 1977. "Conflict Resolution and National Progress." Paper presented at the Fourth Malaysian Economic Convention, Kuala Lumpur.

Rao, V. M. 1969. "Two Decompositions of Concentration Ratio." *Journal of the Royal Statistical Society*, ser. A, vol. 132, pt. 3.

Rawls, John. 1971. *A Theory of Justice*. Cambridge, Mass.: Harvard University Press.

Razak, Abdul. 1971. "With One Mind toward One Objective." Opening address to the MCA general assembly, Kuala Lumpur, August 21, 1971.

Robless, C. L. 1975a. "Some Notes on the Feasibility and Consistency of the New Economic Policy." In Chee and Khoo (1975).

———. 1975b. "Policy Analysis and Development Planning in Malaysia." Kuala Lumpur: Economic Planning Unit, Prime Minister's Department.

Roff, W. R. 1967. *The Origins of Malay Nationalism*. Singapore: University of Malaya Press.

Ross-Larson, Bruce, ed. 1977. *Issues in Contemporary Malaysia*. Kuala Lumpur: Heinemann Educational Books (Asia) Ltd.

Rothschild, Michael, and Joseph E. Stiglitz. 1973. "Some Further Results on the Measurement of Inequality." *Journal of Economic Theory*, vol. 6, no. 2, April.

Rowntree, B. S. 1922. *Poverty: A Study of Town Life*. New ed. London: Longmans, Green.

Sandhu, K. S. 1967. "Indians in the Modern Malayan Economy." *India Quarterly* (New Delhi), vol. 23, April/June.

———. 1969. *Indians in Malaya: Immigration and Settlement, 1786–1957*. Cambridge, Eng.: Cambridge University Press.

Sawyer, Malcolm. 1976. "Income Distribution in OECD Countries." *OECD Economic Outlook*, no. 19, July.

Schutz, R. R. 1951. "On the Measurement of Income Inequality." *American Economic Review*, vol. 41, no. 1, March.

Selvadurai, S. 1968. *A Preliminary Report on the Survey of Coconut Smallholdings in West Malaysia*. Kuala Lumpur: Ministry of Agriculture and Co-operatives.

———. 1972a. *Padi Farming in West Malaysia*. Kuala Lumpur: Kementerian Pertanian dan Perikanan.

————. 1972*b*. *Padi Survey: Sungei Manik and Changkat Jong Irrigation Areas, Perak*. Kuala Lumpur: Ministry of Agriculture and Fisheries.

————. 1972*c*. *Krian Padi Survey*. Kuala Lumpur: Ministry of Agriculture and Fisheries.

————. 1972*d*. *Socio-Economic Survey of Rubber Smallholdings in West Johore*. Kuala Lumpur: Ministry of Agriculture and Fisheries.

————. 1975. *Padi Survey: Sebarang Perak (Stage I)*. Kuala Lumpur: Ministry of Agriculture and Rural Development.

Selvadurai, S., and Ani b. Arope. 1969. *Socio-Economic Study of Padi Farms in Province Wellesley 1968*. Kuala Lumpur: Ministry of Agriculture and Co-operatives.

Selvadurai, S., Ani b. Arope, and Nik Hassan b. Mohammad. 1969. *Socio-Economic Study of the Padi Farms in the Kemubu Area of Kelantan 1968*. Kuala Lumpur: Ministry of Agriculture and Co-operatives.

Selvaratnam, V. 1975. "Some Aspects of Race and Class in Colonial and Post-Colonial Peninsular Malaysia." Institute of Development Studies, University of Sussex.

Sen, Amartya K. 1973*a*. *On Economic Inequality*. Oxford: Clarendon Press.

————. 1973*b*. "Poverty, Inequality and Unemployment: Some Conceptual Issues in Measurement." *Economic and Political Weekly*, Special Number, August.

————. 1976*a*. "Poverty: An Ordinal Approach to Measurement." *Econometrica*, vol. 44, no. 2, March.

————. 1976*b*. "Real National Income." *Review of Economic Studies*, vol. 43.

Shaharuddin bin Haron. 1977. "Restructuring Ownership and Control: Some Recollections on Policy." Paper presented at the Fourth Malaysian Economic Convention, Kuala Lumpur.

Shaplen, Robert. 1977. "Letter from Malaysia." *New Yorker*, April 18, 1977.

Snodgrass, Donald R. 1975. "Trends and Patterns in Malaysian Income Distribution, 1957–70." In Lim (1975).

Squire, Lyn, and Herman G. van der Tak. 1975. *Economic Analysis of Projects*. Baltimore, Md.: Johns Hopkins University Press.

Stenson, Michael. 1976. "Class and Race in West Malaysia." *Bulletin of Concerned Asian Scholars*, April–June.

Stern, Nicholas H. 1977. "Welfare Weights and the Elasticity of the Marginal Valuation of Income." In *Current Economic Problems*. M. Artis and R. Nobay, eds. Oxford: Basil Blackwell.

Stiglitz, Joseph E. 1975. "The Theory of Screening, Education, and the Distribution of Income." *American Economic Review*, vol. 65, no. 3, June.

Suffian, Mohamed bin Hashim. 1972. *An Introduction to the Constitution of Malaysia*. Kuala Lumpur: Government Press.

Tan, B. T. 1975. "Agricultural Subsidy and Price Support Policies." Paper presented at the Second Malaysian Economic Convention, Kuala Lumpur.

Tan, Siew Sin. 1971. "With One Mind toward One Objective." Presidential address to the MCA general assembly, Kuala Lumpur, August 21, 1971.

Theil, Henri. 1967. *Economics and Information Theory.* Amsterdam: North-Holland.

Thillainathan, R. 1970. "The Second Malaysia Plan—Notes on the Objectives of Balanced Distribution of Wealth and Employment." *Kajian Ekonomi Malaysia,* vol. 7, no. 2, December.

———. 1975a. "The Public Enterprise as an Instrument for Restructuring Society: The Malaysian Case." In Chee and Khoo (1975).

———. 1975b. "Planning for Economic Equality and the Role of the Public Sector: The West Malaysian Case." In Lim (1975).

———. 1975c. "Distributional Issues and Policies in Malaysia—A Review." Paper presented at the Second Malaysian Economic Convention, Kuala Lumpur.

———. 1976. "An Analysis of the Effects of Policies for the Redistribution of Income and Wealth in West Malaysia, 1957–75." Ph.D. dissertation, London School of Economics and Political Science.

Thorbecke, E., and J. K. Sengupta. 1972. "A Consistency Framework for Employment, Output and Income Distribution: Projections Applied to Colombia." Development Research Center, World Bank, Washington, D.C.

Todaro, Michael P. 1969. "A Model of Labour Migration and Urban Unemployment." *American Economic Review,* vol. 59, March.

Universiti Sains Malaysia. 1972. "Fishermen and Fisheries Development in Penang and Kedah." Penang.

von der Mehden, F. R. 1975. "Communalism, Industrial Policy and Income Distribution in Malaysia." *Asian Survey,* vol. 15, no. 3, March.

von Vorys, Karl. 1975. *Democracy without Consensus.* Princeton, N. J.: Princeton University Press.

Weisskoff, R. 1973. "A Multi-Sector Simulation Model of Employment, Growth and Income Distribution in Puerto Rico: A Re-Evaluation of Successful Development Strategy." Economic Growth Center, Yale University, New Haven, Conn.

World Bank. 1975. *Rural Development.* Sector Policy Paper. Washington, D.C.

Zagier, D. B. 1977. "On the Decomposability of the Gini Coefficient and Other Indices of Inequality." Unpublished manuscript.

Index

Age, 279; depreciation of human capital with, 239; earnings function and, 265–67; education and earnings and, 255–57; human capital model and, 237; personal income inequality and, 229; poverty and, 132, 151; urban poverty and, 186

Age-income profile, 64, 248, 249, 254, 265

Agriculture, 11, 172, 276, 295; ethnic composition and, 3, 4; poverty measures and, 131, 157–64, 167; racial breakdown of modern, 211–14. *See also* Farmers

Ahluwalia, Montek S., 39, 97, 126 *n*25

Alliance (political party), 8, 9

Anand, Sudhir, 97, 111 *n*1, 135 *n*37, 142 *n*39, 152

Andic, F. M., 286 *n*19, 287

Ani B. Arope, 153 *n*14

Atkinson index, 82–86, 89, 90 *n*38, 92, 103 *n*56, 122 *n*19, 192, 195, 197, 202 *n*19, 274, 310 *n*9, 333, 334, 345

Aziz, Ungku A., 112–13, 152 *n*10

Baling disturbances (1974), 7 *n*12

Barisan Nasional (National Front political party), 9

Barlow, C., 161, 162

Ben-Porath, Y., 239

Between-group component (racial). *See* Ethnic composition, between-group component

Budgets (food and nonfood), poverty line definition and, 114–17

Capital, European (in Malaysia), 4

Census of Population and Housing (1970), 22, 24, 25

Chan, C-K., 161, 162

Chew, A. F. Y., 46 *n*32

Children, 67 *n*13, 132, 151, 276

Chinese. *See* Ethnic composition

Chiswick, B. R., 239 *n*2, 261 *n*43

Coconut subsector, 167, 214, 287 *n*22

Coding of PES income data, 30; estimating household income distribution from, 30–34

Commodity market intervention, 290–92

Constitution, 7

Consumption, 291; economies of scale neglected in, 67 *n*14; farmer's own (of produce), 29, 43, 49, 50; welfare levels and, 63, 64

Corporate ownership, 11–12

Council of Trust for the Indigenous People (MARA), 13

Course of Lectures (Department of Statistics), 44, 47, 48, 49

Data: assessing reliability of PES income, 22–24; coded personal income distribution, 192; coded PES income, 30; estimating household income distribution from coded income, 30–34; fits obtained by, 248; income distribution, 40, 41, 46, 51; income (PES, problems with), 243–47; national accounts, 38 *n*20; noncomparability (between countries) of, 40; PES (1970) as base for study, 21–22, 271, 273; study, 1 *n*1, 4 *n*9

Decomposition: of Gini coefficient, 319–26; incidence-of-poverty measure and, 126, 127; of log-income variance, 330–31; methodology of inequality, 86–92; of poverty, 275; racial inequality and, 99–101; regional inequality and, 97; rural-urban inequality and, 99; strictly decomposable indices and, 88, 102, 274; of Theil second measure *L*, 329–30; Theil *T* index and, 93, 327–29; weakly decomposable indices and, 89–92, 322

Decomposition of personal income distribution, 277; inequality measures and, 198–202; multivariate, 227–29; occupational category and, 216–26; race and, 202–03; region and, 203–06; sector of employment and, 226–27; sex of income recipient and, 206–07

Degree (educational), earnings and, 259–61
Democratic Action party, 8
Department of Statistics, 22, 42, 115, 117
Dependency ratio, 72, 151, 186
Developing countries: income inequality comparisons and, 40, 41; income inequality factors and, 227; inequality and, 21
Development, 21 *n*1; policy for rural, 292–93
de Wulf, L., 287 *n*24
Diploma, earnings and, 259–61
Disaggregation of income (Gini coefficient), 318–19
Doctors, earnings of, 259, 261

Earnings function, 280; age and, 255–57, 265–67; age-income profile and, 248, 249, 254, 265; degree type and, 259–61; estimation of (by race, sex, occupation), 249–53; human capital, 238–41; human capital model and, 237–38; language used in schooling and, 257–59; properties of, 264–67; regional breakdown of, 261–64; return to education and, 241–43
Economic Planning Unit (EPU), 152, 161, 162, 164, 165, 167, 286
Economic welfare, PES income as measure of, 63–65. *See also* Social welfare; Welfare comparisons
Education, 279; age cohort and earnings and, 255–57; age-income profile and, 248, 249, 254; degree type and earnings and, 259–61; estimates of earnings by occupation and, 251–53; estimates of earnings by race and, 247, 249–51; estimates of earnings by sex and, 253–54; ethnic quotas and, 7–8, 294; human capital model and, 237–38; language of instruction and earnings and, 257–59; personal income inequality and, 229; poverty measures and, 131–32, 173, 186; rate of return to, 241–43; rich households and, 142–43; rural poverty and, 276
Employment: ethnic composition of, 3; New Economic Policy and, 10, 11, 13–14; non-agricultural, 160; personal income inequality and, 207–14; personal income inequality and sector of, 226–27; poverty measures and, 131, 135, 150, 172; restructuring of, 294–98; rich households and, 142. *See also* Self-employed individuals; Underemployment; Unemployment; Urban employees
Engineers, earnings of, 259, 261
Enumeration blocks (PES), 24–25
Estates, 157; HBS and, 48; modern agriculture

and, 214; ownership of fixed assets and, 11 *n*17; rubber, 160 163–64
Ethnic composition: Atkinson index of inequality and, 86; between-group component and, 86–92, 96, 97, 102, 198, 200–01, 221, 222, 223, 229, 279, 329, 330, 331; education estimates and earnings and, 247, 249–51, 252; employment restructuring and, 295–98; food budget analysis and, 115; government efforts to balance, 15–17; HBS household choice and, 45–46; HBS and PES comparison and, 52; household income and, 37–38, 72, 76, 82; incidence of poverty and, 125–26, 127, 133, 146–50, 153–56, 160; interracial inequality and, 93–96, 97–99, 273–74, 277; language in schooling and earnings and, 257–59; New Economic Policy and, 10–14, 272; overview of, 1–4; personal income distribution (racial disparity) and, 197–201, 202–03, 206–07, 211, 214, 215–16, 217–23, 226–27, 228–29; political activity and, 6–9; restructuring of society and, 10, 11–14, 15–17, 101–03, 298–301; of rich households, 142; rural household income and, 43; urban-rural inequality and, 100; within-group component and, 86–92, 96, 97, 102, 200, 228–29, 329, 330, 331
Expenditures, 49, 52; consumption, 63
Exports: Malaysian economy and, 4–5; taxes on, 286, 287; tax on rubber, 162, 288–89

Farmers: personal income and race of, 217, 220–21; PES income definition and, 28–29; poverty measures and, 131, 135, 146, 157–64, 167, 276; subsistence, 39, 49–50
Federal Land Development Authority (FELDA), 156, 165
Federation of Malaya Agreement (February 1948), 7
Fei, John C. H., 315–16
Fell, H. A., 46, 50
First Malaysia Plan (1966–70), 6
Fishermen, 165–66, 276
Food budget, poverty line definition and, 114–16, 117

Gerakan Rakyat Malaysia (political party), 8
Gini coefficient, 88, 93, 96 *n*43, 97, 273, 274, 299, 306; decomposition of, 319–26; defined, 34, 311–26; as index based on Lorenz diagram, 304–05; personal income calculation and, 195; Sen's poverty measure and, 119; among states, 97

Goodman, Roe, 26 *n*6
Goodness-of-fit, equations and, 248
Government: employment policy in public
sector and, 220; minimum income and,
281; poverty policy and, 10–11, 14–15;
public assistance and, 283, 285; replanting
(rubber) program of, 161–62, 163; restructuring of society and, 9–14, 15–17
Gross national product (GNP): growth of, 12
*n*20; increase in, 6; savings rate and, 6

Haridas, Mr. (Ministry of Agriculture), 64 *n*4
Hiring: of outside farm labor, 157 *n*23;
preferential (of Malays), 6, 220, 250, 300
Hirschman, Charles, 42
Hoerr, O. D., 242 *n*10
Household Budget Survey (HBS, 1957–58),
21, 22, 42, 273; compared with PES, 51–53;
definition of income and, 47–51; sample
design of, 44–47
Household Expenditure Survey (HES, 1973),
286; poverty budget analysis and, 116
Household heads: PES interviews and, 26;
poverty measures and, 131, 135, 146, 150,
151, 168; rich, 142–43; self-employed, 283
Household income: distribution of households by, 65; distribution of households by
per capita, 66, 69, 77, 79–82; distribution
of households by household size and, 67–
77; estimating distribution (PES) of, 30–34,
272–73; HBS and distribution of, 50–51;
inequality and, 35–38; inequality in per
capita, 188–92; international comparisons
and, 40–41; mapping the household to the
per capita, 346–54; MSSH and, 43; PES and
national accounts comparison and, 38–
39; poverty and, 133; poverty definition
and, 114
Households: as basic income-sharing unit,
66–67; definition of (survey comparisons)
41; distribution of (by household income),
65; distribution of (by household income
and size), 67–77; distribution of (by per
capita household income), 66, 67, 77, 79–
82; HBS and definition of, 44–45; HBS and
rural and urban, 45–46; incidence of poverty and, 132, 276; income distribution
estimation (PES coded income data) for,
30–34; mapping to per capita household
income distribution and, 346–54; PES income definition and farm, 28–29; PES
sample definition of, 24; PES check on undercoverage of, 26; poverty and large urban,
186, 276; rich, 135–43; urban farm, 172
Household size: distribution of households
by, 67–77; food budget analysis and, 116;

inequality and, 80, 81; poverty and, 132,
151; urban poverty and, 186
Houses: HBS and PES compared and, 52; HBS
sample and, 45, 50; PES income definition
and rental of, 29
Huang, Y., 156 *n*18
Human capital, 100; earnings function, 238–
41; income and theory of, 237–38, 265;
traditional sector employees and model of,
251–52

Import duties, 286, 287
Incidence-of-poverty measure, 126, 127, 275;
household composition and, 132; large
urban households and, 186; rural sector
and, 146. *See also* Poverty
Income: coding of PES data on, 30; data in
PES, 22–23, 243–47, 273; definition of HBS,
47–51; definition of PES, 27–29, 272; economic welfare and PES, 63–65; equally
distributed equivalent, 83–85, 92, 120–21,
194, 196, 202 *n*19; estimating household
income distribution from PES coded data
on, 30–34; HBS concept of, 44; MSSH
concept of, 43; human capital model and,
237–38; per capita household, 66, 67, 77,
79–82; poverty measures and, 118; study
choice of concept of, 65–67; surveys
and definition of, 41, 42; underestimation of, 342, 343; underreporting of, 39.
See also Household income; Income
distribution; Personal income distribution
Income distribution: data in PES, 22–23;
estimating household (coded PES data),
30–34; government efforts and, 14–15;
HBS and household, 50–51; HBS and PES
comparison and, 51–52; household
income inequality and, 35–38; international comparisons of inequality and
household, 40–41; PES and national accounts comparisons and household, 38–
39; population unit choice and, 65; poverty measures and, 118–23
Income inequality: Atkinson index and, 82–
86; decomposition of (methodology), 86–
92; distribution of individuals by per
capita household income and, 81–82;
household, 35–38; household income and
per capita household income distribution
and, 79–81; international comparisons of,
40–41; intertemporal comparisons of, 39,
42–53; Lorenz diagram and indices of,
303–10; personal income and, 192–98;
policy analysis and, 101–03; racial disparity and, 197–201, 202–03, 206–07,

Income inequality (*continued*)
211, 214, 215–16, 217–23, 226–27, 228–29; rural-urban, 99–101
Indians. *See* Ethnic composition
Individual per capita household income distribution, 66, 67, 77, 79–82, 102
Industrial Coordination Act (1975), 294
Industrial sector, 5, 11 *n*17, 226, 276; licensing on ethnic bases and, 294. *See also* One-digit industrial and occupational level (poverty); Two-digit industrial and occupational level (poverty)
Inequality. *See* Income inequality
Inflation, 5–6, 43 *n*28
Institute of Medical Research (Malaysia), 114
Intervals (income classification in PES), 30–31
Interviews (HBS), 47–49
Interviews (PES): farmer's income and, 28–29; household assessment by interviewer and, 59–62; questions on income during, 23–24, 53–59; sampling procedure and, 24–26
Irrigation, 157

Jain, Shail, 40

Kajian Ekonomi Malaysia, 112
Kakwani, N. C., 34 *n*16, 40 *n*23
Kanbur, S. M., 97
Kendall, M. G., 313
Kolm, S. Ch., 215 *n*29

Laborers: farm, 252; paddy, 157; landless paddy, 160; rubber, 163–64
Labor market experience, definition of, 239
Land, 100, 287 *n*22; poverty and size of holdings in, 156, 157; rubber, 163 *n*31
Language: Bahasa Malaysia as national, 8; of school instruction (earnings function), 257–59
Lee, E. L. H., 42, 44
Leisure preference, 215, 216
Lim, Lin Lean, 42
Log-income variance, 88, 261, 273, 275, 280, 350; age and education and, 248, 249, 254, 265; decomposition of, 330–31; discrete income distribution (inequality indices defined in), 307–08; inequality across households (personal income calculation), 188–89; inequality measure (personal income) and, 201–02; inequality measures comparisons and, 331–32
Lorenz class (of inequality indices), 339–40
Lorenz curve, 275; Gini coefficient definition and, 34, 316–17; for household and per capita household income, 79–80; inequality in distribution of incomes and, 81–82; inequality indices based on, 303–10; inequality in personal income calculation and, 191–92, 195; lack of welfare comparisons and, 333–40; lemmas on, 341–44; redress of poverty and, 344–45

McNamara, Robert, 113 *n*5, 292 *n*37
Mahathir Mohamad, Dr., 16
Malayan Agricultural Producers Association (MAPA), 164
Malayan Chinese Association (MCA), 7, 8, 9
Malayan Indian Congress, 8
Malay Mail, 112
Malays. *See* Ethnic composition; Restructuring of society
Malaysia: economic overview of, 4–6; estimates of poverty in, 125–26; ethnic pluralism in, 1–4; household income inequality in, 35–38; indigenous people of, 12 *n*19; intertemporal comparisons of inequality in, 42; New Economic Policy in, 9–14; politics in, 6–9; profile of poverty in, 126–32; profile of poverty sensitivity and, 132–35. *See also* Peninsular Malaysia; Regions (states)
Malaysian Socio-Economic Sample Survey of Households (MSSH, 1967–68), 21, 22, 42; income concept in, 43
Mean independence, 89, 103, 192, 275, 306, 341
Men: estimates of earnings function and education and, 247, 249, 253–54, 257; PES sample and military, 25 *n*3
Metropolitan towns. *See* Urban sector, metropolitan towns
Mid-Term Review of the Second Malaysia Plan (MTR), 10, 12–15, 294–98
Migration: to Peninsular Malaysia, 2; rural to urban, 168; urban to rural, 295
Mincer, J., 239 *n*2, 240
Mining, 4, 216 *n*33, 226, 295
Ministry of Agriculture, 64 *n*4, 152
Ministry of Labour and Manpower, 163–64
Ministry of Welfare Services, 114; public assistance program and, 281
Mirrlees, James A., 123 *n*22
Moore, Basil J., 296 *n*44
Muellbauer, John, 65 *n*7

Narkswasdi, U., 153 *n*14
National accounts, PES income estimates comparison and, 38–39
National Corporation (PERNAS), 13
National Operations Council, 8

National Union of Plantation Workers (NUPW), 164
Negative exponential distribution, 353
NEP Prong 1. *See* Poverty
NEP Prong 2. *See* Restructuring of society
New Economic Policy (NEP, 1971): analysis of study results and observations on, 298–301; employment and, 294; objectives of, 9–14, 272
New Villages (Chinese), 150
Nik b. Mohammad, 153 n14
Nonfood budget, poverty line definition and, 116–17
Normalization axiom (Sen), 119–20, 121, 122 n20
Nutrition, poverty budget and, 114–16, 117

Occupation, 279; education estimates and earnings and, 251–53; HBS income concept and, 50; inequality in personal income and, 216–26, 229, 279; PES income questions and, 23. *See also* One-digit industrial and occupational level (poverty); Two-digit industrial and occupational level (poverty)
Oil palm subsector, 4, 164, 167, 214
One-digit industrial and occupational level (poverty): definition of, 236n; personal income inequality and, 216, 220; rural poor and, 145–46, 150, 151, 152; urban poor and, 168
Orshansky, M., 116 n12
Outline Perspective Plan (OPP, 1970–90), 10, 11, 294, 297

Paddy (rice), 5, 287 n22; poverty in sector for, 157–60, 276; price support and, 290
Palan, V. T., 24, 28
Palm oil, 4, 164, 167, 214
Pan Malayan Islamic party, 8
Parabolic age–log-income profile, 248. *See also* Age; Age-income profile
Pareto distribution: personal income calculations and, 192, 193; PES income classification and, 30–31, 33, 353
Participation rate, 72, 186; personal income inequality calculation and, 189–90, 197; underemployment and, 150–51
Payments in kind, 29, 43, 49
Peninsular Malaysia: indigenous people (Malays) of, 12 n19; migration to, 2; rural and urban ethnic groups and, 3–4; study data and, 1 n1. *See also* Malaysia
Personal income distribution, 277–78; decomposition for inequality measures and, 198–202; distribution of income recipients by, 192–98; employment status and, 207–14; income recipient definition and, 187–88; inequality across households in per capita terms (calculation) and, 188–92; interracial differentials (rubber tappers) and, 215–16; male and female decomposition and, 206–07; multivariate decomposition and, 227–29; occupational decomposition and, 216–26; racial decomposition and, 202–03; regional decomposition and, 203–06; sector of employment decomposition and, 226–27
Pigou-Dalton condition, 80, 88 n33, 89, 103, 192, 306, 339
Podder, N., 34 n16, 40 n23
Policy: commodity market intervention, 290–92; direct income transfers and, 281–85; employment restructuring, 294–98; inequality measures and restructuring of society and, 101–03; interracial inequality and, 298–301; poverty and fiscal, 286–89; redressing poverty and, 298–301; rural development and, 144, 292–93
Political issues, 6–9
Political parties, 8–9
Population: adjusting data on, 26; 1970 census and, 22, 24; of Peninsular Malaysia, 2; percentage in poverty, 125
Population-size independence, 89, 103, 192, 275, 306, 341
Population unit, 273, 339; choice of, 65, 127; personal income inequality calculation and, 191; standardizing (international comparison), 41
Post-Enumeration Survey (PES, 1970), 271; coding of income data and, 30; as data base for study, 21–22, 271, 273; design of, 24–26, 272; estimating household income distribution and, 30–34; general analysis of, 22–24; Gini coefficient estimation and, 34; HBS comparison and, 51–53; household income inequality and, 35–38; income definition and, 27–29; income estimates compared with those of national accounts, 38–39; income questions in, 22–23; international comparisons of inequality and, 40–41; intertemporal comparisons of inequality and, 42–51; sample design of, 24–26
Poverty: commodity market intervention and, 290–92; defining, 111–13; definition of poverty line and, 113–18; direct income transfers and, 281–85; distribution of tax burden and, 286–90; education and, 131–32, 173, 186; employment and, 131, 135; employment restructuring and, 294–98;

Poverty (*continued*)
estimating, 125–26; ethnic composition
of, 125–26, 127, 133, 146–50; fishermen
and, 165–66; government focus on, 14–
15; New Economic Policy and, 10–11,
281; profile of Malaysian, 126–32, 276;
redressing, 103, 275, 276, 298–301, 344–
45; rural development and, 144, 292–93;
rural sector and, 127, 131, 133–35, 144–
57; rural sector subgroups and, 157–64,
167, 276; sarong index of, 112; sensitivity
of profile of, 132–35; urban sector and,
127, 145, 167–68, 172–73, 186

Poverty budget, analysis of, 114–17

Poverty gap, 123, 275; racial groups and,
125–26

Poverty line, 275; defining, 113–18; government plans and definition of, 15; poverty
profile and, 132–33; Sen index and, 125;
variations considered in, 135

"The Poverty of the Malays" (Za'ba), 112

Prices: food budget analysis and, 115; HBS
and, 49; PES income definition and, 29, 64;
of rubber, 162; support of, 290–91

Prong 1 (NEP). *See* Poverty

Prong 2 (NEP). *See* Restructuring of society

Public expenditure, 286, 290

Public sector: employment restructuring
and, 294; government employment policy
in, 220

Purcal, J. T., 153 *n*14

Puthucheary, J., 13 *n*23

Pyatt, Graham, 39 *n*21

Race. *See* Ethnic composition

Racial disparity ratios, 82, 86, 197–98, 273–
74

Racial disturbances, 7 *n*12, 8, 9

Ranis, Gustav, 315–16

Rank-order welfare function, 118, 120–22,
314

Rao, V. M., 312–13

Rawls, John, 113

Redress of poverty rule, 103, 275, 276; economic policy and, 298–301; Lorenz dominance and, 344–45

Regions (states), 277; education and income
and, 261–64; ethnic composition and, 2;
interregional inequality and, 93, 97, 99;
personal income inequality and, 203–06;
poverty and, 131, 135, 156, 161, 168; poverty of fishermen and, 165; public assistance and, 283; rich households in, 142

Regression analysis (race, occupation, and
income), 222–23

Religion: Islam as national, 7; taxation and,
286

Rent: HBS and, 48; PES income definition
and, 29

Replanting program (rubber), 161–62, 163

Restructuring of society, 275, 281; as government goal, 15–17; inequality measures
and policy for, 101–03; New Economic
Policy and, 10, 11–14, 272

Rice. *See* Paddy (rice)

Riots, 7 *n*12, 8, 9, 301

Robless, C. L., 11 *n*16

Rothschild, Michael, 335, 338

Round, Jeffrey I., 39 *n*21

Rowntree, B. S., 186 *n*44

Rubber, 4, 5, 214, 287 *n*22; interracial earnings differentials among tappers of, 215–
16; poverty in sector for, 160–64, 276;
price intervention and, 291; tax on export
of, 162, 288–89

Rubber Industry Smallholders Development
Authority (RISDA), 161, 162

Rural and Industrial Development Authority, 166

Rural sector: development policies for, 144,
292–93; ethnic composition of, 3; food
budget analysis and, 115; HBS sample and,
45, 50; household income in MSSH and, 43;
household income in PES and, 37; inequality measurement and, 99–101; inequality of personal income and, 203, 277;
PES income data problems and, 247; PES
sample design and, 25; poverty and, 127,
131, 133–35, 144–51, 276; poverty and
subgroups in agriculture and fishing and,
157–72; rich households in, 142, 143 *n*41

Sabah (state), 1 *n*1, 8, 12 *n*19

Sampling procedure: HBS, 45–47; PES, 24–26,
272

Sarawak (state), 1 *n*1, 8, 12 *n*19

Sarong index of poverty, 112

Savings, 6, 38

Sawyer, Malcolm, 39, 41 *n*26

Screening, education and, 243, 280

Seasonality: off-season crops and, 157 *n*20;
PES income definition and, 28

Second Malaysia Plan (SMP, 1971–75), 9, 10,
12, 157, 281 *n*6, 294

Self-employed individuals, 283; HBS income
concept and, 49, 50; HBS and PES comparison and, 52; personal income inequality and, 207; poverty measures and,
131, 135, 172; understatement of income
and, 39

Selvadurai, S., 64 *n*4, 153, 161 *n*26

Sen, Amartya K., 229 *n*47, 314

Sen poverty measure, 118–23, 125, 126, 133
*n*35, 275

Sex: education estimates (earnings function) by, 253–54; personal income inequality and, 206–07; poverty and, 151. *See also* Men; Women

Shaplen, Robert, 297 *n*46

Singapore, 8

Skilled workers, training of, 296–97

Snodgrass, Donald R., 38, 39, 42, 44

Social welfare, Atkinson index and, 82–86. *See also* Economic welfare; Welfare comparisons

Social welfare function (egalitarian), 338, 345

Special Advisory Committee on Cost of Living Indices, 46

Squire, Lyn, 229 *n*47

States. *See* Regions (states)

Stern, Nicholas H., 84

Stiglitz, Joseph E., 243 *n*12, 335, 338

Stuart, A., 313

Tan, Siew Sin, 9, 10, *n*15

Taxes, 6, 38; direct income transfers and, 284–85; distribution of burden of, 286; HBS income concept and, 50; improvement of welfare of poor and, 286–90; negative income-tax schedule, 283, 284; PES income and, 64; rubber and, 162, 288–89

Tax schedule (Sen's poverty measure), 123

Tea, 167, 214

Teachers, earnings of, 259, 261

Tenure (land), 156 *n*18

Theil entropy index *T*, 93, 96, 102, 273, 274, 299; decomposition of, 327–29; inequality measures analysis and, 308–09; inequality measures comparisons and, 331–32; inequality measures (personal income) and, 198–99, 202, 203, 206

Theil's second measure *L*, 88, 90, 273, 275; decomposition of, 329–30; inequality measures analysis and, 309–10; inequality measures comparisons and, 331–32; inequality measures (personal income) and, 199–200, 202, 203, 206

Thillainathan, R., 215

Third Malaysia Plan (TMP, 1976–80), 10, 133 *n*34, 152 *n*12, 296

Towns. *See* Urban sector, towns

Training of skilled workers, 296–97

Transfer of income, 333, 334; direct, 281–85; Sen's poverty measure and, 122, 123; "weak" principle of, 81 *n*21

Two-digit industrial and occupational level (poverty): fishermen and, 165–66; laborers on rubber estates and smallholders and, 163–64; other subgroups in agriculture and, 167; paddy agriculture and, 157–

60; rubber smallholders and, 160–63; rural poor and, 150, 151–57; urban poor and, 172

Underemployment, 150–51

Unemployment: earnings function and education and, 253; poverty measure and, 131; rate of return to education and, 243; urban poverty and, 172 *n*43

Union of rubber workers, 164

United Malays National Organization (UMNO), 7, 8, 9

Urban Development Authority (UDA), 13

Urban employees, 279; age cohort and, 255–57; age-income profile and, 248, 249, 254; degree or diploma and, 259–61; estimation of earnings function of education (by race, sex, and occupation) and, 249–53; human capital model and, 237–38; language used in schooling and earnings of, 257–59; PES income data and, 243; regional breakdown of, 261–64

Urban sector, 11; ethnic composition of, 3–4; food budget analysis and, 115; HBS sample and, 45; household income in PES and, 37; inequality measurement and, 99–101; inequality of personal income and, 203, 277; metropolitan towns definition (PES) and, 25, 37 *n*18; metropolitan towns and towns as area of, 100; poverty in, 127, 145, 167–68, 172–73, 186; rich households in, 142, 143 *n*41; towns definition (PES) and, 25, 37 *n*18

van der Tak, Herman G., 229 *n*47

Variance of logarithm of income. *See* Log-income variance

"Varlog" measure. *See* Log-income variance

von der Mehden, F. R., 297 *n*45

Wealth distribution vs. income-from-wealth distribution, 210

Welfare. *See* Economic welfare; Social welfare

Welfare comparisons (lack of) and Lorenz dominance, 333–40

Within-group component (racial). *See* Ethnic composition, within-group component and

Women, 67 *n*13, 276; estimates for earnings function and education of, 247, 253–54; salary discrimination and, 261; urban poverty and, 186

World Bank, 38 *n*20, 157, 292 *n*37

Yields: paddy, 156–57; rubber, 162

Za'ba (literary figure), 111–12

Zakat, 286, 288

The full range of World Bank publications, both free and for sale, is described in the *Catalog of World Bank Publications*; the continuing research program is outlined in *World Bank Research Program: Abstracts of Current Studies*. Both booklets are updated annually; the most recent edition of each is available without charge from the Publications Unit, Dept. B, World Bank, 1818 H Street, N.W., Washington, D.C. 20433, U.S.A.

Sudhir Anand is fellow and tutor in economics at St. Catherine's College, Oxford, and formerly an economist at the Development Research Center of the World Bank.